A Guide to the Indian Tribes of the Pacific Northwest

THE CIVILIZATION OF THE AMERICAN INDIAN SERIES

A Guide to the Indian Tribes of the Pacific Northwest

Revised Edition

By Robert H. Ruby and John A. Brown

Foreword by Roland W. Force

Pronunciations of Pacific Northwest Tribal Names by M. Dale Kinkade

UNIVERSITY OF OKLAHOMA PRESS : NORMAN

BY ROBERT H. RUBY AND JOHN A. BROWN

Half-Sun on the Columbia: A Biography of Chief Moses (Norman, 1965)
The Spokane Indians: Children of the Sun (Norman, 1970)
The Cayuse Indians: Imperial Tribesmen of Old Oregon (Norman, 1972)
The Chinook Indians: Traders of the Lower Columbia River (Norman, 1976)
Indians of the Pacific Northwest: A History (Norman, 1981)
A Guide to the Indian Tribes of the Pacific Northwest (Norman, 1986, 1992)
Dreamer-Prophets of the Columbia Plateau: Smohala and Skolaskin (Norman, 1996)
John Slocum and the Indian Shaker Church (Norman, 1996)

Library of Congress Cataloging-in-Publication Data

Ruby, Robert H.
  A guide to the Indian tribes of the Pacific Northwest. ·

  (The Civilization of the American Indian series; 173)
  Includes bibliographies and index.
  1. Indians of North America—Northwest, Pacific—Dictionaries and encyclopedias. I. Brown, John Arthur. II. Title. III. Series: Civilization of the American Indian series; v. 173.
E78.N77R79   1986   979.5'00497'00321   85–22470
ISBN: 0–8061–2479–2 (paper)

5   6   7   8   9   10   11   12   13   14   15   16   17   18   19   20   21   22   23   24   25   26   27

*Dedicated to Edna Phyllis
and to the Sawyer Clan*

Contents

Maps

Foreword

By Roland W. Force
Director, Museum of the American Indian

Why did the people who called themselves Skitswish come to be known as the Coeur d'Alêne Indians? Did the Flathead tribe get their name from flattening the heads of their children? Why are the Kalispel Indians developing an industrial park? How many Klickitat Indians were there in 1806? The answers to these and a host of other questions can be found in the pages that follow.

This is a reference work devoted to the Indian tribes in the Pacific Northwest of the United States, largely those that occupy, or formerly occupied, the states of Oregon, Washington, Idaho, and Montana. It is a companion volume to *Indians of the Pacific Northwest: A History*, by the same authors, which was published by the University of Oklahoma Press in 1981.

The format is encyclopedic. Some 150 tribes are treated in alphabetical order. Brief characterizations provide information about tribal languages, alternative names, house styles, diet, populations at certain dates, contacts with white explorers and traders, treaties, claims against the government of the United States, leading personalities, and significant migrations and settlements. Most of the descriptions end with lists of suggested readings.

The tribal descriptions vary in length and content, at times including comments on kinship organization, economic activities, relations with other groups, and features of cultural contacts with Europeans, such as hostile conflicts, epidemics, and interactions with missionaries. The entries are from one to several paragraphs long.

Reference is made at times to the manner in which non-Indians perceived a particular tribe: as warlike, untrustworthy, good hunters or fishermen, shrewd traders, and so on. Information on contemporary tribal affairs is also provided. Annual special events, such as rodeos, powwows, and the like, are mentioned, as are tribal culture centers, housing programs, and educational medical facilities.

Other traditional aspects of culture, such as whether a group had slaves or practised infanticide, are sometimes noted. The precontact locations of tribes are indicated in relation to features that are identifiable on present-day maps: lakes, rivers, cities or towns, and highways, for example.

In this volume Robert H. Ruby and John A. Brown have compiled a remarkable array of facts and figures about some exceptionally diverse tribal populations. Nothing is more difficult than the treatment of richness and breadth in brief. The dual dangers of over- or understatement are ever present. The reader who consults this book will recognize how skillfully the authors have avoided those inherent pitfalls. A quick scan of a section provides a wealth of data; for more information sources are given.

Much of the richness of the Native American cultures has been lost. Sometimes there was no one to record it. Often the bearers of cultural knowledge died, and with them a wealth of Indian lore passed from the earth. Yet much was set down and has been preserved. In this book, through a painstaking process of review, prodigious reading, and culling, the authors provide a highly useful summary of distinct value to those who seek to know about the native peoples of the Pacific Northwest.

Authors' Preface

A Guide to the Indian Tribes of the Pacific Northwest is prepared for the public at large, including not only residents of the region (many of whom are new to it) but also tourists, scholars, and interested readers. The various tribes described here live, as did their ancestors, in a vast area extending from the Rocky Mountains to the Pacific Ocean and from California to British Columbia. Although we realize that historically the habitations and the movements of the Pacific Northwestern tribes have not been confined within the state and national boundaries established by white men, we have been forced to set arbitrary geographic perimeters for our work. Despite the sedentary tendencies of the region's peoples, from a historical viewpoint they have always been in flux. Continuing archaeological studies will reveal more of that tribal ebb and flow in the earliest times.

As in the past, there are fewer Indian tribes between the Cascades and the Rocky Mountains, but individually the tribes are more populous than those of the coastal regions. On the coast the numerous river valleys, the lush vegetation, and the proximity of ample food supplies facilitated the formation of greater numbers of tribes. Many of the tribes described here became extinct in the nineteenth century. By contrast there has been rebirth and regrouping of tribes in the twentieth century, a time of renewed tribalism and quests for the federal government "acknowledgment" that assures Indians of fishing and other rights. Some have become full-fledged tribes who formerly were classified as subtribes or, in most cases, village bands. To help our readers chart this flux, we have provided comparative population figures. Those given for 1780 are from a 1928 publication by the anthropologist James Mooney. Those of 1805–1806

are from the estimates of the explorers Meriwether Lewis and William Clark. We are aware of the very tenuous nature of these native population figures, yet we note that they have been used by contending parties in claims litigation. They do serve to trace the nineteenth-century decline of native populations and the reversal of that trend in the twentieth century.

In preparing the *Guide*, we have relied on standard ethnological works, such as John R. Swanton's *The Indian Tribes of North America* (1968) and Frederick Webb Hodge's *Handbook of American Indians North of Mexico* (1907 and 1971). We have also relied on numerous other sources of information. We have worked closely with tribal officials, whom we wish to thank for their assistance, along with the anthropologists and the historians who read portions of the manuscript and made helpful suggestions. We would not fail to thank the many librarians and government officials who aided us in our efforts. Our endeavors have been time-consuming and, at times, difficult, especially in the sorting out of linguistic families (noted in parentheses after the tribal name at the beginning of each tribal entry) and other tribal affiliations, yet these labors have been rewarding to us. We are especially appreciative of Dr. M. Dale Kinkade's contribution to this book of the phonetic spellings of the Pacific Northwest tribal names.

We hope the *Guide* will facilitate armchair traveling for those who are unable to visit this part of America in person. In the 1970s numerous centers were built wherein one may detect the resurgent tribal pride. Should one be unable to visit those centers, a visit to the museums that feature tribal cultural items would be most profitable. Visitors may also attend most of the "Special

Events" listed in the *Guide*, at which, despite some innovations, Indians engage in traditional games and ceremonials.

Above all, we hope that because of our efforts you, our readers, will gain knowledge and understanding of the various tribes of which we write and of the individual members of the tribes.

Moses Lake, Washington
Wenatchee, Washington

ROBERT H. RUBY
JOHN A. BROWN

Pronunciations of Pacific Northwest Tribal Names

By M. Dale Kinkade
University of British Columbia

This list includes phonetic transcriptions both of the names by which the Pacific Northwest tribes are generally known and of their own names for themselves. In the lefthand column you will find the generally accepted tribal name. In the left center column, under the heading "Native Phonetics," is the native pronunciation of that generally accepted name. In the right center column, under the heading "Native Name," is th name by which a tribe calls (or called) it self, if that is different from the acceptec name. In the right column is the English pronunciation of the generally accepted name printed in the lefthand column. Some of this information is simply no longer available, and blanks indicate where that is the case.

Pronunciation Key

Symbols are used following the pronunciation guide of *Webster's New Collegiate Dictionary*, 9th ed., except as follows:

ŭ	for the first and second vowels of 'abut'
äy	for the diphthong ī (as in 'ice')
äw	for the diphthong au̇ (as in 'out')
ȯy	for the dipththong ȯi (as in 'boy')
f	in Indian words pronounced with lips close together
hl	a voiceless, very breathy l
tl	a combination of t and hl
q	like k, but pronounced much further back in the mouth
kh	a friction sound such as occurs at the end of 'Bach'
qh	the same, pronounced much further back in the mouth
R	pronounced fully in the throat, with some constriction
ʷ	the preceding sound is pronounced with the lips rounded
'	the preceding sound is pronounced with glottal release
´	primary stress (accent)
`	secondary stress (accent)
·	the preceding vowel is about twice as long as normal

	Native Phonetics	Native Name	English Phonetics
Ahantchuyuk	hánch'ēyŭk		ŭhánchēyŭk
Alsea		wüsí·ⁿ	álsē
Atfalati	ätfálätē		ätfálätē

	Native Phonetics	Native Name	English Phonetics
Bannock			bánŭk
Boise Shoshoni			bȯysē shōshónē
Bruneau Shoshoni			brŭ́nō shōshónē
Calapooya	gäläpŭ́ywē		kalüpŭ́yü
Cascade			kaskȧ́d
Cathlamet	gählȧ́mät		kathlámüt
Cathlapotle	gählȧ́pütl		kathlüpŭ́tül
Cayuse		lḗksēyü	käyŭ́s
Chastacosta			chástükȯ̀stü or
			shastükȧ́stü
Chehalis			shŭhȧ́lŭs
Chelamela			chèlŭmélŭ
Chelan	chŭl'ȧ́n		shŭlán
Chepenafa	(che)p'ḗ·nefü		chŭpénüfä
Chetco			chétkō
Chilluckittequaw	chēlüqʷ'dēgʷä		
Chimakum	chímŭküm(t)		chímŭküm
Chinook			shinúk or chinúk
Clackamas	tlȧ́q'ēmäs		klákŭmŭs
Clallam	nŭ́khʷ(s)tl'ŭ́yüm		klálüm
Clatskanie	hlȧ́ts'qŭnäy		klátskŭnäy
			(locally also
			klatskȧ́nē)
Clatsop	tlȧ́ts'ȯp		klétsüp
Clowwewalla	tlȧ́wēwälä		
Coeur d'Alêne		schétsȯ'ōmsh	kŭrdŭlȧ́n
Colville			kȧ́lvil
Coos			küs or küz
Copalis	kʷ'pēls		kōpȧ́lŭs
Coquille			kokḗl or kōkwíl
Cowlitz	kȧ́wlits		kȧ́wlits
Dakubetede			
Duwamish	dkhʷdüw'ȧ́bsh		düwȧ́mish
Entiat	nt'ēȧ́tkʷ		ántēat
Flathead		sálēsh	flát-hed
Grand Ronde			grand rȧ́nd
Hanis Coos	hȧ́nēs, kŭ́s		hánŭs kŭ́s
Hoh	hȯ́qhʷ		hȯ́
Hoquiam	qhʷŭ́qʷyämts		hȯ́kwēüm
			(locally also
			hȯ́kēüm)
Humptulips	khʷŭntŭ́läpsh,		hŭmtŭ́lŭps
	qhŭmtŭ́läpsh		

	Native Phonetics	Native Name	English Phonetics
Kalispel	qälēspálms		kálŭspel
Kikiallus			
Kittitas	q'tḗtä·s	pshwä́nwäpäm	kítŭtas
Klamath			klámŭth
Klickitat		qhʷä́hlqhʷäypäm	klíkŭtat
Kuitsh			
Kutenai			kǘtŭnā
Kwaiailk	qʷ'äyä́yhl(q')		
Kwalhioqua			kwälēṓkwŭ
Latgawa			lä́tgäwä
Lower Chehalis		ts'ŭqhä́l's, hlŭw'ä́l'mŭsh	lṓŭr chŭhä́lŭs
Lower Elwha			lṓŭr élwä
Lower Skagit	sqä́jŭt		lṓŭr skájŭt
Lower Umpqua			lṓŭr ŭmpkwä
Luckiamute	lä́·k'mäyŭk		lúkēŭmyùt (*locally also* lúkēmyüt)
Lummi		nŭkhʷhlŭmŭchäsŭn	lŭ́mi
Makah			mŭká́
Methow	mḗtqhäw		mét-häw
Mical	mēshä́l		
Miluk Coos			mílŭk kŭ́s
Mishikhwutmetunne			
Modoc	mō·wät'ä·kknē·		mṓdäk
Molala			mōlä́lŭ
Muckleshoot			mŭkŭlshüt
Multnomah	mählnŭmäqh		mŭltnṓmŭ
Naltunnetunne			
Nespelem	nspḗlŭm		nezpḗlŭm
Nez Percé		nēmḗ·pü·	nezpŭ́rs
Nisqually	sqʷä́lē'		niskwä́lē
Nooksack	nŭkhʷsä́'äq		nŭ́ksak
Northern Paiute			pä́yüt
Okanagon	'ṓ'qŭnä'qä́n		ōkŭná́gŭn
Ozette	'ōsē'éhlqʷ		ōzét
Paiute			pä́yüt
Palouse	pälŭ́·s		pŭlŭ́s
Pend d'Oreille			pändŭrä́
Pshwanwapam	pshwä́nwäpäm		
Puyallup	spüy'ä́lŭpŭbsh		pyüélŭp
Queets	qʷ'ḗtsqhʷ		kwḗts
Quileute	kʷṓ'lḗ·yōt'		kwílēüt

	Native Phonetics	Native Name	English Phonetics
Quinault	kwḗnäyhl		kwínȯlt *or* kwinȯ́lt
Sahewamish	s'ähḗwäbsh, sühḗ'wŭbsh		
Salish	sálŭsh		sắlish
Samish			sámish
Sammamish			sŭmámish
San Juan			san wắn
Sanpoil	snpŭRʷḗlkh		sanpōíl
Santiam			sántēam *or* santēám
Satsop	sắtsäpsh		sátsŭp
Sauk-Suiattle	sắ'kʷbḕkhʷ		sók-sū́ēatŭl
Semiahmoo			semēắmü
Senijextee			
Shasta			shástŭ
Shoshoni			shōshṓnē
Siletz			sŭléts
Sinkaietk	(s)nqRḗtkʷ		
Sinkiuse	snq'ä'ắw's		
Siuslaw			sắyüslȯ *or* säyū́slȯ
Skagit	sqắjŭt		skájŭt
Skilloot	sēk'lütkt		
Skin	sk'ēn		
Skokomish	sqō'qṓbŭsh		skōkṓmish
Skykomish	sq'ḗkhʷübsh		skäykṓmish
Snohomish	sdühū́bsh		snōhṓmish
Snoqualmie	sdúkʷälbēkhʷ		snōkwálmē
Spokane	spō·qḗnē		spōkán
Squaxin	sqʷắqhsüd		skwắksŭn
Steilacoom			stílŭkŭm
Stillaguamish	stŭlŭgʷắbsh		stilŭgwắmish
Suquamish	s(y)ü'q'ʷắbsh		sükwắmish
Swallah			
Swinomish	swū́dŭbsh		swínŭmish
Taitnapam	tắytnäpäm		tắytnŭpŭm
Takelma			tŭkélmŭ
Taltushtuntude			
Tenino	tēnắynü		tŭnắynō
Tillamook			tílŭmŭk
Tukuarika			
Tulalip	dkhwlḗläp		tŭlắlŭp

	Native Phonetics	Native Name	English Phonetics
Tututni	dōtōdŭnē		tütütnē
Twana	tüwǎ'dŭkhʷ		twǎnŭ
Umatilla	émätēläm		yümŭtílŭ
Upper Chehalis		qʷ'äyǎyhl(q')	ŭpŭr chŭhǎlŭs
Upper Skagit			ŭpŭr skájŭt
Upper Umpqua			ŭpŭr ŭmpkwä
Wahkiakum	wäqhkēäkm		wŭkǎyŭkŭm
Wallawalla	wäläwǎlä	wälŭ·läpäm	wǎlŭwälŭ
Wanapam	wǎnäpäm		wǎnŭpŭm
Wasco	wäsq'ŭ́		wǎskō
Watlala	wählǎlä		
Wauyukma	wäwyük'mǎ		
Wenatchee	wēnǎ·chäpäm	np'ŭsqʷǎw's	wŭnáchē
Whiskah	khʷŭ́shqä'		wíshkä
Willamette			wilámŭt
Willapa	'äkhʷé·l'äpsh		wílŭpŭ
Wishram	wēshqhäm		wíshràm or wíshrŭm
Wynoochee	qhʷŭnŭ́hlch(ē)		wäynŭ́chē
Yahuskin			
Yakima	syä'ǎqmä'ŭkhʷ	mǎmächätpäm	yákŭmä
Yamel	yǎmhälä		yàmhíl or yámhil
Yaquina	yäqʷṓ·n		yükwínŭ
Yoncalla			yängkǎlŭ or yǎnkälŭ

References

Amoss, Pamela T. 1961. Nuksack Phonemics. Unpublished M.A. Thesis, University of Washington, Seattle.

Aoki, Haruo. 1970. Nez Perce Grammar. University of California Publications in Linguistics 11.

Barker, M. A. R. 1963. Klamath Dictionary. University of California Publications in Linguistics 31.

Carlson, Barry F. 1972. A Grammar of Spokan: A Salish Language of Eastern Washington. Unpublished Ph.D. Dissertation in Linguistics, University of Hawaii, Honolulu.

Frachtenberg, Leo J. 1920. Alsea Texts and Myths. Bureau of American Ethnology Bulletin 67, Washington.

Golla, Victor. 1976. Tututni (Oregon Athapaskan). International Journal of American Linguistics 42:217–27.

Harrington, John P. 1942. Papers. National Anthropological Archives, Smithsonian Institution, Washington.

Hess, Thom. 1976. Dictionary of Puget Salish. Seattle: University of Washington Press.

Jacobs, Melville. 1931. A Sketch of Northern Sahaptin Grammar. University of

Washington Publications in Anthropology 4.2:85–292.

Jacobs, Melville. 1945. Kalapuya Texts. University of Washington Publications in Anthropology 11.

Powell, J. V. 1982. Personal communication.

——, and Fred Woodruff, Sr. 1976. Quileute Dictionary. Northwest Anthropological Research Notes Memoir 3.

Reichard, Gladys A. 1939. Stem-list of the Coeur d'Alene language. International Journal of American Linguistics 10:92–108.

Rigsby, Bruce J. 1965. Linguistic Relations in the Southern Plateau. Unpublished Ph.D. Dissertation in Anthropology, University of Oregon, Eugene.

Silverstein, Michael. 1982. Personal communication.

Speck, Brenda J. 1980. An Edition of Father Post's Kalispel Grammar. University of Montana Occasional Papers in Linguistics 1.

Vogt, Hans. 1940. The Kalispel Language. Oslo: Det Norske Videnskaps-Akademi.

A Guide to the Indian Tribes of the Pacific Northwest

AHANTCHUYUK
(Kalapuyan)

The Ahantchuyuks were popularly known as the French Prairie Indians because that prairie lay in their country in the Willamette valley north of present-day Salem, Oregon. They were also known as the Pudding River Indians for the stream that enters the Willamette River from the east about ten miles south of Oregon City. Meanwhile, other Indians called them the Hanchiuke. Decreased in numbers, the Ahantchuyuks were nudged from around the Molalla River (a tributary to the Willamette from the east) by the Molalas, who, according to tradition, had been driven westward across the Cascade Mountains in wars with other tribes.

Like other Kalapuyan speakers, the Ahantchuyuks were skilled hunters. They used, among other devices, deer-head decoys to catch their quarry. Fur traders of John Jacob Astor's Pacific Fur Company are believed to have been the first white men to enter their lands. The Ahantchuyuks were alarmed when the Astorians first came in 1812 seeking furs and venison to feed the employees at the company headquarters at Astoria on the lower Columbia River. They did not wish to gather pelts for the Astorians; or their successors, the Nor'Westers of the North West Company; or the men of the Hudson's Bay Company, with which the North West Company later merged.

The Bay Company operated a permanent fur trading post at Champoeg until 1825, using the Willamette valley as a thoroughfare for its brigades traveling to and from California. On French Prairie was Chemaway (now Chemawa), one of the first permanent white settlements in the Pacific Northwest. It had received its name from former Hudson's Bay Company employees following Joseph Gervais, who located there in 1828. Tradition has it that a free trapper, named George Montour, had settled on the Prairie about fifteen years earlier. The Ahantchuyuks and other Kalapuyan speakers sold slaves to French-Canadian settlers, who put them to work on farms. They also sold those settlers goods, such as floor-mats and bed coverings.

The Ahantchuyuks witnessed the activities of Methodist and Roman Catholic missionaries, who contested for their souls when the two religious bodies established missions in their lands in 1834 and 1839. In 1841 the Ahantchuyuks were urged to send their children to the Indian Manual Labor Training School that the Methodists had opened at Chemeketa (later Salem) after they abandoned their initial Willamette Mission station.

The Ahantchuyuks realized that the establishment of the Oregon provisional government in 1843 presaged a flood of white settlers onto their lands. Ironically, they facilitated the occupation of their lands by signing on January 4, 1855, a treaty (10 Stat. 1143, ratified March 3, 1855) with Oregon Superintendent of Indian Affairs Joel Palmer, agreeing to remove to a reservation. Having yielded their lands, they had little choice other than to remove west to the Grand Ronde Reservation, which had been established on the west side of the Coast Range in the Yamhill River watershed. The Ahantchuyuks numbered an estimated 200 or more in 1780. They are now extinct.

Suggested Readings: Lloyd Collins, "The Cultural Position of the Kalapuya in the Pacific Northwest," master's thesis, University of Oregon, 1951; Harold Mackey, *The Kalapuyans: A Sourcebook on the Indians of the Willamette Valley* (Salem, Ore.: Mission Mill Museum Association, Inc., 1974).

ALSEA
(Yakonan)

The name Alsea, or Alcea, is derived from Alsi, or Alse, of which the significance is unknown. With the Siletz and Yaquina tribes, the Alseas were sometimes called Southern Tillamooks, because they had been so listed erroneously by Oregon Superintendent of Indian Affairs Joel Palmer when he made a treaty with them in 1855, calling them the Alcea Band of Tillamooks. The name Tillamook, which is sometimes applied to the Alseas, is thus a misnomer, although the Siletzes spoke a Tillamook dialect of the Salish language. Nearly a score of Alsea village sites have been identified on the Alsea River, Alsea Bay, and at nearby locations along the central Oregon coast. The name Alsea has also been given to a town and to an Indian reservation. Peoples of the Yakonan linguistic stock to which the Alseas belonged numbered an estimated 6,000 in 1780. The estimated numbers of Yakonan speakers fell sharply over the generations to twenty-nine in 1910 and to nine in 1930.

The Alseas hunted seals and sea lions for their meat and also netted salmon. Like other natives, they coordinated food gathering with spiritual activities. Calling on animal spirits as well as other powers in nature, their shamans used their powers to promote good salmon runs. The Alseas journeyed into the Coast Range to supplement their diet with camas roots. For cooking they preferred vessels of alder and maple. Before their way of life was changed by whites, they flattened the heads of their infants and placed their dead in canoes at lonely points of land jutting into estuaries.

When the American trader Robert Gray sailed off the Alseas' coasts in 1788, they presented themselves to him and his crew in warlike fashion, dressed in cuirasses and shaking spears. That they kept beyond the range of the guns on Gray's ship indicates that they possibly had had some previous unfortunate encounter with maritime visitors. By the 1820s they had temporized their isolationism to the point of trading with crewmen of the ships of the Hudson's Bay Company along their coasts.

With other western Oregon tribes the Alseas met with Palmer, who on August 11, 1855, made an unratified treaty with them for their lands. Consequently, the Alseas were destined for a reservation along the coast, of which the southern portion bore their name. Nearly a century later their descendants, with those of other western Oregon tribes, would sue the United States for compensation for lands that were taken from the Coast Reservation by executive order on December 21, 1865, and by act of Congress on March 3, 1875 (Case No. 45320). On April 2, 1945, a ruling by the United States Court of Claims was appealed by the Justice Department to the United States Supreme Court, which on November 25, 1946, upheld the decision of the Court of Claims. With the Siletzes, the Yaquinas, and the Neschesnes, the Alseas shared a $1,327,399.20 award. For the Alsea claims against the United States for the lands taken, see **Yaquina** and **Alsea Tribes of the Alsea Reservation.**

Suggested Readings: Stephen Dow Beckham, *The Indians of Western Oregon, This Land Was Theirs* (Coos Bay, Ore.: Arago Books, 1977); Livingston Farrand, "Notes on the Alsea Indians," *American Anthropologist*, n.s. 2 (1901): 239–47; Leo J. Frachtenberg, *Alsea Texts and Myths,* Smithsonian Institution, Bureau of American Ethnology Bulletin no. 67 (Washington, D.C.: Government Printing Office, 1920).

ALSEA TRIBES OF THE ALSEA RESERVATION

The Alsea Tribes of the Alsea Reservation (occasionally referred to as the Yachats Reservation) comprise Hanis and Miluk Coos, Kuitshes (Lower Umpquas), and Siuslaws. In 1859 and 1860 they were removed from their southwestern Oregon homelands to the southern part of the Coast Reservation, later called the Siletz. In 1865 the Siletz Reservation was divided into two parts by the withdrawal of a strip of land around Yaquina Bay. Those Indians in the southern part became known as the Alsea Tribes of the Alsea Reservation. For the history of their reservation, see **Confederated Tribes of the Siletz Indians of Oregon.** Most of the descendants of the Indians composing the Alsea Tribes of the Alsea Reservation live around Coos Bay, Oregon; see **Coos Tribe of Indians, Miluk Coos, Hanis Coos, Kuitsh** and **Alsea.**

Suggested Reading: Stephen Dow Beckham, *The Indians of Western Oregon, This Land Was Theirs* (Coos Bay, Ore., Arago Books, 1977).

ATFALATI
(Kalapuyan)

The name Atfalati was sometimes shortened to Fallatah and Tfalati. The Atfalati people were also commonly known as the Tualatin or Wapato Lake Indians. They spoke the Tualatin dialect of the Tualatin-Yamhill language, one of three Kalapuyan languages. They lived in about twenty-four villages on what are now the Tualatin Plains of northwestern Oregon, in the hills around Forest Grove, along the shores and in the vicinity of Wapato Lake, along the north fork of the Yamhill River, and possibly at the site of Portland. Southwest of Portland, a town, valley and river bear the name Tualatin, which is said to mean "a land without trees" and "slow and sluggish." As was true of other Kalapuyans, their life-style was disrupted by the whites who entered their lands early in the nineteenth century. In precontact times they were fond of adornment and attire and wore red feathers on their heads and long beads and bright dentalia suspended from pierced noses. Both sexes cut holes in their earlobes, from which beads were suspended. They also flattened the heads of their infants more severely than the natives south of them did, and they raised fewer horses than the peoples east of the Cascade Mountains. Their slaves sometimes purchased their freedom with horses. The Atfalatis lived in rectangular houses containing several families. By the 1830s they had begun to clothe themselves in the manner of the Euro-Americans, whose influence extended to other things besides dress. The outsiders disturbed the natives' root and hunting grounds and forced them to follow Euro-American legal codes. Permanent Atfalati villages came to consist of little more than crude plank houses covered with dirt and bark. Contributing greatly to the changes in Atfalati culture was the decrease in their numbers precipitated by smallpox epidemics in 1782 and 1783 and the intermittent fever that raged in the 1830s. As a consequence, they were unable to resist white encroachments.

As the Willamette watershed rapidly filled with whites, the Atfalatis and other Kalapuyan speakers met with white officials seeking to secure their lands. In an unratified treaty with Oregon Superintendent of Indian Affairs Anson Dart on April 19, 1851, the Atfalatis ceded their lands in return for a small reservation at Wapato Lake. This cession definitely reduced their lands, but it was far better for them than the removal east of the Cascade Mountains that the whites demanded. Besides the reservation, they were to receive money, clothing,

Atfalati

The Atfalatis were Kalapuyan speakers. The young Kalapuyan sketched here was a member of one of the several tribes of his linguistic family occupying the Willamette valley of western Oregon. The once-populous Atfalati tribe were all but extinct by the middle of the nineteenth century. The sketch is attributed to A. T. Agate of the United States exploring expedition under Lt. Charles Wilkes, which was in the Pacific Northwest in the early 1840s. The subject was unadorned, though before white contact his people had adorned themselves extensively. Reproduced from Charles Pickering, The Races of Men and Their Geographical Distribution *(1863). Courtesy of Harold Mackey.*

blankets, tools, a few rifles, and a horse for each of their chiefs—Kiacut, La Medicine, and Knolah. At the time of the treaty the tribe numbered but sixty-five persons. Under continuing white pressures, they and other Kalapuyan speakers were asked to renegotiate with the government, this time with Joel Palmer, Dart's replacement. By a treaty dated January 4, 1855 (10 Stat. 1143, ratified March 3, 1855), they were to live in the Willamette valley until a suitable reservation was designated as their permanent home. They agreed to remove to a reservation when the government provided one. Palmer's benevolent influence was seen in the treaty's provisions for medical care for the Indians and help for them in farming and other activities. Palmer believed the Atfalatis to be one of the most influential native peoples in the Willamette valley. How many remained to integrate with the white community is unknown. An 1870 census returned sixty living on the Grand Ronde Reservation, the permanent home given them by the government. The census of 1910 returned but forty-four. A publication of the Smithsonian Institution in 1914 listed but one survivor, who was living on the Yakima Reservation in Washington. How he came to live there the publication did not state.

Suggested Readings: Stephen Dow Beckham, *The Indians of Western Oregon, This Land Was Theirs* (Coos Bay, Ore.: Arago Books, 1977); S. A. Clarke, *Pioneer Days of Oregon History* (Portland, Ore., 1905); Leo J. Frachtenberg, "Ethnological Researches Among the Kalapuya Indians," Smithsonian Institution, *Miscellaneous Collections* 65, no. 6 (1916); John Adam Hussey, *Champoeg: Place of Transition* (Portland, Ore.: Oregon Historical Society, 1967); Melville Jacobs, *Kalapuya Texts*, University of Washington Publications in Anthropology, vol. 13 (Seattle, 1945); Harold Mackey, *The Kalapuyans: A Sourcebook on the Indians of the Willamette Valley* (Salem, Ore.: Mission Mill Museum Association, Inc., 1974); W. W. Oglesby, "The Calapuyas Indians" (188?) Mss. P-A 82, Bancroft Library, University of California, Berkeley; James L. Ratcliff, "What Happened to the Kalapuya? A Study of the Depletion of Their Economic Base," *The Indian Historian* 6, no. 3 (Summer, 1973).

BANNOCK
(Shoshonean of Uto-Aztecan)

The modern name Bannock derives from the tribe's own name, Banakwut. The Bannocks were also called "the Robbers" by early nineteenth-century fur men and others. They were erroneously called Snake Indians (a name that whites gave to the Shoshonis) because they were closely associated with the Shoshonis and because they belonged to the same linguistic family. The name Bannock has been applied in Idaho to a river, a mountain range, and a county. A small community in Montana bears the name Bannack.

The Bannock Indians were, in fact, a branch of the Northern Paiutes. They left their homelands in present-day southeastern Oregon in the eighteenth century, after they had acquired horses, and moved to south-central Idaho, where they associated with the Pohogwes, a branch of the Northern Shoshonis, and acquired traits of the horse culture. Horses enabled them to range into present-day southern Montana and western Wyoming and into the Salmon River country of Idaho. Exposed to the Indian cultures of the Great Plains, to which they traveled with their Shoshoni allies to hunt buffalo, they exchanged their sagebrush and willow clothing for the skins worn by natives of the plains. They also replaced their permanent pole-supported conical lodges of bundled grass, bark, and tule mats for skin-covered tipis of the kind used by the Plains Indians. With horses the Bannocks coalesced their rudimentary family units into larger groups to cope with the emergencies that arose on the plains, and their chiefs came to be chosen for aggressiveness and fighting abilities.

The estimates of Bannock numbers by nineteenth-century observers are tenuous because they often included in their estimates other Shoshonean peoples with whom the Bannocks allied. In 1845 the Bannocks were said to number about 1,000, and in the late 1850s about 400 to 500. In 1870 they numbered roughly 600 to 800; in 1901, 513; in 1910, 413, of whom all but 50 lived in Idaho; in 1930, 415, of which 313 lived in Idaho; and in 1937, 342.

In early January, 1814, under a chief called The Horse, the Bannocks destroyed the Astorian fur post commanded by John Reed on the lower Boise River. The Horse led his people on other forays against white fur traders and their posts until 1832, when he assumed a peaceful posture. After that Le Grand Coquin became the Bannocks' chief. In 1843 during Le Grand Coquin's chieftaincy, Fort Hall was built as a fur post by the American trader, Nathaniel Wyeth near the mouth of the Portneuf River above Idaho's American Falls. The post was later sold to the Hudson's Bay Company. On October 14, 1863, Le Grand Coquin, with the Eastern Shoshonis under their chief, Washakie, signed the unratified treaty of Soda Springs, Idaho. The Bannock chief Tahgee (or Taghee) also signed the treaty for his people, who agreed to allow whites to pass peacefully through their lands.

In 1864 the Bannocks were at Fort Bridger (Wyoming), where they did not receive the annuities promised them under the Soda Springs Treaty. When they had signed that treaty, they had been asked to remove to Wyoming's Wind River Reservation under Washakie. Although allied with that chief's people, Tahgee did not want to take his people to Wind River. Another treaty (15 Stat. 673) was signed at Fort Bridger on July 3, 1868, after a similar agreement signed at Long Tom Creek, Idaho Territory on August 26, 1867. The second treaty would have located the Bannocks on a reservation, but it went unrecognized by the United States. The American officials then promised the Bannocks a suitable reservation in their own country in the Portneuf and Kansas (Camas) prairie regions southeast of the Fort

Bannock

This woman was of the Bannock Tribe, who with the acquisition of horses ranged not only in present-day south-central Idaho but also on the Great Plains. The Bannock clothing and trappings reveal the Plains influence. Courtesy of the Idaho State Historical Society.

tection against the whites, who were taking their game and pasture and other lands and were offering bounties on the scalps of local Indians. In September, 1865, in council with Idaho Territorial Governor Caleb Lyon, the Boise-Bruneaus indicated their readiness to move to a reservation. The area selected for them was that of Fort Hall. They were relatively poor in horses, compared with other Shoshonean peoples. At this time the Boise-Bruneaus included 300 Boises, 850 Bruneaus, and 150 Bannocks, plus members of other tribes. They consented to remove to the Fort Hall Reservation in 1869, in part because they sought annuities like those that the Eastern Shoshonis had received as a result of their Fort Bridger Treaty. Very few Bannocks traveled to Fort Bridger to receive annuity goods, which were to be dispensed to them at that agency until one of their own was provided for them.

At Fort Hall the Bannocks' fear of starving was heightened when government officials urged them to abandon their off-reservation searches for buffalo and other native foods. The tribe faced starvation when goods promised for delivery did not arrive. Their plight became evident on May 30, 1878, when some drunken Indians wounded two white cattlemen in the absence of troops at the military Fort Hall (which had been established May 27, 1870, about twenty-five miles from the old fur post of the same name and fifteen miles from Fort Hall Agency headquarters). The Bannocks' grievances culminated in the Bannock-Paiute War. The first engagement occurred on June 8, 1878, when a twenty-six-man force of volunteers and Northern Paiute scouts fought fleeing Bannocks south of the small mining town of South Mountain (Idaho). Several Bannocks were killed, including their war chief, Buffalo Horn. The Bannocks swung west from South Mountain to join some Northern Paiutes, who were urged on by a subchief, Oytes, who was a Dreamer prophet. The Bannocks and Paiutes by then numbered about 700, including about 450 warriors. They joined their forces near Juniper Lake east of Steens Mountain in southeastern Oregon. Among the assembled tribesmen was the peaceful Northern Paiute chief

Hall Reservation in Idaho, whenever they or the president deemed wise. The same treaty set aside the Wind River Reservation for Washakie's Eastern Shoshonis. Instead, by executive order on July 30, 1869, President Ulysses S. Grant assigned the Bannocks also to the Fort Hall Reservation, which had been originally established by executive order on June 14, 1867, for the Boise-Bruneau Shoshonis. By the middle of the nineteenth century these peoples from the Boise Basin in southwestern Idaho had mixed with the Northern Paiutes for mutual pro-

8

Winnemucca, who faced Bannock threats for not engaging in hostilities against the Americans. He was rescued from his predicament by his daughter, the famed Sarah Winnemucca.

Those Paiutes who had left the Malheur Reservation in southeastern Oregon to join the Bannocks fought soldiers on June 23, 1878, near Camp Curry in Silver Creek valley, about sixty miles west of Fort Harney and thirty miles west of Burns, Oregon. After that fight the Bannock-Paiutes moved north. Thirty-five miles south of Pendleton, Oregon, they forced a volunteer outfit to retreat on July 4. Two days later they fought another engagement at Willow Springs near Pendleton, and on the following day, July 7, they engaged volunteers and regulars at Birch Creek. From there the fighting moved north to the Umatilla Indian Reservation, where their leader, the Northern Paiute Egan, was killed by Indians from the reservation. Some Bannocks and Paiutes were shot down by government gunboats as they attempted to escape farther north across the Columbia River, as were innocent natives of the area. Other Bannocks and Paiutes were scattered far and wide to the south in disarray. After the war the Bannocks gathered at Fort Hall. There they were later joined by neighboring Northern Shoshonis and eventually by the Lemhi Bannocks and Shoshonis, after their Lemhi Reservation in east-central Idaho was abandoned in 1907. For an account of the Bannocks on the Fort Hall Reservation, see **Shoshone-Bannock Tribes of the Fort Hall Reservation.**

Suggested Readings: George F. Brimlow, *The Bannock Indian War of 1878* (Caldwell, Idaho: Caxton Printers, Ltd., 1938); Brigham D. Madsen, *The Bannock of Idaho* (Caldwell, Idaho: Caxton Printers, Ltd., 1958); Omer C. Stewart, "The Question of Bannock Territory," in *Languages and Cultures of Western North America* (Pocatello, Idaho: Idaho State University Press, 1970).

BOISE SHOSHONI
(See **Shoshoni**)

BRUNEAU SHOSHONI
(See **Shoshoni**)

BURNS PAIUTE INDIAN COLONY

The Burns Paiute Indian Colony is a viable tribe which originated from the homeless Northern Paiutes who gathered in the Burns, Oregon, area, where they were allotted in 1897. Their reservation was established on October 13, 1972 (Public Law 92-488) in two locations. In 1935 a 760.32-acre parcel was purchased for them under authority of section 208 of the National Industrial Recovery Act of June 16, 1933. It lies northwest of the Burns city limits. Another parcel of approximately ten acres, known as Old Camp, lies about a half mile west of Burns. Less than twenty-five miles east of the Burns city limits 71 scattered allotments remain of the 115 that were made in 1897. The allotted land totals 11,014 acres. The tribe is governed by a general council composed of all adult members, and it operates under a constitution and by-laws that were approved on June 13, 1968. Tribal membership stood at 223 in 1985. See **Northern Paiute.**

9

CALAPOOYA
(Kalapuyan)

The Calapooyas lived in what is present-day west-central Oregon. They spoke Central Kalapuyan, which was one of three Kalapuyan languages and shared common elements with the Takilman linguistic family. The Calapooya tribe and other Kalapuyan speakers were said to have migrated from the south into the Willamette valley in pre-contact times, replacing the valley's natives. Some early-day white observers identified these displaced natives as the Multnomahs, from an early name for the Willamette River. The five subdivisions of the Calapooyas were located on the headwaters of the Willamette River, on the Middle and West forks of its tributary the McKenzie, and at the confluence of the Willamette and McKenzie rivers near present-day Eugene, Oregon. From March to May, 1812, the Astorian Donald McKenzie, for whom the river is named, explored the homelands of the Calapooyas, seeking furs. Fur traders subsequently established a post, often referred to as "McKay old house," at or near the mouth of the McKenzie. Other geographical features bearing the tribal name are the Calapooya River on the north, near present-day Brownsville, Oregon; Calapooya Creek, an affluent of the Umpqua River in southwestern Oregon; and the Calapooya Mountains in that area.

Like other Willamette-valley natives, the Calapooyas lived by fishing, hunting, and gathering. Occasionally their routines were interrupted, as were those of other Kalapuyan speakers, by the inroads of other natives. Warlike Klamaths often came over the Calapooya Mountains to fight, plunder, and capture women. In 1849, Oregon Territorial Governor Joseph Lane found that the Calapooya tribe was reduced to only sixty members, who were living poorly. See **Atfalati.**

Calapooya

This Calapooya was sketched by A. T. Agate of the expedition led by Lt. Charles Wilkes in the Pacific Northwest in the early 1840s. He wears a robelike costume of elk skin and holds a bow and a quiver made of seal skin. His cap is fox skin with the ears attached. Reproduced from Charles W. Wilkes, U.S., Narratives of the United States Exploring Expedition During the Years 1838, 1839, 1840, 1841, 1842 *(Philadelphia: Lee and Blanchard, 1845), volume 5.*

Their ranks had been thinned primarily by diseases brought by whites, such as the smallpox that struck in the 1780s and the intermittent fever of the 1830s.

The Calapooyas were among those involved in the January 9, 1855, treaty (10 Stat. 1143, ratified March 3, 1855). By its terms they were removed to the Grand Ronde Reservation. Removal there did not check their decline in numbers (nor that of other Kalapuyans sent there). In 1870 the Calapooyas numbered only forty-two. In 1880 the total of all Kalapuyan speakers on the Grand Ronde Reservation was 351; in 1890, 164; and in 1905, 130. In 1910 there were but 5 Calapooyas out of the total of 106 Kalapuyan speakers on the Grand Ronde. That 106 were reduced to 45 in 1930. The government allowed various peoples on the Grand Ronde Reservation to keep their tribal identities in enclavelike settlements and returned their numbers separately. In time that segregation broke down, and by August 13, 1954, when the reservation was dissolved, the remnants of the former Kalapuyan speakers had lost their tribal identities. There are no Kalapuyan speakers today.

Suggested Readings: Stephen Dow Beckham, *The Indians of Western Oregon, This Land Was Theirs* (Coos Bay, Ore.: Arago Books, 1977); S. A. Clarke, *Pioneer Days of Oregon History* (Portland, Ore., 1905); Leo J. Frachtenberg, "Ethnological Researches Among the Kalapuya Indians," Smithsonian Institution, *Miscellaneous Collections* 65, no. 6 (1916); John Adam Hussey, *Champoeg: Place of Transition* (Portland, Ore.: Oregon Historical Society, 1964); Melville Jacobs, "Kalapuya Texts," *University of Washington Publications in Anthropology* 11 (1945), pt. 3; Harold Mackey, *The Kalapuyans: A Sourcebook on the Indians of the Willamette Valley* (Salem, Ore.: Mission Mill Museum Association, Inc., 1974); W. W. Oglesby, "The Calapooyas Indians" (188?), Mss. P-A 82, Bancroft Library, University of California, Berkeley; James L. Ratcliff, "What Happened to the Kalapuya? A Study of the Depletion of Their Economic Base," *Indian Historian* 6, no. 3 (Summer, 1973).

CASCADE INDIANS
(See **Watlala**)

CATHLAMET
(Upper Chinookan Division of Chinookan)

The Cathlamets (or Kathlamets) were the westernmost speakers of the Upper Chinookan linguistic stock whose language was spoken from present-day Rainier, Oregon, down the Columbia River to the Cathlamet homelands. These lands lay on the south bank of the Columbia upstream from Tongue Point (which is about thirteen miles from the Pacific Ocean near Astoria, Oregon) to the vicinity of Puget Island. They also claimed lands on the Columbia north bank from the mouth of Grays Bay (opposite Tongue Point) upstream to just beyond Oak Point. Despite the differences in languages, the Cathlamets were culturally similar to Lower Chinookan peoples. Around 1810, Cathlamet villagers moved north across the Columbia to settle in a village of the Wahkiakums, who were Upper Chinookan linguistically but, like the Cathlamets were closely related culturally to Lower Chinookan peoples. Around the middle of the nineteenth century some Cathlamets were still living with the Wahkiakums at Grays Bay under a Chief Selawish. Early fur men believed the Cathlamets had belonged among the Chinooks proper and with the Chinooks' closely related neighbors, the Clatsops, before splintering into their own

Cathlamet

Mrs. Wilson of the Cathlamet Tribe of the lower Columbia River, circa 1900. Her head reveals evidence of head-flattening, a practice among the aristocracy of lower Columbia River natives. Courtesy of the Smithsonian Institution.

villages sometime around the middle of the nineteenth century. The Astorian trader Ross Cox thought the Cathlamets who traded at Fort Astoria the most "tranquil" of the tribes around the post, which was established in 1811. In 1810 the American Winship brothers, because of unfriendly natives and high Columbia waters, had failed to establish a trading post near the Cathlamet lands.

In a treaty dated August 9, 1851, the Cathlamets ceded to the United States the lands on which stood Fort Astoria and its British replacement, Fort George, and lands about forty miles upstream and to the south for about twenty miles. In exchange they received from the government money, clothing, and other assorted items and retained two small islands in the Columbia River. On August 24, 1912 the United States Court of Claims awarded the tribe's descendants $7,000 for loss of their aboriginal lands (37 Stat. 518). The Wahkiakums were awarded the same amount. Nonreservation descendants of Cathlamets shared in a November 4, 1971, award to the Chinook Nation (see **Chinook**).

Cathlamet numbers were estimated at 450 in 1780. The American explorers Meriwether Lewis and William Clark estimated that there were 300 in 1805–1806. By 1849 the tribe had shrunk to 58, according to the figures given by Oregon Territorial Governor Joseph Lane. Since they were contemporaries of the Cathlamets whose numbers they recorded, Lewis and Clark and Governor Lane would have reported figures less tenuous than those of the ethnologist James Mooney, who estimated the 1780 Cathlamet populations in 1928. Largely because of disease and dispersal, the Cathlamets no longer have a tribal identity.

Suggested Readings: Franz Boas, *Kathlamet Texts.* Smithsonian Institution, Bureau of American Ethnology Bulletin no. 26 (Washington, D.C., 1901); Melville Jacobs, "Historic Perspectives in Indian Languages of Oregon and Washington," *Pacific Northwest Quarterly* 28, no. 1 (January, 1937); Albert Buell Lewis, *Tribes of the Columbia Valley and the Coast of Washington and Oregon*, Memoirs of the American Anthropological Association, vol. 2, pt. 2 (Lancaster, Pa., 1906); Fred Lockley, *History of the Columbia River Valley from The Dalles to the Sea* (Chicago, 1928); Thomas Nelson Strong, *Cathlamet on the Columbia* (Portland, Ore.: Binfords and Mort, 1906).

CATHLAPOTLE
(Upper Chinookan Division of Chinookan)

The Cathlapotles were one of several early-day peoples speaking the Clackamas dialect of the Upper Chinookan linguistic stock. The tribal name means "people of the Cathlapotle River." The river, now called the Lewis, is a tributary entering the Columbia near the town of Woodland, Washington, on Interstate 5. The main Cathlapotle village of Nahpooitle (or Nohpooitle) lay at the mouth of the Lewis River. Another Cathlapotle village, called Wakanasisi, was perhaps on the Columbia north bank opposite the mouth of the Willamette River. In 1792, Lt. William Broughton of British Capt. George Vancouver's expedition found the Cathlapotles with iron battle-axes and copper swords. Lewis and Clark noted some unusual iron swords among these people in 1805–1806. These explorers estimated the tribe's population at 900 in fourteen large wooden houses. They have been estimated at 1,300 in 1780. The reduction in numbers, which continued during the nineteenth century, was probably due mostly to various plagues. An article appearing in the August 8, 1915, issue of the *Portland Oregonian* told of a Cathlapotle woman, Wahl-la-Luk Umtux, who was among the first of her area to receive Christian baptism at Fort Vancouver. Bearing a new name, Catherine Cosike, she was in 1915 one of not more than a dozen of her people remaining. Today the Cathlapotles are extinct. See also **Clackamas.**

CAYUSE
(Waiilatpuan)

Early nineteenth-century French-Canadian fur men called the Cayuses the *cailloux,* a French word for stones or rocks. The name may possibly have derived from the character of the area that the tribe inhabited, or it may have been a gallicized rendering of the name by which they called themselves which meant "superior people." Early-day whites called them "proud and haughty." One early American traveler called them an "imperial tribe." Closely related culturally and geographically to the Nez Percés, they eventually adopted the language of the latter. Like the Nez Percés, they were noted for their horse culture. Originally the Cayuses had lived in what is now north-central Oregon. After moving away from their linguistically related neighbors, the Molalas, who were not horse-oriented, they eventually reached a new homeland on the upper reaches of the Walla Walla, Umatilla, and Grande Ronde rivers of present-day Oregon and Washington. Their lands stretched westward from the Blue Mountains to the John Day River, a tributary of the Columbia. Their affiliation with the Molalas has been disputed by some scholars. It was during their expansion that they abutted Nez Percé lands.

The Cayuse horse, a sturdy animal standing about thirteen hands high, was named for the tribe. According to their tradition, the Cayuses received their first horses from the Shoshonis. The horses, grazing on the lush grassy Cayuse lands, enabled their masters to ride down on and intimidate sedentary peoples nearby on the Columbia River. The Cayuses would force their victims to perform menial tasks and fish for them. With horses the Cayuses were able to journey as far east as the Great Plains to trade, hunt, and fight. Like other Columbia Plateau peoples, they acquired cultural elements of the Plains tribes. Horses remained among the most prized possessions of their aristocracy, and it was common for warriors to be buried with their favorite mounts. Besides the Cayuse horse, a small station

Cayuse

A Cayuse brave mounted on his cayuse. The name of the native breed of horse attests to the horsemanship of the Cayuse tribesmen. A proud people, the Cayuses were described by early white travelers as an "imperial tribe." The Umatilla Reservation was carved out of their lands in northeastern Oregon. Courtesy of the Smithsonian Institution.

on the Union Pacific Railway east of Pendleton, Oregon, bears the tribal name, as do many other things, ranging from conveyances to a mountain pass in Washington state.

Fur men entering Cayuse country in the early nineteenth century failed to make fur gatherers of these proud tribesmen. In 1818 personnel of the North West Company built Fort Nez Percés (later called Fort Walla Walla) in the lands of the Wallawallas, who were neighbors of the Cayuses. From that fort men of the Hudson's Bay Company (with which the North West Company merged in 1821) sought the Cayuses' goodwill, as the Nor'Westers had, in order to traverse Cayuse lands and tap the furs of the rich Snake River country on the east. Previously, at the urging of Nor'Wester officials, the Cayuses had effected a tenuous peace with enemy tribes on the upper Snake River, whose furs the British sought to collect before competing Americans took them.

The Cayuse reputation was tarnished after their November 29, 1847, massacre of immigrants and missionaries of the American Board of Commissioners for Foreign Missions, including the Reverend Marcus Whitman and his wife, Narcissa, at their Waiilatpu Mission on Cayuse lands near present-day Walla Walla, Washington. Today the massacre site is a national monument where life and death at the mission are depicted. The underlying causes of the massacre were squabbles between the Cayuses and their missionaries over ownership of mission lands, Cayuse unhappiness at immigrants traversing their lands in the Umatilla and Walla Walla valleys, Cayuse fears that these travelers were carrying measles (which broke out among both the immigrants and the Cayuses immediately before the massacre), the Cayuse practice of killing doctors who failed to cure patients (Whitman was a doctor), and finally Cayuse agitation among Walla Walla valley "half-bloods," some of whom assisted in the deed. The ensuing Cayuse War of 1848 culminated in the hanging in Oregon City on June 3, 1850, of five Cayuses whom officials of the Oregon provisional and territorial governments deemed guilty. The massacre ended American Board mission work among the Cayuses and other interior tribes. Roman Catholic missionaries continued ministering to natives of the area, with varying degrees of success.

Because of losses from war and disease and the inroads of whites trying to impose their laws on them, the Cayuses, despite hostile feelings, signed a treaty on June 9, 1855 (12 Stat. 945), which was ratified March 8, 1859, and proclaimed April 1, 1859. According to its terms, they submitted to the United States and were to live on a reservation to be established in their homelands. Four months later, however, some Cayuses joined an Indian confederation in fighting the Yakima War of 1855–56 against American volunteer and regular army forces. The Cayuses vented less hostility toward the few remaining British, with whose traders they remained on speaking terms, even tolerating British interference in the choice of their chiefs. Suffering much and broken in spirit after their defeats in war, they settled on the Umatilla Reservation with the Umatillas and the Wallawallas.

In 1780 the Cayuses had numbered about 500. In 1904 they numbered 404; in 1923, 337; and in 1937, 370. The merging of Cayuses with Umatillas, Wallawallas, and Nez Percés continued into the twentieth century. Today no one speaks their original Waiilatpuan language. As a final indignity to the proud Cayuses, white men rounded up and sold many of their horses and converted into wheat farms the lands on which these animals once grazed. See also **Confederated Tribes of the Umatilla Reservation.**

Suggested Readings: Albert S. Gatschet, "The Molale tribe raided by the Cayuses," ms. no. 2029, National Anthropological Archives Collection, Smithsonian Institution, Washington, D.C.; Robert H. Ruby and John A. Brown, *The Cayuse Indians: Imperial Tribesmen of Old Oregon* (Norman: University of Oklahoma Press, 1972); Theodore Stern, Martin Schmitt, and Alphonse F. Halfmoon, "A Cayuse-Nez Percé Sketchbook," *Oregon Historical Quarterly* 81, no. 4 (Winter, 1980).

CHASTACOSTA
(Athapascan)

The name Chastacosta (or Shasta Scoton) derives from the tribe's name for themselves. The Chastacostas belonged to a group known as the Coast Rogues. Like other Pacific Coast Athapascan speakers, they perhaps migrated into the region from the north in some remote time. They lived in southwestern Oregon on the lower course of the Illinois River, a tributary of the Rogue River. They also lived on both sides of the Rogue above its confluence with the Illinois and upstream on the Rogue north bank as far as the mouth of Applegate River. They were among those who met with Oregon Superintendent of Indian Affairs Anson Dart in 1851. On November 18, 1854, one or two bands of Chastacostas, along with the Grave Creek Umpquas, signed an unratified treaty with Oregon Superintendent of Indian Affairs Joel Palmer. Under its terms they agreed to go to a temporary reservation at Table Rock on the upper Rogue River until removed to a permanent reservation. Early in 1856 they joined other Athapascan speakers in attempting to drive whites from their lands. After futile fighting that summer, 153 Chastacostas (53 men, 61 women, 23 boys, and 16 girls) were removed northward to the Coast Reservation (later called the Siletz). Their attrition at that place, like that of the other Indians there, was severe. They and ten other Athapascan tribes had been estimated to number 5,600 in 1780. In 1856 there were only 153 Chastacostas, and in 1937 only 30. By 1950 they were virtually extinct.

Suggested Reading: Frederick Webb Hodge, ed., Handbook of Indians North of Mexico, pt. 1 (Washington, D.C.: Government Printing Office, 1907).

Chastacosta

George Harvey, a chief of the Chastacostas, belonged to the group known as the Coast Rogues. In 1856 his people were involved in the later stages of the Rogue Wars against whites in southwestern Oregon. Courtesy of the Smithsonian Institution.

CHEHALIS
(See **Lower Chehalis, Kwaiailk,** and **Confederated Tribes of the Chehalis Reservation**)

CHELAMELA
(Kalapuyan)

The Chelamelas, popularly known as Long Tom Indians, lived in the watershed of the Long Tom River, a Willamette River tributary west of present-day Eugene, Oregon. The name Long Tom is said to be a modification of the native word *lungtumler*. Like other Kalapuyan speakers, early in the nineteenth century the Chelamelas came into contact with white fur traders, who considered them indolent because of their unwillingness to abandon their native economy of hunting, fishing, and gathering in order to collect furs. The Chelamelas also suffered from diseases as they encountered missionaries, settlers, and other whites. They had already been pressured by native peoples, such as the Klickitats, who strengthened their position in the Willamette valley after the ravages of the intermittent fever. They had encountered Alseas and others raiding eastward from the Pacific Coast. Meanwhile, horse-riding Nez Percés and Cayuses from east of the Cascade Mountains entered the Willamette valley on animal hunts. Under provisions of the January 4, 1855, treaty with government agents, (10 Stat. 1143, ratified March 3, 1855) the Chelamela remnant moved from its ancestral homeland to the Grand Ronde Reservation.

Suggested Reading: Stephen Dow Beckham, *The Indians of Western Oregon, This Land Was Theirs* (Coos Bay, Ore.: Arago Books, 1977).

CHELAN
(Interior Division, Salishan)

The Chelans lived in north-central Washington east of the Cascade Mountains in the vicinity of the southern end of Lake Chelan. They spoke the Wenatchee dialect of the Interior Salishan language. The name Chelan has been given not only to the lake but also to a mountain range, a county in north-central Washington, a short river tumbling from the lake to the Columbia River, and the towns of Chelan on the Lake and Chelan Falls on the Columbia (both towns are on or near U.S. Highway 97). The early nineteenth-century fur trader Alexander Ross mentioned the "Tsill-anes" in his writings, as he did other area tribes whom he grouped together as the "Oakinacken nation." The Chelans were known to have paddled about fifty miles to the upper end of Lake Chelan, from which they crossed over a steep, poor trail to the summit of the Cascade Mountains and down the Skagit River, an affluent of Puget Sound, with whose natives they traded. According to Chelan tradition, their people in early times engaged in combat with tribes west of the Cascade Mountains.

Some geologists believe that the epicenter of the large earthquake of November 14, 1872, was in the Chelan area and northward. Natives in its path were frightened in the belief that the Earth Mother was angry with them. Roman Catholic priests utilized the quake to intensify their missionary efforts among the Chelans. A defender of the native religion, Chelan chief Nmosize (Innomoseecha Bill) burned down a mission house that the Reverend Alexander Diomedi, S.J., had built during the chief's absence. Shortly thereafter, however, the Indians built a Catholic church along the lake near the present town of Manson. Chief Nmosize was greatly displeased with the behavior of white men, especially soldiers such as those of Camp Chelan, which was established in 1880 at the lower end of Lake Chelan. That post was built to oversee the Moses, or Columbia, Reservation (established April 19, 1879), which extended from

Chelan

Peter Wapato, whose father, John Wapato, fled from the Columbia River to nearby Lake Chelan in north-central Washington at the time of the great earthquake of 1872. The Wapato family came to be identified as Chelan Indians. They had a record of friendship with white men who settled in the vicinity of Lake Chelan. Courtesy of the North Central Washington Museum Association.

the lake north to the Canadian border.

Under the terms of the Chief Moses Agreement of July 7, 1883 (approved July 4, 1884), several Chelans took up allotments around the lake and at other places on the southern end of the Moses Reservation. Under the leadership of Long Jim about forty or fifty Chelans who were living on the northern shores of the lake, the Chelan River, and at its mouth refused allotments, insisting that they were a people separate from those of Chief Moses. During further conflict between these Indians and white homesteaders, who claimed lands on failure of Indians to take allotments under the Moses Agreement, three Chelans were sent in 1890 to the guardhouse on the Colville Reservation. Conflict continued over several years, reaching the United States Supreme Court in the case of *Starr* v. *Long Jim* (227 U.S. 613), which that chief failed to win.

The Chelans were said to have been a numerous people in the eighteenth century, but by 1870, with the neighboring Methows and Entiats (with whom they were lumped by government officials), they had been reduced to about 300. During a threatened Indian outbreak in 1879 the March 27 *Portland Oregonian*, stated that the Chelans could muster between 50 and 100 warriors. Then and thereafter the Chelans, like Long Jim, fought whites only in the courts. Chelan descendants live primarily in the Chelan area and in other parts of north-central Washington, including the Colville Reservation. See also **Confederated Tribes of the Colville Reservation.**

CHEPENAFA
(Kalapuyan)

The Chepenafas were popularly known as the Mary's River Indians because of their location at the forks of Saint Mary's Creek near present-day Corvallis, Oregon. They spoke the Mary's River dialect of the central Kalapuyan language. Some ethnologists have classified them as a subdivision of the Luckiamute Indians, another Kalapuyan-speaking people.

Like other natives of the Willamette watershed, the Chepenafas lived in harmony with their environment before the coming of the whites. Their male youth sought spirit powers by fasting five days and nights and swimming in a lake. For routine travel the Chapenafas propelled dugout canoes with long poles and decorated wooden paddles. Wood, which is abundant in their country, also figured in their ceremonials. For example, they suspended moss- and hide-covered drumsticks and boards from their lodge roofs, which they beat with fire-hardened clubs to produce humming sounds. Like other natives between the Rogue River valley and the mouth of the Columbia River on the north, they played a game of shinny that was much like field hockey. The game, pitting bands against each other, took several days to play amidst much wagering.

Much Chepenafa culture was disturbed by whites, especially the settlers who began occupying their lands in the 1830s. Weakened by starvation and such diseases as smallpox and the intermittent fever of the 1830s, the Chepenafas were unable to prevent white incursions. The few Chepenafas who remained were included in the January 4, 1855, treaty with the United States (10 Stat. 1143, ratified March 3, 1855), which provided for their removal to a reservation. With other Kalapuyan speakers they ceded their lands in the Willamette valley to go to the Grand Ronde Reservation, to which their remnant removed in 1856. In 1870 they numbered forty-nine on that reservation and in 1910 only twenty-four.

Suggested Readings: Stephen Dow Beckham, *The Indians of Western Oregon, This Land Was Theirs* (Coos Bay, Ore.: Arago Books, 1977); Albert Gatschet, "The Kalapuya People," *Journal of American Folklore* 12 (1899), pp. 212–14; Harold Mackay, *The Kalapuyans: A Sourcebook on the Indians of the Willamette Valley* (Salem, Ore.: Mission Mill Museum Association, Inc., 1974).

Chepenafa

William Hartless, a Chepenafa Indian, circa 1890. The Chepenafas were unable to stem the tide of white settlers into their homelands beginning in the 1830s. After enduring diseases and incursions not only by whites but also by more powerful Indian tribes, the Chepenafa tribal remnant was sent to the Grand Ronde Reservation in 1856.

CHETCO
(Athapascan)

The Chetcos were among the natives referred to as the Coast Rogues. The name Chetco, meaning "close to the mouth of the stream," refers possibly to the tribe's forty-two–house village, which was at the mouth of the Chetco River where it enters the Pacific Ocean in extreme southwestern Oregon. The Chetcos also lived along the Winchuck River, another Pacific Ocean affluent. Their territory also included an undefined region along the coast north of the Chetco River probably extending to Cape Farrelo. Except for the narrow Chetco River valley their settlements were confined mainly to the coast. They were closely allied with the Tolowas, a tribe of Athapascan stock who

Chetco

Seafoods were important to the Chetcos, as was demonstrated by this "Rock Oyster Queen" of southwestern Oregon, photographed at the turn of the last century. The basket into which she placed the oysters and the strap attaching it to her head were skillfully made by Chetco women. Courtesy of the Lincoln County Historical Society.

lived in extreme northwestern California at Crescent Bay, Lake Earl, and the Smith River. Like other Athapascan speakers of the Pacific Coast, the Chetcos' ancestors entered that region at some remote time possibly from the north.

The Chetcos lived in wood-plank houses with dirt floors and traveled in shallow Klamath-type canoes. Their country abounded in game, berries, acorns, surf fish, molluscs, and sea mammals. They trapped deer in deep pitfalls. Like the Tolowas, Chetco women were skilled at making baskets, which they decorated with porcupine quills. Among their items of personal adornment were beads of Olivella. As whites increasingly traveled across their lands, the Chetcos supplemented their livelihood by ferrying travelers across the Chetco River. Later they lost their ferrying business to whites. Among the latter they had a reputation for unfriendliness as early as 1828, when they abandoned several lodges because of the appearance of the northbound Jedediah Smith party.

Whites filed 7,437 320-acre land claims in western Oregon Territory under the Donation Land Act (passed by Congress on September 29, 1850), appropriating 2.5 million acres of the natives' land base. Among those claims was one filed by A. F. Miller on the site of the principal Chetco village. In 1853, after Miller and other whites had persuaded the Indians to surrender their arms, they attacked the Indians, killing twelve men and burning houses in which two other Chetcos died.

At the mouth of the Chetco River, on March 29, 1856, about sixty Chetcos in revenge attacked Lt. E. O. C. Ord, U.S.A., and his troops on route to Crescent City, California. A soldier was killed in the attack, and three were wounded. After losing six braves in that engagement, the Chetcos were forced from the area. Like other Coast Rogue Athapascan speakers, the Chetcos moved up the Rogue River to help its Indians in their futile war against the Americans. Afterwards they were removed to the Grand Ronde Reservation and then to the Coast Reservation (later called the Siletz). Chetcos were among the natives with whom Oregon Superintendent of Indian Affairs Anson Dart treated for their lands in council at Port Orford in 1851. The Chetcos also treated with Oregon Superintendent of Indian Affairs Joel Palmer in 1855. Both treaties were unratified. After skirmishing whites between 1852 and 1856, the stubbornly resisting Chetcos were the last Indians of southwestern Oregon to surrender.

20

With certain western Oregon tribes, the Chetcos were plaintiffs in a case (No. 45230) tried in the United States Court of Claims, in which the tribe sued for the loss of aboriginally owned lands that it estimated at 433,150 acres. They received an award but appealed to the United States Supreme Court. On November 25, 1946, that court upheld an April 2, 1945, ruling of the Court of Claims. The tribe was awarded $489,085.20 for recovery of the Coast Reservation lands that the Chetcos had lost by executive order on December 21, 1865, and by act of Congress on March 3, 1875.

In 1854 the Chetcos numbered 241, having suffered losses not only in wars but also from diseases from early white contacts. In 1861 they numbered 262; in 1877, 63; and in 1910, only 9. In 1960 fewer than five Chetco speakers remained. Their descendants try to retain their tribal heritage. For a history of the Chetcos on their reservation, see **Yaquina.**

Suggested Reading: Stephen Dow Beckham, *The Indians of Western Oregon, This Land Was Theirs* (Coos Bay, Ore.: Arago Books, 1977); Joel Berreman, *Chetco Archaeology: A Report of the Lone Ranch Creek Shell Mound on the Coast of Southern Oregon,* American Anthropological Association, General Series in Anthropology, no. 11 (Menasha, Wis.: George Banta Publishing Company, 1944).

CHILLUCKITTEQUAW
(Upper Chinookan Division of Chinookan)

The Chilluckittequaws were Upper Chinookans living along the Columbia River, which divided them into two bands—those of the White Salmon estuary on the north and those of the Hood River estuary on the south.

The Chilluckittequaws' numbers in 1780 have been estimated at 3,000. Their reduction to an estimated 2,200 in 1805–1806 (of whom 1,400 were north-shore bands and 800 Smock-shops of the south shore) suggests the prevalence of disease among them, especially the smallpox plague of 1782–83. Their native name is not perpetuated in place-names. Whites gave the northern division, the name White Salmon, the name of a town and the river. A Chilluckittequaw remnant lived near White Salmon, Washington, until 1880, when its members removed downstream to The Cascades of the Columbia, where a few still lived in 1895. A tribal remnant was also found on the Yakima Reservation (see **Wishram**).

The Chilluckittequaws on the Columbia north bank were the Woocksockwilliacums, or White Salmons. They comprised several bands whose homelands were in what are today Washington's Klickitat and Skamania counties, an area extending roughly from ten miles below The Dalles west to the White Salmon River. They were not confined to the shores of the Columbia, for at least one of their important villages was about five miles south of the mouth of Hood River.

The Chilluckittequaws of the Columbia south bank were called Hood Rivers. Lewis and Clark called them the Smock-shops. The photographer and observer of American Indians Edward S. Curtis called them the Ninuhltidihs. Ethnologist James Mooney called them the Kwikwuilits. For the most part the southern Chilluckittequaws lived in permanent fishing villages on the Columbia where they caught several species of salmon between May and October. Like other Upper Chinookan peoples, they received pay from the local users of fishing stations, which were passed down according to inheritance customs. The Chilluckittequaws had first use of the stations. They were followed by users from neighboring villages and then by those from more distant points. Individuals and family groups were free to come and go from village to village within their own ethnic groups.

Someone remained in attendance at a village on occasions when all of the natives left it. Villages tended to be autonomous. The tribal political organization was minimal.

The Hood River Chilluckittequaws traded freely with the Shahaptian-speaking Tenino tribe. The association between the two peoples was perhaps strengthened by mutual fear of their ancient foe, the Northern Paiutes. In time the Hood Rivers became absorbed by and were grouped with the Wascos, another Upper Chinookan people. The few Hood Rivers remaining in the middle of the nineteenth century treated with Oregon Superintendent of Indian Affairs Joel Palmer on June 25, 1855. By their treaty they yielded their lands for a promised reservation. In that year they numbered eighty souls. Chief Wallachin claimed leadership over the scattered bands, who migrated back and forth across the Columbia between the Hood and Salmon rivers and downstream to The Cascades. He declined to sign the treaty, saying, "I have said that I would not sell my country and I have but one talk." Most descendants of the Hood Rivers live on the Warm Springs Reservation in north-central Oregon.

Suggested Readings: Leslie Spier and Edward Sapir, "Wishram Ethnography," *University of Washington Publications in Anthropology* 3, no. 3 (1930); Robert H. Suphan, "Ethnological Report on the Wasco and Tenino Indians," in *Oregon Indians*, vol. 2 (New York: Garland Publishing, Inc., 1974).

CHIMAKUM
(Chimakuan)

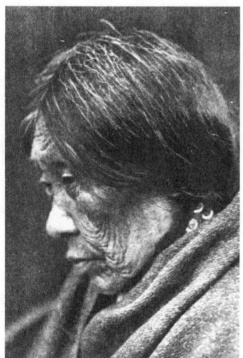

According to tribal tradition, the Chimakums were a remnant of a Quileute band who had fled the Pacific Coast from a high tide that took four days to ebb. That they were of the same linguistic stock as the Quileutes lends credence to that tradition. In any case, they migrated to an area around the southern shores of the Strait of Juan de Fuca and the western shores of Puget Sound near the present-day towns of Port Townsend, Discovery Bay, Port Hadlock, Port Ludlow, and Chimacum, Washington.

Chimakum

This Chimakum is a descendant of a band who, according to tradition, fled the Pacific Coast from a high tide to settle on the eastern side of Washington's Olympic Peninsula. Although the Chimakum Tribe is now extinct, some Indians trace their ancestry back to it. Photograph by Edward S. Curtis from Curtis's The North American Indian *(1907–1930), volume 9.*

The latter community is located near U.S. Highway 101. A creek also bears the name Chimakum. One of their villages, Tsetsibus, near Port Hadlock, was an important gathering place for area natives.

The Chimakums developed a reputation as a warlike people. Shortly before 1790 they were fighting tribes such as the Snohomishes, Snoqualmies, Clallams, Makahs, and Nitinats of Canada. Around 1850 they fought the Suquamishes. By that time the Chimakum population had fallen from 400 to less than 100. Their chief, known as Kulkakhan or General Pierce, was a signatory to the Point-No-Point Treaty of 1855, under which they were to remove to the Skokomish Reservation on the southern end of Hood Canal. There was, however, no able

Chimakum movement to that place because of their decline, which was caused not only by war but also by disease and absorption among the Clallams, most of whom refused to remove to the Skokomish. In 1890 the anthropologist Franz Boas found but three speaking the Chimakum language, and they spoke it imperfectly. Yet some descendants still identify themselves as Chimakums today.

Suggested Readings: Franz Boas, "Notes on the Chemakum Language," *American Anthropologist* 5 (January, 1892); Edward S. Curtis, *The North American Indian* (1912; New York, 1970), vol. 9; Myron Eells, *The Twana, Chemakum, and Klallam Indians of Washington Territory* (1889; Seattle: Shorey Book Store, 1971).

CHINOOK
(Lower Chinookan Division of Chinookan)

The Lower Chinooks, or Chinooks proper were given their name by the Chehalis Indians, their Salish-speaking neighbors on the north. The Chinooks spoke the Lower Chinookan dialect of the Chinookan language and lived in what is now Washington state on the north bank of the Columbia River. Their lands stretched from the Columbia estuary to Willapa (Shoalwater) Bay on the Pacific Ocean. Some anthropologists believe that in early times Chinookan peoples had drifted down the Columbia River, making a wedge between the Salish peoples at the mouth of that river. Culturally the Chinooks exhibited a few of the patterns of the Columbia Plateau peoples on the east as well as the patterns of peoples of the Northwest Coast.

The mouth of the Columbia River was, of course, an important entry point to the Pacific Northwest hinterland. In their villages there the Chinooks traded with both natives and whites. From the latter they contracted diseases, especially those venereal in nature, and obtained liquor, which also reduced their numbers.

In precontact times the Chinooks' strategic location had enabled them to maintain a mercantile hold on their homeland, but with the advent of the white land- and sea-based traders in the late eighteenth and early nineteenth centuries, the economic patterns and prominence of the Chinooks were disturbed. The Euro-Americans traded manufactured goods for native items, such as the elk-hide cuirasses known as *clamons*. Then the Euro-Americans traded the Columbia River articles to warring tribes on the upper Northwest Coast for sea otter pelts, which they in turn traded in China for products such as teas and silks. By this trade the status of the Chinook women was changed from mild subservience to dominance because they played a more active role in dealing with the white traders than their men did. When the maritime trade gave way to the land-based trade in beaver and other furs, the position of the Chinook women did not alter. They simply moved their operations from shipboards to forts across the Columbia River on the south. The Chinook name has been applied to a variety of things, including a wind, a salmon, a trade jargon, a canoe, vehicles, and business establishments.

Location: Today the Chinooks live primarily in southwestern Washington state, though some are widely scattered around the Pacific Northwest.

Numbers: In 1980, at a time of revived tribalism, Chinook membership stood at around 900. Between 1780 and 1805, Chinook numbers declined from about 800 to 400. In the latter half of the nineteenth century they numbered scarcely 100.

History: No one knows when Chinooks first met white men. Their tradition and that of the Clatsops, their Lower Chinookan-speaking neighbors on the south near the mouth of the Columbia River, tells of Spanish ships wrecking on their beaches in the second half of the eighteenth century. In May, 1792, the Chinooks met the American trader Capt. Robert Gray, who sailed into the Columbia River in the *Columbia Rediviva*, from which the river received its name. According to the Chinooks, Gray was the first white man to enter the river. In 1792, they also met the crew of the British vessel *Jenny*, which entered the Columbia, and the crewmen of HMS *Chatham* under the command of William Broughton, who was exploring the lower Columbia River for Britain. The Chinooks were among the Indians who traded with the American explorers Meriwether Lewis and William Clark, whose party wintered among Clatsops in 1805–1806. In 1811 the Chinooks traded with the Astorians of John Jacob Astor's Pacific Fur Company at Fort Astoria (Astoria, Oregon). After the merger of Astor's firm with the North West Company in 1813, the Astorian post became Fort George. After the Hudson's Bay Company merged with the North West Company in 1821, Fort George became a subpost for that firm, which in 1824 moved its main operations up the Columbia right bank to Fort Vancouver. After that move the Chinooks experienced a loss of prestige, as well as a loss in their trade.

On August 9, 1851, agents of the United States dealt with the Chinooks for their lands

Chinook

The Chinook Tribe traded extensively in their lands on the north bank of the Columbia River near its mouth. Much of their trading with whites was done by their women. The head of this woman reveals head-flattening performed in infancy, a badge of Chinook aristocracy. Photograph by Edward S. Curtis, circa 1900.

in an unratified treaty at Tansey Point (Oregon). After that the survivors of the once-influential tribe, bereft of numbers, lands, and power, dispersed to neighboring white communities. Some of them removed to area reservations.

Government and Claims: In 1953 the Chinook Tribe with no reservation, established an organization, The Chinook Indian Tribe Inc., for the political, educational, and social welfare of the tribe. On July 23, 1979, that organization petitioned the federal government for acknowledgment, which would give it fishing and other rights.

After the neighboring Tillamooks on the south were awarded a settlement of their claims in 1897 (30 Stat. 62) for lands taken by the United States, the Chinooks, Clatsops, Cathlamets, and Wahkiakums (Upper Chinookans) presented a claim to the United States on March 2 and 28, 1899, for compensation for their alienated lands. On August 24, 1912, they were awarded $20,000 by act of Congress (37 Stat. 518, 535). After the establishment of the Indian Claims Commission on August 13, 1946, those Chinooks who were enrolled on reservations of identifiable tribes filing claims were included in any forthcoming awards. The nonreservation Chinooks, Clatsops, and some Wahkiakums and Cathlamets combined as identifiable tribes into The Chinook Nation to press their claim (Docket 234), which they filed on August 8, 1951. In doing so, they maintained that the $26,307.95 that they had been awarded in 1912 for the 762,000 acres that they had yielded in the unratified

treaty of August 9, 1851, was unconscionable. The Indian Claims Commission on November 4, 1971, awarded them $75,000, which, after the previous award had been deducted, entitled them to recover $48,692.05. The Chinook Nation group had been organized to press those claims and it was after that group broke up that The Chinook Indian Tribe Inc. was organized.

Contemporary Life and Culture: Although integrated within the white community, the Chinooks are planning a museum and cultural center to keep alive tribal spirit and heritage. While awaiting an answer to their petition for federal acknowledgment, the tribe promotes fishing enterprises, an industry as old as the Chinookan peoples themselves. Today no one speaks the tribal language.

Suggested Readings: Mildred Colbert, *Kutkos Chinook Tyee* (Boston, 1942); Verne F. Ray, "Lower Chinook Ethnographic Notes," *University of Washington Publications in Anthropology* 7, no. 2 (1938); Verne F. Ray, "The Historical Position of the Lower Chinook in the Native Culture of the Northwest," *Pacific Northwest Quarterly* 28, no. 4 (October, 1937); Robert H. Ruby and John A. Brown, *The Chinook Indians: Traders of the Lower Columbia River* (Norman: University of Oklahoma Press, 1976); James G. Swan, *The Northwest Coast; or, Three Years' Residence in Washington Territory* (1857; Fairfield, Wash.: Ye Galleon Press, 1966); Reuben Gold Thwaites, ed., *Original Journals of the Lewis and Clark Expedition, 1804–1806*, vols. 3 and 4 of 8 vols. (Cleveland, 1904–1907; New York: Antiquarian Press, 1959).

CLACKAMAS
(Upper Chinookan Division of Chinookan)

The Clackamases, after whom one dialect of the Upper Chinookan linguistic stock is named, occupied about twelve villages, which were located mainly on the south bank of the lower Columbia River downstream from present-day Troutdale, Oregon,

roughly to a point opposite present-day Kalama, Washington, and on the east side of the Willamette River from a few miles above its mouth to Oregon City east to the Cascade Mountains. Other river valleys in their lands were the Clackamas, a Willamette

25

tributary; and the Sandy, which flows into the Columbia. Besides the Clackamas River, an Oregon county and town bear the tribal name.

Clackamases and other speakers of their dialect lived in wooden houses, of which the larger ones sheltered three or four families of as many as twenty or more people in a communal setting. The Clackamas villages, varied in size but were fairly permanent. Their inhabitants migrated in summer to procure salmon, roots, and berries. An important item in their diet and trade was the *wappato* root, which they harvested in swampy places along the lower Columbia. Clackamases were skilled in handling canoes fashioned from logs. From platforms on rocks they netted, gaffed, and speared fish as the latter tried to leap over Willamette Falls. The Clackamases and their neighbors came into earlier contact with white traders and travelers than did other Willamette valley natives. The regional headquarters of the Hudson's Bay Company during the second quarter of the nineteenth century were at nearby Fort Vancouver, which was a short way upstream on the Columbia north bank opposite the mouth of the Willamette. In February, 1841, the Clackamas chief, Popoh, was converted to the Roman Catholic faith by the Reverend François Norbert Blanchet. Also contesting for Clackamas souls was the Reverend Alvin F. Waller of the Methodist Mission station near present-day Salem, Oregon.

A treaty that the Clackamases signed with Oregon Superintendent of Indian Affairs Anson Dart in the fall of 1851 went unratified. They signed another on January 10, 1855 (10 Stat. 1143), ratified March 3, 1855. At the time of the latter treaty the Clackamas signatories to it represented only eighty-eight people. By its terms the Clackamases were promised $2,500 in annuities, of which $500 was to be in cash and the remainder in food and clothing. The treaty was considered one of Dart's most important because the lands obtained by the United States lay along the much-coveted Columbia south bank east of the Willamette, including the Clackamas and Sandy river valleys. In the fall of 1851 twenty mills were operating in that area. Those Clackamases who were not integrating with whites and other Indians in the Willamette valley were, as stipulated by treaty, removed westward to the Grand Ronde Reservation. On that confine in 1871 the Clackamases numbered but fifty-five. Their numbers in 1780 have been estimated at 2,500. In 1805–1806 they were estimated at 1,800. Although early twentieth-century newspaper accounts describing certain Indians as the last of their tribe should be read with caution, they do reveal the decline in native populations that was evident at that time. One such article, appearing in the Portland, Oregon, *Journal*, May 9, 1915, told of Soosap, the "last" Clackamas, whose mother was of that tribe and whose father was a Klickitat.

Suggested Readings: Stephen Dow Beckham, *The Indians of Western Oregon, This Land Was Theirs* (Coos Bay, Ore.: Arago Books, 1977); S. A. Clarke, *Pioneer Days of Oregon History* (Portland, Ore., 1905); John Adams Hussey, *Champoeg: Place of Transition* (Portland, Ore.: Oregon Historical Society 1967); Melville Jacobs, *Clackamas Chinook Texts* (Bloomington, Ind.: Indiana University Press, 1958–59), 2 vols.

CLALLAM
(Coastal Division, Salishan)

The Clallams (or Klallams) called themselves by a name meaning "strong people" or "mighty tribe." The early twentieth-century photographer-observer of Indians Edward S. Curtis regarded them as the most warlike and powerful of all the Salish-speaking peoples on the coasts of Washington state, where they occupied the territory stretching along the Strait of Juan de Fuca between Clallam and Port Discovery Bays, including territory formerly held by the Chimakums. Much Clallam tradition, indeed, concerns raids and counterraids involving themselves and neighboring Makahs, Suquamishes, and Chimakums, plus Canadian tribes, such as the Haidas, Tsimshians, and Cowichans. To defend themselves from raiding foes, the Clallams built strong double palisades of split logs. The fierce appearance of knife-wielding members of their Black Society was heightened by charcoal painted on their faces. Some scholars believe that, like the Makahs west of them, the Clallams had migrated south to their location on the southern shores of the Strait of Juan de Fuca. They were closely related to Canadian tribes such as the Songishes, of lower Vancouver Island, whose Lkungen dialect was similar. Clallams continued to migrate to lower Vancouver Island, and a smaller group moved to the United States mainland near present-day Marietta, in Lummi Indian territory. One Clallam group was said to have settled on the upper west coast of Whidbey Island in northern Puget Sound. Even into the contact period, the Clallams attempted to secure lands on that island from Skagit Indians living there. The Clallams were believed to have occupied at least fifteen villages in all, mostly in the southern Strait of Juan de Fuca area.

The Spanish explorer Manuel Quimper discovered Dungeness Bay on the Strait on July 4, 1790, marking what may have been the earliest contact of Clallams with Euro-Americans in their homelands. On April 30, 1792, British Capt. George Vancouver anchored in, and named, Dungeness Bay. As later explorers did, Quimper noted the impaled heads of Clallam foes on Clallam beaches.

The Clallams were not only a warring people but also tradesmen. They carried on considerable trade with their close neighbors, such as the Twanas, and with natives of Vancouver Island, in items such as skins and oils, for which they received goods such as blankets. Besides their trade with neighboring tribes, they would trade, for example, strings of clams for horses from the Yakima

Clallam

This Clallam couple, Charles and Nellie Jackson, revealed in their persons the influence of the whites, ranging from mill owners to missionaries, who had come among this once-powerful tribe of the Strait of Juan de Fuca. The picture, taken circa 1890, is typical of those posed by photographers in studio settings. Courtesy of Whitman College.

Indians east of the Cascade Mountains. The members of the Vancouver expedition were aware of the Clallams' trading propensities. They received from them venison and fish in exchange for coppers and trinkets.

During the period of the Hudson's Bay Company dominance in the region, the Clallams came into the company's orbit, but not always on peaceful terms. On July 1, 1828, Bay Company trappers under Alexander Roderick McLeod killed two Clallam families in retaliation for the killing by

Clallams of five company trappers. As late as 1868, as a result of Clallam-Tsimshian feuding, a party of twenty-six Clallams was taken to the Skokomish Reservation and kept at hard labor by its agent. To compensate for Tsimshian deaths in the feuding, the United States, in Indian fashion, paid the Tsimshians off in gold coins and other gifts. The Clallams and the United States generally remained on good terms, because of the peaceful inclinations toward Americans of Clallam chiefs such as the intemperate Chitsamakkan (Chetzmokha), who was dubbed Duke of York and possessed two wives named Queen Victoria and Jenny Lind.

The ethnologist George Gibbs, when told that the Clallams formerly numbered 2,240, stated that he believed that in 1853 they numbered no more than 800. Official government records of that same year placed their number at 400. A decade earlier Lt. Charles Wilkes of the United States Exploring Expedition estimated them at 425. During the 1850s Clallam population losses were hastened by smallpox and alcohol, which were, according to an elderly Clallam chief, more devastating than their desultory wars.

In the Treaty of Point-No-Point, January 26, 1855, the Clallams were scheduled to remove to the Skokomish Reservation at the southern end of Hood Canal. They shunned that reservation because of its poor soils and its distance from their own lands, and because it lay in the territory of the Twanas, their traditional rivals. Very few Clallams removed to the Skokomish. Many Clallams were scattered in small villages around Hood Canal, Puget Sound, and the Strait of Juan de Fuca at distances from 50 to 150 miles from the Skokomish Reservation. Some Clallams acquired land by purchase or homestead entry. One small group purchased 210 acres of land at Jamestown on the Strait of Juan de Fuca, where they managed their holdings as a communal venture. A less ambitious village venture was that of a Clallam band at Port Gamble. The statistics available indicate that before 1914 the average Clallam population was at Jamestown about 240 and at Port Gamble about 90. Many Clallams worked in sawmilling, fishing, and canoeing and were pictured by Indian agents as independent, self-supporting, industrious, and relatively prosperous.

Bearing the tribal name are a town, a bay, a river, and a county.

In 1936–37 the United States purchased and placed in trust 1,604.44 acres of land for the Clallams. The historic relative independence of the Clallam bands from each other came into play in the division of the trust acreage. In essence, the United States recognized the de facto Clallam separateness in the establishment of reservations for the Lower Elwha Tribal Community and the Port Gamble Indian Community.

As a result of a relief act of March 3, 1925 (43 Stat. 1102, 44 Stat. 173), the Clallam band received $399,277.68. The Indian Claims Commission did not consider this a gratuitous offset to the claim (Docket 134) that the Clallams had filed for themselves and the Chimakums for additional compensation for lands ceded to the United States. The Clallams had claimed that the Chimakums were nearly extinct at the time of the Point-No-Point Treaty. They asserted that the few Chimakums who remained had been absorbed within the Clallam tribe, which had occupied the Chimakum lands and claimed them as well as their own. On December 2, 1957, the commission recognized the Clallam claim that they had taken possession of the Chimakum lands between 1855 and 1857. Finding the claim to have involved 438,430 acres, the commission on October 1, 1970, awarded the Clallam bands $440,000. After $39,180 were excluded because of a previous consideration, their award was $400,820. The commission then deducted from that sum the value of aboriginal Clallam land holdings, or $15,000, which the United States had paid for the Port Gamble Reservation tract. This made the net award $385,820. A small group of Clallams, apart from the other three groups (Jamestown, Lower Elwha, and Port Gamble), are organized as the Clallam General Council, but without federal acknowledgement. See also **Jamestown Clallam Indian Tribe; Lower Elwha Tribal Community, Lower Elwha Reservation; and Port Gamble**

Indian Community, Port Gamble Reservation, Washington.

Suggested Readings: Myron Eells, The Twana, Chemakum, and Clallam Indians of Washington Territory (1889; Seattle: Shorey Book Store, 1971); Robert H. Ruby and John A. Brown, Myron Eells and the Puget Sound Indians (Seattle: Superior Publishing Company, 1976); Erna Gunther, "Klallam Ethnography," University of Washington Publications in Anthropology 1, no. 5 (1927).

CLATSKANIE
(Athapascan)

The Clatskanies split off from a band of Athapasan speakers, the Kwalhioquas, who lived in the hills north of the lower Columbia River in present-day Washington. Probably before 1775, a band of these Kwalhioquas migrated to the south side of the Columbia River in search of more favorable subsistence and became the Clatskanies. Their Kwalhioqua relatives, languishing in their homeland, eventually disappeared, while the Clatskanies flourished a while longer. The migrants explained their exodus from their homelands in one of their traditions. According to the legend, some young men with a magic spindle had started a forest fire that burned for two years, driving the elk away. About five years later, after the grass returned, some hunters following the trail of the elk crossed the Columbia River on a raft. When they crossed, they sent a messenger north with the news of their success before moving south across the river.

About fifty miles east of the mouth of the Columbia, the Skilloots, an Upper Chinookan people, eventually moved south across the river and pushed the Clatskanies back from it about twenty miles. Those Clatskanies remained primarily a hunting people. The Clatskanies on the river were possibly a mixed group of Chinookan and other speakers. Among native and white traders they developed a reputation for violence because of their attempts to exact tribute from those passing their shores. Like other white fur traders before them, the men of the Hudson's Bay Company traveled past the Clallam shores only in large, armed convoys. While the Lewis and Clark expedition wintered at Fort Clatsop in 1805–1806, the Clatskanies planned to storm the fort. Clatsops seem to have thwarted the plan. Some anthropologists maintain that the Clatskanies were the "Clackstar Nation" whose numbers Lewis and Clark placed at 1,200. Anthropologist Herbert C. Taylor, Jr. has estimated their numbers at that time more conservatively at 400. George Simpson of the Hudson's Bay Company estimated their population at 175 in 1825. Oregon Territorial Governor Joseph Lane stated in 1849 that they numbered about 300 on lands stretching along the coast northward to the Columbia River. It is very likely that Lane included Clatsops in his enumeration. According to Oregon Superintendent of Indian Affairs Anson Dart, with whom they signed an unratified treaty on August 9, 1851, ceding their lands, they numbered no more than 3 men and 5 women in 1851. In 1910 they were said to number only 3. Such diseases as smallpox and the intermittent fever, desultory fighting, and intermingling with others finally took their toll.

Suggested Readings: Melville Jacobs, "Historic Perspectives in Indian Languages of Oregon and Washington," Pacific Northwest Quarterly 28, no. 1 (January, 1937); Herbert C. Taylor, Jr., and Lester L. Hoaglin, Jr., "The 'Intermittent Fever' Epidemic of the 1830's on the Lower Columbia River," Ethnohistory 9, no. 2 (Spring, 1962): 165.

CLATSOP
(Lower Chinookan Division of Chinookan)

Today an Oregon town and county bear the name Clatsop, which is derived from a native word for dried salmon. Culturally the Clatsops were much like the Chinooks proper across the Columbia River from them on the north. Both peoples held slaves and flattened the heads of infants of the aristocracy. Both performed similar rituals, such as those associated with the first salmon runs. The Clatsops were more dependent on hunting than the Chinooks, to whom they sold elk skins for processing into cuirasses *(clamons)*. Less skilled in trade than the Chinooks, the Clatsops nonetheless competed with them in such endeavors and occasionally engaged them and their other neighbors in petty conflicts. The Clatsops' exposure to Euro-Americans was also similar to that of the Chinooks, though the earliest ships entered the Columbia at Bakers Bay in Chinook waters. Later these craft crossed the treacherous bar of the Columbia and passed into the stream along its southern shores, where the Clatsops resided.

The Clatsops stole a march on the Chinooks when the Lewis and Clark party camped in their country at Fort Clatsop during the winter of 1805–1806. In 1811, Astorians of John Jacob Astor's Pacific Fur Company established Fort Astoria in Clatsop country at present-day Astoria, Oregon. Two years later British fur traders of the North West Company established Fort George at that same place. The post was under Hudson's Bay Company management after 1821, and save for a few buildings, it was moved up the Columbia right bank to Fort Vancouver in 1824.

Disease, drink, and debauchery rendered the Clatsops unable to recover their numbers. The practice of abortion and infanticide by their women added further to their decline, as did their marriages to fur traders and others, including neighboring tribesmen. The Clatsops struggled to survive by trading with the whites, butchering whales cast up on their beaches, and salvaging goods from wrecked ships. In 1829 their appropriation of goods from the Hudson's Bay Company ship *William and Ann* caused that firm to send a punitive expedition to their villages. Cold statistics reveal the relentless decline in their numbers later: 220 in 1841, 180 in 1848, 56 in 1871, and 26 in 1910.

Attempting to rescue Clatsop souls were the Reverend John E. Frost and others of the Missionary Society of the Methodist

Clatsop

This mother and child, photographed circa 1880, are representatives of those Clatsops who, after extensive contact with whites, remained in their tribal homeland, which was on the south bank of the Columbia River at its entrance into the Pacific Ocean. The American explorers Lewis and Clark wintered among the Clatsops in 1805–1806. Courtesy of the Oregon Historical Society.

Episcopal Church, which ministered to tribal members in their country beginning in 1840. Like Pacific Northwest Methodist missions in general, the Clatsop Mission ended in failure. Frustrating such activity was the continuing Indian attrition from liquor-induced violence and the loss of native lands. As missionaries shifted their efforts from the Indians to white settlers, some Clatsop families, evaluating the situation, married their daughters to whites, including French-Canadian former fur men such as those who settled on French Prairie in the Willamette valley.

On the heels of the settlers, the United States sent an Indian subagent to Astoria. On August 5, 1851, Oregon Superintendent of Indian Affairs Anson Dart signed an unratified treaty with most of the Clatsops. Two days later he signed another with a small Clatsop band, the Nucqueclahwemuks. On August 24, 1912, Congress awarded these two Clatsop bands $15,000 and $1,500 respectively (37 Stat. 518) to satisfy claims arising from nonratification of their treaty. A descendant of a Clatsop signatory to the treaty named Dunkel claimed that none of Dunkel's heirs had received the monies due them under its terms. Clatsops who intermarried with other tribesmen were also involved in claims against the United States. In 1897 the Nehalem "band" of Tillamooks,

which included Indians of Clatsop blood, was awarded a $10,000 settlement by the government for its unratified treaty of August 6, 1851. This was one of many belated adjustments that the government made to descendants of the Clatsops who had extended hospitality to whites in their lands. Nonreservation Clatsop descendants also shared with Chinooks, Wahkiakums, and Cathlamets a November 4, 1871, award (see also **Chinook**). By 1980 the Clatsops had not regained the status of a viable or identifiable tribe, but those remaining attempted to retain the memory of their ancestry and complained of intrusion of industrial firms on ancient tribal burial places.

Suggested Readings: Franz Boas, *Chinook Texts,* Bureau of American Ethnology Bulletin no. 20 (Washington, D.C., Government Printing Office, 1894); Grace P. Morris, "Development of Astoria, 1811–1850," *Oregon Historical Quarterly* 37, no. 4 (December, 1937); Verne F. Ray, "Lower Chinook Ethnographic Notes," *University of Washington Publications in Anthropology* 7, no. 2 (1938); Verne F. Ray, "The Historical Position of the Lower Chinook in the Native Culture of the Pacific Northwest," *Pacific Northwest Quarterly* 28, no. 4 (October, 1937); Robert H. Ruby and John A. Brown, *The Chinook Indians: Traders of the Lower Columbia River* (Norman: University of Oklahoma Press, 1976).

CLOWWEWALLA
(Upper Chinookan Division of Chinookan)

The Clowwewallas were of the Clackamas division of the Upper Chinookan linguistic stock. They lived along the Willamette River from its mouth south about twenty miles to and around Willamette Falls. They were found on the west bank of the falls across from present-day Oregon City. At the falls they built platforms from the rocks, from which they netted, gaffed, and speared the fish trying to leap up the falls. They also traded with such peoples as the Tillamooks on the west, from whom they obtained oil from sea animals. Because they lived in the

lower Columbia–Willamette river area, the Clowwewallas, like their neighbors, came into early contact with white fur traders. Until truces were effected, they were initially on poor terms with the whites. One consequence of their contacts with fur traders and later with settlers was a severe population loss due to the epidemics that followed the Columbia and Willamette river valleys in the late eighteenth and early nineteenth centuries. In 1780 the Clowwewallas numbered roughly 300; and in 1805–1806, 650. The latter estimate probably included others of the Clackamas division of Upper Chinookans. Those living at the Willamette Falls were said to have numbered only 13 in 1851. Clowwewallas and Clackamases, along with Kalapuyan speakers, such as Molalas, were included in treaties effected with Oregon Superintendent of Indian Affairs Anson Dart on January 10 and 19, 1855 (10 Stat. 1143, ratified March 3, 1855). In accordance with the terms of their treaty, a Clowwewalla remnant was removed west to the Grand Ronde Reservation. They shortly became extinct. See also **Clackamas**.

COEUR D'ALÊNE
(Interior Division, Salishan)

Originally the Coeur d'Alênes called themselves Skitswish, a word believed to be simply the name of one place, perhaps meaning "foundling." The name Coeur d'Alêne, meaning in French "heart of an awl," was said to have been given the Skitswish by early nineteenth-century French-Canadian fur traders, who believed them to be stingy-hearted with a sharpness in trade like that of a pin or an awl. They were a fiercely independent people who roamed over four million acres from Spokane Falls in present-day Washington on the west to the Clark Fork River in present-day Montana on the east, and from Lake Pend Oreille in present-day Idaho on the north to the Clearwater River in Idaho on the south. They were composed of three major bands, which were based in present-day Idaho on Coeur d'Alene Lake, the Coeur d'Alene River, and the Saint Joe River. Bearing their name today, besides the lake and the river, are the Coeur D'Alene Reservation, a mountain range, and a city on Interstate 90 on the northern shores of the lake. The successor to the original Coeur d'Alêne tribe is known today as The Coeur D'Alene Tribe, Coeur D'Alene Reservation, Idaho.

Location: The Coeur d'Alênes settled on and in the environs of their reservation of about 69,000 acres, which is in the panhandle of northern Idaho about thirty-five miles south of the city of Coeur d'Alene, Principal settlements are at Benewah, Desmet, Plummer, Sanders, Tensed, and Worley.

Numbers: In 1827 a Hudson's Bay Company trader, John Warren Dease, gave the Coeur d'Alêne numbers at 400, about 600 fewer than in 1780. In 1835–36, Samuel Parker, a missionary for the American Board of Commissioners for Foreign Missions placed them at 700, but Parker was given to exaggeration. In 1841 Lt. Charles Wilkes, commanding a naval expedition to the Pacific Northwest, listed them more realistically at 450. In 1870 they were listed officially at 300; and in 1888, at 516.

History: As noted, the Coeur d'Alênes were an independent people. Occasionally they engaged in combat with other tribes, such as the Nez Percés on the south and the Spokanes on the west, but generally they had good relations with their neighbors, with whom they shared fishing, gathering, and gaming places. Although they discouraged white traders from entering their lands, the Coeur d'Alênes in the early nineteenth century traded with them outside Coeur d'Alêne country at posts such as Fort Spokane and Fort Colvile and Kullyspell (Kalispel) House and Spokane House. Three Coeur d'Alêne Indians visited the American explorers Meriwether Lewis and William Clark in Nez Percé country as those men journeyed homeward in 1806.

In April 1842, the Reverend Pierre De Smet, S.J., laid the groundwork for a Coeur d'Alêne mission, which began operating in November of that year when the Reverend Nicholas Point, S.J., and a Brother Huet built a log church on the Saint Joe River. Point characterized his native parishioners as noted for "dissimulation, egotism and cruelty." The tribesmen confessed their "pagan" practices to the clerics, who set about establishing them in the Catholic faith. Despite the opposition of some Coeur d'Alênes, such as Chief Stellam, in response to the efforts of churchmen to have them become farmers, the priests prevailed. In 1879 one priest hailed them as "the tribe which has now made the greatest advance in civilization." In May, 1858, the Coeur d'Alênes led neighboring tribes in repulsing the command of U.S. Army Col. Edward Steptoe moving northward toward the Canadian border. During the Yakima War, which broke out in 1855, the Coeur d'Alênes remained neutral, but in September, 1858, along with several other tribes of the interior they unsuccessfully engaged the army command of Col. George Wright in two fights in the Spokane country. One provision of a "treaty" that Wright blustered from them was the right to build the Mullan road through their lands. In 1859 they submitted to the building of the road despite threats of some tribesmen to kill its builder, Capt. John Mullan.

With the executive orders of June 14, 1867, and November 8, 1873, of the 598,500-acre Coeur d'Alene Reservation, the tribe ceded to the United States 2,389,924 acres, which extended from the central Idaho panhandle west ten or twelve miles into Washington Territory, east to the Bitterroot Mountains, north to the Pend Oreille River, and south to the dividing point between the drainage basins of Coeur d'Alene Lake and the Snake River. The Coeur d'Alene Reservation was established only after the failure (for lack of ratification by the United States) of the agreement into which the Coeur d'Alênes had entered on July 28, 1873, to relinquish their right and title to their lands. After petitioning for a commission to treat for their lands outside the reservation, the tribe, by an agreement dated March 26, 1887 (26 Stat. 989, 1027, ratified March 3, 1891) ceded to the United States 184,960 acres of the northern part of the reservation for $231,884.97, which opened those acres to

Coeur d'Alêne

Chief Seltice of the Coeur d'Alênes of northern Idaho, photographed circa 1890. Like his predecessors, he vigorously sought to protect his people from white encroachments on their lands. His people had a reputation among whites as shrewd traders. Courtesy of Jerome Peltier.

non-Indian occupancy and settlement under United States mineral laws. By an agreement concluded at Spokane Falls, in Washington Territory, on March 18, 1887, the nonreservation Spokanes living in the vicinity of Spokane Falls, after deeding to the United States all right, title, and claim that they had or ever would have to any and all lands outside the Spokane Reservation, agreed to remove to the Coeur d'Alene and Flathead reservations. In exchange, the United States agreed to assist them in moving and becoming established in their new homes. Thus in January, 1894, thirty-two largely Roman Catholic Spokane families were relocated on the Coeur d'Alene Reservation, which some of them later left. Between 1905 and 1909, 97 Spokanes and 541 Coeur d'Alênes were allotted quarter sections of land, de-

33

spite the opposition of important Coeur d'Alênes, such as Chief Moctelme.

Government and Claims: On November 17, 1934, the successor of the historic Coeur d'Alêne tribe, the Coeur D'Alene Tribe, Coeur D'Alene Reservation, Idaho, rejected by a narrow margin the Indian Reorganization Act (48 Stat. 984). The tribe has an elective council, from which its principal officers are elected. Committees deal with problems related to land, law and order, education, welfare, credit, and domestic affairs.

The Coeur D'Alene Tribe, Coeur D'Alene Reservation, Idaho, claimed (Docket 81) additional payment for the 2,389,924 acres that the tribe had ceded to the United States for $231,884.97 pursuant to the agreement of March 26, 1887. The Indian Claims Commission decided that as of March 3, 1891 (the ratification date of the 1887 agreement) the value of the land had been $4,659,663 and ordered that the tribe be paid this amount minus the previous award, or $4,427,778.03. With twenty-four other tribes throughout western United States the tribe in 1970 filed claims (Dockets 523-71 and 524-71) with the Court of Claims for mismanagement of Indian Commission judgment funds and other funds, such as Individual Indian Money accounts held in trust by the United States. The Coeur D'Alene Tribe in 1981 was awarded $173,978.79.

Contemporary Life and Culture: Of great importance to the Coeur D'Alene Tribe is its Development Enterprise, which was begun in 1970 and boasts one of the largest farms in northern Idaho. Profits from this farm were used in developing the Swine Enterprise. Other businesses under the Development Enterprise were the Utility Service Enterprise (a construction company), the tribal service station at Tensed, the Timber Enterprise, and the Tribal Distributors. The tribe has sought to repurchase as much land as possible. Members lease their lands. The tribe also seeks to exchange lands with private interest groups to unify its holdings from its various enterprises. Older tribal members cling to some of their traditional

means of livelihood, such as hunting, fishing, and gathering. Nearly everyone speaks English. To preserve the fast-disappearing native language, a tribal language program was instituted. Children attend the Sacred Heart Mission school at Desmet and public schools in the reservation towns and Tekoa, Washington. Tribal authorities are trying to encourage continuing school attendance.

Special Events: The Whaa-laa Days, held during the second week of July at Worley, feature Indian games and war-dance contests.

Suggested Readings: Ross R. Cotroneo and Jack Dozier, "A Time of Disintegration: The Coeur d'Alene and the Dawes Act," *Western Historical Quarterly* 5, no. 4 (October, 1974); Edward S. Curtis, *The North American Indian* (1912; New York: Johnson Reprint Corporation, 1970), vol. 7; Jack Dozier, "Coeur D'Alene Country: The Creation of the Coeur D'Alene Reservation in Northern Idaho," *Idaho Yesterdays* 6, no. 3 (Fall, 1962); Jack Dozier, "The Coeur d'Alene Indians in the War of 1858," *Idaho Yesterdays* 5, no. 3 (Fall, 1961); Jack Dozier, "The Coeur d'Alene Land Rush, 1909–10," *Pacific Northwest Quarterly* 53, no. 4 (October, 1962); Jack Dozier, *The Coeur D'Alene Indian Reservation* (1970); William T. Geoffroy, "The Coeur d'Alene Tribe: A Contemporary View," *Idaho Heritage* 1, no. 10 (October, 1977); Sven Liljeblad, "The Indians of Idaho," *Idaho Yesterdays* 4, no. 3 (1960); Lawrence Palladino, S.J., *The Coeur d'Alene Reservation and Our Friends the Coeur d'Alene Indians* (Fairfield, Wash.: Ye Galleon Press, 1967); Jerome Peltier, *A Brief History of the Coeur d'Alene Indians, 1806–1909* (Fairfield, Wash.: Ye Galleon Press, 1982); Jerome Peltier, *Manners and Customs of the Coeur d'Alene Indians* (Moscow, Idaho: Peltier Publications, 1975); Gladys A. Reichard, "An Analysis of Coeur D'Alene Myths," *Memoirs of the American Folklore Society* 41 (1947); James A. Teit, "The Salishan Tribes of the Western Plateaus," ed. Franz Boas *Forty-Fifth Annual Report of the Bureau of American Ethnology* (Washington, D.C.: Government Printing Office, 1930); Deward E. Walker Jr., *American Indians of Idaho,* Anthropological Monographs of the University of Idaho, no. 2 (1973).

COEUR D'ALENE TRIBE, COEUR D'ALENE RESERVATION

The Coeur D'Alene Tribe, Coeur D'Alene Reservation, Idaho, is composed of Coeur d'Alênes and those Spokanes who wish to live on the Coeur d'Alene Reservation. The Spokanes, by a treaty of March 18, 1887, were allowed their choice of living on the Coeur d'Alene or the Flathead reservation. Those Spokanes who joined the Coeur d'Alênes were for the most part Upper Spokanes of the three Spokane groups living nearest to the Coeur d'Alênes. Many Upper Spokanes shared the Roman Catholic faith with the Coeur d'Alênes.

In 1960 approximately 400 tribal members were listed as living on the Coeur d'Alene Reservation. In 1965 about 360 people were living there. As of 1982 there were about 822 enrolled tribal members, and in 1985 there were 853. Since 1984 a quarter of Indian blood has been required for tribal enrollment.

In 1991 the 1,100-member Coeur D'Alene Tribe filed a lawsuit over ownership of Coeur d'Alene Lake, claiming that it had been granted to them in an 1873 treaty. The tribe has a model modern medical facility, a $3 million tribal school, plans to build a $2 million bingo palace, and plans for a new tribal headquarters and to construct a resort. See also **Coeur d'Alêne.**

Coeur D'Alene Tribe, Coeur D'Alene Reservation

Peter Moctelme, a Coeur d'Alêne chief. After early difficult years Roman Catholic fathers persuaded many Coeur d'Alênes, such as Moctelme, to become farmers. Around the turn of the century he opposed allotting on the Coeur D'Alene Reservation in northern Idaho. Courtesy of the Eastern Washington Historical Society.

COLVILLE
(Interior Division, Salishan)

The Colvilles were called by other Salishan peoples by a name that has been written Scheulpi, or Chualpay, in English letters. French-Canadian fur men called them La Chaudières, or Kettles, for the kettlelike depressions in the rocks at the Kettle Falls on the Columbia River just south of the Canadian border in present-day Washington state. Besides living at the falls, the Colvilles also lived south of them farther down the Columbia River as far as present-day Hunters, Washington, and in the Colville River valley a short distance to the east. The designation "basket people," given them by

Colville

Chief Oropaughn of the Colvilles proper, a very popular leader of the 1880s and 1890s. His people lived in the general area of Kettle Falls on the Columbia River, below the Canadian border. They are not to be confused with other Indians of the Colville Reservation also called Colvilles, though the Colvilles proper did live on the reservation bearing their name, which derives from that of Andrew Colvile, a governor of the Hudson's Bay Company. Photograph in the authors' collection.

a white observer in 1846, refers to the fifteen- to twenty-foot baskets of woven osiers, roots, and hard, twisted cords in which they netted up to three thousand salmon daily at Kettle Falls. Their name, Colville, is derived from that of a Hudson's Bay Company governor, Andrew Colvile, after whom was named a nearby company post, Fort Colvile, which was established in 1825. The United States military's Fort Colville was established nearby in 1859. Also bearing the name Colville are a river and its

valley, a reservation, and a town on U.S. Highway 395.

Colville numbers in 1780 have been estimated at 1,000. In 1882 only 6 or 7 were reported by a reservation census taker. The number of Colvilles was 321 in 1904, 334 in 1907, and 322 in 1937. It would seem that those figures include people from other tribes on the Colville Reservation. Among the causes of the attrition of the original Colvilles was a smallpox epidemic in 1782–83 and subsequent outbreaks of that disease, which would have been more widespread if some natives in the Kettle Falls area had not been vaccinated by their Roman Catholic priests. No one knows for certain when Colvilles first met white men. Two whom they very likely met around 1800 were the trappers Le Blanc and La Gasse sent westward by David Thompson of the North West Company. A Colville Indian, Alexander Daylight, who died in 1913, claimed to have talked with Thompson at Kettle Falls in July, 1811. Because of the falls, the area was not only a fishing, trading, and military center but also a center for missionary activity as well. Three years after meeting their first Catholic missionaries near the falls in 1838, the Colvilles were ministered to by the Reverend Pierre De Smet, S.J., then the best-known cleric of his faith in the interior of the Pacific Northwest. For years Indians from miles around visited the Saint Francis Regis Mission near the falls. Although opposed to miners, soldiers, and settlers in their country, the Colvilles refrained from engaging in the Indian wars of the 1850s, at least partly because of the influence of their priests. Their chiefs also saw that with such small numbers they stood little chance of success in combat with soldiers who carried superior weapons.

By executive order of April 8, 1872, the Colville Reservation was established east of the Columbia River for tribes of the area. Before that year had ended, settlers in the fertile Colville valley within the reservation had pressured the government into opening it again to white settlement and establishing another reservation for the Colvilles. This second Colville Reservation was established by executive order on July 2, 1872, west of the Columbia River. The tribesmen belonging to this Colville Reservation today are called Colvilles and are incorporated as the Confederated Tribes of the Colville Reservation. See **Confederated Tribes of the Colville Reservation, Washington.**

Suggested Readings: David H. Chance, "Balancing the Fur Trade at Fort Colville," *The Record*

(Washington State University, Pullman) 34 (1973); Edward S. Curtis, *The North American Indian* (1912; New York: Johnson Reprint Corporation, 1970), vol. 7; Pierre Jean De Smet, S.J. *Life, Letters, and Travels of Father Pierre-Jean De Smet, S.J., 1801–1873,* ed. Hiram Martin Chittenden and Alfred Talbot Richardson (New York: Francis P. Harper, 1905), 4 vols.

COLVILLE CONFEDERATED TRIBES
(See **Confederated Tribes of the Colville Reservation, Washington.**)

CONFEDERATED SALISH & KOOTENAI TRIBES OF THE FLATHEAD RESERVATION

The roots of the Confederated Salish & Kootenai Tribes of the Flathead Reservation in Montana lay in the Hell Gate, Montana Council of July 16, 1855, where the Flatheads (Salishes), Pend d'Oreilles (or Upper Kalispels), and Kutenais signed with the Washington territorial governor and superintendent of Indian Affairs, Isaac Stevens, a treaty ratified March 8, 1859. The Flatheads and Pend d'Oreilles were of the Interior Division of the Salish linguistic stock. The Kutenais were of Kitunahan linguistic stock. The treaty provided the tribes a reservation, called the Flathead or Jocko, on the western slopes of the continental divide in western Montana. The original Flathead Reservation totaled 1,242,969 acres, but by a government act of April 23, 1904, 2,378 of its Indians were allotted 80 or 160 acres each; 404,047.33 acres were patented to settlers; 60,843.04 acres were granted to the state of Montana for school purposes; 18,523.85 acres were reserved for the United States; and 1,757.09 acres were reserved for the tribes for church, school, agency, railroad, and biological-station purposes. The total acreage thus disposed of was 485,171.31 in 4,834 parcels. Allotting for

the tribes was completed in 1908. Eighty acres were allotted if the lands were classified as agricultural, and 160 acres were allotted if the lands were classified for grazing. Before the opening of the reservation some Indian families had had as many as 3,000 head of horses.

By proclamation on May 22, 1909 (36 Stat. 2494) the president opened to entry and settlement all nonmineral and unreserved lands on the reservation that were classified as agricultural lands of the first class, as well as agricultural lands of the second class and grazing lands. The reservation was officially opened to holders of lands in those categories on May 2, 1910. Although the reservation's boundaries remain as originally designated, its Indian-owned lands as of September 30, 1977, had been reduced to 618,758.51 acres by allotment and homestead sales. Of that acreage 567,319.54 acres were in tribal ownership. The balance, except for 1,017 acres in government reserve, was in individual ownership.

Among the tribes who later came to live on the reservation were about ninety Upper Spokanes who came there in 1887 under

Confederated Salish & Kootenai Tribes
of the Flathead Reservation

Johnny Arlee, 1982, a medicine man who practices native traditional religion and healing with which Catholics have found reconciliation of a onetime scorn. He uses the sweat house. Rock, earth, fire, and water are elements of the rite. Today's Salish and Kutenai tribal members are descendants of the Flathead and Kutenai peoples, who were distinct linguistic groups when put on the Flathead Reservation in western Montana. Photo courtesy of Larry Reisnouer, Spokane, Washington.

the leadership of Baptiste Peone. They subsequently signed an agreement with the United States allowing them to remain.

Location: Slightly less than 50 percent of the enrolled tribal members live on the Flathead Reservation. Those off the reservation live principally in the Pacific Northwest, but also in other areas, such as California.

Numbers: Tribal membership in 1980 was approximately 5,937. In 1985 membership was 3,225, and in 1989 it was 6,669.

Government and Claims: The Confederated Salish & Kootenai Tribes of the Flathead Reservation, were organized under the Indian Reorganization Act, and their constitution and bylaws were approved by the secretary of the interior on October 28, 1935. Their corporate charter was ratified on April 25, 1936. The governing body is a council, whose members are nominated reservationwide. Elections of council members are held biennially. Many tribal members have held public office at the state, county, and local levels.

A compromise settlement between the petitioning Confederated Tribes and the defending United States was reached for an entry of a final judgment by the Indian Claims Commission in the amount of $4,431,622.18 on the condition that the claim (Docket 61), which had been appealed to the Court of Claims (Docket 1-66), be dismissed and remanded to the commission which was done. For 12,005,000 acres of lands ceded to the United States under the 1855 treaty, a final judgment was entered on August 5, 1966, for the value of the land as of March 8, 1859. This amounted to $5.3 million less the consideration that had already been paid the tribes ($593,377.82) and an offset of $275,000. Thus the final award was $4,431,622.18. On July 24, 1951, the tribes filed a claim with the Indian Claims Commission (Docket 156) for an accounting of their trust funds, erroneous boundary surveys, the opening of the Flathead Reservation, and taking of its lands and waters. The docket was dismissed because the claims were similar to those filed with the Court of Claims (No. 50233) under the act of July 30, 1946, which had authorized the suit by the tribes a year before the Indian Claims Commission was established. The claims for compensation for waters and lands taken were for the waters of Hell Roaring Creek, which had been taken for a power plant for the city of Polson, Montana; for reservation lands taken without adequate compensation for a power site under an act of March 3, 1909; and for waters from Flathead Lake taken for constructing and operating the Flathead Irrigation Project under the act of April 3, 1908, without the compensation agreed upon. The court dismissed those claims, but on December 18, 1967, it awarded the tribes $190,399.97 as reimbursement for the expenses of surveys and classification of tribal lands sold and otherwise disposed of under the act of April 23, 1904 (33 Stat. 302) in breach of the Hell Gate Treaty. On March 8, 1971, a judgment was made for $6 million that was a compromise settlement for the general accounting of tribal monies and property. On April 23, 1971, a judgment of $7,410,000 was made. It included the 1912 value of 485,171.31 acres of reservation land minus the $1,343,331.22 already paid plus interest of $16,294,880.29, for a total of $22,361,549.07. On November 11, 1971, a judgment of $550,000 was made for erroneous surveys of the northern and southwestern reservation boundaries.

Contemporary Life and Culture: Much of the tribal land consists of valuable stands of timber, sales of which have averaged about $3 million annually. Two large sawmills, which are of non-Indian ownership but located on the reservation, provide employment to tribesmen, who also work in other area mills and in allied logging operations. Additional tribal revenue comes from yearly rent paid for the site of Kerr Dam, a hydroelectric facility of the Montana Power Company, on the Flathead River on reservation lands. The power company also uses waters from Kerr Dam under lease. The Bureau of Indian Affairs operates an irrigation system on the reservation serving about 125,597 acres. The project was established in 1908 to help the Indians become farmers. As of 1980, less than 12 percent of the lands

irrigated by the project belonged to tribal members. The tribes own a tourist resort at Blue Bay on Flathead Lake, as well as recreational facilities at Hot Springs. Points of interest on the reservation include the National Bison Range at Moiese, waterfowl refuges, and historic Saint Ignatius Mission, which was established in 1854. Tribal children have attended both mission and public schools since both began operations on tribal lands. Considerable intermarriage has rendered many tribal members indistinguishable from non-Indians in speech and lifestyles. Since 1976 two cultural committees have operated, one by Salishes and one by Kootenais. Among their various activities has been the gathering of several hundred cassette tapes of tribal stories, songs, and general language information. The committees work with the Northwest Reading Laboratory in developing Indian reading materials. The involvement of youth in these activities—part of a trend toward "being Indians"—is a source of great satisfaction to their elders.

Special Events: On a weekend around the second week of May a Cherry Festival is held at Polson. At the same place on Memorial Day weekend the Blue Bay Regatta is held. In June at Hot Springs the Homesteader Days are held, featuring an Indian rodeo and powwow. Also held at that time the Pioneer Days are in Ronan, featuring a rodeo and powwow. Around the Fourth of July the Arlee Powwow is held at Arlee. The Babb Rodeo is held around the same time at Babb. In mid-July the Wagon Burner Regatta is held at Polson. On Labor Day weekend the Indian Summer Regatta is held at Polson.

Suggested Readings: See suggested readings under **Flathead** and **Kutenai**.

CONFEDERATED TRIBES OF THE CHEHALIS RESERVATION, WASHINGTON

The Confederated Tribes of the Chehalis Reservation, originated from the establishment of the 4,224.63-acre Chehalis Reservation for Kwaiailks (Upper Chehalises) and

Lower Chehalises at the confluence of the Chehalis and Black rivers in southwestern Washington state.

Location: Tribal members live on the Chehalis Reservation or near it in towns such as Elma and Rochester, which are west of the cities of Chehalis and Centralia. Some live at points as distant as the state of Florida.

Numbers: In 1906 there were about 149 Chehalises. The tribe numbered 382 in 1984.

History: The area designated for the Chehalis Reservation was selected by the government as early as 1860. Two years later 230 Chehalises were living in the area, which was established as a reservation by executive order on July 8, 1864. In 1868 there were but forty families on the reservation, but many more Chehalises lived nearby. Those on the reservation became concerned about the uncertain status of their lands. In 1873, when their agent, R. H. Milroy, requested that the reservation be enlarged, the commissioner of Indian affairs replied that additions were impossible because parts of the land requested for the enlargement had already been granted to the Northern Pacific Railroad. A nontreaty people, the Chehalises received less federal help than did treaty tribes. Because of their nontreaty status, they received no patents for the lands allotted them and therefore had to apply for lands under the homestead laws. By an executive order signed by President Grover Cleveland on October 1, 1866, 3,753.63 acres of the reservation were restored to the public domain for homestead entry, and 471 acres were set aside for school purposes. Thirty-six Indians on the reservation selected homesteads. A third executive order dated November 11, 1909, restored an additional section of the reservation to the public domain.

Government and Claims: The Confederated Tribes of the Chehalis Reservation, Washington, are a self-governing, independent political unit within the United States with a constitution and bylaws adopted on July 15, 1939, and approved by the commissioner of Indian affairs on August 22, 1939. The tribes had voted to reject organization under the Indian Reorganization Act of 1934 (48 Stat. 984). Their governing body, the Chehalis Community Council, is composed of all qualified voters. It elects a business committee that manages all of the Confederated Tribes, real property and other assets and administers the funds within tribal control. The committee also enforces tribal ordinances.

In 1906, because the reservation's natural resources were being diminished by encroaching whites, the Chehalis Tribe petitioned the United States government for payment for the lands that the U.S. had appropriated. Not having signed a treaty relinquishing the lands, the Chehalises had to wait a long time for compensation for their loss. In a 1908 report the acting commissioner of Indian affairs, C. F. Larrabee, denied the validity of the Chehalis claims, maintaining that the Chehalises had participated in the Tansey Point (Oregon) Treaties in 1851. Those treaties had been drawn up by Oregon Superintendent of Indian Affairs Anson Dart. Several Chehalises complained bitterly in depositions in an 1929 investigation of native land use in the Indian claims case *Duwamish et al. v. the United States* (No. F-275). On August 8, 1951, a century after the Tansey Point treaties, the Chehalis Tribe again filed with the Indian Claims Commission a petition against the United States (Docket 237) for lands that the U.S. had appropriated, including 3,753.63 acres removed from the Chehalis Reservation by executive order in October, 1886. The plaintiffs were the Upper and Lower Chehalis, Satsop, Humptulips, Upper and Lower Chinook, and Clatsop tribes, as well as the Confederated Tribes of the Chehalis Reservation. Problems arose when the Claims Commission initially questioned the plaintiffs' right to prosecute the claim on behalf of the various tribes. Finally, however, the commission decided that the Confederated Tribes of the Chehalis Reservation were the successors in interest to the tribes who were the original owners of lands. The Confederated Tribes were seeking compensation for the lands because the government in the

1860s had ordered the Indians to go to the Chehalis Reservation.

There is no proof that the Satsops, Humptulipses, Wynoochees, and Lower Chehalis villagers (such as Hoquiams, Ohyuts, and others) ever merged with the Chehalises on the Chehalis Reservation after those groups were ordered by the government to remove to that confine. Even the Lower Chehalises for the most part did not remove there. In 1873 the Humptulipses still refused to leave their lands and go on the reservation. In 1879 the 164 Lower Chehalises living along the Pacific Coast on the tributaries of Grays Harbor refused to remove. In 1885 most of the Lower Chehalises were reported to be under the jurisdiction of the Quinault Agency, and many of their families eventually moved to the Quinault Reservation. Some Lower Chehalises were on the Shoalwater Reservation. Some Kwaiailks refused to remove to the Chehalis Reservation, though it lay in their own territory. They chose to live, instead, with the Cowlitz and Nisqually Indians. Thus, contrary to government reports of the period, the Chehalises were not all brought together on the reservation as the government planned that they should be. The Indian Claims Commission, unable to determine who the claimant Indians, or their ancestors, were, decided unfavorably for the petitioners. The latter took their case to the United States Court of Claims (140 C.Cl. 192), which returned the case to the Claims Commission for reconsideration. The petitioners then changed their case to delete the Clatsops and Chinooks as directed by the Court of Claims. The Claims Commission reheard their case and determined that the band of Kwaiailks had held aboriginal title to 320,500 acres and the Lower Chehalises to 517,700 acres. The final judgment, entered October 7, 1963, was an award of $754,380 to the Confederated Chehalis Tribes.

Contemporary Life and Culture: Many Chehalises are engaged in the timber and fishing industries, the building trades, and social services. Some Chehalises carve wood items and do beadwork for sale. Much reservation land that once produced good timber has been cleared for pasture and other agricultural uses. Some Chehalises lease individual allotments on the reservation, of which about 1,780 acres remain in trust or otherwise restricted in status. One source of tribal income, as on other reservations, was eliminated by a June, 1980, United States Supreme Court ruling forbidding the sale of non-state-taxed cigarettes to non-Indian buyers at reservation smokeshops. The first major reservation housing program was begun in 1976 and completed in 1978. In 1980 another housing project was begun. Among other tribal projects are water-system and river-cleanup operations. A tribal center was built in the mid-1970s with facilities for children, a health clinic, a meeting room for the elderly, a library, classrooms, and tribal offices. Law enforcement is from the office of the Grays Harbor county sheriff. Medical and dental services are provided by visiting doctors and nurses. Most children attend Oakville elementary and secondary schools. Many participate in summer classes and recreational activities at the Chehalis Tribal Hall. There is a program to preserve native language. They have produced Chehalis history films, and published a tribal history. They belong to the Northwest Coalition of Gaming Tribes.

Special Events: The Chehalises hold their Tribal Days around the last weekend of May.

Suggested Readings: George Gibbs, Tribes of Western Washington, vol. 1 of Smithsonian Institution, Contributions to North American Ethnology (Washington, D.C.: Government Printing Office, 1877); Hermann Haeberlin and Erna Gunther, "The Indians of Puget Sound," University of Washington Publications in Anthropology 4, no. 1 (1930); Carolyn Marr, Donna Hicks, and Kay Francis, The Chehalis People (Oakville, Wash.: Confederated Tribes of the Chehalis Reservation, 1980); Leslie Spier, Tribal Distribution in Washington, American Anthropological Association, General Series in Anthropology, no. 3 (Menasha, Wis.: George Banta Publishing Company, 1936); Herbert C. Taylor, "Anthropological Investigation of the

Chehalis Indians Relative to Tribal Identity and Aboriginal Possession of Lands," in *Coast Salish* *and Western Washington Indians,* vol. 3 (New York: Garland Publishing, Inc., 1974), pp. 117–58.

CONFEDERATED TRIBES OF THE COLVILLE RESERVATION, WASHINGTON

The Confederated Tribes of the Colville Reservation, Washington, are composed primarily of descendants of the following Salish and Shahaptian-speaking peoples: Colvilles, Entiats, Methows, Nespelems, Nez Percés, Sinkaietks (Southern Okanagons), Palouses, Sanpoils, Senijextees, Sinkiuses, and Wenatchees.

Location: A large portion of tribal members live on the Colville Reservation in north-central and northeastern Washington state. A slightly higher number live off the reservation, particularly in bordering towns, such as Omak, Okanogan, Brewster, and Grand Coulee.

Numbers: In 1985 tribal membership stood at 3,799. In 1989 it was 3,880.

History: The Confederated Tribes of the Colville Reservation, Washington, had their inception in the April 19, 1872, executive order of President Ulysses S. Grant establishing the Colville Reservation east of the Columbia River. The boundaries of the reservation were changed by another executive order on July 2, 1872. The western boundary was then the Okanogan River; the eastern and southern boundaries were the Columbia River; and the northern boundary was the Canadian border. The entry of the bands of Chiefs Moses and Joseph onto the reservation in the 1880s caused considerable anguish, especially among the Sanpoils and the Nespelems, the original residents of the reservation. In an agreement completed May 23, 1891, that was never ratified by the United States Senate, the Okanagons, Sinkiuses, Nez Percés, Colvilles, and Senijextees agreed to sell the United States 1.5 million acres, the North Half of the reservation, for $1.5 million in five annual installments of $300,000. An act of July 1, 1892 (27 Stat. 62) restored the North Half to the public domain and provided that Indians not wanting to move to the South Half of the reservation be allotted from the vacated lands in the North Half. Before the North Half was opened to white settlement on October 10, 1900, 600 Indians had been allotted 51,653 acres from it by a presidential proclamation dated April 10, 1900. The North Half had been opened for mineral entry by an act of February 20, 1896. The 1,449,268 acres of the diminished reservation (its South Half) were opened to mineral entry on July 1, 1898 (30 Stat. 571). On December 1, 1905, 350 of the estimated 551 adult Indians living on the reservation signed the so-called (James) McLaughlin agreement relinquishing to the United States all rights, title, and interest to lands within the diminished reservation. The agreement also provided that the Indians be remunerated the as-yet-unpaid $1.5 million for the North Half. An act of March 22, 1906 (34 Stat. 80) provided for the allotment of 80 acres to each Indian belonging to the reservation and for sale of the surplus lands. The act was amended, August 31, 1916, to reserve lands for schools, mills, cemeteries, and missions. By presidential proclamation on May 3, 1916 (39 Stat. 1778) the unallotted, unreserved nontimber and mineral lands within the diminished reservation were opened to white settlement. As a result of the Indian Reorganization Act of 1934, undisposed lands (about 818,000 acres) within the Colville Reservation were temporarily withdrawn from further disposition or sale by a Department of Interior order of September 19, 1934. An act of July 24, 1956 (70 Stat. 626–627) restored ownership of the undisposed lands to the Confederated Tribes.

Government and Claims: After considerable intratribal conflict the Business Council of the Confederated Tribes of the Colville Reservation, Washington, was established. The Council derived its powers from the Confederated Tribes' constitution and bylaws, which were adopted by referendum vote on February 26, 1938. A most serious point of contention in the 1950s and 1960s was possible termination of the Confederated Tribes' relationship with the federal government. Termination was generally favored by tribal members living off the reservation and others who had a lesser quantum of native blood. Today the Colville Tribal Council opposes termination. It does, however, seek sovereignty in tribal matters in which state and federal governments have been involved, such as law enforcement and protection of water rights.

After the Yakima Tribe filed a claim (Docket 161) for additional recovery for lands ceded to the United States in the June 9, 1855, Yakima Treaty, the Confederated Tribes of the Colville, on their own behalf and that of the thirteen other tribes under that treaty, filed two intervenor claims for additional compensation for ceded lands of five of the fourteen tribes. One of the intervenor claims (Docket 222) was on behalf of certain Palouses and others who had removed to the Colville Reservation. The other (Docket 224) was filed on behalf of Sinkiuses (such as the Moses Columbia Tribe et al.). The intervenor dockets were consolidated with Docket 161 on July 28, 1959, and November 10, 1961. Among the various tribes, besides the Moses Columbias, were Chelans, Entiats, and Wenatchees. They all had been represented at the Yakima Treaty Council by Chiefs Tecolekun and La-Hoom who signed for them. (In 1954, five years before the Confederated Tribes had been permitted by the Indian Claims Commission to intervene, there were on the Colville Reservation 301 Sinkiuses, 113 Entiats, and 253 Wenatchees.)

The Yakima Tribe tried to block the claims filed by the Confederated Tribes of the Colville, maintaining that the fourteen tribes assigned to the Yakima Reservation (of which eleven are now identifiable) were a

Confederated Tribes of the Colville Reservation, Washington

Mel Tonasket, a tribal official who in 1979 reflects the progressiveness of the Confederated Tribes of the Colville Reservation in north-central Washington. The Confederated Tribes are an amalgam of nearly a dozen Pacific Northwest tribes. Not all of the tribal members live on their reservation, where the tribes operate several businesses.

confederation for which the Yakimas were the spokesmen. The Indian Claims Commission, opposing the Yakima convention, maintained that the lands of the various tribes had been ceded to the federal government, which had tried unsuccessfully to make the fourteen Salishan tribes and certain Palouses remove to the Yakima Reservation as provided by the treaty. When peoples under the Chief Moses agreement had not removed to the Moses, or Columbia, Reservation, the government had made an agreement with them in 1883 to remove to the Colville Reservation. The commission decided that they were entitled to additional compensation separate from that of the Yakimas, whose nation the commission found to be nonexistent, should the compensation $593,000 for the combined cession of 8,176,000 acres plus additional gratuities of $48,300 be found unconscionable. After it was so found, the commission awarded the tribes concerned $4,088,000 less offsets, making its final April 6, 1965, award $3,446,700.

On July 31, 1951, the Confederated Tribes filed a claim (Docket 178) before the Indian Claims Commission for mismanagement of Colville funds and property held in trust by the United States. An agreed-upon settlement of $5,540,598 was reached by the Confederated Tribes and the defending United States and approved by the commission in a final judgment on September 17, 1970. The order allowed the Colvilles to file a claim for accounting from July 1, 1951, which was to be set in a separate docket (178-A). This claim was transferred to the Court of Claims on February 24, 1977. In 1982 the tribes accepted an out-of-court settlement of $7 million for mismanagement of range and forestry lands and fiscal mismanagement from 1952 to 1982 (Docket 178-A). On July 31, 1951, the Colville Tribes filed a petition (Docket 177) alleging that the Bureau of Indian Affairs had accepted insufficient compensation for lands sold on the South Half of the Colville Reservation and that the handling of the funds had been improper. Docket 177 had also stemmed from the act of March 22, 1906, whereby the government had reduced the payments it required for surplus lands and had permitted entry on them before they were paid for, thus violating its fiduciary duties as trustee for the Indians and injuring them. The Claims Commission dismissed that claim because of its similarity to Docket 181-B described below. Also filed on July 31, 1951, was a petition (Docket 181) of multiple claims made not only by the Confederated Tribes but also by individuals. Subsequently, the claims were put into separate dockets (181, 181-A, 181-B, and 181-C). Docket 181 was for loss of aboriginal

lands to the United States: 130,590 acres taken from the Colvilles proper; 513,050 acres taken from the Sanpoil-Nespelems; 395,152 acres taken from the Okanagons; 379,665 acres taken from the Methows; and 311,305 acres taken from the Senijextees. The lands alienated were calculated as those that the tribes claimed at the time of the executive order of July 2, 1872, by which the tribes were to remove to the Colville Reservation. On March 1, 1960, the Claims Commission awarded the Colvilles proper $104,600; the Sanpoil-Nespelems $410,900; the Okanagons $223,400; the Methows $143,300; and the Senijextees $117,800. The total recovered by the Colville Tribes was $1 million after deduction of offsets of $61,000.

In Docket 181-A it was claimed that certain tribes under Chief Moses of the Sinkiuses (referred to as Columbias, Chelans, Entiats, and Wenatchees), who had received his Moses, or Columbia, Reservation (established by executive order on April 19, 1879, and amended by executive orders on March 6, 1880, and February 23, 1883), had been forced under the agreement of July 7, 1883, to leave that reservation for the Colville. As the Columbia Reservation had been restored to the public domain by executive order on May 1, 1886, the Colville Tribes claimed that the removal had been uncompensated.

Docket 181-B had its roots in an agreement dated May 9, 1891, whereby the North Half of the Colville Reservation was ceded to the United States. The agreement was to have gone into effect after ratification by Congress, but by an act of July 1, 1892 (27 Stat. 62) Congress opened the North Half to settlement without ratifying the agreement and delayed the payment of the agreed compensation of $1.5 million until June 21, 1906. The Colville Tribes contended that the payment was, in retrospect, unconscionable. A portion of the same docket (181-B) also alleged that the act of March 22, 1906 (34 Stat. 80) provided for sale of surplus lands on the South Half of the Colville Reservation and that the government had failed to provide adequate and fair compensation for those lands. For purposes of a final judgment the Claims Commission consolidated dockets 181-A and 181-B, making an award of $3.5 million.

Docket 181-C was for several claims: for spoilation and depletion of fisheries due to construction of Grand Coulee Dam; for removal of resources (this claim is sometimes labeled "Docket No. 181-C, Mineral Claims"); for failure to safeguard hunting grounds; and for failure to safeguard rights to compensation for the taking and using of lands for railroads. The last two claims were not compensated, but in 1980 the Court of Claims heard the docket (because by law the Claims Commission had ceased to exist) and awarded the Colville Tribes compensation plus interest amounting to $3,257,000 for loss of fisheries and $140,000 for loss of mining operations. One claim, the Grand Coulee Dam claim (Docket 181-D) had been separated from Docket 181-C to allow the above award to be made. Docket 181-D originally included claims for the taking of tribal lands in connection with the construction of the Chief Joseph Dam on the Columbia, as well as the Grand Coulee, but was later amended to exclude reference to the former project. With twenty-four other tribes throughout the western United States, the Confederated Tribes filed other claims (Dockets 342-70 and 343-70) that reached the Court of Claims, for mismanagement of Individual Claims Commission judgment funds and for other funds, such as Individual Indian Money accounts held in trust by the United States. The tribes were awarded $1,213,027.79 in 1980 for their claim in Docket 181-D.

Contemporary Life and Culture: The effort to acquire power revenues from Columbia River dams is part of a wider effort by the Colville Tribes to control resources, not only the waters of the Columbia and other rivers but also a variety of others ranging from wildlife to lands. In 1981 the Colville Tribes budgeted $4 million for land purchases. A failed molybdenum mining venture dashed the Colvilles' hopes for riches. Other failed enterprises were Package Log Cabin sales, a meatpacking plant, and a modern greenhouse operation. After ridding the reservation of non-Indian businesses in 1973, they started a thriving Trading Post. Timber is a viable resource. In 1984 the tribes dedicated their new $10 million sawmill located near Omak. In 1991 they continued an ongoing fight of federal (tribal) vs. state jurisdiction—e.g., the right of the State Patrol to arrest drivers on reservation highways. The Colvilles, who started a bingo parlor in 1991 to which they bus off-reservation people, resisted the state's plans to establish rules for reservation gambling under the 1988 Gambling Regulatory Act. They plan a casino at Wenatchee, Washington, near the famous Clovis site, discovered in 1990, to which they claim connections and on which dig they put a damper.

There has been considerable assimilation of various tribes on the reservation. One goal of the Pascal Sherman elementary school, which is on the reservation east of Omak, is the perpetuation of tribal heritage. High school students attend school at Grand Coulee. An increasing number of young people attend higher education centers, such as community colleges and state universities.

Special Events: The annual Trophy Powwow is held the first weekend of early March on the reservation at the Nespelem Community Center. An all-Indian rodeo is held at Nespelem on the last weekend of April. The Circle Celebration, featuring Indian stick games and tribal dances, continues for several days in early July. Another rodeo is held on the reservation at Inchelium on the Fourth of July. There is an Indian powwow at the Omak (Washington) Stampede, which is held on the weekend near mid-August. Indians from the Colville also participate in the Suicide Race run in conjunction with the Stampede.

Suggested Readings: Jessie A. Bloodworth, "Human Resources Survey of the Colville Confederated Tribes," Field Report of the Bureau of Indian Affairs, Portland Area Office, Colville Agency, Nespelem, Washington, 1959; Ann Briley, *Lonely Pedestrian: Francis Marion Streamer* (Oroville, Washington, 1986). M. Gidley, *Kopit: A Documentary of Chief Joseph's Last Years* (Seattle: University of Washington Press, 1981); M. Gidley, *With One Sky Above Us: Life on an Indian Reservation at the Turn of the Century* (New York: Putnam, 1979); Robert H. Ruby and John A. Brown, *Half-Sun on the Columbia: A Biography of Chief Moses* (Norman: University of Oklahoma Press, 1965); Ruth Scofield, *Behind the Buckskin Curtain* (Seattle: Seattle Pacific College, 1977).

CONFEDERATED TRIBES OF COOS, LOWER UMPQUA & SIUSLAW INDIANS, INC.

Confederated Tribes of Coos, Lower Umpqua & Siuslaw Indians, Inc.

Chief Edgar Brown of the Confederated Tribes is of Coos descent. In 1984 the tribe obtained federal recognition entitling them to federal services, but not federal acknowledgment, since it had previously been terminated in 1954. Courtesy of the Confederated Tribes of Coos, Lower Umpqua & Siuslaw Indians, Inc.

The Hanis Coos, Kuitshes, and Siuslaws have recently regrouped as the Confederated Tribes of Coos, Lower Umpqua and Siuslaw Indians, Inc. These tribes are those formerly placed at Yachats on the southern end of the Siletz Reservation after the middle of the nineteenth century. They drifted from there, banded together, and have remained associated with a continuous organization to the present. See **Hanis Coos, Kuitsh,** and **Siuslaw.** In 1975 the Coos separately petitioned for federal recognition (see **Coos Tribe of Indians**). The Coos, Lower Umpquas, and Siuslaws in 1983 petitioned the government to recognize their confederation. Provision for restoration of recognition was submitted to Congress in H.R. 5540 on April 26, 1984. It became law when President Ronald Reagan signed the bill, October 10, 1984. Their population that year was just short of 500.

CONFEDERATED TRIBES OF THE GRAND RONDE COMMUNITY OF OREGON

The Confederated Tribes of the Grand Ronde Community of Oregon grew out of several tribes representing a half dozen linguistic groups on the Grand Ronde Reservation. They were confederated under the 1934 Indian Reorganization Act (48 Stat. 984). On March 8 and 9 of that year the tribes met at the Chemawa Training School near Salem, Oregon, where they were reported to be eager for self-government and the establishment of their native identity. After receiving on May 13, 1935, a charter of incorporation, they expected many governmental aids and the restoration of their alienated reservation lands. Their expectations were not realized. Their disappointment was perhaps one reason why they voted to

terminate their relations with the government under a congressional act of August 13, 1954 (68 Stat. 732). With termination on August 13, 1956, they lost health and school funds and other government-supported programs. In the 1970s the successors of the Confederated Tribes of the Grand Ronde Community came together as the Confederated Tribes of Grand Ronde Indians, a loosely organized group not acknowledged by the federal government.

Numbers: In 1984 the population of the Confederated Tribes was about 1,500. In 1856, after most of the tribes destined for the Grand Ronde Reservation had been removed there, a census revealed that there were 1,925 Indians on the reservation, of whom 909 were Takelmas, Latgawas, or Shastas. In May, 1857, after most of those three peoples had moved to the Siletz Reservation, 922 Upper Umpquas, Kalapuyan speakers, and Molalas remained on the Grand Ronde with a few Takelmas, Latgawas, and Shastas. A few Clatsops were added to Grand Ronde membership rolls in 1875, making a total enrollment from all tribes of 424 in 1886. In 1902 there were 398.

History: The organization of the Confederated Tribes of the Grand Ronde Indians has a history going back to January 11, 1856, when eight wagons carried some old and infirm Upper Umpquas and Kalapuyan speakers from the Umpqua River valley north to the Grand Ronde. These Indians had been gathered on the temporary Umpqua Reservation, from which a remainder, numbering about 300, walked to the Grand Ronde through winter cold and snow. In February, 1856, the bands composing the Rogue River Indians were moved from the Table Rock Reservation to the Grand Ronde. The Molalas and Kalapuyan-speaking tribes of the Willamette valley were also removed there. In late summer two boatloads of Rogues and coastal tribesmen were brought to the Grand Ronde, where they remained until May, 1857, at which time the coastal Indians and over half of the Rogues were moved to the Siletz Reservation. To prevent the Indians from escaping from confinement at the Grand Ronde, and to prevent their clashing with settlers, Fort Hoskins was established on July 26, 1856, in Kings Valley (near Hoskins, Oregon) on the Luckiamute River near the mouth of Bonner Creek. In that same year Fort Yamhill was established a half mile north of Valley Junction. After 1866, when those posts were no longer manned, the whiskey trade became rampant, taking its toll of the Indians.

The first schools opened on the Grand Ronde in August, 1856. Unlike the Kalapuyan speakers and Umpquas, the Takelmas and Latgawas asked for pay to send their children to school. Such institutions were established to destroy Indianness. Use

Confederated Tribes of the Grand Ronde Community of Oregon

Jackie Colton and Clara Riggs, 1981. In 1983 these women and their fellow tribes-people of the Confederated Tribes of the Grand Ronde Community of Oregon received the recognition of the federal government, after previously terminating relations with it.

of native tongues was discouraged in the schools, and children were forced to cut their hair, wear shoes, and abandon much of their native culture. Their male elders were taught to farm, and the women were taught to do household chores. Unsuitable conditions on the Grand Ronde produced intertribal conflict among the traditionalist elderly. When, for example, a Molala killed an Umpqua on the reservation, the matter was settled by payment of blood-feud money to the victim's relatives. The establishment of the Manual Labor Training School early in 1880 at Forest Grove was an amalgamating catalyst among Pacific Northwest Indians (within five years the school was transferred near to Salem, where it became the Chemawa Training School). Marriages further broke down intertribal barriers. During the 1870s, the Peace Policy era of President Ulysses S. Grant, the Grand Ronde was administered by officials of the Roman Catholic faith.

In 1871 about thirty families on the Grand Ronde were given individual plots to farm. Property ownership and work, government officials believed, would help them develop self-esteem. As the system of land tenure and work was unfamiliar to the Indians, the plan failed. Under the Dawes Indian Severalty Act of February 8, 1887 (24 Stat. 388), Indians took up 33,148 acres on the reservation. After a June, 1901, conference the Indians with government approval, on April 21, 1904, ceded 26,111 acres of the reservation to the United States. By 1928 the land base of these reservation Indians was virtually nonexistent. Most of the allotments had been sold off; only sixty-seven allottees remained, holding a mere 440 acres.

Government and Claims: On August 26, 1935, a congressional act (49 Stat. 810) was passed pertaining to the western Oregon tribes. Those with whom unratified treaties had been made in 1851 and 1855 were to bring suit for certain lands taken from the Siletz Reservation. The Confederated Tribes of the Grand Ronde Indian Community were included with the petitioners from the Siletz Reservation (Case No. 45230). Because the Grand Ronde Indians were not coastal tribes formerly affected by the withdrawal of the tracts from the Siletz Reservation, the Court of Claims excluded them from the suit, along with certain petitioning Chinooks and Clatsops and the Willamette Valley Confederated Tribes, a loosely organized group of nonreservation Indians.

The Grand Ronde tribes were included with petitioning Kalapuyan-speaking descendants and others in filing a claim (Docket 238) with the Indian Claims Commission on August 8, 1951. Their case was dismissed on November 17, 1954. Emulating other Oregon tribes that had restored themselves as separate and legal entities, the present-day Tribes of the Grand Ronde Indians Incorporated effected a similar restoration after termination by formally organizing and holding regular meetings. Their loose organization lacked federal acknowledgment until November, 1983, when Congress voted to recognize the Grand Ronde Indians, paving the way for them to receive federal aid for housing, health, and education and to develop a plan for the establishment of a reservation on Bureau of Land Management land. Thus their termination status was ended.

CONFEDERATED TRIBES OF THE SILETZ INDIANS OF OREGON

The Confederated Tribes of the Siletz Indians of Oregon initially evolved from several tribes representing about a half dozen linguistic groups on the Siletz Reservation. They took their name from the reservation, which had been named for the Siletz Indian tribe. Their relationship with the federal government was terminated on July 20, 1956, by an act of Congress (Public Law 588, signed August 13, 1954), which declared in essence that on August 13, 1956, there would be no Indian tribal entities in western Oregon. A nucleus of the former Confederated Tribes reorganized in the 1960s, and in 1973 they filed as a nonprofit corporation working to regain federal recognition. On November 18, 1977, an act (91 Stat. 1415) called for the secretary of the interior to submit to Congress within two years a plan for locating a reservation in Oregon's Lincoln County for the Confederated Tribes. That reservation, held in trust by the United States, was established on September 4, 1980 (Public Law 96-340; 94 Stat. 1072). The tribes were given two parcels of land: 3,633 acres of Bureau of Land Management timberlands in Lincoln County and 38.44 acres of the original Siletz Reservation, known as Government Hill, where the town of Siletz is located. The November

18, 1977, act had allowed transfer of public-domain lands from the BLM to the BIA to be held in trust for the Confederated Tribes of the Siletz Indians of Oregon. By that act tribal members were to receive the federal services and benefits awarded other Indian tribesmen of similar status.

Location: Tribal members live in the area of their reclaimed holdings in such towns as Newport, along the north-central coast of western Oregon.

Numbers: In 1985 there were 867 registered Confederated Siletzes. Many more were unregistered. At the time of termination in 1956 the Confederated Tribes had numbered 929. When a new tribal council was formed in the fall of 1973, they numbered 200. In 1989 their numbers stood at 1,309.

In 1857 there had been on the Siletz Reservation, 590 Latgawas and Takelmas, Shastas, and a few Umpquas from a total of 909 who had been on the Grand Ronde Reservation the previous year. By July, 1858, 205 of the 590 had died and 35 had returned to the Grand Ronde. Of the Indians on the Siletz at that time, only 259 treaty Takelmas received subsistence. That left 1,766 others there in starving condition. Included among the latter were 279 Kuitshes (Lower Umpquas) and Coos and 181 Siuslaws and Alseas, most of whom did not become part of the Siletz Confederated Tribes. On the Siletz Reservation in 1865 were 123 Chastacostas and Umpquas, 121 Takelmas, and 1,824 coastal tribesmen, including Chetcos, Tututnis (Rogues), Yaquinas, Upper Coquilles, and others. All of those peoples were greatly reduced in number from the time when they first came into contact with whites.

History: In 1856, at the end of the Rogue Wars, the Tututnis, Takelmas, Shastas, Latgawas, and a few Dakubetedes and Taltushtuntudes were all counted as Rogues and included with the Takelmas after removal to reservations. Members of those tribes, plus Chetcos, Chastacostas, and Upper Coquilles, were rounded up at Port Orford as combatants in the war. From there 600 of them were shipped on the steamer *Columbia* in June, 1856, up the Pacific Coast and

Confederated Tribes of the Siletz Indians of Oregon

Art Bensell, 1980, as chairman of the Confederated Tribes of the Siletz Indians of Oregon, which received federal recognition in 1977. Bensell was inducted in 1987 into the American Indian Athletic Hall of Fame. Before him, Rube Sanders from the same tribe received the same honor.

the Columbia and Willamette rivers to Dayton, Oregon, from which they were marched to the Grand Ronde Reservation. In July another boatload of 592 Rogues was shipped north in the same manner. Another 215 Indians, mostly from coastal tribes, walked the 125 miles to the north portion of the Coast Reservation (the future Siletz Reservation) north of Yaquina Bay. Some Latgawas and Takelmas from the Table Rock Reservation reached the Grand Ronde via the Willamette valley by walking or riding in wagons. By May, 1857, nearly all of the Rogues and Shastas had been moved to the

49

Coast Reservation except for Chief Sam and 58 of his men and their families, who remained on the Grand Ronde. Sam had remained neutral during the Rogue Wars.

The original Siletz Reservation, established by executive order on November 9, 1855, had been designated the "Coast Reservation." It contained 1,383,000 acres running roughly 102 miles north and south along the Oregon coast and 20 miles east and west, between the summit of the Coast Range and Cape Lookout on the north to about midway between the Siuslaw and Umpqua rivers on the south. In August, 1856, the Siletz Agency was staffed at headquarters north of Yaquina Bay. By 1860 the reservation had come to be called the Siletz. A subagent, stationed at Yachats Prairie in 1861, oversaw Indians on the southern portion of the reservation, which became known as the Alsea. The Indians of that southern portion, including Coos and Kuitshes along with the Siuslaws, were removed to near the Yachats River estuary on the coast, where the Alsea Indians were. The Umpqua Subagency (located in 1856 on the south near the mouth of the Umpqua River), which formerly had supervised them, was closed late in 1859.

By executive order on December 21, 1865, a strip of land about twenty-five miles wide running from east to west across the Siletz Reservation, including Yaquina Bay, was withdrawn to give whites lands that they wanted. This cut the Siletz Reservation in two. The south half, which then became the Alsea Reservation, ran about thirty-one miles from north to south. On March 3, 1875 it was turned over to the public domain (18 Stat. 420). After the withdrawal of the Alsea Reservation and the Yaquina strip, the Siletz was reduced to about 223,000 acres. Acts of October 31, 1892 (28 Stat. 286 and 323) and of August 15, 1894 (28 Stat. 286 and 323) ceded to the public domain 191,798.80 acres from the Siletz. This was the total unallotted acreage except for five sections that were withheld for the Confederated Tribes. A proclamation by President Grover Cleveland on May 16, 1895, ceded the remaining lands of the Siletz to the public domain after its Indians were allotted. When the reservation was terminated in 1954, it comprised approximately 7,900 acres. All but 38.44 of its acres reverted to the public for sale. In time those 38.44 acres were given to the town of Siletz in lieu of payment of taxes.

The first year after removal to the Coast Reservation, 1856–57, was disastrous for the Indians. Several hundred died from exposure, starvation, and disease. Prospects were no better with time. In 1865, for example, the Siletz agent spent $46.23 on each of the treaty Chastacostas and Umpquas and the 121 treaty Takelmas. Each of the other 1,824 Indians, parties to unratified treaties, received a mere $2.50 per year. The disparity in the amounts of goods that the Indians received aggravated intertribal conflict. Troubles increased when relatives sought revenge on native doctors who had failed to cure the diseases that ran rampant on the reservation. By 1859 about 100 of these native healers had been killed. The government sought to reduce these killings by removing arms from the Indians, which only caused more trouble. To keep the Indians in line, prevent them from escaping, and lessen the burden on the agents, the military established two forts. One of these was Fort Hoskins in Kings Valley (closed 1866), and the other was Fort Yamhill near Valley Junction (closed 1866). A third post, Fort Umpqua (abandoned 1862), had been established near the mouth of the Umpqua River during the Rogue Wars. Despite the efforts of the military to contain the Indians, they continued to escape down the coast or across the Coast Range. For example, in 1857, after the Rogue wars, about a hundred Rogues, Coos, and Umpquas were gathered up. In July, 1864, a hundred Coos and Umpquas were captured in the mountains of southern Oregon and at Coos Bay. The military proved as objectionable to the Indians as the reservations were. The troops harassed their women and introduced diseases amongst them.

A more subtle development eroded native culture on the reservations. Indians lost their individual tribal characteristics. For example, as the short, stocky, dark-complexioned, peacefully inclined Yakonan-speaking peoples mixed with the tall, round-headed, intellectual Takilmas, both groups lost their original characteristics.

Helping make reservation life unbearable were agents who stole from the Indians on the Siletz. The few goods supplied to the Indians by treaty were of poor quality. In the schools the children learned only the English language and other aspects of American culture. By the twentieth century the tribal languages had virtually disappeared. The efforts of officials to curb consumption of alcohol among their charges were ineffective. The requirement that they obtain passes, when leaving the confines for their old haunts, in no way reduced their access to strong drink, which they secured from the whites who had appropriated their old village sites. Only in 1871, when General Joel Palmer became agent, was the whipping post abolished that had formerly been used when Indians rebelled against their plight or followed old tribal practices. Also abolished was the chieftaincy. Instead of chiefs acting as spokesmen for their people, tribal courts and juries were instituted. In the 1870s, the era of the President Ulysses S. Grant Peace Policy, when churches ran the agencies, the Methodist influence on the Siletz, like that of other churches at other agencies, only served to hasten the process of acculturation. To help prevent reversion of the Indians to the old ways, the church tried to neutralize the teachings of the messiah cults that surfaced during this period. An Indian police force established on the Siletz on August 15, 1878, was also used as a vehicle of acculturation, as was a boarding school established there the following year.

Government and Claims: On March 3, 1901, after Indian allottees on the Siletz had petitioned Congress for full titles to their properties, that body passed a law ending trust control of allotted lands. By 1953 only seventy-six allotments remained on the Siletz, or 5,390 acres of the lands formerly held in trust for individuals. Of a voting population of 233 members in April, 1935, 53 voted to accept the Indian Reorganization Act (48 Stat. 984). Voting against it were 123 mem-

bers. On October 31, 1892, the Confederated Tribes of Siletz Indians had been party to an agreement ratified by act of Congress on August 15, 1894 (28 Stat. 286, 323) to cede to the United States the unallotted lands on the Siletz Reservation except for the five timbered sections near the Siletz River that had been withheld and reserved as tribal land. For a total of 191,798.80 acres ceded, the Confederated Tribes were paid $142,600. The ceded portion had been opened to homestead entry by presidential proclamation on May 16, 1895. The land was disposed of slowly because a fee was required of $1.50 per acre in addition to the regular Homestead Act filing fee. Once this acreage fee was removed by Congress on May 17, 1900, the land was disposed of more rapidly.

Eventually the Confederated Tribes attempted to sell the five reserved timbered sections except for one section at Depoe Bay. An act of Congress of May 13, 1910 (36 Stat. 367), amended May 18, 1916 (39 Stat. 123, 149), permitted the government to offer the timbered sections for sale. Only one was sold, and the other four were disposed of at the time of termination of the reservation in 1954. The Confederated Tribes claimed (Docket 239) that the $142,600 that they had received for the 191,798 acres was far too little. The Indian Claims Commission decided on November 23, 1955, that the Confederated Tribes were entitled to a payment of $573,396 less their original payment of $142,600. Some of the individual tribes comprising the Confederated Tribes of Siletz Indians were petitioners for various claims before the Court of Claims and the Indian Claims Commission (see **Coos Tribe of Indians, Coquille, Hanis Coos, Siuslaw** and **Tututni**).

On Aug. 13, 1954, President Dwight D. Eisenhower signed Public Law 588 terminating forty-three bands west of the Cascade Mountains in Oregon, effective August 13, 1956. Although the Confederated Tribes of Siletz Indians and the Grand Ronde Indian Community had passed resolutions favoring termination, other Indians opposed it, including the Coos, Kuitshes, and Siuslaws, as well as the Chinooks and several Tillamooks. After termination the Indians were expected to pay taxes, which resulted in the sale of some allotments and further alienation of Indian lands. In the fall of 1973, as noted, 200 persons of the Siletz formed a new council. Their objective was to move toward restoration of their Indian status. The minimum native-blood quantum for membership was set at one-eighth. On March 30 and 31, 1976, Siletz council members appeared in Washington, D.C., to testify before the Senate Subcommittee on Indian Affairs. In 1975 the Siletzes opened a manpower office with a Comprehensive Employment Training Act (CETA) grant. They also operated an alcohol and drug-abuse program. Despite the opposition of commercial and fishing interests, Congress passed an act (91 Stat. 1415) on November 18, 1977, which was signed by President Jimmy Carter, restoring the Confederated Tribes of Siletz Indians of Oregon as a federally recognized Indian tribe. This permitted them to receive the federal services and benefits accorded recognized tribes and their members. The act did not establish a reservation for the Siletz Indians or hunting and fishing rights, but on October 4, 1980, 3,630 acres of land in scattered blocs were transferred from the Bureau of Land Management for a reservation for them, as described above.

Special Events: After mid-November the Confederated Tribes hold their annual Siletz Restoration Powwow.

Suggested Readings: Stephen Dow Beckham, *The Indians of Western Oregon, This Land Was Theirs* (Coos Bay, Ore.: Arago Books, 1977); J. Owen Dorsey, "Indian of Siletz Reservation, Oregon," *The American Anthropologist* 2, (January, 1889); William Eugene Kent, *The Siletz Indian Reservation, 1855–1900,* thesis Portland State University, 1973; *Siletz Restoration Act, Hearings . . . S. 2801* (1976), Jerome Sayer and John M. Volkman, "Statistical Profile of the Confederated Tribes of Siletz Indians, January, 1976," in *Siletz Restoration Act . . . S. 2801* (1976).

CONFEDERATED TRIBES OF THE UMATILLA INDIAN RESERVATION, OREGON

The roots of the Confederated Tribes of the Umatilla Indian Reservation, Oregon, go back to the June 9, 1855, Walla Walla Treaty (12 Stat. 945, ratified March 8, 1859) between the Cayuses, the Umatillas, and the Wallawallas and the United States. In that treaty those tribes agreed to remove to the Umatilla Reservation in northeastern Oregon. They also ceded to the United States 2,151,680 acres in Oregon Territory and 1,861,120 in Washington Territory to create the 245,699-acre reservation. For a time each of the tribes kept a measure of separateness on the reservation, although bearing in common the name Umatilla. Besides the descendants of the three tribes, a few Northern Paiutes were removed to the reservation late in the nineteenth century. The Umatilla Tribes became officially confederated with the adoption on November 4, 1949, of a constitution and bylaws, which were approved by the Department of the Interior on December 7, 1949.

Location: Approximately half of the total tribal membership lives on the Umatilla Reservation. Agency headquarters are just east of Pendleton on Interstate 80 and U.S. Highways 395 and 37.

Numbers: Tribal membership in 1985 stood at 1,578. In 1989 the numbers were 1,652.

History: Before the beginning of wheat growing on the reservation, the Indians used its lush grasslands primarily as range for their horses. In the later nineteenth and early twentieth centuries many of those animals were rounded up and slaughtered for animal food or used for other purposes, such as pulling trolley cars in Chicago. The Indians also grew gardens along the Umatilla River. The Slater Act of March 3, 1885, reduced the reservation and provided for allotment of the lands to the Indians on it, but it also limited allotment to 120,000 acres. An act of October 17, 1888, replacing that legislation, allowed the secretary of the interior to set aside more lands for Indians on the eastern part of the reservation. A total of 82,742 acres was allotted to 1,118 Indians, and an additional 980 acres were reserved for school and mission purposes. Acts of July 1, 1902, and March 2, 1917, provided for allotment of 73,130.76 more acres between 1921 and 1926. By an act of May 29, 1928, about 7,000 acres of the reservation were reserved for tribal grazing purposes. By an act of August 5, 1882, 640 acres were withdrawn from the reservation to add to the existing townsite of Pendleton. A cession on December 4, 1888, removed a considerable portion of the southern part of the reservation. Of the roughly 157,000 acres reserved for the Indians, only 95,273 remained in 1969, of which 15,438 were tribally owned and 79,835 allotted. For the early histories of the tribes composing the Confederated Tribes of the Umatilla Reservation, Oregon, see **Cayuse, Umatilla,** and **Wallawalla.**

Government and Claims: Before adopting their constitution and bylaws, the Umatilla Tribes rejected organizing under the Indian Reorganization Act (48 Stat. 984). Tribal affairs are administered by a general council of adult enrollees and a nine-member board of trustees elected from the council.

On August 9, 1951, the Umatilla Tribes filed four claims against the United States. Filed under Docket 264, they were later separated. The first and fourth claims in that docket were for additional compensation for lands ceded to the United States under the 1855 treaty. One claim was for compensation for three parcels of land totaling approximately 3,840,000 acres, outside the ceded area for which aboriginal title was claimed. The Indian Claims Commission found insufficient evidence that the Umatilla Tribes had aboriginal title to and non-exclusive use of the parcels. This docket was heard by the Claims Commission with Docket 198 filed by the Confederated Tribes of the Warm Springs Reservation, Oregon, because the same area was involved. The decisions on the two dockets were, however, made separately. An unfavorable decision

Confederated Tribes of the Umatilla Reservation

David Steve Hall, a leader among the Umatilla Confederated Tribes of the Umatilla Reservation, 1968. The reservation, which was originally occupied mainly by Umatilla, Cayuse and Wallawalla tribesmen, lies just east of Pendleton, Oregon.

by the commission on the issue of title, entered June 10, 1960, caused the Umatilla Tribes to file a motion for a rehearing. The 1960 decision was vacated, and new findings were entered. The petitioner appealed these to the United States Supreme Court (Appeal Docket 1-65), but on November 24, 1965, petitioner and defendant agreed to dismiss the appeals pending before the Court of Claims and to combine separated claims (Dockets 264, 264-A, and 264-B) to make one lump settlement. The final judgment entered with the commission favored the tribes, who were awarded $2,450,000 after all allowable deductions, credits, and offsets. Docket 264-A was a claim for loss of salmon, steelhead, and eel because of construction of diversion dams on the Umatilla River and for the loss of Umatilla River water rights in a 1916 state court decision. Docket 264-B was a claim for an errone-

53

ously established boundary survey in 1871, which had excluded about 19,000 acres of land promised to the tribes under their 1855 treaty. Final judgment of the three dockets was entered on February 11, 1966. In 1970 the tribes filed in the Court of Claims Dockets 342-70 and 343-70 for petitions, claiming damages arising from government policies and practices in the investment of tribal trust funds and Individual Indian Moneys. The tribes combined with twenty-four others having similar claims. A judgment for $172,059.39 was awarded in November, 1981. For still another loss, that of fishing rights at Celilo when The Dalles Dam was built in 1957, the tribes had received $4,198,000 in 1953.

Contemporary Life and Culture: Most tillable Umatilla Reservation lands are leased for farming. Also leased is the McNary Dam townsite near Umatilla, Oregon, to which the Umatilla Tribes obtained title under provisions of Public Law 85-186—a transaction that was effected after the dam was built in 1957 on the Columbia River. On February 18, 1959, the Indians leased the townsite to S & S Steel Products Inc. of Los Angeles, a manufacturer of ten-by-fifty-foot mobile homes. Under the provisions of the lease, tribal members are given first preference for employment with the company. Other Indians have second preference for employment. An on-the-job training contract with S & S provided training for other Indians as well. More than 50 percent of the S & S employees were Indians in 1983.

That some of the elderly speak the Nez Percé and other Shahaptian dialects gives the reservation peoples a measure of unity. The tribes administer a scholarship fund for enrolled members to pursue academic and vocational-technical training. The latter has helped tribal members to find work on logging and construction projects. Special tribal committees handle enrollment, credit, recreation, and summer-work programs. The reservation has an office for general and adult education, a day-care center, employment and health facilities, alcohol and drug treatment programs, a housing authority, and an educational program for the elderly. A forest and range enterprise is tribally owned, as are a store and a lake for camping and fishing. The tribe has received a half-million-dollar grant from the Meyer Memorial Trust for the Oregon Trail Interpretive Center they are developing. Major denominations are Roman Catholic and Presbyterian. Some tribal members follow the traditional *washat* religion, and a few are Shakers.

Special Events: Indians of the Umatilla participate in a powwow in conjunction with the Pendleton (Oregon) Roundup, which is held during the second full week in September.

Suggested Readings: J. M. Cornelison, "The Seed of the Martyrs," manuscript, Oregon Historical Society, Portland, Oregon; Lessie L. Cornelison, "Allen Patawa", manuscript, Umatilla County Library, Pendleton, Oregon; Maj. Lee Moorhouse, "The Umatilla Reservation," *The Coast Alaska and Greater Northwest* 15, no. 2 (April, 1908); Col. William Parsons; *An Illustrated History of Umatilla County . . .* (Spokane, Wash.: W. H. Lever, 1902); Robert H. Ruby and John A. Brown, *The Cayuse Indians: Imperial Tribesmen of Old Oregon* (Norman: University of Oklahoma Press, 1972); *Umatilla Indian Reservation Then and Now* (Pendleton, Ore.: Umatilla Indian Agency, n.d.).

CONFEDERATED TRIBES OF THE WARM SPRINGS RESERVATION OF OREGON

The Confederated Tribes of the Warm Springs Reservation of Oregon had their origin in the treaty of June 25, 1855 (12 Stat. 963, ratified March 8, 1859) that Oregon Superintendent of Indian Affairs Joel Palmer, representing the United States, signed with the Teninos (including Teninos proper, Tyighs of the upper Deschutes River,

Confederated Tribes of the Warm Springs Reservation of Oregon

These children of the Confederated Tribes of the Warm Springs Reservation of Oregon, photographed in the 1970s, are typical of Indian children who receive lessons not only in the three R's but also in tribal heritage. Courtesy Rockey/Marsh Public Relations, Portland, Oregon.

Wyams of the lower Deschutes, and Dockspuses [Tukspushes] of the John Day River), and Wascos (of the Kigaltwalla, Dog River, and Dalles bands). These peoples were confederated with a view to locating them on the Warm Springs Reservation south of The Dalles of the Columbia River in Jefferson and Wasco counties of north-central Oregon.

Location: Many members of the Confederated Tribes live near the Warm Springs Agency headquarters, which is about fourteen miles northwest of Madras on U.S. Highway 97. Tribal members also live as far away as Simnasho, twenty-five miles north of agency headquarters.

Numbers: After the 1855 treaty the Indians scheduled to go on the Warm Springs Reservation numbered 1,355. In 1985 there were 2,200 members of the Confederated Tribes.

History: The treaty with the tribes and bands destined for the Warm Springs Reservation was precipitated by the increasing number of white settlers who wished them removed from their ancestral lands. With promises of government payments and of retention of fishing and hunting privileges, they were induced to surrender title to about 10 million acres in exchange for a reservation of about 464,000 acres. The area was later increased after long-festering disputes over the northern and western reservation boundaries were settled in 1972. Fortunately for the Warm Springs Tribes, the treaty (14 Stat. 751) signed November 15, 1865, with Oregon Superintendent of Indian Affairs J. W. Huntington, and ratified March 2, 1867, did not threaten their right to fish in traditional places along the Columbia River. The peoples of the Warm Springs continued fishing there, and on February 9, 1929, a government act (45 Stat. 1158) set aside a village site near Celilo Falls for a small band who had been assigned to the Warm Springs. In addition to harassment from whites, the tribes on the Warm Springs Reservation were subjected to Northern Paiute raids as early as 1859. The raids continued until 1866, when the army began a campaign to exterminate or subdue the raiding Paiutes. Warm Springs In-

dian scouts served the army in campaigns against the Paiutes, as they did in 1873 in the campaigns against the Modocs of southern Oregon and northern California.

During the President Ulysses S. Grant Peace Policy era of the 1870s, Warm Springs agent Capt. John Smith tried not only to advance the white style of education among the Indians but also to eliminate native practices, such as slavery, shamanism, and polygamy. The economic level of the Confederated Tribes remained low. They tried to subsist by fishing, which became more difficult with each year, and by farming lands that were poorly suited to agriculture. After the Bannock-Paiute War of 1878 thirty-eight Paiutes were moved in September, 1879 to the Warm Springs from Vancouver Barracks in Washington Territory, where they had been imprisoned since as early as 1866 to 1868 during the Snake War to exterminate the Paiute raiders. After Gen. Nelson Miles, commanding the Department of the Columbia, recommended that the Paiutes captured in the Bannock-Paiute War and still held on the Yakima Reservation be allowed to leave, about seventy under their leader, Oytes, went to the Warm Springs in August, 1884. That, in essence, completed the establishment of the more important tribes on the reservation: Teninos, Wascos, and Northern Paiutes.

Government and Claims: After adopting the Indian Reorganization Act (48 Stat. 984) in 1937, the Confederated Tribes in the following year incorporated themselves with a constitution that recognized self-management. The BIA was retained in an advisory capacity.

Because the ancient Columbia River fishing grounds at Celilo Falls were inundated by the waters behind The Dalles Dam, the Confederated Tribes in 1958 received a $4 million indemnity. A part of that sum was distributed on a per capita basis to tribal members, but most of it was held in the tribal treasury. The tribes submitted a claim (Docket 198) to the Indian Claims Commission to recover additional compensation for lands in north-central Oregon ceded to the United States on June 25, 1855. For what was determined to have been the tribes' aboriginal ownership of 1,605,000 acres, they were awarded by the Claims Commission on October 17, 1973, a compromise settlement of $1,225,000. A related claim, separated from Docket 198 and docketed 198-A, was dismissed on the motion of the tribes. The Warm Springs Indians also filed a claim (Docket 524-71) that reached the Court of Claims for mismanagement of Indian Claims Commission judgment funds and other funds, such as Individual Indian Money accounts, held in trust by the United States. The tribes were awarded $88,249.98 in 1981 for their claim Docket 524-71.

Contemporary Life and Culture: Because of the demand for lumber during World War II, the tribes in 1942 entered into their first contract for the sale of timber logged along the western edge of their reservation. Revenues derived from such sales raised per capita payments. Members also receive pensions beginning at age sixty. In 1967 the tribes purchased a privately owned sawmill on the reservation and a plywood plant, Warm Springs Forest Products Industries. With their $4 million settlement in 1958 they opened a resort and convention center, Kah-Nee-Ta Lodge, in the early 1970s. This enterprise increased employment and revenues. Among their various other projects were a modern administrative and tribal center, a housing program, and a $5.5 million trout and salmon hatchery near Kah-Nee-Ta. The tribes have their own laws for fish and game management. Additional income is derived from employment in a small electronics plant on the reservation and the sale of wild horses. The tribes authorized the building of Pelton Dam by the Department of the Interior on the Deschutes River and shared some of the expense. On July 16, 1982, they dedicated their $30 million Pelton Re-regulating Dam hydroelectric project. The license for that project was the first issued to an Indian tribe by the United States Federal Energy Regulatory Commission, and the dam was the first low-rise hydroelectric project ever built by an Indian tribe. The generated power, which is sold to Pacific Power and Light Company, is produced from waters reserved by the Pelton and Round Butte dams on the Deschutes. Junior and senior high school students attend schools in Madras. On the reservation are a Catholic and an Indian Shaker church and churches of Protestant denominations. The tribe is adding a $4.5 million Interpretive Indian museum to their tourists' offerings.

Special Events: Warm Springs tribal members practice the *washat*, a religious ceremony in which drums and feathers are used at funerals, feasts, and Sunday services. There is also an Indian feather religion, whose rituals are closed to the public. A First Roots Feast is usually held in early spring at Warm Springs. In the second or third week of May the Tygh Valley All Indian Rodeo and Celebration is held. In June the Pi-Ume-Sha Pow-wow at Warm Springs and Kah-Nee-Ta features competitive dancing. Fun Days are held at Warm Springs around the Fourth of July. There is also a Huckleberry Feast in early fall at the He-he Mill. Rodeos are often held in conjunction with those celebrations. Other gatherings and powwows are held at Thanksgiving and Christmas and on New Year's Day. Lincoln's Birthday is celebrated at Simnasho, and there is an Indians' Night Out honoring the elderly at some time during the year.

Suggested Readings: David S. Boyer, "Warm Springs Indians Carve Out a Future," *National Geographic* 155, no. 4 (April, 1979); Confederated Tribes of the Warm Springs Reservation of Oregon, *A Brief Look at the Warm Springs Indian Reservation* (Portland, Ore., 1975); Confederated Tribes of the Warm Springs Reservation of Oregon: Cynthia D. Stowell, *Faces of a Reservation* (Portland, Ore.: Oregon Historical Society Press, 1987); Martha (Ferguson) McKeown, *Come to Our Salmon Feast* (Portland, Ore.: Binfords and Mort, 1959); Gordon MacNab, *A History of the McQuinn Strip* (Portland, Ore., 1972); Gordon MacNab, *A Short History of the Confederated Tribes of the Warm Springs Reservation* (Portland, Ore., 1972); Ralph Shane and Ruby D. Leno, *A History of the Warm Springs Reservation, Oregon* (Portland, Ore.: U.S. Department of the Interior, Bureau of Indian Affairs, 1949).

CONFEDERATED TRIBES OF THE YAKIMA INDIAN RESERVATION OF WASHINGTON

The origins of the Confederated Tribes of the Yakima Indian Reservation of Washington lay in the Yakima Treaty signed in the Walla Walla valley on June 9, 1855. After that treaty some of the signatory bands, primarily Klickitats, joined the Yakimas proper on the Yakima Reservation of the Simcoe Agency. Most of the tribes who belonged to what the Yakima Tribes call the Yakima Nation subsequently located with and became associated with other tribes. Today the Yakima Tribes stress their nationhood because, unlike tribes on reservations established by executive orders, they were party to a treaty in the manner of sovereign nations.

Location: Yakima tribesmen live on their reservation of over one million acres in south-central Washington state, on farms in the Yakima River valley, or in reservation towns, such as Toppenish, Wapato, Parker, and White Swan. Others live in off-reservation towns in the valley, such as the city of Yakima.

Numbers: Tribal membership in 1984 was about 6,853, more than double the 3,000 estimate of the numbers of the Yakimas proper in 1780. Among the reasons for the larger number in more recent times is the inclusion of peoples, such as the Klickitats, who historically did not belong to the Yakima tribe. Less exposure than many other tribes to endemic diseases also helped sustain the Yakima Tribes' population.

History: Under the Yakima Treaty of 1855 the Klickitats became the most numerous people on the Yakima Reservation next to the Yakimas proper. Many Klickitats were removed there in 1867 under the pressure of whites who wanted them out of the Willamette valley of Oregon, where for many years they had gone to trade, hunt, and farm. An indication of the close cultural ties between Klickitats and Yakimas was the election of the influential Klickitat White Swan, or Joe Stwire, as head Yakima chief

during the early reservation period. During that time Yakima Reservation peoples came under the strong hand of the Reverend James ("Father") Wilbur, a Methodist minister, who became agent in 1864. Except for a brief period, the Reverend Wilbur retained that office throughout the President Ulysses S. Grant Peace Policy era of the 1870s and early 1880s. Wilbur ruled under the standard of "The Plow and the Bible," and his administration was regarded by the white-Protestant community as a model of Indian agency management. The Indians, however, were unenthusiastic about accepting farming, and the teaching of the Bible led to friction between Protestants and Roman Catholics over management of the Simcoe Agency. Clerics of the latter faith had initially worked among the Yakima peoples. Friction also developed between the original inhabitants of the reservation, their descendants, and the Northern Paiutes, of whom 540 were exiled to the Yakima Reservation in the wake of the Bannock-Paiute War of 1878. The Paiutes' stay was brief, extending only from early 1879 into the early 1880s.

In the late nineteenth century whites began encroaching on the Yakima Reservation with projects such as a dam that was built across the Yakima River in 1891 for irrigation purposes. In 1894 the agent, L. T. Erwin, attempted to bring his charges into the white world by constructing for them the Erwin Ditch with funds secured from the sale of the Wenatshapam Fishery that had been reserved for them under the Yakima Treaty (see **Wenatchee**). Controversies among Yakimas and whites, involving fishing, water, and land-use rights, continued into the twentieth century, when advancing technology and the increasing numbers of the whites aggravated the problems. Allotment of the reservation began in the early 1890s and was mostly completed in 1914. Between 1892 and 1915 about 4,506 allotments were made. By 1914 440,000 acres of the reservation had been allotted, and 798,000 acres remained unallotted. As the twentieth century advanced, Yakima peoples were brought more closely into the white world, but not always on friendly terms. At the time of World War I, for example, Yakima traditionalists believed their youth were sent to fight so that Americans could destroy them. The relationship of the Yakima tribes with the federal government in the twentieth century centered around the settlement of tribal claims.

Government Organization and Claims: Despite pressures on them to do so, the Yakima peoples did not formally organize their government until 1935. One reason why they first rejected organization under the Indian Reorganization Act of 1934 (48 Stat. 984) was a long heritage of dissatisfaction with the United States. The council of the Confederated Tribes of the Yakima Indian Reservation of Washington is composed of fourteen members representing the fourteen peoples who were signatories to their treaty. A general council includes all tribal members over eighteen years of age. A close liaison exists between these two bodies. The tribal and agency headquarters are located at Toppenish, Washington, about twenty miles south of Yakima on U.S. Highway 97 and Interstate 82. Under Washington state law (Chapter 36, *Laws of Washington*, dated March 13, 1963) and federal law (Public Law 280, 83rd Congress, 1st Session, passed August 15, 1953), the state assumed jurisdiction over Yakima Indians on tribal and allotted lands held in trust by the United States, with respect to eight categories of activity: compulsory school attendance, public assistance, domestic relations, mental illness, juvenile delinquency, adoption proceedings, dependent children, and operation of motor vehicles on public streets, alleys, roads, and highways.

On June 21, 1949, the Yakima Tribes filed a claim (Docket 47) with the Indian Claims Commission for a compensation for or recovery of any of five areas on and adjacent to the Yakima Reservation. Denying their claim to one tract, designated as Tract A, which was adjacent to the eastern reservation boundary in the Mabton area, the commission accepted the boundary line established by the Harry A. Clark survey

Confederated Tribes of the Yakima Indian Reservation of Washington

Watson Totus, a leader of the Yakima people, was renowned in not only business but also religious affairs. Totus was a leader of the Seven Drum religion, which is deeply rooted in Yakima worship. This picture was taken in 1977.

of 1885. The commission also denied the tribes' claim to two other tracts, designated B and D, but established the value of the 17,669.10 Tract C in the Ahtanum Creek area at $22,086.38 plus interest from 1923. Tract C lay north of the pre-1953 western end of the northern reservation boundary, which began at the confluence of Reservation Creek and the South Fork of the Ahtanum and extended up Réservation Creek to its headwaters and thence in a straight line to Spencer Point. The acreage in Tract C had been involved in a dispute over which fork of Ahtanum Creek served as the western portion of the northern boundary. That creek has a very small branch now designated as the North Fork. Upstream the south fork has a large tributary, now known as Reservation Creek. In his 1890 survey George A. Schwartz had established the boundary along the present-day Reservation Creek, which he called the South Fork. In an 1899 survey E. C. Barnard had followed Schwartz's definition of the boundary along Reservation Creek, which he too called the South Fork of the Ahtanum. In his report Barnard wrote that he thought that the boundary should follow a natural line west from the headwaters of the creek. That "natural line" was from the crest of the divide around the headwaters of the Klickitat River via Darling (or Darland) Mountain to Spencer Point.

At the time of its hearings the Claims Commission possessed the map made at the time of the 1855 treaty, which was lost until 1930. The commission sided with the Yakimas by establishing the present-day South Fork of the Ahtanum as the boundary and by designating natural contours between the present-day South Fork headwaters and Spencer Point as the boundary. This placed the boundary north of the old one, adding 18,094.42 acres to the reservation. This additional acreage had been settled by whites except for a 425.32-acre land grant that the Northern Pacific Railroad had received under the act of July 2, 1864 (13 Stat. 365). Those 425.32 acres were returned to the Yakimas, since the patent had not been finalized by the General Land Office. Schwartz had also surveyed the western and southwestern boundaries of the reservation. His surveys were accepted by the General Land Office, October 21, 1891. The southwestern boundary followed the crest of the Simcoe Mountains. Barnard's surveys, accepted by the General Land Office on April 7, 1900, pushed the boundary line farther west in a straight line from Spencer Point to Goat Butte (usually referred to as The Hump) just east of Mount Adams and from there to Grayback Peak, adding 293,837 acres to the reservation. Within the area between the two lines, formerly believed to be public domain and sold to settlers, lay 27,647.7 acres in a twenty-square-mile area within the southwestern corner of the reservation.

About three-fifths of this acreage lay in an almost solid block in Klickitat County. The rest lay scattered in Yakima County. The acreage was mountainous between Simcoe Ridge on the south and Toppenish Ridge on the north. On November 6, 1953, the Claims Commission fixed the value of those lands at $69,119.28 as of December 21, 1904, when the settlers' rights to ownership were validated.

On November 29, 1957, the Claims Commission entered an interlocutory order of an award for the Tract C lands of $22,086.38 plus interest from 1923, and for the Cedar Valley tract, the value plus interest from 1904. On November 6, 1953, after the commission denied the Yakimas any recovery for Tracts A, B, and D, the Indians appealed the decision to the Court of Claims (Appeals Case No. 4-61, 158 C.Cls. 672). That court affirmed the decision of the Claims Commission in all cases except those of tracts B and D, in which two considerations were reversed and remanded to the commission for consideration of the liability of the United States. On its return from the Court of Claims, Tract C was redocketed 47-A; and on June 25, 1965, the Yakimas were awarded $61,991.40 for the 17,669.10-acre tract. The commission later found that 121,465.69 acres in Tract D should be added to the Yakima Reservation. Tract D, shaped like an isosceles triangle, lay on the southwestern boundary of the reservation on a line running southeast from a terminal point of the western boundary west of the summit of Mount Adams in the Cascade Range, to a point beginning on the southern boundary at Grayback Mountain, in lands between the watersheds of the Klickitat and White Salmon rivers south of Mount Adams. The commission found that the boundary had been laid out erroneously in 1907 by the Campbell, Germond, and Long surveys, which had followed the survey of Barnard, who used the socalled White Swan map that Governor Stevens had made of the reservation in March, 1857, just four years before the unreliable first survey of the reservation's eastern and southeastern boundary lines by Thomas F. Berry and James Lodge in 1861. The commission determined that in Tract D the Yakimas were entitled to compensation for 97,908.97 acres that had been sold to white settlers. To be returned to the Indians were 2,548 acres of vacant and unpatented lands, as well as 21,008.66 acres of the Gifford Pinchot National Forest including the eastern half of Mount Adams. The treaty call had placed the western reservation boundary just east of that mountain, but the original map (which was discovered in 1930 filed with maps from Montana in the National Archives) placed the boundary west of the mountain. The Department of Agriculture reluctantly released the acreage, claims for which were redocketed separately (Docket 47-B). That docket was dismissed when the defending United States agreed to transfer the 21,008.66 acres to the Yakimas by executive order on May 26, 1972. Claims for recovery of the remaining 97,908.97 acres in Tract D and the Cedar Valley tracts were consolidated with the claim (Docket 164) for the erroneous allotment of nearly 411 80-acre tracts to non-Yakimas on the reservation. Finally $2,160,000 was awarded for the remaining portions of Dockets 47 and 164 less $60,000 that the Yakimas had retained from other claims (Dockets 161, 222, and 224). The settlement called for dismissal of Dockets 147 and 160. Docket 147 had been a claim for loss of fish in the Yakima River.

For a second time the Claims Commission denied the Yakima claim for Tract B, which is known as the Lake Walupt area. This 7,705-acre pear-shaped area west of the western boundary of the reservation included the lake and berry grounds. The E. D. Calvin survey of 1939, however, found the lake area to be on the western slopes of the Cascade Range and thus outside the reservation, which was established by the 1855 treaty at the crest of those mountains. The Tract B claim was denied by the commission in a decision on February 25, 1966. The Chester W. Pecore boundary line was established as the western reservation boundary. This line dated from a 1920–24 survey along the west of the Cascade Range and had been accepted by the General Land Office, August 6, 1926. Thus 47,593 acres were added to the reservation. This addition included 346.44 acres of Northern Pacific Railroad Company mineral lands that that company had filed on. The filing was withdrawn and the land returned to the Yakimas. The company released its claim to the 346.44 acres on March 28, 1941.

The Yakima Tribes filed a claim (Docket 162) for additional compensation for 23,000 acres of timber land near Leavenworth, Washington, where the Wenatchee Tribe (one of the fourteen Confederated Tribes under the 1855 Yakima Treaty) resided and had their fishery. On January 8, 1894, by an agreement with the United States the Yakimas had signed away the land for $20,000. Money from the sale, as noted above, had been used to build the Erwin Ditch. The Indian Claims Commission decided that the lands had been worth $69,000 in 1894, and on August 31, 1965, it awarded the Yakimas an additional $49,000. With twenty-four other tribes throughout western United States the Yakima Tribes filed a claim (Docket 310-74) that reached the Court of Claims. The claim was for mismanagement of Individual Claims Commission judgment funds and for other funds held in trust by the United States, such as Individual Money accounts. The Yakima Tribes were awarded $1,306,390.11 in 1980.

On behalf of the Wishram Tribe, one of the fourteen groups under the Yakima Treaty, the Yakima Tribes filed a claim (Docket 165) on July 24, 1951, alleging that after the 1855 treaty the United States had not intended to pay for the lands ceded by the tribes and thus had forced them into war with that country. Although the Wishrams had remained friendly, turning over their weapons to the commandant at Fort Dalles at his request, they had been mistakenly attacked by American troops, who destroyed much of their properties in the belief that they were combatants. Despite promises by the military command that the Wishrams would be compensated for their losses, they were not so compensated, and their weapons were not returned. When the defending United States asked for an accounting of Indian losses, none was forthcoming. The Claims Commission then dismissed the docket.

The Yakima Tribes also filed a claim (Docket 161) for additional recovery for lands ceded to the United States by the fourteen tribes confederated under the Yakima standard. See **Confederated Tribes of the Colville Reservation, Washington.**

Contemporary Life and Culture: In 1975 1,118,149.04 acres of tribal lands were held in trust on the Yakima Reservation. In 1983 about 15,000 acres were under cultivation. No other Pacific Northwest tribes have been more active in promoting business enterprises than the Yakima Tribes. About 150 million board feet of timber are taken annually from their sustained-yield-managed reservation holdings. A tribal furniture manufacturing operation bears the name of their sacred mountain, Mount Adams. Other enterprises involve tribal heritage, agriculture, fishing, and banking. The oldest and largest reservation irrigation undertaking is the Wapato Project, which delivers water to nearly 150,000 acres of croplands, including 90,000 acres of Indian lands. Reservation lands also include more than 2.7 million acres of range for domestic livestock. The Yakima Tribes also derive income from claims for lost fishing rights and lands taken without compensation. On November 8, 1979, the tribes succeeded in getting the Ninth Circuit Court of Appeals to order returned to them some legal ground that they had lost in a Supreme Court decision ten months previously; the circuit court ruled that the tribes have concurrent jurisdiction with the state of Washington in several reservation matters. There is a Yakima Tribal Housing Authority. Health needs are met primarily through facilities operated by the Indian Health Service. In summer children at Camp Chaparral on the reservation near Mount Adams prepare for fall public school. For years the Yakimas opposed nuclear waste dumping at nearby Hanford. The 6,706-member tribe in 1992 fought the U.S. Supreme Court ruling that owners of fee patent Yakima Reservation lands were subject to property taxes levied by the county. On June 9, 1980, the Yakimas opened their beautiful cultural center containing a museum, theater, library, restaurant, longhouse, and

offices. In 1989 the Yakima blamed a smaller salmon run (by 100,000) on the March 24 Exxon oil spill at Valdez and filed suit for $25 million. That same year they became aware of a $123-million loss in BIA mismanagement of their timber sales. A November 1990 judgment given in Yakima County Superior Court to a case filed in 1977 limited tribal irrigation rights while prescribing and assuring a stream flow sufficient to maintain fish life. Their suit for 2.5 million acre-feet of Yakima River water was kept at 655,000 acre-feet.

Special Events: The Yakima Tribes have a full schedule of cultural events. These include the annual George Washington Birthday Celebration at Toppenish in the third week of February; the Speely-mi Annual Arts and Crafts Fair at Toppenish on a weekend near the middle of February; the Celilo Salmon Feast and Pow-wow at Celilo, Oregon, in April; the Rock Creek Root Feast at Rock Creek in April; the Satus Pow-wow at Satus in the fourth weekend of April; the Weaseltail Club event at White Swan on Memorial Day weekend; the Treaty-day Golf event in the first week of June; the Tiinowit Pow-wow at the ancient ceremonial grounds at White Swan during the first weekend of June; the All-Indian Rodeo and Treaty Day at White Swan in the first weekend of June; the American Indian Days Celebration at White Swan in the third weekend of September; the Veterans Day Pow-wow at Toppenish in the second week of November; the Christmas and New Year's Pow-wow at Wapato, of which the final night's activities are held at White Swan.

Suggested Readings: Richard D. Daugherty, *The Yakima Peoples* (Phoenix, Ariz.: Indian Tribal Series, 1973); Melville Jacobs, *Northwest Sahaptin Texts* (New York: Columbia University Press, 1934–37), 2 vols.; Lucullus V. McWhorter, *The Crime Against the Yakimas* (Yakima, Wash.: Republic Printers, 1913); Robert E. Pace, *The Land of the Yakimas* (Toppenish, Wash.: Yakima Indian Media Services, 1977); Robert E. Pace, *Yakima Indian Nation Bibliography* (Toppenish, Wash.: Yakima Indian Media Services, 1982); Click Relander, *Strangers on the Land* (Yakima, Wash.: Franklin Press, 1962); Helen Hersh Schuster, *The Yakimas: A Critical Bibliography* (Bloomington, Ind.: Indiana University Press, 1982);

Helen Hersh Schuster, *Yakima Traditionalism: A Study in Continuity and Change*, dissertation (Ann Arbor, Mich.: University Microfilm International, 1977); A. J. Splawn, *Ka-Mi-Akin, The Last Hero of the Yakimas* (Yakima, Wash.: Binfords and Mort, 1944).

COOS

(See **Coos Tribe of Indians, Hanis Coos, Miluk Coos,** and **Confederated Tribes of Coos, Lower Umpqua & Siuslaw Indians, Inc.**)

COOS TRIBE OF INDIANS

The Coos Tribe of Indians originated from four tribes: the Hanis Coos, the Miluk Coos (or Lower Coquilles), the Kuitshes (or Lower Umpquas) and the Siuslaws. The present-day Coos Tribe was composed for the most part of descendants of members of those tribes who lived on the Alsea Reservation.

Location: The Coos Tribe of Indians lived mainly around Coos Bay, Oregon.

Numbers: In 1975 the tribal membership numbered approximately 125.

Government and Claims: In 1938 the Coos Tribe adopted its first constitution and bylaws.

There was a schism in the tribe in the 1950s when a few members were included in an award to the Upper Coquilles and other tribes of the Siletz Reservation, lumped together as Tillamooks for the award. In 1851, when Oregon Superintendent of Indian Affairs Anson Dart had made his two treaties at Port Orford, Oregon, with Athapascan-speaking tribes, he rounded up Indians as far north as the estuary of the Coquille River. A few Nasomahs of the southernmost division of the Miluk Coos were in the group near present-day Bandon. Also in the group who treated with Dart were Upper Coquilles who were related to certain Nasomahs through intermarriage. Thus as successful litigants before the Court of Claims (Case No. 45320), the Upper Co-

quilles, the Chetcos, the Tututnis, and the Alcea Band of Tillamooks received awards. Those Coos who could prove Upper Coquille ancestry became eligible for some of the awards from the claims. Since the 1950s those Coos have broken away from the now-incorporated Coos Tribe of Indians and joined the Coquille Tribe. The relationship between the two groups is uneasy because the Coos Tribe of Indians was unable to receive an award from the United States for its land cession. Even before the Coquilles did so, the Coos Tribe had petitioned the Court of Claims for a settlement (Case No. K-345), but received none. The Coquilles, when they subsequently petitioned the Court of Claims, were successful. The Coos Tribe then petitioned the Indian Claims Commission again, but the commission refused to hear its case. Continuing tension between members of the Coos Tribe and Coos members of the Coquille Indian Tribe also has stemmed from competition for federal programs. The Coquille Indian Tribe is landless and without federal acknowledgment. The Coos Tribe has 6.1 acres of land and several cemeteries. Believing that its claims were strengthened by this land case, it sought federal acknowledgment in 1975. Today the Coos have federal recognition within their confederation with the Lower Umpquas and Siuslaws. See **Confederated Tribes of Coos, Lower Umpqua & Siuslaw Indians, Inc.;** and **Hanis Coos.**

COPALIS

(Coastal Division, Salishan)

The Copalises lived on the Pacific Coast of Washington state from north of the entrance to Grays Harbor to the lands of the Quinault Indians and in the valley of the Copalis

River, a Pacific Ocean affluent. In 1805–1806 Meriwether Lewis and William Clark reported that the "Pailsk," who were perhaps the Copalis, numbered 200 in ten houses. Not only the Copalis River bears the tribal name but also the towns of Copalis, Copalis Beach, and Copalis Crossing.

The Copalis River yielded what were regarded as the most succulent of all Pacific Coast salmon. The Copalises ate other fish also, including sculpin that were noted for their large heads and wide mouths. Neighboring tribes came to the Copalis villages to obtain razor clams, which today are as highly prized as they were in prerecorded times. It is said that the Copalises never let their fires die out because they always expected visitors. The Copalises' contacts with whites were evident in the potatoes grown in the 1850s by one of their chiefs, Herkoish.

In the 1850s the Copalises had no special designation in most official tabulations. As a nontreaty people, their few remaining tribesmen depended on the Quinault Agency for such aids as medicines and vaccinations against smallpox. The Chehalises claimed that the Copalises were one of their subdivisions, though they attacked the Copalises so often that the latter had deserted some of their villages. The Quinaults also claimed the Copalises as part of their tribe, but the Indian Claims Commission, in *The Quinaielt Tribe* v. *United States* (Docket 242), held that the Copalises were no part of the Quinaults. The same estimation was also given in the 1850s by on-the-spot observers James Swan and George Gibbs. Archaeologists have unearthed old Copalis villages in recent years.

COQUILLE
(Athapascan)

Originally, the Coquilles were known by their native name, which was spelled in English Mishikhwutmetunne and meant "people living on the stream called Mishi, or Misha." Whites called them Upper Coquilles and Coast Rogues. Although Athapascan speakers entered southern Oregon from the north at some early period, the Coquilles are believed to have entered the valley of the Coquille River only shortly before white contact. The Coquille River flows into the

Coquille

Susan Wasson, whose Indian name was Adulsa (also spelled Adethsa), was born about 1841. Her first husband, a white miner, died at sea. She then married another white man, George Wasson, and they had nine children. Her Coquille people, however, were unfriendly to early-day whites in their country. Courtesy of Roberta Hall.

Pacific Ocean where the town of Coquille, Oregon, is today. The origin of the tribal name is disputed. Some say it is the French word meaning "shell." Others say that it is a native word with a French spelling.

The Coquilles' dwellings were made of willow frames covered with sod or grass reeds over wood frame poles. Some houses were lean-tos of cedar planks. During the precontact period females were matched with spouses in arranged marriages. Although women had no role in village government, they did go out on spirit quests, and some became shamans. During the precontact period governance was at the village level. Later whites grouped the native villagers together to better deal with them. After the Coquilles moved away from the coast, they depended for much of their subsistence on acorns and on deer, which they hunted with dogs. They did, however, fish occasionally along the coast near present-day Port Orford. They caught salmon in nets and baskets. They also caught eels in willow-twig baskets.

The Coquilles had little to do with coastal natives, although they did raid the Coos for slaves. Coquille tradition, however, has it that during early times a marriage united the Coquille and Coos peoples when a Coos chief, Kitzunginum, took a Coquille woman, Nestilcut, as one of his five wives. To commemorate their marriage, the couple marked a cedar tree as high as they could reach. Eventually Kitzunginum's own people killed him during an elk hunt, shooting him with arrows when his back was turned. Another tradition has it that the chief had forcibly wrested tribal leadership from his brother.

Coquille contacts with whites were especially unfriendly. After an Indian guide misled W. G. T'Vault and his party, who were searching for an overland route between the coast and the Willamette valley, the Coquilles on September 14, 1851, attacked the party with bows and arrows, war clubs, and knives made from iron from the vessel *William G. Hagstaff*, which had previously wrecked near Port Orford. Wading into the water, the natives (who may, in fact, have been Lower Coquilles, or Miluk Coos) attacked the party before it could ready its

rifles (for an account of this incident, see **Miluk Coos**). Aggravating the conflicts between the tribes of the upper and lower Coquille River were the unratified treaties effected with them by Oregon Superintendents of Indian Affairs Anson Dart and Joel Palmer in 1851 and 1855. The Coquilles and other so-called Rogue peoples were rounded up in June, 1856, and moved, mostly by ship, from Port Orford to Portland and then to the Grand Ronde Reservation, where many of them succumbed to smallpox. Eventually those who did not escape to their homelands from the reservation were moved to the Siletz Reservation. Those who escaped had previously buried their canoes in the sand in their homelands, hoping to find them on returning there. After fleeing the reservation, they discovered that they could no longer live in their traditional manner, because whites had occupied their old lands. Many intermarried with whites.

With certain other descendants of western Oregon tribes, the Coquilles were plaintiffs in a Case No. 45230 in the Court of Claims, seeking to recover compensation for lands that were taken from the Coast Reservation by executive order on December 21, 1865, and by act of Congress on March 3, 1875. After receiving an award that did not include interest, the Coquilles appealed to the United States Supreme Court for payment of the same, but that court on November 25, 1946, upheld the April 2, 1945, ruling of the Court of Claims. In the end, the Coquilles received an award of $847,190.40. For the history of a suit before the Court of Claims in which the Coquilles were named as defendants, see **Yaquina** and **Alsea**. For other claims, see **Confederated Tribes of the Siletz Indians of Oregon.** Anthropologist John R. Swanton states that the 1910 census listed fifteen Mishikhwutmetunnes under the name Upper Coquille. Today there are no full-blood Coquilles. See also **Coquille Indian Tribe.**

Suggested Readings: Stephen Dow Beckham, *The Indians of Western Oregon, This Land Was Theirs* (Coos Bay, Ore., Arago Books, 1977); Roberta L. Hall, *Oral Traditions of the Coquille*

Indians, pamphlet, 1978, Department of Anthropology, Oregon State University; Roberta L. Hall, *The Coquille Indians: Yesterday, Today and Tomorrow* (Lake Oswego, Ore.: Smith, Smith and Smith Publishing Company, 1984); Beverly Mecum Ward, "White Moccasins," n.d., manuscript in possession of author, Coos Bay, Ore.

COQUILLE INDIAN TRIBE

The genetic and cultural origins of the Coquille peoples are mixed. The Upper Coquilles (see **Coquille**) were Athapascan speakers. The Lower Coquilles, or Miluk Coos (see **Miluk Coos**), were Yakonan speakers. According to those today identifying themselves as Coquilles, the spelling of their tribal name until the early twentieth century was Coquelle. In 1952, Indians of Coquille descent organized with a few Coos to seek a judgment from the Court of Claims in their land claims case. The tribe disbanded in 1956 but reformed in 1975 as the Coquille Indian Tribe. On July 28, 1989, President George Bush signed a bill, Public Law 101–42, restoring Coquille tribal status after thirty-five years of nonrecognition, their tribal status having been lost with the 1954 Western Oregon Termination Act. The 631-member tribe acquired a gift of 1.2 acres from Port of Bandon, and the tribe purchased 4 acres adjacent to that. They plan a museum.

Coquille Indian Tribe

Jerry Running Foxe, a modern Coquille of the Oregon coast, circa 1980. His ancestors vigorously opposed invasion of their coasts by white men.

COW CREEK BAND OF THE UMPQUA TRIBE OF INDIANS

The Cow Creek Band of the Umpqua Tribe of Indians was created when Oregon Superintendent of Indian Affairs Joel Palmer affixed his signature to a treaty on September 19, 1853 (10 Stat. 1027), which was ratified April 12, 1854. That was the second ratified treaty in the Pacific Northwest to be negotiated with Indians of several villages of different linguistic groups. In this case the villages were along Cow Creek, a tribu-

tary of the South Fork of the Umpqua River in southern Oregon. Among the Indians included in the treaty were Athapascan-speaking Upper Umpqua Targunsans and Miwaletas. The Miwaletas took their name, meaning "small long-time-ago people," from that of their chief. Also included in the treaty were Takilman speakers and possibly a few Waiilatpuan-speaking Southern Molalas.

Location: The descendants of those Cow Creek peoples, who formed the nucleus of the present-day tribe, live in Oregon towns such as Drew, Tiller, Riddle, and Canyonville. The Cow Creeks formerly lived on the creek that bears their name. The Upper Umpquas were their neighbors downstream on the South Fork of the Umpqua River. Beyond them were the Yoncallas. Far into the nearby Cascade Mountains, along the headwaters of the North and South Umpqua rivers, lived the Southern Molalas.

Numbers: In 1985 the Cow Creeks numbered 221. In 1990 there were 755.

History: By terms of their 1853 treaty the Indians ceded nearly 800 square miles of their land for $12,000 in twenty-one payments and a small temporary reservation on their lands on Cow Creek. Later they were removed to another reservation at the decision of the federal government. In contrast to such confinement, they previously had been a mobile people who moved their villages seasonally from place to place. When the Rogue Wars were renewed in October, 1855, many Cow Creeks fled to the hills, joining others who had fled when the government threatened to move them to the temporary reservation established for Upper Umpquas (see **Upper Umpqua**). Those who fled had no wish to be moved north with Upper Umpquas, Yoncallas, and Southern Molalas to the Yamhill country, where the Grand Ronde Reservation was to be established for them. The journey to the reservation in January, 1856, was indeed very difficult for those who made it. Many were forced to walk because the eight wagons commissioned to remove them were inadequate. Many of those who did remove later managed to escape to their former homes, where, hiding out in the mountains, some died from starvation and exposure. Half the Miwaletas died, some expiring so fast that their survivors could not bury them but burned them instead. Several were killed by Oregon mounted volunteers foraying through the hills.

After 1868 white settlers pushed the Cow Creek Indians ever farther up the South

Cow Creek Band of the Umpqua Tribe of Indians

Susan Thomason of the Cow Creek Band of the Umpqua Tribe of Indians of the southern Oregon coast. This picture was taken about 1860, a few years after her people signed a treaty with the United States in which they yielded their lands. Courtesy of the Douglas County Museum, Oregon.

Umpqua, where they came to rest in headwater country above and around Canyonville, along the route of north-south travel between the Pacific Northwest and California. Some of their women married French-

Canadian fur trappers. The settlers who occupied their former lands built fences to prevent the Indians from burning their lands as they had for generations to nurture the growth of berries. They were thus deprived of that source of food. Two attempts were made to round up the Cow Creeks still at large. In May, 1856, Agent James P. Day failed to corral those Cow Creeks who were around Canyonville. In 1860 the military were likewise unsuccessful in attempting to confine them. Twenty-five years later volunteers were still pursuing them. Faced by starvation, the Cow Creeks raided Douglas County settlers' farms and killed their livestock. When the pursuits of volunteers tapered off, the Indians emerged from hiding for a while. They also sent runners to the Grand Ronde Reservation to assay the conditions of the Indians there. The runners returned with reports of starvation and exposure.

Government and Claims: The Cow Creek Band of the Umpqua Tribe of Indians is a nonprofit organization incorporated in the state of Oregon. Although it is landless without a reservation, since late 1910 the tribe has sought through legislation to obtain compensation for lost ancestral lands. In 1932, President Herbert Hoover vetoed a bill that would have compensated the tribe. In 1936 the Cow Creeks were named in the group of litigants in *Rogue River Tribe of Indians* v. *United States* (64 F. Supp. 339, Ct. Cl.) and also, four years later, in a second hearing (89 F. Supp. 789, Ct. Cl.). The Cow Creek Band of the Umpqua Tribe of Indians claims, however, that it was improper to list them as litigants because they lacked knowledge of the litigation and had not participated in it. They had not, for example, negotiated a contract with an attorney. Of the seventeen petitioning tribes only two were successful. The Cow Creek claim was dismissed.

The tribe claims that the Cow Creeks listed in the petition were descended from the Cow Creeks who were on the Grand Ronde Reservation before removal to the Siletz. The Court of Claims decided on April 3, 1950 (Case No. 45231), that the total of $12,000 paid in installments to the Cow Creek Band that had removed to the Grand Ronde was adequate compensation for the Cow Creek lands and thus tribal members were not entitled to any further awards. In fact, most of the tribe had received the first two payments before the band was rounded up and removed to the Grand Ronde. The Cow Creek Band of the Umpqua Tribe of Indians failed to petition the Indian Claims Commission (which was established by an act of Congress on August 13, 1946) before August 13, 1951, the deadline for the renewal of past claims. The Cow Creeks claimed that they had not only not been notified but also were unaware of the existence of the commission. For those reasons they sought congressional permission to litigate their claim before the Court of Claims. Their request, in the form of Senate and House bills (S. 688 and H.R. 2882), was for Congress to extend for them the statute of limitations in the Indian Claims Commission act against filing claims against the government, thus permitting them to file suit in the Court of Claims. The tribe insisted that the majority of its ancestors had fled to the hills and had received none of the eighteen remaining payments, which it claimed were paid only to about forty-five members of the tribe on the Grand Ronde. Both the congressional bills finally passed May 26, 1980 (94 Stat. 372), giving the tribe authorization to sue the United States in the Court of Claims for compensation for its alienated lands, for which, the tribe claims, the previous payment was unconscionably low. (See **Upper Umpqua**). By a congressional act dated December 29, 1982, the tribe was granted federal recognition. A decade later the tribe was looking to produce tribal income. One of the considerations was a bingo parlor.

Special Events: The tribe holds its annual Cow Creek Band of Umpqua Pow-wow usually in the last two weeks of July at South Umpqua Falls.

Suggested Reading: Stephen Dow Beckham, *The Indians of Western Oregon: This Land Was Theirs* (Coos Bay, Ore.: Arago Books, 1977).

COWLITZ
(Coastal Division, Salishan)

The name Cowlitz is said to mean "capturing the medicine spirit" because the Cowlitzes visited a small prairie on the Cowlitz River (a Columbia River affluent in Washington state) to commune with the spirit world and receive "medicine" power. During the early nineteenth century the Cowlitzes became divided into four groups. One group were the Lower Cowlitzes, who occupied the middle and lower courses of the Cowlitz River from Cowlitz Landing south to the mouth of the river, plus the river's tributaries and adjacent lands. Because their lands bordered on the Columbia River, these Cowlitzes relied more on salmon for subsistence than did other Cowlitz groups. Another group were the Mountain Cowlitzes, who combined with the Kwalhioquas, who subsequently gave up their language for that of the Cowlitzes. The Mountain Cowlitzes lived on the upper reaches of the Chehalis River and eventually combined with the Kwaiailks (Upper Chehalises). The Upper Cowlitzes (sometimes called the Stick Indians) lived on the upper Cowlitz River and below Mount Rainier. They intermarried with the Shahaptian-speaking Klickitats and assumed their language. The western movement of the Klickitats from just east of the Cascade Mountains was accomplished by individuals, mostly women, and not by the tribe in general. The Upper Cowlitzes traveled widely for mountain game and grazed horses on their mountain meadows. Another Cowlitz group, the Lewis Cowlitzes, were so named because of their location on the Lewis River, a Columbia affluent. They too combined with the Klickitats and adopted the Klickitat language.

With no access to the sea, the Mountain and Upper Cowlitz groups became skilled hunters. The anthropologist Verne F. Ray believed that the Cowlitzes were the most cohesive tribe in western Washington, partly at least because of their isolation. Their women were excellent basket makers, who worked cedar roots horizontally and bear and straw grass vertically into their utensils. Possibly those techniques were learned from the Klickitats or at least improved by the Cowlitzes' association with that tribe. The Cowlitzes held and traded slaves, which they obtained mostly by barter and war.

Besides the Cowlitz River, Cowlitz County, Washington bears the tribal name.

Location: Many Cowlitzes remain in the general area of their ancestral homelands. Others have scattered, especially to western Washington and into Oregon.

Numbers: The Cowlitz tribe lists as members those having one sixteenth or more Cowlitz blood. In 1980 tribal membership was 1,689. In 1973 the tribal population had been 278, and in the following year there were about 320 adult Cowlitzes. In 1780 the tribal population, along with that of the Chehalises, the Humptulipses, and some others, was about 1,000. In 1842 there were 350 Upper Cowlitzes, about 100 Mountain Cowlitzes, and 330 others, presumably including the Lower Cowlitzes and perhaps the Lewis River group. Epidemics, such as the intermittent fever of the 1830s, reduced the total Cowlitz numbers to less than 1,000. The smallpox of the 1850s reduced their numbers to between 600 and 700. In 1879 there were only 66 Cowlitzes near the mouth of the Cowlitz River under the supervision of a Nisqually agent. In 1887 there were 127 Cowlitzes, whom the government classified as part of the Chehalis tribe. In 1893 the Puyallup agent reported that those Cowlitzes had scattered onto small farms or were absorbed within the white community.

History: During the early contact period the Cowlitzes were sometimes unfriendly to whites. One special agent wrote that they were "independent, fearless and aggressive and refused to subordinate themselves to the white man." Because they were also on unfriendly terms with the natives on the Pacific Coast, the Cowlitzes in 1813 asked the traders of the North West Company's Fort George, near the mouth of the Columbia River, to trade with them in their own

Cowlitz

Joseph E. Cloquet, a chairman of the Cowlitz Tribal Council, photographed circa 1980. The Cowlitzes were among the southwestern Washington tribes who opposed removal to reservations outside their homelands. The Cowlitz Tribe has sought to maintain tribal traditions and to obtain settlement of claims.

In December, 1838, the Roman Catholic priest François Norbert Blanchet established the Saint Francis Xavier Mission near present-day Toledo, Washington, on the route between the Columbia River and southern Puget Sound. In that same year the Anglican minister Rev. Herbert Beaver vaccinated nearly 120 Lewis River Cowlitzes. Others of the tribe were vaccinated by a Hudson's Bay Company medical officer. In February and March, 1855, the Cowlitzes attended the Chehalis River Treaty Council with Washington Territorial Governor and Superintendent of Indian Affairs Isaac Stevens, but did not sign a treaty. They were disgruntled that the proposed treaty did not provide for a reservation in their own country. With most of the other mountain tribes, such as the Snoqualmies, the Upper Cowlitzes fought Americans in the 1855–56 Indian wars. Other Cowlitzes in 1856, under the watchful eye of Indian Agent Sydney S. Ford, were rounded up on a temporary reservation on lands of one Simon Plomondon, a former Hudson's Bay Company employee, who was the first settler on Cowlitz Prairie. During the wars large numbers of Lewis River Cowlitzes were confined at Fort Vancouver. During their captivity their horses and other properties were stolen or destroyed. In 1860 the Indian agent of the Columbia River district, R. H. Lansdale, removed Lewis River Cowlitzes because of conflicts with whites who were driving them from place to place, taking their lands and burning their properties. Among those removed were forty-three who with their livestock were sent eastward across the Cascade Mountains to the Yakima Reservation.

On March 20, 1863, a presidential proclamation offered Cowlitz lands for public sale, though the tribe had never signed a treaty relinquishing them. Subsequently, tribal members defied the wish of the government that they remove to the Chehalis Reservation, which was established July 8, 1864, between the Chehalis and Black rivers. The Cowlitzes never recognized the reservation and continued to hold out for one of their own. In 1868 they refused presents offered them by government offi-

lands, where such activity could be carried on more safely. In 1818, after a party of Iroquois in the employ of the North West Company massacred thirteen innocent Cowlitzes, the chief trader at Fort George brought the Cowlitz chief How How to the post, hoping to arrange a marriage between the chief's daughter and one of the men. Thinking that the chief and his braves had come to attack them in retaliation for the killings, the natives at the post engaged them in a short fracas until the matter was clarified. During the 1830s the Lower Cowlitzes moved in to possess the environs of the mouth of the Cowlitz River, replacing the Chinookan speakers formerly living there. Intermarriage continued between Cowlitzes and Chinookan peoples, as it did between Cowlitzes, Klickitats, and Chehalises. During this period the intermittent fever struck with great severity.

cials, fearing that acceptance meant surrender of their lands. In 1872, when it was definitely ascertained that the Chehalis Reservation was for all nontreaty Indians of southwestern Washington Territory, the Cowlitzes continued refusing to recognize it as their home.

Government and Claims: The Cowlitz tribe is an unincorporated association formed by a group of Cowlitz Indians to maintain tribal traditions and to obtain settlement of tribal claims. The association's constitution and bylaws provide that membership should consist "solely of Cowlitz Indians and their descendants." The constitution and bylaws also provide for an executive committee of five to supervise tribal affairs. The organization accepts for its membership rolls those persons claiming Cowlitz descent.

In 1931 the United States Supreme Court, in *Halbert* v. *United States*, held that the Cowlitzes were entitled to take allotments on the Quinault Reservation and that the Cowlitz tribe was recognized and protected by the Treaty of Olympia (1855). On June 23, 1971, the Indian Claims Commission (Docket 218) held that the United States had exercised such "domination and control" over Cowlitz lands that the tribe had been deprived of its aboriginal title without its consent and without payment of any consideration. On April 12, 1973, the tribe entered into a compromise settlement, for which the Claims Commission on July 1, 1973, awarded it $1,550,000 (fifty-eight years after the tribe's first bills for a set-

tlement had been introduced in 1915). A total of 280 members voted to accept the award. Forty voted to reject it because they wanted lands instead of money. The group voting negatively broke from the Cowlitz Tribe of Indians to become the Sovereign Cowlitz Tribe. There followed a controversy with the government over plans for distribution of the funds, especially over distribution to Cowlitz-descendant members of the Yakima Tribe, who under federal legislation were eligible for Cowlitz tribal enrollment. Meanwhile, many of the Klickitats who had formerly lived in the Cowlitz country, and with whom the Cowlitzes had intermarried, had removed eastward across the Cascade Mountains to join other Klickitats on the Yakima Reservation. As a landless tribe the Cowlitzes still seek a land base, which would give them federal acknowledgment and the rights enjoyed by several tribes of treaty Indians. See **Klickitat** and **Taitnapam.**

Suggested Readings: "Cowlitz Indians Yesterday and Today," *Longview* (Wash.) *Daily News*, August 14, 1976; Edward S. Curtis, *The North American Indian* (1912; New York: Johnson Reprint Corporation, 1970), vol. 9; Judith Irwin, "The Cowlitz Way A Round of Life," *Cowlitz Historical Quarterly*, Spring, 1979, pp. 5–24; Verne F. Ray, "Handbook of Cowlitz Indian," in *Coast Salish and Western Washington Indians*, vol. 3 (New York: Garland Publishing Inc., 1974), pp. 245–315; State of Washington Indian Affairs Task Force, *Are You Listening Neighbor?. . . The People Speak. Will You Listen?* (Olympia, Wash.: 1978).

DAKUBETEDE
(Athapascan)

The now-extinct Dakubetedes lived in southwestern Oregon on the Applegate River, an upper Rogue River tributary entering that stream from the south. They were also called the Applegate River Indians. They spoke a dialect similar to that of the Taltushtuntudes, who were Athapascan speakers inhabiting nearby Galice Creek. The Dakubetedes were also neighbors of the Shastas, whose lands extended from Oregon into California. The Dakubetedes' history during the later nineteenth century parallels that of the Takil-man-speaking Takelmas, with whom they became culturally assimilated. The Dakubetedes have always been counted in conjunction with other tribes. One ethnologist, James Mooney, estimated their 1780 population at 3,200, which included Taltushtuntudes and a portion of the Umpquas (probably the portion that spoke the Athapascan tongue). For an account of Dakubetedes's confrontations with whites, including wars, treaties, and removal to a reservation, see **Takelma**.

DUWAMISH
(Coastal Division, Salishan)

The name Duwamish is said to mean "inside [the bay] people." The tribe lived in autonomous winter-village groups on the Duwamish, Black, and Cedar rivers and their tributaries, as those watercourses existed before the changes wrought by the U.S. Army Corps of Engineers in 1916. According to the nineteenth-century ethnologist George Gibbs their "proper seat" was at the outlet of Lake Washington and along the Duwamish river, where their most important villages were located.

A prominent subdivision, the Sammamishes, was autonomous, as were all other groups within the Duwamish River basin. The Sammamishes spoke a dialect similar to that of the Duwamishes proper and were intimately connected with other tribes of the area. It was reported that, instead of going to the Suquamish (Port Madison) Reservation, as other Duwamish subdivisions did, the Sammamishes were assigned to the Tulalip (Snohomish) Reservation, but apparently they did not go there either.

In the Duwamish homelands, because of the changes wrought by engineering, the Black River is today nonexistent, and the northern half of the Duwamish River, transferred to the Duwamish Waterway, is a vital link in the busy waterfront complex of Seattle. The Duwamishes left their mark not only on that waterway but also in the names of several other places, such as the large boat moorage area Shilshole Bay and the city of Seattle, which was named for their chief Sealth, or Seattle.

Because of the flexibility of Duwamish resident kinship ties, it was common for individuals to affiliate with other settlements. It was also common for upper-class Duwamishes to marry into other tribes, a practice followed by Chief Seattle. The chief's father was a Suquamish headman, while his mother was a Duwamish woman.

Location: Many Duwamishes are descended from those who remained in their aboriginal homelands. Like their ancestors, they are assimilated within the greater Seattle community.

Numbers: In 1980 the membership of the Duwamish Tribe stood at about 325 active members, from a judgment roll of 1,200. In 1854, Washington Territorial Governor and Superintendent of Indian Affairs Isaac Stevens placed the Duwamish numbers at 162, a number far short of the rough estimate of 1,200 listed for 1780. A listing in 1856 placed them at 378. A 1910 census listed only 20.

History: After providing leadership in wars against neighboring native peoples, Chief Seattle signed the Point Elliott Treaty in 1855. At that time he reaffirmed his friendship to Americans, including those who were settling on his people's lands. From a Duwamish winter village that became Pioneer Square white men laid the foundations of Seattle. Several Duwamishes worked for whites in the Seattle area and traded such items as potatoes to them. When Duwamish, Taitnapam, Puyallup, Nisqually, and Suquamish elements attacked the fledgling Seattle community in 1856, Chief Seattle proved his loyalty to whites. To remove the Duwamishes from the Indian-white hostilities on the mainland, the tribe was assigned by their treaty to the Fort Kitsap (later the Suquamish and Port Madison) Reservation on the Kitsap Peninsula, which is across Puget Sound from Seattle. They were anxious to leave the reservation, not only because of barely subsisting there but also because they were on poor terms with the Suquamishes, for whom the confine came to be named. They also infringed on the Suquamishes' rights to and use of their own home land. All but four or five Duwamish families fled the reservation in the summer of 1856. They stayed on the eastern shores of Bainbridge Island for five months before moving to the western shores of Elliott Bay, from which they were removed to Holderness Point (Duwamish Head). By winter, the Duwamishes had returned to their old home land on the Duwamish River. Under pressure from local whites, the Duwamish agent suggested that his

Duwamish

George, a Duwamish who lived in the general area of Seattle, which was named for the Duwamish chief Sealth. Today many Duwamishes are assimilated within the greater Seattle community, though they seek to retain their tribal identity. Courtesy of the Smithsonian Institution.

charges be assigned to the Muckleshoot Reservation, because its Indians were from the nearby Green and White rivers and were related to Duwamishes. Some Duwamishes did settle on the Muckleshoot. In 1893 a large group, avoiding confinement, gathered on Ballast Island in Seattle after whites had burned them out of their homes in west Seattle. In 1910 the Duwamishes still had a village at Foster, south of Seattle.

Government and Claims: In 1925 the Duwamishes adopted a constitution and formed

73

a government. Like so many other landless tribes, under the direction of their tribal council they sought acknowledgment by the federal government. A proposal that they join forces with the Suquamishes to obtain that acknowledgment was opposed by some members of the latter tribe. In seeking acknowledgment, the Duwamishes also sought rights enjoyed by certain other Puget Sound tribes, including eligibility to catch up to 50 percent of the annual harvestable salmon and steelhead trout of Washington state. In a 1974 decision they were denied those rights because of lack of acknowledgment and their landlessness.

After Congress authorized some Puget Sound tribes on February 12, 1925 (43 Stat. 836), to take legal action for compensation for the loss of their lands, *Duwamish et al. v. U.S.* (79 C. Cls. 530) was filed in 1926 and was in the Court of Claims for over a decade. During that time the Duwamishes did business with the government through the Tulalip Agency. Their case, which involved a claim of $900 for each of fifty-six longhouses destroyed, was dismissed without recovery. The court was of the opinion that the sums that had been appropriated for and disbursed to the Duwamishes by the United States had exceeded their legal and equitable claims. In 1946 the tribe filed a claim (Docket 109) with the Indian Claims Commission for additional compensation for lands ceded to the United States. The Commission determined that the tribe's aboriginal lands had amounted to 54,790 acres as of March 8, 1859. After a $12,000 offset the commission on July 20, 1962, made a final award to the Duwamishes of $62,000. The payment amounted to $1.35 for each acre lost—in essence, for acreage that had become the city of Seattle. The tribe appealed to the Court of Claims, which on July 12, 1963, confirmed the commis-

sion's findings and dismissed the Duwamish appeal on motion of the tribe on December 10, 1963. The commission entered an amended final judgment the following day.

Contemporary Life and Culture: Some members of the Duwamish tribe are enrolled on the Suquamish and Muckleshoot reservations. They are treated by the Bureau of Indian Affairs as either Suquamishes or Muckleshoots—not Duwamishes. If they were to identify themselves as members of the Duwamish tribe, they could not receive the services of the BIA and the Indian Health Service, though some Duwamish Indians not enrolled on a reservation have received some federal services. Like the Puyallups, who are assimilated in the Tacoma community, many Duwamishes are assimilated into the society of the greater Seattle area. Besides its efforts to achieve acknowledgment and fishing rights, the tribe has established a nonprofit corporation to facilitate retention and reclamation of tribal culture and development of self-determined projects. In the late 1970s archaeologists unearthed some Duwamish settlements. Others, however, were beyond recovery because of industrial development. See **Suquamish Tribe, Port Madison Reservation.**

Suggested Readings: Edward S. Curtis, *The North American Indian* (1912; New York: Johnson Reprint Corporation, 1970), vol. 9; George Gibbs, *Tribes of Western Washington,* vol. 1 of Smithsonian Institution, *Contributions to North American Ethnology* (Washington, D.C.: Government Printing Office, 1877); Hermann Haeberlin and Erna Gunther, "The Indians of Puget Sound," *University of Washington Publications in Anthropology* 4, no. 1 (1930); State of Washington Indian Affairs Task Force, *Are You Listening Neighbor? . . . The People Speak. Will You Listen?* (Olympia, Wash.: 1978).

ENTIAT
(Interior Division, Salishan)

The Entiats, also known variously as the Sintiatqkumuhs and the Intietooks, lived mainly along the Entiat River, of which the lower banks at the confluence with the Columbia River were known to Canadian voyageurs as *Point de Bois*. The Entiat River drainage area in north-central Washington extends from the Columbia west into the Cascade Mountains, between the drainage areas of the Wenatchee River and Lake Chelan. One Entiat band, the Sinialkumuhs, lived on the Columbia between the Entiat and Wenatchee rivers. The Entiats have been classified as a subdivision of Wenatchees, though Verne Ray, a leading student of Pacific Northwestern Indians, believes that they were a separate people.

During the spring and fall the Entiats were at fishing stations, catching mainly salmon. At other seasons they gathered roots and berries or hunted deer, bear, and other game at higher elevations. Their first contacts with whites were with fur men, missionaries and government explorers in the early and middle nineteenth century. An Entiat chief, named La-Hoom, or La Hoompt, signed the Yakima Treaty of 1855. Some Entiats removed from their lands and took allotments on Lake Chelan. One who moved there was Wapato John (Nicterwhilicum), who abandoned a store on the Columbia River upstream from the Entiat River, when the earthquake of 1872 dislodged what became known as Ribbon Cliff along U.S. Highway 97, temporarily damming the Columbia and flooding him out. One Entiat chief, the centenarian Shilhohsaskt (Standing Cloud), remained near the mouth of the Entiat River until he died ca. 1900. Today some Entiat descendants live on the Colville Reservation. See **Confederated Tribes of the Colville Reservation, Washington.**

Entiat

Entiat chief Shilhohsaskt and his wife, Spokokalx. The Entiats were an Interior Salish people of the Entiat River, a Columbia River tributary in north-central Washington. Shilhohsakt died ca. 1900, shortly after this photograph was taken. Courtesy of the North Central Washington Museum Association.

FLATHEAD
(Interior Division, Salishan)

The Flatheads were known by various names, including Selish, or Salish, a designation that came to be applied to their linguistic family. In somewhat the same manner, the term Flathead was applied to any of the native peoples who practiced head flattening of their infants. The Flatheads, however, denied that their ancestors flattened heads. They believed that they were called Flatheads because the sign language identified them by pressing both sides of the head with the hands. A mountain man claimed that Salish meant "we the people." which was signified by striking the head with the flat of the hand, from which gesture the Flatheads were said to have received their name. It has also been suggested that the tribe were called Flatheads because, unlike other tribes west of them, they left their heads in the normal configuration, flat on the top, instead of deforming them to slope toward the crown. Translating the English name, the French-Canadian fur traders called them *Têtes-Plates*.

For hundreds of years the Flatheads were among the Salish peoples living west of the Rocky Mountains. Some scholars believe that it was after they traveled east of those mountains that they came under pressure from the Blackfeet Indians, who had firearms and in the early eighteenth century drove the Flatheads west across the Rocky Mountains to what became their homeland in the Bitterroot valley of western Montana. Other authorities believe smallpox plagues on the plains were a more important force driving the Flatheads toward the Bitterroot. It was at the head of the Bitterroot that their chief Three Eagles (Cheleskaiyimi) met the American explorers Meriwether Lewis and William Clark in 1805. The two explorers noted that the Flatheads had about 450 lodges and about 500 horses. Their numbers in 1780 have been estimated at 600. After obtaining horses, mainly from the Shoshonis, the Flatheads became expert horsemen and hunters. Despite Blackfoot hostility they routinely traveled to go after the buffalo across the Rocky Mountains on the plains. In the late eighteenth century the father of Three Eagles, Chief Big Hawk, was killed in the buffalo country in the upper Missouri River country. The Flatheads also journeyed to the plains to steal horses, avoiding whenever possible conflict with their owners. They not only bravely faced Plains Indian tribesmen but also were a buffer separating their Salish allies from them. Over the years the Flatheads impressed whites with both their bravery and their friendliness. During the Indian wars of the nineteenth century they remained loyal to Americans.

In the first half of the nineteenth century the Flatheads were involved in the fur trade. Saleesh House, later called the Flathead Post, operated to the northwest of their country. The Flatheads' fur trapping was mainly in the spring when the Blackfoot raids abated. In retaliation for those raids, the Flatheads and other Salish peoples fought the Blackfeet whenever the latter interrupted their hunting and horse-stealing enterprises on the plains. The British fur men, with whom the Flatheads did their early trading, tried to keep them from the American traders approaching from the East.

It was from the East that an important personage came to the Flatheads, Shining Shirt, possibly an Iroquois, who reportedly antedated the coming of horses to them in the eighteenth century. He was said to have been the first to introduce them to Christianity, prophesying the coming of white men with long black robes "to teach them religion." Other Iroquois followed. Coming from Quebec, they lived among Flatheads in the early nineteenth century after their defeat in the War of 1812 as partisans of the British. Under their leader, Old Ignace La Mousse, two dozen of them came to live among Flatheads in 1820 and exerted considerable influence. By intermarrying, these Iroquois eventually lost their tribal identity. Their Christianity had a strong nativist cast. It was among Salish peoples that the nativist Prophet Dance resurged. In the 1830s, Flathead delegations, usually led by Iroquois, visited Saint Louis seeking the black robes. As white publicists described their quest, the predictions of Shining Shirt were fulfilled in the person of the Reverend Pierre De Smet, S.J., who established the Saint Mary's Mission in the lower Bitterroot valley in 1841. From the Bitterroot, De Smet and his associates ministered to the natives in a wide area. The Blackfeet were among those receiving their ministrations. That set poorly with the Flatheads, who associated the Christian faith with the "medicine" power needed to overcome their plains foes. The church fathers sought to make farmers of the Flatheads to keep them from their dangerous buffalo hunting ventures. By the 1850s Blackfoot attacks both east and west of the Rockies had reduced the Flatheads to 300 or 400, or roughly half the numbers given by Hudson's Bay Company trader John Warren Dease in 1827.

Under their chief, Victor, the Flatheads and the Pend d'Oreilles (or Upper Kalispels) met in council with Washington Territorial Governor and Superintendent of Indian Affairs Isaac Stevens at Hell Gate, near Missoula, Montana, in July, 1855. From that council a treaty was effected setting aside the 2,240-square-mile Flathead, or Jocko, Reservation north of the Bitterroot valley. An important consideration in its establishment was the presence there of the Jesuit Saint Ignatius Mission. Initially most Flatheads opposed removing to the reservation. On November 14, 1871, James Garfield, later president of the United States, was empowered to represent the government to negotiate a contract with the Flatheads for their removal. Victor's successor, his son Charlot, despite government proddings and promises, refused to sign the contract for removal. Finally, as more whites entered

Flathead

Chief Charlot, also known as the Bear Claw. For a long time he refused to move from his homeland in Montana's Bitterroot valley to the Flathead Reservation on the north. He finally removed there in 1891 and died there in 1910. Courtesy of the Smithsonian Institution.

the Bitterroot valley, Charlot in 1891 removed to the Flathead Reservation, where he regained his head chieftaincy and remained a traditionalist until he died in 1910. See **Confederated Salish & Kootenai Tribes of the Flathead Reservation.**

Suggested Readings: Robert Bigart, "The Salish Flathead Indians During the Period of Adjustment, 1850–1891," *Idaho Yesterdays* 17, no. 3 (Fall, 1973); Robert Bigart, "Patterns of Cultural Change in a Salish Flathead Community," *Human Organization*, Fall, 1971; W. L. Davis, S.J., "Peter John De Smet: The Journey of 1840," *Pacific Northwest Quarterly* 35, no. 1 (January, 1944); John Fahey, *The Flathead Indians* (Norman: University of Oklahoma Press, 1974); Olga Wedemeyer Johnson, *Flathead and Kootenay: The Rivers, the Tribes, and the Region's Traders* (Glendale, Calif.: Arthur H. Clarke Co., 1969); Gloria Ricci Lothrop, *Recollections of the Flathead Mission* (Glendale, Calif.: Arthur H. Clark Co., 1977); Peter Ronan, *Historical Sketch of the Flathead Indian Nation* (1890; Helena, Mont., 1965); Claude Schaeffer, "The First Jesuit Mission to the Flathead, 1840–1850: A Study in Culture Conflicts," *Pacific Northwest Quarterly* 28, no. 3 (July, 1937); Allan H. Smith, "The Location of Flathead Post," *Pacific Northwest Quarterly* 48, no. 2 (April, 1957); Harry Holbert Turney-High, "The Flathead Indians of Montana," *American Anthropologist* 39, no. 4, Pt. 2 (1937).

GRAND RONDE CONFEDERATED TRIBES
(See **Confederated Tribes of the Grand Ronde Community of Oregon**)

HANIS COOS
(Yakonan)

The Hanis Coos (Kowes) constitute the northern dialect division of the Kusan linguistic family, of which the Miluk Coos are the southern division. The Hanis Coos lived around Coos Bay on the southern Oregon coast. They also claimed lands beginning at Ten Mile Creek (ten miles south of the Umpqua River) and extending down the coast to Coos Bay and east to the summit of the Coast Range. The word *coos* is said to mean "on the south," "lagoon" or "lake," and "place of pines." Although no present-day places bear the name Hanis, Coos Bay, Coos County, and the city of Coos Bay bear the tribal name. Combined with the Miluk Coos, the Hanis Coos were estimated to have been 2,000 in 1780, about 500 more than were believed to exist in 1805 and 1806. In 1871 there were 136 Coos on the Alsea Subagency of the Siletz Reservation. In 1910 the population of the combined Coos tribes was given as 93; in 1930, as 107; and in 1937, as 55. Like the Miluk Coos, the Hanises depended for subsistence on foods from the sea, where they skillfully operated their canoes. In summer they camped in the Coast Range to hunt, fish, pick berries, and dig roots.

When Congress passed the Donation Land Act on September 29, 1850, whites staked out claims to Coos Bay without having to make any purchases of land or any treaty with the Indians. Like the Miluk Coos, the Hanises remained peaceful toward whites during the Rogue Wars, which lasted through 1856, despite provocations. On August 11, 1855, Coos groups, along with several other tribes on the Oregon coast, evinced their peaceful disposition by signing a treaty with Oregon Superintendent of Indian Affairs Joel Palmer, even though whites had staked out Coos Bay after passage of the Donation Land Act. During the Rogue Wars, Coos peoples were under the guard of Coos County Volunteers of Empire City (present-day Coos Bay). After the wars the Hanis and Miluk Coos were rounded up and brought to a temporary reservation on the north side of the Umpqua River at its mouth, where they were kept under military surveillance. With closure of the Umpqua Subagency on September 3, 1859, they were marched north to the mouth of the Yachats River, where, with the Kuitshes (Lower Umpquas) and Siuslaws, they were placed under the newly located (1861) Alsea Subagency (sometimes referred to as the Yachats Reservation) on the Siletz, or Coast, Reservation. In April and May, 1864, soldiers from Fort Yamhill rounded up thirty-two families at Coos Bay and returned them to the mouth of the Yachats River on the reservation. In 1875, while they were living on the southern portion of the Coast Reservation, which by then was named the Alsea, that reservation was turned over to whites, forcing the Hanis Coos, the Kuitshes, and a few Siuslaws to return to their original homelands.

In 1916 and 1917 the descendants of the Coos, who had organized before 1900, met with a remnant of Kuitshes and Siuslaws at Coos Bay to institute a suit against the government for claims for lands lost. Their suit (Case No. K-345) was not decided until May 2, 1938, when the United States Court of Claims handed down an opinion that their Indian testimony was inadmissable. Oblivious to records of fur trappers, diarists, Indian agents, and others, the United States Supreme Court on November 14, 1938, refused to hear their appeal. The Coos experienced a similar refusal by the Indian Claims Commission between 1947 and 1951, despite additional evidence. The commission maintained that they already had their day in court. After those rebuffs the Coos, Kuitshes, and Siuslaws unsuccessfully petitioned the United Nations to permit them

Hanis Coos

Chief Dalouse ("Jack") Jackson, in the 1890s. In the first quarter of the century his descendants in southwestern Oregon suffered several reversals as they sought compensation from the United States for the lands that they had lost in the nineteenth century. In 1972 the Hanis, along with other Coos, incorporated as the Coos Tribe of Indians and instituted tribal programs. Courtesy Coos-Curry Museum and Historical Association.

entrance into that organization. Having acquired a 6.1-acre "reservation" and a tribal hall at Coos Bay, the Hanis and Miluk Coos, joined by others of Kuitsh and Siuslaw ancestry, opposed termination under the congressional enabling legislation during the 1950s. In 1975 a bill (S.B. 945) was drafted to reopen the case of the Coos, Kuitshes, and Siuslaws, but failed to pass.

The three tribes' failure to win those claims did not deter them from instituting programs on their own. In 1972 they incorporated as The Coos Tribe of Indians under the laws of the state of Oregon. In 1973 they opened the Tribal Trading Post to sell groceries at low cost to low-income families. In 1974 the Willow River Benevolent Association secured a Comprehensive Employment Training Act (CETA) grant and became a clearinghouse for a manpower program, establishing a successful job-placement staff run by Indians. Also in 1974 the Indians established the Coos and Curry County Indian alcohol and drug-abuse program and a detoxification center in Coos Bay.

In 1967 only one Coos spoke the native language, but in the 1970s several programs were begun to preserve Coos culture. In 1974 the Coos Tribe of Indians formed the Oregon Coast Indian Archaeological Association, perhaps the first such society organized by Native Americans. In January, 1975, a Native American research group opened the Research Center Museum in the Indian hall on the reservation belonging to the Confederated Tribes of the Coos, Lower Umpqua, and Siuslaw. Wishing to share the endangered culture of her people, Esther Waters secured baskets, artifacts, photos, and other materials for the museum. The tribe also secured the services of Peter J. Stenhouse, who in 1974 began excavating a former Indian village on private land on the lower Umpqua River estuary. The artifacts collected were deposited in the Research Center Museum in Coos Bay. In 1975, Indians of southwestern Oregon began stressing the importance of Indian history and culture in the Coos Bay Public Schools by instituting a series of mini-courses, including demonstrations of basket making, dancing, story telling, and other folklore programs.

In 1977 the program was expanded to other areas of Coos County. In 1976 a Cheyenne, James Thornton, was hired to initiate and coordinate programs relating to Native Americans. Among other activities, he edited a newsletter, *Indian Education.* See **Confederated Tribes of Coos, Lower Umpqua & Siuslaw Indians, Inc.;** and **Coos Tribe of Indians**.

Suggested Readings: Stephen Dow Beckham, *The Indians of Western Oregon: This Land Was Theirs* (Coos Bay, Ore.: Arago Books, 1977);

Leo J. Frachtenberg, *Coos Texts,* Columbia University Contributions to American Anthropology, vol. 1 (New York, 1913); Leo J. Frachtenberg, *Lower Umpqua Texts and Notes on the Kusan Dialect,* Columbia University Contributions to American Anthropology, vol. 4 (New York, 1914); Melville Jacobs, "Coos Myth Texts," *University of Washington Publication in Anthropology,* vol. 8, no. 2 (Seattle, 1940); Melville Jacobs, "Coos Narrative and Ethnologic Texts," *University of Washington Publications in Anthropology* vol. 8, no. 1 (Seattle, 1939); Henry Hull St. Clair and Leo Frachtenberg, "Traditions of the Coos Indians," *Journal of American Folklore* 23 (1909).

HOH
(Chimakuan)

The Hohs were formerly considered a band of the Quileute tribe, who are also of Chimakuan linguistic stock. The Hoh Tribe, Hoh Indian Reservation, Washington, is today the successor of that band.

Location: The members of the Hoh Tribe primarily live on and around their 443-acre reservation, which was established by executive order on September 11, 1893. The reservation lies on the Pacific Coast of the Olympic Peninsula of northwestern Washington, about fifteen miles south of the Quileute Reservation and about twenty-five miles from the town of Forks, near U.S. Highway 101.

Numbers: The Hohs and Quileutes combined were estimated to have been 500 in 1780. In 1905 the Hohs were reduced to 62, primarily because of disease and assimilation with other peoples. In the early 1970s there were about 15 or 20 permanent residents of the Hoh Reservation. In 1985 the tribe numbered 91.

History: According to Indian tradition, the Hohs, Quileutes, and Quinaults of the Olympic Peninsula managed their own affairs in a confederation that was strong enough virtually to control all of the tribes from Cape Flattery at the entrance to the Strait of Juan de Fuca on the north to Grays Harbor along the Pacific on the south. Centrally located in this confederation, the Hohs and the neighboring Queets Indians controlled the hunting grounds of the area, guarding them from the encroachments of other peoples, such as the Clallams. Like the other tribes of the confederation, the Hohs had both war and peace chiefs. In July, 1787, they encountered the British trader Charles Barkley, who dispatched a boat up the Hoh River to trade with its natives. It never returned. Natives killed all of the hands aboard. The Hohs were among the tribes who fought a party of about twenty Russians and Aleut Indians late in 1808, holding them captive before trading them among the coastal tribes, as was their custom with captured natives. The captives were finally ransomed by an American trader in May, 1811.

The Hohs were among the tribes north of Grays Harbor who met with Washington Territorial Governor and Superintendent of Indian Affairs Isaac Stevens to effect the Quinault River Treaty, which was negotiated on July 1, 1855, and signed by Stevens at Olympia on January 25, 1856 (12 Stat.

Hoh

The Hoh Tribe, to which this turn-of-the-century man belonged, lived on the Pacific shores of Washington's Olympic Peninsula. Today the tribe occupies a tiny reservation in that area and depends heavily, as its ancestors did, on fishing. Photograph by Edward S. Curtis from Curtis's The North American Indian *(1907–1930), volume 9.*

971, ratified March 8, 1859). By executive order on September 11, 1893, a small reservation was set aside for the Hohs at the mouth of the Hoh River. It was insufficient for allotment. On March 4, 1911, Congress passed an act (36 Stat. 1345) directing the secretary of the interior to make allotments to Hohs, Quileutes, and Ozettes on the Qui-

nault Reservation as stipulated in their 1856 treaty, rather than have them allotted on the reservations that had been set aside for them. By 1913 lack of farming and grazing lands had halted allotment on the Quinault.

Government and Claims: The Hoh Tribe, Hoh Indian Reservation, Washington, having approved the Indian Reorganization Act of 1934 (48 Stat. 984) adopted a constitution on May 24, 1969. Elections of tribal officers are held biennially. The Hoh Tribal Business Committee is the governing body. Under the 1963 Washington State Indian Jurisdiction Act, the state assumed control over several social programs. Some services are provided by the federal government.

With the Quileutes, the Hohs claimed (Docket 155) additional compensation for the lands ceded to the United States under the Quinault River Treaty. The Hoh, Quileute, Queets, and Quinault tribes had each received $25,000, which they claimed were unconscionably small amounts. The Indian Claims Commission determined that the four tribes had had aboriginal title to 688,000 acres as of March 8, 1858. On April 17, 1963, it awarded the Hohs and Quileutes $112,152.60 as their share of compensation for those lands. Congressional legislation on October 14, 1966, provided for division of the funds between the two tribes on the basis of the total tribal memberships.

Contemporary Life and Culture: Hoh Reservation residents depend heavily on fish in the Hoh River for their income. To help maintain fish production, the tribe has constructed enhancement facilities. The reservation, which was logged in 1954, will not provide merchantable timber again until the 1990s (a reasonably short interval in that region of heavy rainfall). Some Hoh men supplement their incomes by logging on the Olympic Peninsula. The tribe's picturesque ocean frontage has potential for economic development. In the 1980s one or two tribesmen were still making traditional dugout canoes for river and ocean travel, and some women made baskets to sell to tourists. The children attend schools in Forks. Religious preference is Protestant, and some Hohs are Shakers.

Suggested Readings: George Gibbs, *Tribes of Western Washington,* vol. 1 of Smithsonian Institution, *Contributions to North American Ethnology* (Washington, D.C.: Government Printing Office, 1877); Harry Hobucket, "Quileute Indian Tradition," *Washington Historical Quarterly* 25, no. 1 (January, 1934); Albert B. Reagan, "Tradition of the Hoh and Quillayute Indians," *Washington Historical Quarterly* 20, no. 3 (July, 1929); Steve Wall and Harvey Arden, *Wisdomkeepers: Meetings with Native American Spiritual Elders* (Beyond Words Publishing, 1990).

HOQUIAM
(See **Humptulips**)

HUMPTULIPS
(Coastal Division, Salishan)

The name Humptulips derives from a native word said to mean "chilly region." The tribe was also called the Grays Harbor Indians because it held the north shore of that body of water in Washington state, from near the middle of North Bay possibly as far east as Junction City, plus Hoquiam Creek and the Humptulips and Whiskah rivers, which are affluents of Grays Harbor. Besides the river, a town on U.S. Highway 101 bears the name Humptulips. Because of their location, the Hoquiam and Whiskah groups of Indians were classified by ethnologist John R. Swanton as Humptulips villagers. Some scholars regard the Humptulipses as having been closely related to the Lower Chehalises. They spoke a dialect of the Lower Chehalis language, but politically they were a separate people. Like the Chehalis peoples, they had no treaty with the United States, though like other nontreaty peoples, received some government assistance. Several received vaccinations and other medical aids from the Quinault Agency on their north. Their nineteenth-century chief Chinoose refused government goods, fearing that, if the Humptulipses accepted them, the goods might be construed as payment for their lands. The Humptulipses kept a semblance of tribal identity by having their own chiefs and by refusing as late as 1873 to remove to a reservation. Through disease and assimilation with other peoples, they were reduced to sixteen in 1885 and twenty-one in 1904. See **Confederated Tribes of the Chehalis Reservation.**

JAMESTOWN CLALLAM INDIAN TRIBE

The Jamestown Clallams received their name from the settlement of Jamestown, which was seven miles north of Sequim, Washington, on the upper Strait of Juan de Fuca. The Clallams called the place *nuxia'antc*, or "white firs." Formerly most Jamestown Clallams lived at nearby Dungeness, from which whites pressured them to remove.

Jamestown Clallam

Cookhouse Billy, his wife (with the beaded bag), and Mary Hall Hunter (seated with baby). They were of the Jamestown Clallam Indian Tribe, which received its name from their settlement, Jamestown, near Sequim, Washington, on the eastern Strait of Juan de Fuca. Courtesy of Virginia Keeting.

Some lived at Washington Harbor and Port Discovery. Like other Clallams, they did not wish to go to the Skokomish Reservation, where they were scheduled to remove under the provisions of the Point-No-Point Treaty of 1855. In June, 1874, under their chief Lord Jim Balch, for $500 they bought 210 acres of logged-off land, which they surveyed and divided amongst themselves according to the amount contributed by each purchaser. The new site of Jamestown was named in honor of Balch who had engineered the transaction. According to the late nineteenth- and early twentieth-century missionary Rev. Myron Eells of the Congregationalist Church, which had a mission outstation amongst the Jamestown Clallams, they were the "most civilized and prosperous band" of the Clallam peoples. In 1892 a Clallam, Jacob Hall, established a prosperous business selling crabs in the Seattle market. Other Clallams fished, farmed, and worked for local whites at various tasks, including canoeing. About 1890 the Indian Shaker religion was introduced into Jamestown, from which it spread to nearby places such as Neah Bay in the lands of the Makahs.

Location: About 75 percent of the Jamestown Clallam Indian Tribe live in or within a 150-mile radius of Port Angeles, the largest city of the area, which is about twenty miles east of the old Jamestown location on U.S. Highway 101. The remainder are scattered from various points in the Pacific Northwest to the East Coast of the United States.

Numbers: In 1985 there were about 188 tribal members. A century earlier there had been about 100. In 1989 there were 389.

Government and Claims: In 1981 the Jamestown Clallams joined the Port Gamble and Lower Elwha Clallams and Skokomishes as members of the Point-No-Point Treaty

Council, which makes fishery management decisions. On February 10, 1981, the Jamestown Clallam Indian Tribe was acknowledged as an entity having a government-to-government relationship with the United States. That acknowledgment gave it fishing treaty rights and other privileges. With the success of the Hoopa Tribe of California, the Mille Lacs of Minnesota, and the Cherokee and Absentee-Shawnee of Oklahoma for self governance, the Jamestown Clallam Indian Tribe, along with the Quinaults and Lummi of Washington state, declared their independence of Bureau of Indian Affairs paternalism, a system they claim gives them only eleven cents of every dollar appropriated for them. The balance, they say, is skimmed off on the way down for administration. For claims see **Clallam.**

Suggested Reading: Virginia Keeting, ed., *Dungeness: The Lure of a River* (Sequim, Wash.: Sequim Bicentennial Committee, 1976).

KALISPEL
(Interior Division, Salishan)

Kalispel

Louis Male Wolf. Although there is no record of it, this photograph was probably taken by Frank A. Rinehart of the Bureau of American Ethnology in Omaha, Nebraska, in 1898. The Kalispels were an Interior Salish people. In precontact times the Upper Kalispels, also known as the Upper Pend d'Oreilles, lived east of the Rocky Mountains, but they were driven west into modern-day Washington, Idaho, and Montana. Courtesy of the Smithsonian Institution.

The Kalispels, or Pend d'Oreilles, were called "boat" or "canoe people" and "paddlers" by other natives. The designation Pend d'Oreille was given them by French-Canadian fur men. It means literally either "to hang from, at, or around the ear" or "ear pendants." The Kalispels were divided into upper and lower groups with little dialectic variation in their common language. The Lower Kalispels were known for their low-riding canoes, which had distinctive snubbed prows to meet the buffets of gusty winds on Lake Pend Oreille in northern Idaho. They were also noted for their horsemanship and for their proficiency in making a bread out of the camas root, which caused them also to be called "camas people." The Upper Kalispels were sometimes called by a name meaning "people of the confluence," from a place at the outlet of Lake Pend Oreille where a considerable band formerly wintered.

It was said that at one time the Upper Kalispels lived east of the Rocky Mountains, but were driven west by Blackfeet to become the neighbors of the Lower Kalispels, or Kalispels proper, who lived in the Pend Oreille River valley in northeastern Washington state and northern Idaho. The Lower Kalispels also lived in northern Idaho on Lake Pend Oreille, from which the Pend Oreille River flows, and on Priest Lake; and in Montana and Idaho along the lower Clark Fork River, which flows into Lake Pend Oreille. The Upper Kalispels lived east of the Lower Kalispels in Montana; on Thompson Lake and the Flathead Lakes; on the Flathead River, west past Thompson Falls to Lake Pend Oreille; on Horse Plains; and around present-day Missoula.

Some have considered the Chewelahs of northeastern Washington (sometimes called the Slate'use or Tsent) a Kalispel group. They were culturally related to the Kalispels, but spoke a slightly different dialect and remained aloof. The Chewelah Mountains east of the upper Colville valley in Washington have also been called the Calispell Mountains. A city in western Montana also bears the name Kalispell. There is a Calispell Lake in Washington state.

The Kalispel numbers (both Uppers and Lowers) in 1780 have been estimated to have been 1,600. In 1805–1806 they were estimated at 853, and in 1850 at 1,000. In recorded times the Kalispels hunted as far east as the Great Plains, as far north as Canada, and as far south as the Salmon River country of Idaho. The Kalispels' development resembled that of their Kutenai neighbors. Both tribes were divided into upper and lower branches, and both came under the influence of white fur traders after David Thompson of the North West Company selected the site of his Kullyspell House on the eastern shores of Lake Pend Oreille in September, 1809. Like the Kutenais, the Kalispels were visited by the Roman Catholic missionary Reverend Pierre De Smet, S.J., who in 1846 established the Saint Ignatius Mission near what is now Cusick, Washington. In the spring of 1845 the Reverend Adrian Hoecken, S.J., had begun the Saint Michael's Mission on the Pend Oreille River at Albeni Falls, from which it was removed downstream a short way and renamed Saint Ignatius. The mission was moved to the Flathead, or Jocko, Reservation in Montana in 1854. The Upper Kalispels followed the mission, unlike the Lower Kalispels, who refused to move from their homeland. Also unlike the Lower Kalispels, the Upper Kalispels under their chief, Alexander, were among those who met Washington Territorial Governor and Superintendent of Indian Affairs Isaac Stevens in council at Hell Gate, Montana, in July, 1855, after which they were assigned with the Kutenais and the Flatheads to the Flathead Reservation. From then on developments among the Upper Kalispels followed closely those of the other peoples on that reservation. See **Confederated Salish & Kootenai Tribes of the Flathead Reservation.** See also **Pend d'Oreille.** For developments among the Lower Kalispels thereafter, see **Kalispel Indian Community, Kalispel Reservation.**

Suggested Reading: Robert Carriker, *The Kalispel People* (Phoenix, Ariz.: Indian Tribal Series, 1973).

KALISPEL INDIAN COMMUNITY, KALISPEL RESERVATION

The Kalispel Indian Community, Kalispel Reservation, Washington, is descended from Lower Kalispels, or Lower Pend d'Oreilles, who lived in what is now northeastern Washington state and northern Idaho.

Location: The members of the Kalispel Indian Community live on and near their reservation, which contained 4,620 acres when it was established by executive order on March 23, 1914, on the western shores of the Pend Oreille River about forty miles north of Spokane.

Numbers: In 1985 membership of the community stood at 259, and in 1989 at 232.

History: The Yakima Indian War, which broke out in 1855, prevented Lower Kalispels, Spokanes, Coeur d'Alênes, and Colvilles from meeting with Dr. R. H. Lansdale, whom Washington Territorial Governor and Superintendent of Indian Affairs Isaac Stevens had instructed to effect a treaty with them. The Upper Kalispels, or Upper Pend d'Oreilles, however, were among those who met with Stevens at Hellgate near Missoula, Montana, where on July 16, 1855, they signed a treaty that assigned them, the Kutenais, and the Flatheads to the Flathead, or Jocko, Reservation in Montana. Advised that the Saint Ignatius Mission had been moved to the Flathead, Stevens assumed that

Hometown Newport Wash.
CON...

**Kalispel Indian Community,
Kalispel Reservation**

Renee Pierre, a candidate for Queen of the Kalispel Indian Community in northeastern Washington, 1980. Her people were among the most traditional of the Pacific Northwest tribes, but recently they have developed along modern lines while seeking to retain their traditional tribal values.

selow) disdained to live on the Flathead Reservation with Indians of other tribes, and for the most part, the Lower Kalispels remained in their homeland. Ironically, at that time the Lower Kalispels were an amalgam of Kalispel, Spokane, and Flathead peoples.

During the Spokane–Coeur d'Alène phase of the Indian War of 1858, most Kalispels refrained from hostilities. In the 1880s, despite the pressure of railroad surveyors and white settlers in the Pend Oreille River valley, about 400 Kalispels still remained in that country. Their days of freedom were numbered because of such developments as the Northern Pacific Railroad's acquisition of their lands under that railroad's 1864 congressional charter. By 1881 about seventy-five miles of track had been laid around Lake Pend Oreille, and the railroad was selling its government-granted lands to white settlers. Under such pressures Victor in 1884 requested compensation for the lands lost. He also requested a reservation in his people's homelands. Public land surveys followed in 1886, and in that same year cavalry troops arrived to control Indian-white conflicts over lands. Chief Marcella refused to remove to the Flathead Reservation, though one band of sixty-three Kalispels under Chief Michel removed to that reservation after Michel agreed with the government to sell his lands in 1887. Michel's band feared that, if they did not remove there, they would be forced onto the Coeur d'Alène Reservation. A white traveler among the Lower Kalispels (or Calispels, as he termed them) noted that, though they were a small tribe, they had powerful relatives and backers among other tribes, who would not let them be "eaten up by their enemies." In 1890 large numbers of whites entered the Pend Oreille country. By then the natives were concentrated on the eastern shores of the Pend Oreille River (opposite Usk, Washington).

As the twentieth century approached, nontreaty (nonreservation) Lower Kalispels were displaced by white settlers. The Indian commissioner in 1895 therefore ordered their lands surveyed and legal descriptions filed with the General Land Office. Most Kalispels did not live on the lands surveyed

the Lower Kalispels would also sign a treaty to remove there. In August and September, 1855, some of both Kalispel branches removed to the area around the transplanted mission. Victor, or Happy Man, was the successor of the Roman Catholic chief Loyola, or Standing Grizzly, of the Lower Kalispels. Both Victor and his son Marcella (Mas-

for them, but in communal enclaves that moved about on these lands. A problem arose when it was realized that the Northern Pacific Railroad had been granted odd sections on which some Kalispels lived. In 1906, Congress gave the Northern Pacific lands in lieu of 2,711 acres occupied by Kalispels, thus minimizing the threat of their removal to a reservation. Continuing white pressures for land in the early twentieth century precipitated renewed surveys and allotting. Since the time of the 1895 surveys, deaths of over a score of Kalispels had been offset by their increased numbers; hence only forty acres of agricultural or eighty acres of grazing lands could be allotted each member. In December, 1911, the Spokane agent was ordered to allot them following the resurvey the next year. Individual trust patents were not issued, since many allotted lands were withdrawn for power-site development on the Pend Oreille River. Nevertheless, a reservation, as noted, was established in 1914 on the allotted land, even before land patents were issued. The first patents were received in May, 1924, and the remainder nine years later.

Government and Claims: With but two of their thirty-eight members voting against it, the Kalispels accepted the Indian Reorganization Act of 1934 (48 Stat. 984) and organized. In 1939 they chartered themselves under a new constitution (approved in 1938) as the Kalispel Indian Community, of which the governing body is the Kalispel Indian Council. Their constitution was revised on July 27, 1967. In 1974 the Kalispel federal tribal jurisdiction was transferred from the Northern Idaho Indian Agency at Lapwai to the Spokane Indian Agency at Wellpinit.

In 1927 the Kalispel Indian Community filed a claim (Docket 94) with the Indian Claims Commission and on March 21, 1963, was awarded $3 million for 2,247,000 acres taken mostly in northeastern Washington and the Idaho panhandle, as well as 126,000 aquatic acres. In 1970 the Community, with twenty-four other western tribes, filed claims (Dockets 532–71 and 524–71) with the Court of Claims for mismanagement of Indian Claims Commission judgment and other funds as Individual Indian Money accounts held in trust by the United States. The Community was awarded $114,127.80 in 1981. In 1991 the U.S. Supreme Court ruled for the Kalispels that they had lost a ten-mile strip along the Pend Oreille River between Usk and Cusick when the Box Canyon Dam was built (1955). Compensation is yet to be agreed upon. A gift of 436 acres from the Northwest Power Planning Council is for a wildlife refuge. The tribe operates an aluminum box factory; they raise buffalo to sell to organizations for banquets; they belong to the Upper Columbia United Tribes, which is a fish and wildlife management program; and they have developed a fish hatchery and aqua farm for raising perch, which they package for market.

Contemporary Life and Culture: As late as 1950 tribal members were jobless and lived in houses built by the Civilian Conservation Corps. Public assistance and land leases to local cattlemen were the sole sources of individual and tribal support. As late as 1965 only one tribal member had graduated from high school, and an interpreter was needed at tribal meetings. The key to its development program is the Kalispel Indian Development Enterprise, which seeks to acquire for the Kalispel Indian Community a manageable land base (in addition to its own 4,557.41 acres of trust land) on which to preserve for future generations the soils, water, plants, animals, and Kalispel life-style.

Special Events: In early August near Usk the Kalispel Powwow Days, featuring Indian games and war dances, are held.

Suggested Readings: Robert Carriker, *The Kalispel People* (Phoenix, Ariz.: Indian Tribal Series, 1973); Robert Carriker, "The Kalispel Indian Tribe and the Indian Claims Commission Experience," *Western Historical Quarterly* 9, no. 1 (January, 1978); O. J. Cotes, ed., *The Kalispels: People of the Pend Oreille* (Usk, Wash., 1980); John Fahey, *The Kalispel Indians* (Norman: University of Oklahoma Press, 1986); Sonny Tuttle, *Kalispel Indian Development* (Usk, Wash.: Kalispel Indian Community, n.d.).

KIKIALLUS
(Coastal Division, Salishan)

The Kikiallus Tribe of Indians descended from the Kikiallus subdivision of the Skagits. The Skagit River, a Puget Sound affluent in northwestern Washington, was formerly called the Kikiallus river. The Kikialluses lived primarily in two villages in the Fir-Conway area south of present-day Mount Vernon and on nearby Camano Island. They also migrated beyond present-day Arlington on Jim Creek on the Stillaguamish River, another Puget Sound affluent. Thus they had close ties with the Stillaguamish Indians on the Stillaguamish.

Location: Tribal members today live at various places in the Pacific Northwest, particularly in northwestern Washington state.

Numbers: In the middle of the nineteenth century the Kikialluses numbered about 140. In 1980 they numbered roughly 150.

History: The Kikialluses held no slaves. In that respect they differed from other coastal peoples holding them in their class system. At the time of white settlement of the Conway area, the tribe lived in four longhouses. The Kikiallus chief Sd-zo Mahtl signed the Point Elliott Treaty with the United States in 1855. Their last aboriginal chief was Bill Jack. The Kikialluses were helped to assimilate with whites by the marriage of a girl of the Jack family to an Irishman, John O'Brien, who came to the tribe's area in the late 1850s. From that marriage stemmed a numerous progeny.

Government and Claims: The Kikialluses have a tribal organization, but by 1980 they still had not received federal acknowledgment. In 1951 they filed a claim (Docket 263) with the Indian Claims Commission for additional payment for the 8,060 acres that they had ceded to the United States under the Point Elliott Treaty, for which they had been paid $5,973.31 after the 1855 treaty. Their aboriginal lands had been in two tracts: 4,560 acres on the northern tip of Camano Island, and a 3,500 acre heart-shaped tract on the mainland abutting Skagit Bay. The commission found the tribe entitled to a payment of $12,000 for their lands, and after deducting the amount already paid them, awarded them on June 7, 1972, an entitled recovery sum of $6,026.69.

Suggested Readings: Martin J. Sampson, *Indians of Skagit County* (Mount Vernon, Wash.: Skagit County Historical Society, 1972); "Susie Sampson Peter—Oldest of the Kikiallus," *Spokesman-Review,* November 2, 1959.

KITTITAS
(See **Yakima**)

KLAMATH
(Lutuamian)

The anthropologist A. L. Kroeber suggests that the name Klamath stems possibly from the Calapooya name, Athlameth, for this people. Anthropologist Albert Samuel Gatschet reported that the tribe's own name for themselves, Maklaks, means "people," "community," and the like. It has also been reported, by anthropologist Leslie Spier, that the name Klamath is reserved for the Klamath-Marsh–Williamson River subdivision—the Auksni. Other Klamaths use the name only by courtesy. From the Canadian trappers has come down a hybrid French-English name, La Lakes.

Oregon's Klamath Lake and Klamath County bear the Klamath name today. Within Klamath County is the city of Klamath Falls on Interstate 97. A river in Oregon and California, and a town in the latter state also bear the name. Before their treaty with the United States in 1864, the Klamaths—with two other tribes who signed the treaty, the Modocs and the Paiute Yahuskins—claimed over twenty million acres in present-day Oregon and California. The Klamaths gained much attention when the United States terminated its trust relationship with them by an act dated August 13, 1954 (25 Stat. 718 USC X 564).

Location: In 1957, 404 of the 2,038 Klamaths lived outside Oregon. Three hundred of those who remained in Oregon lived mostly in the south-central part of the state, but off the reservation. In the post-termination era the Klamaths have tended to live in the general area where the Klamaths proper formerly lived. The former village sites were on Klamath Lake and Klamath Marsh and on the Williamson and Sprague rivers.

Numbers: On the final tribal roll at the time of termination in 1958 there were 2,133 members. In 1977 the same number were listed as Klamaths. In 1848, Klamath numbers had stood roughly at 1,000. Estimates of their 1780 numbers have varied from 400 to 1,000. In 1923, there were 1,201 Klamaths, Modocs, and other Indians under the Klamath superintendency. In 1930, 2,034 were listed as Klamaths and Modocs. In 1937 1,912 were listed as Klamaths, probably including members of other tribes.

History: Because of their interior location in present-day south-central Oregon and north-central California, the Klamaths were able to avoid white men until late in the contact period. The Hudson's Bay Company trader Peter Skene Ogden, who met them in 1826, called them a "happy race." They would not be so for long, he believed, after they began associating with whites. Among the goods that the Klamaths ob-

tained from whites were guns and horses. At The Dalles on the north they obtained from other natives horses, blankets, buffalo skins, and dried salmon, in exchange for slaves that they captured from California tribes. They also exchanged beads, and the seeds of the *wocus*, which they gathered in marshy places in their homelands. They processed the seeds into a nutritious food that was used in soups or mixed into flour to make cakes. The Klamaths also met annually with other tribes to trade at such places as Yainax east of Klamath Lake. They harpooned fish and shot waterfowl with bows and arrows. The clothing of both sexes consisted of fiber skirts and basket caps, plus in cold weather tule leggings and sandals, mantles of skin and fiber, and fur mittens. Not until early in the nineteenth century did they adopt buckskin clothing and footwear, which they obtained through trade. They wore dentalia shells in nasal-septum perforations and flattened the heads of their infants. They also adopted the practice of tattooing the body. Their winter habitations were semisubterranean earthen lodges, which were circular pits as much as four feet deep.

On October 14, 1864, the Klamaths' treaty (16 Stat. 718) was signed by twenty-one of their chiefs, along with four Modoc and two Yahuskin headmen. These peoples traded to the United States their high, semiarid lands east of the Cascade Mountains for the Klamath Reservation. This reservation of about 1,107,847 acres was proclaimed on February 17, 1870 (16 Stat. 383). The Klamath Agency had been instituted on May 12, 1866, at the upper end of Agency Lake, a few miles south of Fort Klamath and north of Klamath Lakes. The Klamaths settled at the agency with a few disgruntled Modocs. Most of the latter tribe refused to join the Klamaths on the reservation, preferring to remain in their own homelands. Because of intertribal friction, the Modocs and some Upland Klamaths and Yahuskins were placed at Yainax, where a subagency was established in 1870 some thirty-five miles east of the main Klamath Agency.

The boundaries of the Klamath Reservation had been established by surveys in

1871 and 1888 and were reported on December 18, 1896. An act (30 Stat. 571) was passed on July 1, 1898, authorizing negotiations for a settlement with the Klamaths for the lands that had been excluded from the reservation by erroneous surveys. It was agreed on June 17, 1901, that the Klamaths were to be paid $537,007.20 for 621,824.28 acres of "Klamath Reservation-Excluded Lands." Because many Klamaths sought allotments on sections of the reservation that originally had been intended for a military road company, the allotment process, which had begun on the reservation in 1895, was interrupted two years later by conflicts that remained unresolved until 1906. Allotment resumed three years later. By an act of May 27, 1902 (32 Stat. 260), Klamath children born after allotting had been completed in 1895 were authorized to receive further allotments, but their elders were unhappy that those born after April 15, 1910, could not do so, though as tribal members they retained an equity in tribal properties.

In 1902 the Modocs, who had been exiled to the Quapaw Agency in Oklahoma after their defeat in 1872–73 in their war with the United States, sent representatives to the Klamaths seeking permission for certain of the Modoc tribe to receive allotments on the Klamath Reservation if they returned to the area. The Klamath Council approved the request, and in 1903 twenty-one Modocs settled at the upper end of the northeast portion of the reservation. Forty-seven others wanted to come at a later time. In 1909, Congress authorized allotments to Quapaw Modocs on the Klamath Reservation, but then the Klamaths opposed letting them have the land. Sixteen Modocs, however, were certified for allotments when allotting resumed in 1909. In all 177,719.62 acres were allotted to 1,174 Indians, and 6,094.77 acres were reserved for agency, school, and church purposes.

Unlike most Oregon Indians the Klamaths were not victimized by great epidemics, nor did they come into violent confrontations with whites. Yet in the roughly 100-year history of the Klamath Reservation Indians, perhaps nothing changed their lives more than the termination of their trust relationship with the United States.

Government and Claims: The roots of the modern Klamath General Council, as the tribe was called, lay in the establishment in 1909 of a council to deal more effectively with agency staff. In 1929 the tribe established a business committee. On June 15, 1935, a majority of Klamaths voted to reject the provisions of the Indian Reorganization Act (48 Stat. 984). The termination of the 861,125-acre Klamath Reservation came about as members were permitted to vote for themselves and for their children to be either "withdrawing" members (who would receive about $50,000 each for their share of the tribal assets) or "remaining" members (who would hold tribal interests in common under state law). There were two factions wanting termination. One represented those wanting immediate creation of individual Indian rights, dissolution of the tribe, and distribution of its assets. The other, the tribal governing body, sought tribal identity and tribal rights. Of the 2,133 members on the final roll in 1958, there were 1,660 electing to withdraw and 473 electing to remain. The individual holders of lands no longer in trust became subject to taxation. In 1980 the "remaining" Klamaths and their heirs, a total of about 600, received about $173,000 for each of the remaining 473 shares in the thousands of acres of forest lands taken by the federal government through condemnation in 1974 and added to the Winema National Forest.

Before the treaty with the Klamaths, Modocs, and Yahuskins, Congress by an act on July 2, 1864 (13 Stat. 355), granted the state of Oregon three alternating sections of public lands on each side of a military road that was to be constructed from Eugene to the eastern boundary of the state. Having been assigned by the Oregon legislature to construct the road, the Oregon Central Military Road Company began the project. In 1867, 1871, and 1873 the state of Oregon issued patents to the company for a total of 402,240.67 acres, which by conveyances became vested in the California & Oregon Land Company. Of the acreage, with the exception of that required for a right-of-way for the road, 111,385 acres lay within the Klamath Reservation. Before the establishment of the Indian Claims Commission in 1947, Indian tribes were permitted to sue the United States only on consent of the Congress to recover for losses. An act of May 26, 1920 (41 Stat. 623) permitted Klamaths, Modocs, and Yahuskins to bring suit. The government would not stop tribal attempts to reclaim that portion of the reservation given to the Military Road Company. The tribe's long journey to recovery began after the United States unsuccessfully instituted three suits against the company to annul patents to the Indian lands that the company held. In February, 1904, the United States Supreme Court ruled that the Indians had indeed lost 111,400.48 acres. Congress therefore passed an act (33 Stat. 1033) directing the secretary of the interior to ascertain the value of the acreage and to ask the California & Oregon Land Company how much it would be willing to accept in return for the lands or whether it would accept other unallotted lands within the reservation in exchange. Eventually the land company conveyed to the United States the 111,400.48 acres, accepting in lieu 86,418.06 acres of unallotted choice timber lands near Yamsey Mountain. That exchange was concluded on August 22, 1906, in accordance with provisions of the act of June 21, 1906 (34 Stat. 325, 367) without the knowledge of or any compensation to the tribe. In 1913 the Internal Revenue Service valued the tribe's timber at $3,550,000. That land exchange had reduced the reservation by 86,418.06 acres. On November 2, 1907, the secretary of the interior suggested that the Indians be paid $108,750 for the lost acreage, and on April 30, 1908, Congress appropriated the monies (35 Stat. 70, 92). In councils about 150 adult Klamath males, of a total of 287 adult males, signed the release that relinquished lands for the monies offered. After the May, 1920, act enabling the Klamaths to sue for a more equitable payment for the 86,418.06 acres, the case was argued in 1934 before the Court of Claims. On April 8, 1935, that body decided against the Indian plain-

Klamath

Yu-mai-poo-tas, also called Tecumseh or Medicine Man. When this photograph was taken in 1875, the Klamaths of south-central Oregon were becoming less isolated from white settlement. In 1864 they had signed a treaty with the United States, which provided a reservation for them. Courtesy of the Klamath County Museum.

93

tiffs. An act of May 15, 1936, authorized and directed the Court of Claims to reinstate and rehear the case. On April 25, 1938, the Supreme Court confirmed a Court of Claims award of $2,980,000 for the lands plus interest, for a total of $5,313, 347.32. Ironically, the military road that set off all of the above developments was never used.

On January 31, 1964, one hundred years after their initial treaty with the government, the Klamaths, after presenting to the Indian Claims Commission their claim (Docket 100) for lands ceded in 1864, were awarded $2.5 million, for which Congress specified methods of distribution in an act of October 1, 1965 (79 Stat. 879). Various other claims were put into separate dockets. The Klamaths filed a claim (Docket 100-A) for additional compensation for the 621, 824.28 acres of the reservation excluded by erroneous surveys. An award was made by the Claims Commission on September 2, 1969, for $4,162,992.82 above the original consideration paid for the boundary-survey errors. For mismanagement of their funds and properties the Klamaths filed a claim (Docket 100 B-1), on which the commission made its final judgment on January 21, 1977, by awarding the tribe $18 million, after the case had been appealed to the Court of Claims (Docket 389-72). A claim for mismanagement of tribal forest and sawmill operations was filed (Docket 100 B-2), and on May 1, 1982, the members by a twelve-vote margin accepted the government's offer of $16.5 million to settle that claim. Far less than the tribe wanted, the monies were distributed to those living of the 2,133 members of record on August 13, 1954, or their descendants. Claims for mismanagement of Klamath grazing and agricultural lands and irrigation projects, as well as for rights-of-way conveyed through tribal lands at less than fair market value (Docket 100-C), were disposed of by a final award of $785,000, for which the Klamath Executive Committee passed a resolution on January 16, 1976, asking that the proceeds from the docket be disbursed to pay off tribal loans used for litigating funds. After Congress had twice put off the termination of

federal supervision as a result of the Termination Act of August 13, 1954 (from the initial date of August 13, 1958, to August 12, 1961), two suits were filed in 1961 and 1962 before the Court of Claims for additional compensation for the tribal lands disposed of during termination (Antelope Desert, Klamath Marsh, and ten units of Klamath forest land). The property selected for sale as a result of termination constituted 77.825 percent of the value of the total estate. Of that, 78 percent was forest land, which had the greatest value of all. These suits, Dockets 125-61 and 87-62, were consolidated, becoming Docket 387-72. The result was an award to the majority of Klamaths of $21,235,496.80 (Docket 125-61). The other 162 tribal members (represented by Docket 87-62) were awarded $2,220,793.20.

Contemporary Life and Culture: The problems attending termination were severe for the Klamaths. Claiming no responsibility for the effects, Congress had made no provision for a follow-up program for the tribe except to assist in hunting and fishing activities through contracts with the BIA, since with termination there was no abrogation of those contracts. Receipt of the monetary awards made many recipients victims of white men wishing to cash in on the Indians' payments. Individual tribal identity problems followed in the wake of termination. The withdrawal of federal services aggravated the situation. Many BIA programs came to an end.

In 1969 the remaining and withdrawing Klamaths and three whites formed the Organization of Forgotten Americans, which sought social benefits for the Klamaths, including their tribal reinstatement. The organization also tried to protect Klamath tribes from squandering compensation from any future claims. Most important, it worked toward reinstatement of the tribe to make it eligible to receive federal funds and services of the BIA. In the early 1980s a court ruling required the U.S. Forest Service to consult the tribe over land-management issues. The tribe also entered into an agreement with the Forest Service to establish traditional cultural camps at the head of the Williamson River in the Winema National Forest. The 2,313-member tribe had its tribal status restored in 1991. In 1984 one tribal member had kept a fire that he vowed never to extinguish until his people regained their lost lands. See also **Modoc.**

Suggested Readings: S. A. Barrett, *The Material Culture of the Klamath and Modoc Indians,* University of California Publications in American Archaeology and Ethnology, no. 5 (Berkeley, Calif., 1907–1910) pp. 239–92; Charles Crane Brown "Identification of Selected Problems of Indians Residing in Klamath County, Oregon— An Examination of Data Generated Since Termination of the Klamath Reservation," disserta-tion, University of Oregon, 1973; Luther Shee-leigh Cressman, *The Sandal and the Cave: The Indians of Oregon,* Studies in History, no. 8 (Corvallis, Ore.: Oregon State University Press, 1981); Edward S. Curtis, *The North American Indian* (1912; New York, Johnson Reprint Cor-poration, 1970), vol. 13; Albert Samuel Gatschet, *The Klamath Indians of Southwestern Oregon* vol. 2 of Smithsonian Institution, *Contributions to North American Ethnology* (Washington, D.C.: Government Printing Office, 1890), pts. 1 and 2; Carrol B. Howe, *Ancient Tribes of the Kla-math Country* (Portland, Ore.: Binfords and Mort, 1968); Leslie Spier, *Klamath Ethnography,* University of California Publications in Ameri-can Archaeology and Ethnology, vol. 30 (Berke-ley, Calif., 1930); Theodore Stern, "The Klamath Indians and the Treaty of 1864," *Oregon His-torical Quarterly* 57 (March, 1956–December, 1956); Theodore Stern, *The Klamath Tribe: A People and Their Reservation* (Seattle: Univer-sity of Washington Press, 1965).

KLAMATH AND MODOC TRIBES AND YAHOOSKIN BAND OF SNAKE INDIANS

The Klamath and Modoc Tribes and Ya-hooskin Band of Snake Indians is composed of descendants of the Klamaths, Modocs, and Yahuskin Paiutes who treated with the United States on October 14, 1864. Under provisions of their treaty the three tribes were assigned to one reservation, the Klamath. For an account of this tribe see **Klamath.**

KLICKITAT
(Shahaptian)

It is believed that the Klickitats (Klikitats), or the Wah-how-pums, as they were called by explorers Meriwether Lewis and William Clark, were given the name by which they are known today by Chinookan peoples. The name Klickitat is derived from one vil-lage name meaning "beyond the [Cascade] Mountains." The Klickitats were said to have moved in precontact times either from the south or the western slopes of the Rocky Mountains to their lands near the Cascade Mountains of Washington state. Their re-moval was hastened by pressures from the Cayuse Indians. After coming to their new homeland, they divided into eastern and western divisions, both of which retained their Shahaptian language. Besides the Klick-itat River, a town and a county in Wash-ington bear the tribal name.

The Western Klickitats (also called the Cowlitz Klickitats) mixed with the Cowlitzes west of the Cascade Mountains and became the Taitnapams. They settled on the head-waters of such streams as the Cowlitz and Lewis rivers, which are Columbia River trib-utaries in southwestern Washington. The Eastern Klickitats primarily occupied the upper drainage systems of two other Colum-bia tributaries, the Klickitat and White Sal-mon rivers of south-central Washington. They were skilled horsemen noted for their weaponry, especially their superb bows and arrows, which helped earn them the reputa-tion of good hunters. They were also skilled

Klickitat

*The Klickitat tribe, to which this early twen-
tieth-century man belonged, lived mostly in
south-central Washington, but a branch of
the tribe lived on the west in the foothills of
the Cascade Mountains and hunted extensively in the Willamette valley of Oregon.
Many Klickitat descendants live on the
Yakima Reservation and have been important among its leaders. Photograph by Edward S. Curtis, from Curtis's* The North
American Indian *(1907–1930), volume 7.*

traders, serving as intermediaries between
interior and coastal peoples. Their women
were skilled at basketry.

After the epidemics of the 1820s and
1830s had reduced the populations of the
Willamette valley tribes, the Klickitats' aggressiveness strengthened their position in
that valley, where they migrated to hunt
and trade. They were also found as far south
as the Umpqua River of southern Oregon

and as far west as Puget Sound and the
Coast Range of Oregon. Among the natives
of the lower Willamette valley they developed a reputation as "robbers" and "plun-
derers." Under their chief, Socklate Tyee,
and armed with Hudson's Bay company
guns, they fought the Rogue Indians of
Oregon in the 1840s. During the Rogue
Wars of the 1850s, under their chief, Quatley (Quarterly), they scouted for the United
States military. When the American government subsequently made treaties with Oregon Indians, the Klickitats unsuccessfully
sought redress in the white man's courts
for their losses of lands in the Willamette
valley. The Eastern Klickitats were one of
fourteen tribes under the Yakima standard
signing a treaty on June 9, 1855, with Washington Territorial Governor and Superintendent of Indian Affairs Isaac Stevens.
Angered at the treaty, some of them fought
Americans in the ensuing Yakima and Puget
Sound wars of 1855 and 1856. Under the
pressure of whites in the Willamette valley,
where the Western Klickitats had returned
after the war, they were sent up the Columbia to the Yakima or Simcoe Agency in
1867. Evidence of their close alliance with
the Yakimas was the election of one of their
number, Joe Stwire, or White Swan, to the
Yakima chieftaincy during the reservation
era. The government had handpicked for
the chieftaincy his predecessor, the Klickitat Spencer.

Lewis and Clark estimated Klickitat numbers at 700 in 1805 and 1806. The 1910
census listed them at 405, a reduction less
severe than that suffered by other tribes
who had greater exposure to the whites'
diseases. In 1962 there were between 10
and 20 Klickitats in Washington. In 1970
there were only 21 Klickitats remaining, of
whom 5 were on the Yakima Reservation.
Their reduction appears to have been due
primarily to intermarriage with other peoples, such as the Yakimas, with whom they
were grouped. See **Yakima** and **Taitnapam.**

Suggested Readings: Delia M. Coon, "Klickitat
County: Indians of and Settlement by Whites,"
Washington Historical Quarterly 14, no. 4 (Octo-
ber, 1923); Melville Jacobs, *Northwest Sahaptin
Texts* (New York: Columbia University Press,

1934–37), 2 vols.; H. O. Lang, ed., *History of the Willamette Valley . . .* (Portland, Ore.: G. H. Himes, 1885); Lucullus V. McWhorter, *The Crime Against the Yakimas* (Yakima, Wash.: Republic Printers, 1913); J. G. Maddock, "The Klickitat Indians," *Travel*, August 1895, pp. 306–311. University of Washington Pacific Northwest Collections; Selma Neils, *The Klickitat Indians* (Portland, Ore., 1985);

Click Relander, *Strangers on the Land* (Yakima, Wash.: Franklin Press, 1962). For a bibliography of the Yakimas (with whom the Klickitats were assimilated), see Robert E. Pace, *Yakima Indian Nation Bibliography* (Toppenish, Wash.: Yakima Indian Media Services, 1978); Helen Hersh Schuster, *The Yakimas: A Critical Bibliography* (Bloomington, Ind.: Indiana University Press, 1982).

KOOTENAI TRIBE OF IDAHO

The Kootenai Tribe of Idaho is made up of Lower Kutenais who did not join others of the tribe living in Canada nor join Upper Kutenais who had moved to the Flathead Reservation in Montana. In 1989 they numbered 108. In February 1991 they joined other area tribes in special ceremonies honoring Indian troops in the Desert Storm war in the Persian Gulf. See **Kutenai.**

KUITSH
(Yakonan)

The Kuitshes, commonly referred to as Lower Umpquas, lived on the lower Umpqua River of Oregon. Sand dunes along the coast separated them from their neighbors on the south, the Coos. The Kuitshes seem never to have been enumerated separately before modern times. The estimate of their numbers in 1780 included tribesmen of Yakonan stock—Coos, Siuslaws, Alseas, and Yaquinas. Only 9 Kuitshes were counted in the 1930 census.

Because of their coastal location, the Kuitshes were exposed to white influences earlier than the natives of the interior on the east. At an early date they adopted American culinary utensils and dress. Before coming under white influences, they had worn skirts and basket hats. Large beads worn in their noses concealed their mouths. They flattened the heads of their infants. The double-pitch roofs of their houses resembled those of whites. Like white men, they wrapped their dead and enclosed them in boxes or, in native fashion, in inverted canoes. They placed burial containers beneath small plant shelters.

One summer day in 1791 the Kuitshes discovered the British schooner *Jenny* in the estuary of the Umpqua River. During her stay of several days they traded some sea otter skins to her captain, James Baker. The following year they were visited by the British vessel *Ruby*, commanded by Charles Bishop. This vessel entered Winchester Bay at the mouth of the Umpqua River. In 1821 they were visited by J. Birnier of the Hudson's Bay Company, who was said to be the first white man to descend the course of the Umpqua River. Five years later, still embittered by the killing of several natives along the Umpqua by some Iroquois Indians who had been gathering furs to sell to the Hudson's Bay Company, they chased a free trapper upstream. On July 14, 1828, they pounced on the northbound party of seventeen Americans led by Jedediah Smith, killing all but four of its members. Before that attack, after a chief had stolen an axe from the party, Smith had ordered him tied as though to be hanged. The axe was recovered, but the chief had been humiliated and was resentful. Smith, who was absent at the time of the killings, finally reached Fort Vancouver with the help of Tillamook Indians. There, sanctuary was provided by the chief factor, Dr. John McLoughlin.

The Kuitshes succumbed to the intermittent fever outbreak of 1829 and 1830 at an alarming rate. Angered by their attrition, they ascended the Umpqua River in 1838,

Kuitsh

Midnineteenth-century chief Solomon Riggs of the Kuitsh tribe. The Kuitshes inhabited the southern Oregon coast and in 1860 were removed north to coastal reservations. Before coming under white influence, they wore skirts and basket hats and flattened the heads of their infants.

going about forty miles from the Pacific Ocean to the mouth of Elk Creek, where they attacked the Hudson's Bay Company post, Fort Umpqua. In the fracas they killed no fort personnel, but wounded three. Their hostilities caused the Methodist missionaries Rev. Jason Lee and Rev. Gustavus Hines to cancel a trip to the mouth of the Umpqua in 1840. Because of their losses from the whites' diseases and the marriage of their women to white men, the Kuitshes were largely immobilized during the Rogue Wars of the 1850s. On July 28, 1856, the American military Fort Umpqua was established on the Rogue River two miles upstream from its mouth. It was meant to keep the natives submissive and protect miners and settlers. Because of such protection pro-

moters entered Kuitsh country. Samuel Roberts entered the Umpqua River on August 4, 1850. Herman Winchester and others of the Umpqua Land Company settled in the Lower Umpqua country at Umpqua City, Scottsburg, Elkton, and Winchester. When they were too weak to repel a marine invasion of about seventy-five vessels calling at the Umpqua River, the Kuitshes contented themselves with peacefully boarding the craft. During the gold discoveries in the Rogue River valley and the ensuing Rogue Wars, they and some Coos and a few Siuslaws were expelled from Scottsburg and forced onto the beach at Empire City (present-day Coos Bay), where they were guarded by the Coos County Volunteers.

Immediately after the Rogue Wars the Kuitshes were moved north to the Umpqua Subagency (one of four subagencies in western Oregon in 1856), where a village of Kuitsh, Coos, and Siuslaw refugees was established on the right bank of the Umpqua and extended about two miles upstream from its mouth. The village houses, furnished by the agency, were of split cedar planks atop three- to five-foot pits. They were walled a short way above ground and covered by gable roofs. From fires on the mat-covered ground, smoke escaped through rooftop apertures. Occupants slept in bunk beds. The Indians aspired to own tables and other furniture in the manner of whites. In 1858, two years before their removal to the Coast Reservation (later to become the Siletz and the Alsea) the villagers numbered about 460, over half the number that had belonged to the Umpqua Subagency. Two years after the September 3, 1859, closing of that subagency, the Kuitshes were marched north to the Yachats River, where the Alsea Subagency was established on the Siletz Reservation.

Artifacts unearthed in former Kuitsh lands near Reedsport in 1979 were heralded as the oldest ever found on the Oregon coast.

For information about Kuitsh land claims, see **Hanis Coos** and **Siuslaw**. For more information about more recent cultural developments among them, see **Confederated Tribes of Coos, Lower Umpqua & Siuslaw, Inc.,** and **Hanis Coos.**

Suggested Readings. Stephen Dow Beckham, *Requiem for a People: The Rogue Indians and the Frontiersmen* (Norman: University of Oklahoma Press, 1971); Joel V. Berreman, *Tribal Distribution in Oregon*, American Anthropological Association Memoir no. 47 (Menasha, Wis.: George Banta Publishing Company, 1937); Leo J. Frachtenberg, *Lower Umpqua Texts and Notes on the Kusan Dialects*, Columbia University Contributions to American Anthropology, vol. 4 (New York, 1914); Leslie Spier, "Tribal Distribution in Southwestern Oregon," *Oregon Historical Quarterly* 28, no. 4 (December, 1927).

KUTENAI
(Kitunahan)

The Kutenais (Kootenays) called themselves by a name meaning "people of the waters, or lakes." Like other tribal names, Kutenai has been subjected to variation and controversy. Some authorities claim Kutenai is a Blackfoot term meaning "big stomach." In that vein, natives of the Great Plains were said to have referred to the Kutenais as "those who are soft" because by Plains standards they lacked aggressiveness. Many authorities agree that the word *Kutenai* stems from the Piegan word *ktonai*, ktunai. Although there is agreement that the tribe migrated west across the Rocky Mountains and subsequently became a linguistic island, there is some question when they migrated. Some scholars, disputing the claim that they were pushed west by fire-armed Blackfeet, claim their migrations were too ancient for their traditions to be historically valid. One Kutenai tradition has it that they migrated from around Lake Michigan about six hundred years ago.

After migrating across the Rocky Mountains, the parent Kutenai villages and activity centers were said to be on Tobacco Plains on the Kootenai River of Montana and on that (same) river in southeastern British Columbia. From those points their migrations resumed as they splintered into upper and lower divisions. The Upper Kutenais were influenced by the horse-buffalo-hunting Plains Indian culture complex. In contrast, the Lower Kutenais were a sedentary people who subsisted to a great extent on fish, roots, and game. Before about 1850 the Upper Kutenais of the aboriginal Agiyiniks, or Jennings band, numbered more than 700. They lived in the area of Jennings, Montana, and migrated east to present-day Kalispell and then south to Elmo. Their descendants live on the Flathead Reservation in Montana. Another Upper Kutenai band, the Aganahoneks, or Tobacco Plains band, live on a reservation in Canada. A third band, the Agukuatsukings, or Tweed-Warlands, once lived on the Kootenai River between Tweed and Warland, Montana, but are now extinct. Yet another band, the Libby Montanas, moved to the Fort Steele area near Cranbrook, British Columbia. Before the 1855 treaty of the Kutenais with the United States, the Libby and Jennings bands had moved to the upper Flathead Lake country of Montana.

The Lower Kutenais were known as canoe Indians. They were also called Arc-à-plats, meaning "flat bows," by French-Canadian fur men because of their straight, broad flat bows. They were also called the Skalizises. One Kutenai group broke away from those in the area of Bonners Ferry, Idaho, and went north to Creston, British Columbia. Some Lower Kutenais of the Arrow Lakes of the Columbia River became part of the Senijextees, a Salishan people. After quarreling with the Salish speakers, most of these Lower Kutenais moved to Kootenay Lake in southeastern British Columbia. The few who remained with the Senijextees went on the Colville Reservation in north-central Washington state.

The Kutenais came into the white fur trade early in the nineteenth century. They

Kutenai

A Kutenai woman of the early 1900s. The Kutenais were among the tribes pushed west by the Plains Indians. Their homes were mainly in present-day northern Montana and British Columbia. They were divided along geographic and economic lines. The Upper Kutenais were influenced by Plains culture; the Lower Kutenais were oriented toward rivers and lakes in seeking subsistence. Photograph by Edward S. Curtis from Curtis's The North American Indian *(1907–1930), volume 7.*

traded at various posts after July, 1807, when David Thompson of the North West Company braved the Piegans' wrath to establish his Kootenay House north of Lake Windermere in British Columbia. At that time the Upper Kutenais had many horses, which they introduced to other natives. Ironically, they were subsequently relieved of many of them by raiders of the plains. Like other peoples of the horse, the Kutenais used the animals variously as a means of transportation and a source of wealth. Horses facilitated their travels to the plains, from whose peoples they adopted secret societies. Their sun dance was simpler than that of the Plains tribes and lacked the element of self-torture. The last such dance among the Kutenais is said to have been held around the beginning of World War I.

It was through the fur trade that the Kutenais came into contact with Christianity. They were introduced to that faith by Iroquois Indians whom the trading companies had brought west. Two Kutenai youths were among the first to attend an Anglican mission school near the Hudson's Bay Company's Fort Garry (later Winnepeg, Manitoba). Among the early Roman Catholic clerics who ministered to them was the intrepid Pierre De Smet, S.J. The Kutenais were attracted to the Saint Ignatius Mission in the lower Flathead valley in Montana, where they raised crops. Their move to that place early in 1855 had been facilitated by the marriage of Kutenai women to white men. In July, 1855, Washington Territorial Governor and Superintendent of Indian Affairs Isaac Stevens met with Kutenais, Flatheads, and Kalispels at Hell Gate near Missoula, Montana, to treat for their lands. Absent from the council was Edward, or Edwald, who had been the chief of the original Tobacco Plain Kutenai tribe before it separated in the Upper and Lower divisions. Attending the council was a Tobacco Plains band under Michelle, who, after unsuccessfully seeking to have one large reserve established for all Kutenai bands, became disillusioned with the promises of white men and went north to Canada with his band. Claiming that Michelle had not represented them at the council, the Lower Kutenais retained a non-treaty status. Gold discoveries in the 1860s proved a mixed blessing to them and to the other Kutenais.

At the time of the 1855 treaty the Kutenais numbered about 500, about 130 less than the figure given by the Hudson's Bay Company trader John Warren Dease in 1827. In 1881 the Kutenais on the Flathead Reservation numbered 395. Their numbers increased between 1895 and 1910 with migrations to that reservation of Kutenais from Bonners Ferry, Idaho, and Libby, Montana. At the middle of the twentieth century most of the 600 Kutenais lived in Montana and British Columbia. A smaller number, about 99, lived near Bonners Ferry. Today the main centers of Kutenai population are southeastern British Columbia at Creston, Cranbrook, Windermere, and Grasmere; western Montana, on the Flathead Reservation; and northern Idaho, around Bonners Ferry.

After they refused to remove to the Flathead Reservation, the Kutenais near Bonners Ferry (later the Kootenai Tribe of Idaho) were allotted by the government in 1895. Each family received an eighty-acre tract. Tribal members filed a claim (Docket 154) with the Claims Commission asserting title to 1,160,000 acres in northeastern Idaho and northwestern Montana because their aboriginal title had been extinguished by the United States on March 8, 1859, without treaty or compensation. A judgment was rendered on April 25, 1960, in which members of the Kootenai Tribe of Idaho were awarded $425,000. (For other Kutenai claims, see **Confederated Salish & Kootenai Tribes of the Flathead Reservation**.) On September 20, 1974, the tribe gained national attention by its "Declaration of War . . . between the Kootenai Nation and the United States of America." In October of that year President Gerald Ford signed a bill creating a 12.5-acre reservation for the tribe. As a result of the "war" these Kootenais also received some new houses, some paved roads, and a community center. Their constitution had been approved on June 16, 1947. Tribal membership in 1982 was 115. The tribe has done considerable planning under the direction of its council, which is notable for the youth of its members. Education is conducted through the Boundary County and Bonners Ferry school districts of Idaho.

Suggested Readings: Paul E. Baker, *The Forgotten Kutenai* (Boise, Idaho: Mountain States Press, 1955); Franz Boas, *Kutenai Tales*, Bureau of American Ethnology Bulletin no. 59 (Washington, D.C.: Government Printing Office, 1918); Clara Graham, *Fur and Gold in the Kootenays* (Vancouver, B.C.: 1945); "An Interview with Joe Mathias (Director of Kootenai Tribe, Outreach)," *Idaho Heritage* 1, no. 10 (October, 1977); Olga Wedemeyer Johnson, *Flathead and Kootenay: The Rivers, the Tribes, and the Region's Traders* (Glendale, Calif.: Arthur H. Clark Co., 1969); Frank B. Linderman, *Kootenai Why Stories* (New York: Scribners, 1926); Carling Malouf, "Early Kutenai History," *Montana Magazine of History* 2, no. 2 (Spring, 1953); Harry Holbert Turney-High, *Ethnography of the Kutenai*, Memoirs of the American Anthropological Association, no. 56 (Menasha, Wis.: George Banta Publishing Company, 1941).

KWAIAILK
(Coastal Division, Salishan)

The Kwaiailks were also known as Upper Chehalises. The name Kwaiailk was that of one of at least four bands in the upper Chehalis River country, an area from Cloquallam Creek to the upper reaches of the Chehalis River in southwestern Washington state. The name is now used to designate all of those bands collectively. They all spoke dialects distinct from those of Lower Chehalis peoples. The boundary dividing the Kwaiailk and the Lower Chehalis dialects was at the confluence of the Chehalis and Satsop rivers. If dialect is considered to mean mutually intelligible forms of the same language, it may be said that the Kwaiailks spoke at least two distinct dialects, though the variations between them were not great. The boundary between the two Kwaiailk dialects was at Grand Mound: Chehalis 1, or Oakville Chehalis, was spoken west of the mound; Chehalis 2, or Tenino Chehalis, was spoken southeast of that point.

While the Lower Chehalises depended primarily on the sea and the lower Chehalis River country for subsistence, the Kwaiailks in the prairie and foothill country subsisted on roots, game, and berries, as well as fish. To encourage growth of berries and camas roots, they burned prairie lands every two or three years. Such areas were shared by peoples from several villages. The Kwaiailks fished for salmon and traveled up Black River to Mud Bay on southern Puget Sound to gather clams and catch flounders. Among the different game that they hunted were deer and elk. Successful hunters feasted their friends and relatives. Well-established trade routes lay between the Lower Chehalis and the Kwaiailk lands. Over those routes the Kwaiailks obtained goods, such as dentalia and seal oil, that were traded along the Pacific Coast from Neah Bay southward to the Columbia River. Trade routes also ran from the Kwaiailk country to east of the Cascade Mountains. At some time before 1800 the Kwaiailks acquired horses, which they grazed on their prairie lands. In 1824 the Hudson's Bay Company trader John Work noted that, unlike the peoples near the coast, those inland had horses, including a people whom he called the Halloweena Nation which some believe to have been a Kwaiailk band. When, nine years later, Work's company established Fort Nisqually on the southern reaches of Puget Sound, the Kwaiailks began to trade there, as well as trading with that firm on the Columbia River. Some Kwaiailks tended sheep for the Puget Sound Agricultural Company, a subsidiary of the Hudson's Bay Company. Among the natives with whom Kwaiailks had close ties were the neighboring Cowlitzes and Nisquallis. Combined with them and other nearby tribes, the Kwaiailks were believed to number about 1,500 to 2,000 at the beginning of the nineteenth century. Epidemics reduced them to about 215 shortly after midcentury. The survivors of those plagues sometimes burned entire villages, trying to escape the contagion. American naval Lt. Charles Wilkes placed Kwaiailk and Lower Chehalis numbers at 700 in 1841, before a severe smallpox epidemic of the early 1850s. The ethnologist George Gibbs placed Kwaiailk numbers at 216 in 1854.

The Kwaiailks were among the natives who in February and March, 1855, met Washington Territorial Governor and Superintendent of Indian Affairs Isaac Stevens, who sought unsuccessfully to treat with them for their lands. During the immediately ensuing Indian war, some Kwaiailks in the vicinity of present-day Centralia, Washington, were moved by their agent, Sydney S. Ford, to a temporary reservation on Ford's Prairie. Among the 400 Indians confined there were some who had served as scouts for the Americans during the war. After the war the government succeeded in obtaining title to Kwaiailk lands without their consent and without compensating them. Finally, the 4,224.63-acre Chehalis Reservation was set apart physically at the confluence of the Chehalis and Black rivers and established by executive order on July 8, 1864, for Chehalises, Chinooks, and other small bands. By an executive order dated October 1, 1886, 3,753.63 acres of the reservation were restored to the public domain for Indian homestead entry, and 471 acres were set aside for school purposes. Thirty-six Indians on the reservation selected homesteads covering all of the lands not reserved for school purposes. Many natives who had been scheduled to remove to the reservation became absorbed within the white community or were removed to other reservations. Today no Kwaiailk tribe exists as such, but Kwaiailks were among the Chehalis Confederated Tribes. See **Confederated Tribes of the Chehalis Reservation, Washington.**

Suggested Readings: George Gibbs, *Tribes of Western Washington and Northwestern Oregon,* vol. 1 of Smithsonian Institution, *Contributions to North American Ethnology* (Washington, D.C.: Government Printing Office, 1877); Hermann Haeberlin and Erna Gunther, "The Indians of Puget Sound, *University of Washington Publi-*

cations in *Anthropology* 4, no. 1 (1930); Carolyn Marr, Donna Hicks, and Kay Francis, *The Chehalis People* (Oakville, Wash.: Confederated Tribes of the Chahalis Reservation, 1980); Leslie Spier, *Tribal Distribution in Washington*, American Anthropological Association, General Series in Anthropology, no. 3 (Menasha, Wis.: George Banta Publishing Company, 1936); Herbert C. Taylor, *Anthropological Investigation of the Chehalis Indians Relative to Tribal Identity and Aboriginal Possession of Lands*, in *Coast Salish and Western Washington Indians*, vol. 3 (New York: Garland Publishing Inc., 1974), pp. 117–58.

KWALHIOQUA
(Athapascan)

The name Kwalhioqua (also Quillequeoqua or Willopah) is a Chinookan designation meaning "at a lonely wooded place." The Kwalhioquas were unique in that, as Athapascan speakers, their language for a period was an island in a sea of other tongues. They were of the Pacific division of the Athapascan language, one of three Athapascan language divisions in North America. Like others of the Pacific division, they are believed to have migrated into the Pacific Northwest in the distant past. In the eighteenth century they moved into the Willapa Hills of southwestern Washington state. Probably before 1775, one of their bands migrated to the south and became the Clatskanies. Those who remained diminished in numbers. Others meanwhile had migrated to the Chehalis and Cowlitz river watersheds and eventually came to rest on the upper reaches of the Chehalis River as part of the Cowlitz tribe living there. As they slowly admixed with the Cowlitzes, those Kwalhioquas assumed their language and lost their own. This intermingling, which began in the 1820s and 1830s, was complete at the end of the century, when they became indistinguishable from Cowlitzes. Those few who did not mix with the Cowlitzes moved west to Shoalwater (Willapa) Bay on the Pacific Coast, where they admixed with Chinooks and Chehalises and assumed the Chehalis dialect of the Salishan language. Some anthropologists have speculated that the Kwalhioquas had been unable to secure footholds on the lands of the once populous lower Columbia River and coastal peoples. Having no seines for fishing, they borrowed these implements from those peoples and arranged with them for brief stays in their lands. In their own lands the Kwalhioquas subsisted by hunting, fishing, and gathering.

On August 9, 1851, Oregon Superintendent of Indian Affairs Anson Dart treated with the Kwalhioquas on the Willapa River. He erroneously called them the "Wheelappa Band of the Chinook Indians." They ceded to the United States their lands: those between Willapa Bay and the Cowlitz valley, those in the hill country between the Chehalis and Willapa valleys, and those bordering on the lands of the Cathlamets on the Columbia River. In 1853 an Indian agent listed the Kwalhioqua numbers as probably no more than 10 or 15, no doubt because of a smallpox epidemic that had sharply reduced them. About that time only two or three Indians among the tribes at Shoalwater Bay were identified as Kwalhioquas. In 1856 only three or four families on the headwaters of the Chehalis River identified themselves as Kwalhioquas. In 1910 there were said to be but two survivors, a woman on the Nisqually Reservation and her aunt living near Rochester, Washington.

Suggested Readings: Jean Hazeltine, *The Historical and Regional Geography of the Willapa Bay Area, Washington* (South Bend, Wash.: South Bend Journal, n.d.); Frederick Webb Hodge, *Handbook of American Indians North of Mexico*, pt. 1 (Washington, D.C.: Government Printing Office, 1907); Melville Jacobs, "Historic Perspectives in Indian Languages of Oregon and Washington," *Pacific Northwest Quarterly* 28, no. 1 (January, 1937).

LATGAWA
(Takilman)

The Latgawas lived in southwestern Oregon on the upper Rogue River, around Table Rock and Bear Creek on the east, and in the neighborhood of Jacksonville. The tribal name, deriving from their location on the upper Rogue, means "those living in the uplands." They have also been called Upland Takelmas, but they were culturally distinct from the Takelmas, and there was a dialectic difference as well. In precontact times the Latgawas often raided the Takelmas for slaves, whom they traded to the Klamaths. The Takilman linguistic stock to which they belonged numbered an estimated 500 in 1780, but in 1910 only one remained. A 1937 enumeration counted 104 "Rogue River" Indians. The Latgawas' history from the middle of the nineteenth century parallels that of the Takelma bands, with whom they had become closely associated and intermixed when the two tribes joined together to war on white settlers and gold miners. Both resisted treaties with the United States, fought against the whites, and opposed removal to the Siletz Reservation. For an account of those developments see **Takelma.**

Latgawa

This man, John Ponsee, was classified as a Rogue River Indian because his tribe, the Latgawas, were located on the upper Rogue River in southwestern Oregon. In 1910 only one Latgawa remained. Courtesy of the Lincoln County Historical Society, Oregon.

LOWER CHEHALIS
(Coastal Division, Salishan)

The Lower Chehalises lived in what is now southwestern Washington. Their name derives from *tshels*, a native word meaning "sand." Tshels was also the name of a large village at Hanson's Point at the entrance to Grays Harbor, near the modern-day town of Westport. The Chehalis name is now applied to formerly autonomous villagers who spoke a similar language in a much wider area along the Chehalis River and around Grays Harbor. The Lower Chehalises lived principally around the south sides of the Chehalis River and Grays Harbor. In later times, after the Chinookan speakers had been reduced by epidemics, such as the intermittent fever of the 1830s, the Lower Chehalises occupied territory to and around Shoalwater (Willapa) Bay that had been held by the Chinooks. Among the pressures to which the Lower Chehalises were subjected in early times, according to some anthropologists, were the movements of Chinookan peoples down the Columbia River, who pressed the Lower Chehalises into their historic positions. Besides being closely related culturally if not linguistically to the Chinooks, the Lower Chehalises were closely related to other peoples of the lower Chehalis River watershed and Grays Harbor, into which the Chehalis River flows. These peoples were the Humptulipses, Copalises, Wynoochees, and Satsops. Some ethnologists maintained that the Satsops were a subdivision of the Lower Chehalises, because they were part of the same political group. The Satsop language, however, was a Kwaiailk (Upper Chehalis) dialect. The Lower Chehalises had close ties with the Quinaults on the north along the Pacific Coast and with the Chinooks on the south. They had ties with Kwaiailks, but spoke a distinctly different Salish language.

The Lower Chehalises' villages were their largest social groupings and their only political and land-use units. In contrast to the Kwaiailks, they subsisted primarily on sea foods. They traded such products as dried sturgeon, clams, and seal oil to their inland neighbors. During the maritime fur-trading

Lower Chehalis

Tillie Atkins, a Chehalis woman of the 1890s shows white influences in her attire. The Chehalis peoples lived along the lower Chehalis River and the adjoining Washington coast. They were first exposed to white mariners and traders late in the eighteenth century. Courtesy of Whitman College.

era they encountered whites such as the American Robert Gray, who in 1792 sailed into the harbor bearing his name. They also were among those who traded with Meriwether Lewis and William Clark in 1805 and 1806 at the American explorers' winter quarters near the mouth of the Columbia River. During the early nineteenth century the Lower Chehalises traded with Astorians of John Jacob Astor's Pacific Fur Company at Fort Astoria and with traders of the North West and Hudson's Bay companies. It was evidence of their importance to white traders that the latter sometimes set aside rooms on their ships anchored in Bakers Bay on the lower Columbia River for important Chehalis men and women. A Hudson's Bay Company trader, John Work, in the latter part of 1824 found the usually friendly Lower Chehalises not so friendly because of rumors that whites planned to attack them. Work quickly dispelled the rumors by distributing tobacco among them. In 1858 an Indian agent complained that Lower Chehalises were intermediaries in a liquor trade extending from Shoalwater Bay to the Quinault country. The Lower Chehalises and neighboring peoples, including those of the upper Chehalis River, were estimated at between 1,500 and 2,000 at the beginning of the nineteenth century and at 400 shortly after midcentury. In 1854 the ethnologist George Gibbs placed their numbers at 100 in Grays Harbor and on the lower Chehalis River. The estimate of 217 in 1855 may have included other peoples of the lower Chehalis River country.

In February and March 1855, Washington Territorial Governor and Superintendent of Indian Affairs Isaac Stevens met the Lower Chehalises in council with neighboring tribes to treat for their lands. Although the council ended in failure, the government later succeeded in obtaining title to the Lower Chehalises' lands without compensating them. Without their consent and with no treaty, it also determined that a reservation should

be established for them. Few Lower Chehalises removed to the 4,224.63-acre Chehalis Reservation that was established by executive order on July 8, 1864, farther up the Chehalis River at its confluence with the Black River. Today the Lower Chehalises do not exist as a tribe, having been incorporated within other tribes (primarily with those near them). Some Lower Chehalises became assimilated within the white community. The Lower Chehalises were grouped with their non-Quinault neighbors (Chinooks, Humptulipses, Hoquiams, and Satsops) who allotted on the Quinault Reservation. Their descendants belong to the Quinault Allottees Association, which is opposed by the Quinault tribal government. At the time of the allotting, only about 10 percent of the original Quinaults allotted on the reservation that bore their name. See **Confederated Tribes of the Chehalis Reservation, Washington.**

Suggested Readings: George Gibbs, *Tribes of Western Washington and Northwestern Oregon,* vol. 1 of Smithsonian Institution, *Contributions to North American Ethnology* (Washington, D.C.: Government Printing Office, 1877); Hermann Haeberlin and Edna Gunther, "The Indians of Puget Sound," *University of Washington Publications in Anthropology* 4, no. 1 (1930); Leslie Spier, *Tribal Distribution in Washington,* American Anthropological Association, General Series in Anthropology, no. 3 (Menasha, Wis.: George Banta Publishing Company, 1936); Herbert C. Taylor, "Anthropological Investigation of the Chehalis Indians Relative to Tribal Identity and Aboriginal Possession of Lands," in *Coast Salish and Western Washington Indians,* vol. 3 (New York: Garland Publishing Inc., 1974) pp. 117–58.

LOWER ELWHA TRIBAL COMMUNITY, LOWER ELWHA RESERVATION

The Lower Elwha Tribal Community, Lower Elwha Reservation, was formerly one of three Clallam bands, and like the other two the community is today recognized by the federal government as a tribe. The other two are the Port Gamble and the Jamestown Clallam bands. The Lower Elwha Reserva-

tion was begun in 1936–37 when the United States purchased and put in trust for the tribe 372.74 acres of land on the northeastern Olympic Peninsula in Washington state. The purchase, amounting to $58,701.54 was made pursuant to section 5 of the Indian Reorganization Act of June 18, 1934

(48 Stat. 984). The tract, known as the Lower Elwha Tract, lay on aboriginal Clallam lands. It consisted of fifteen parcels near the mouth of the lower Elwha River west of the city of Port Angeles.

Location: The Lower Elwhas live primarily on or adjacent to their Lower Elwha Reservation in Clallam County, Washington, where the Elwha River, flowing north from the Olympic Mountains, enters the Strait of Juan de Fuca. The reservation, consisting of bottom lands, has about a mile of beach along the strait. The nearest city, Port Angeles, lies about nine miles to the east on U.S. Highway 101.

Numbers: Tribal membership was given as 250 in 1978, 413 in 1984, and 1,099 in 1989.

Government and Claims: The reservation, which originally had been assigned to fourteen families living on a sand spit, was proclaimed on January 19, 1968. On it the Lower Elwhas developed their own constitution and bylaws, which they adopted on April 6 and approved on April 29, 1968. Their governing body is the Lower Elwha Tribal Community Council, composed of all of the qualified voters of the community. Officials are elected from among the council members to a business committee for two-year terms. To seek recompense from the United States for alleged wrongs, the three Clallam groups consolidated their claims. See **Clallam**.

Contemporary Life and Culture: The religious preference of tribal members has been Protestant. Children attend public schools. Local, state, and federal agencies provide health care and other services. Residents earn their livelihood by fishing, logging, and seasonal farm labor. The Tribal Community conducts a fisheries enhancement and management program coordinated through the Point-No-Point Treaty Council. The tribe is working to have the Elwha dam removed from the Elwha River so as to restore salmon runs. See **Clallam**.

LOWER SKAGIT
(Coastal Division, Salishan)

The meaning of the name Skagit is unknown. The Skagits proper, or Lower Skagits (sometimes called the Whidbey Island Skagits), were one of several peoples to whom the name was applied. In modern-day Washington state, they occupied tracts in the central portion of Whidbey Island in Puget Sound and on the mainland, including the mouth of the Skagit River and a triangular 56,300-acre area adjacent to the North Fork of that stream. They were long at enmity with northern, British Columbia tribes, who raided them for slaves, and with the Clallams on the south shore of the Strait of Juan de Fuca, who encroached on their lands. The Hudson's Bay Company trader John Work described them as a fine-looking people, whose heads were not so flattened as the Chinooks' and who were quite naked save for blankets or little fur or feather cloaks. During the fur-trading era they traded at Hudson's Bay Company posts, such as Fort Langley (founded in 1827 on the lower Fraser River of British Columbia), Fort Nisqually (founded in 1833 on southern Puget Sound), and Fort Victoria (founded in 1843 on lower Vancouver Island). Roman Catholic priests began ministering to the Lower Skagits in their homelands early in the 1840s. Like other Puget Sound natives, they were suspicious of whites. In the later nineteenth century they were helpless to stem the tide of white settlers occupying their lands, especially the fertile bottomlands of the lower Skagit River valley, some of which were reclaimed from Puget Sound. In 1853 the ethnologist George Gibbs believed that, when their chief S'neet-lum had died, they

Lower Skagit

A woman, circa 1900, of the Lower Skagit tribe, which inhabited the lower Skagit River in the upper Puget Sound Basin. She is completing a mat that might have served her people for many purposes, including the preparation and consumption of foods. Among the materials from which mats were made were rushes and inner, fibrous layers of bark. Mats were also an item of trade. Courtesy of the Skagit County Historical Museum.

had lost much of their former prestige. One of their prominent chiefs was Goliah, who signed the Point Elliott Treaty of January 22, 1855. At the time of that treaty, government officials reported that the Lower Skagits numbered around 300. As a result of the treaty they were placed under the Tulalip Agency and moved to the Swinomish Reservation, which was set aside in western Skagit County by executive order on September 9, 1873. The descendants of the Lower Skagits and other tribesmen on that reservation are members of the Swinomish Tribal Community.

One of twelve Skagit subdivisions listed by ethnologist John R. Swanton was the Nuwahas (Duwahas), who figured very prominently in Skagit history. The division of Skagits into an Upper Skagit Tribe and a Lower Skagit Tribe is a separation of modern origin. While some believe the Nuwahas were a subdivision of the Upper Skagits, the Claims Commission in hearing the Upper Skagits' claim (Docket 92) for compensation for lost lands found the Nuwahas not to be Upper Skagits. At the time of the Point Elliott Treaty the Skagit and Samish tribes were organized for mutual defense under Satbabutkin, the head chief of the peoples around present-day Concrete, Washington, in the middle-upper Skagit watershed. Satbabutkin was the son-in-law of the Nuwaha chief Pattehus (Pateus), who lived around Bay View on the eastern shores of Padilla Bay across from Anacortes. The Lummi, Nooksack, and Semiahmoo Indians called the Nuwahas "cliff dwellers." The Swinomish, Samish, and other Indians called them Stucktabshes, which the whites translated as "Stick Samishes" because the Nuwahas were from the forested mainland.

Under a former chief, Sathill, the Nuwahas fought the "last war" between the Puget Sound tribes and those of Vancouver Island when Sathill and his braves invaded that island near present-day Sydney, British Columbia. In an ensuing fight the Nuwahas recovered the head of a former chief, Chadaskadim, which had been stolen the previous year by a Canadian tribe. These events were said to have occurred after a great plague during the eighteenth century, perhaps the smallpox, which destroyed most of the Nuwahas except those in the upland reaches of their territory. Other epidemics of the early nineteenth century also attacked them, reducing their numbers to about 200. At one time they were said to have numbered several hundred. The succeeding generations were powerless to resist the white settlers who arrived in the latter part of the nineteenth century to occupy the Nuwahas' lands, which today are considered among the most fertile in America. The Nuwahas were converted to Roman Catholicism, which helped change their posture from a warlike character to that of a peaceful people. Their descendants are proud that Chief Pattehus signed the Point Elliott Treaty. The "up Samish River" Nuwahas became associated with Upper Skagit peoples. The Lower ("Samish Flat") Nuwahas around 1918 merged with Samishes (see **Samish**). Although efforts have failed to recognize the Nuwahas as a tribal entity and achieve federal recognition, a Nuwaha remnant seeks to keep alive tribal history and maintain its identity. Descendants live on reservations, such as the Lummi, and at such places as the Bow-Edison area below Bellingham.

The Lower Skagit aboriginal lands totaled 56,300 acres, including 50,300 acres on central Whidbey Island and the triangular 6,000-acre mainland tract extending along Skagit Bay from the mouth of Brown's Slough to north of the mouth of the North Fork of the Skagit River. In the middle of the nineteenth century these lands were valued at $100,188. As the Lower Skagits had received $25,331.50 as a result of the Point Elliott Treaty, they were entitled to recover $74,856.50. The Indian Claims Commission on October 13, 1971, ordered them paid that amount for the acreage they had yielded. See **Swinomish Indian Tribal Community.**

Suggested Readings: Lee Ann Bennett, *Effect of White Contact on the Lower Skagit Indians,* Occasional Paper no. 3 (Seattle: Washington Archaeological Society, 1972); Martin J. Sampson, *Indians of Skagit County* (Mount Vernon, Wash.: Skagit County Historical Society, 1972).

LOWER UMPQUA
(See **Kuitsh.**)

LUCKIAMUTE
(Kalapuyan)

The Luckiamutes were one of the Willamette valley tribes. They spoke one of several dialects of Central Kalapuyan, one of the three Kalapuyan languages. There were probably six Luckiamute bands who lived on the Luckiamute River, a Willamette River tributary in west-central Oregon. Like other Kalapuyan peoples, they obtained their subsistence directly from nature, depending mainly on roots, especially the camas, which they cooked in holes dug for the purpose. They ate fish, but any salmon that they ate had to be caught north of their country, because the fish could not ascend above the Willamette Falls. The Luckiamutes also ate insects, berries, and nuts. Excellent bowmen, they hunted deer and bear, plus smaller game and wildfowl. Since they owned but few horses, they crossed rivers on reed mats and conducted their hunts largely on foot. Like other Kalapuyan peoples, their women were expert makers of baskets, buckskin clothing, and robes of fine otter and weasel fur. They imported garments of mountainsheep wool and clothing ornamented with porcupine quills and beads. Wealthy Luckiamute men often possessed several wives—evidence of their well-developed class system, which included slavery. The men wore buckskin headbands, to which were attached redheaded-woodpecker scalps. To match that ostentatious adornment, they wore necklaces, wrist bands, and plugs fastened in their earlobes.

On April 30, 1851, the Luckiamutes met with federal commissioners, who, unbeknownst to themselves, were no longer authorized by Congress to treat with Oregon Indians. Luckiamute chiefs Daboe (or Jim), Scholaque (or John), and Nuhkow staunchly opposed the plan to move their people east of the Cascade Mountains. On May 2, 1851, they agreed to yield their sovereignty to the United States and never to countenance nor aid tribes or bands who were at enmity with the United States. With other Kalapuyan peoples, they agreed to settle on a small reserve on lands that they had ceded. The lands had, however, already been settled by whites, who had taken them under the Donation Land Act of September 29, 1850, which, in essence, gave settlers free lands even before the lands had been ceded by the Indians. In exchange for ceding their lands, the Luckiamutes were to receive money, clothing, and a few farming tools. Oregon Superintendent of Indian Affairs Anson Dart tried to resettle them on the agreed-upon tract, though their treaty was never ratified.

Increasing pressure from whites made it impossible for officials to isolate the Indians. Consequently the Luckiamutes were asked to negotiate a new treaty. With the Molalas and a few Clackamases from below Willamette Falls they met in council at Dayton, Oregon Territory, where on January 4, 1855, they effected a treaty (10 Stat. 1143, ratified March 3, 1855) with Oregon Superintendent of Indian Affairs Joel Palmer, who wished to help them with medical care and other aids. They agreed to remove to a reservation at such a time and place as the government designated. As a result they removed to the Grand Ronde, which lay immediately north of the Luckiamute homelands. On that reservation in 1870 they numbered thirty-six. In 1910 only eight remained. Integrated with other peoples and depopulated by disease, they lost their tribal identity. On June 30, 1957, the Grand Ronde Reservation itself was dissolved.

Suggested Readings: Stephen Dow Beckham, *The Indians of Western Oregon: This Land Was Theirs* (Coos Bay, Ore., Arago Books, 1977); S. A. Clarke, *Pioneer Days of Oregon History* (Portland, Ore., 1905); Leo J. Frachtenberg, *Ethnological Researches Among the Kalapuya Indians,* Smithsonian Miscellaneous Collections 65, no. 6 (1916); J. A. Hussey, *Champoeg: Place of Transition* (Portland: Oregon Historical Society, 1964); Melville Jacobs, "Kalapuya Texts," *University of Washington Publications in Anthropology* 12 (1945), pt. 3; Harold Mackey, *The Kalapuyans: A Sourcebook on the Indians of the Willamette Valley* (Salem, Ore.: Mission Mill Museum Association, Inc., 1974); W. W. Oglesby, "The Calapooyas Indians," [188?], Mss. P-A 82, Bancroft Library, University of California, Berkeley; James L. Ratcliff, "What Happened to the Kalapuya? A Study of the Depletion of Their Economic Base," *The Indian Historian* 6 no. 3 (Summer, 1973).

LUMMI
(Coastal Division, Salishan)

The Lummis spoke the same Straits, or Lkungen, dialect as the Songishes of southern Vancouver Island, who called themselves Lkungen, according to anthropologist Franz Boas. Another anthropologist, Wayne Suttles, has stated that the name is derived from that of a native house, on Gooseberry Point west of Bellingham, Washington, which was in Lummi territory. Possibly the name of the house came to designate the peoples of a larger area after their concentration on the Lummi Reservation across from Gooseberry Point.

Location: Successors of the Lummis, The Lummi Tribe, Lummi Reservation, Washington, live primarily in northwestern Washington in the general area of Bellingham, which is on Interstate 5 below the Canadian border. The largest number of Lummis live on their reservation, which is on the mainland on the northwestern shores of Bellingham Bay and along eastern shores of the Strait of Georgia.

Numbers: As of 1989 tribal numbers were 2,846. Including neighboring Samishes and Nooksacks, the Lummis numbered about 1,000 in 1780. In the 1850s they were listed variously from 386 to 500. In 1905 they numbered 412. According to the 1910 census, they numbered 353. In the official reports, they were 505 in 1923 and 661 in 1937. Estimates of their numbers during the 1950s were around 400.

History: Sometime before 1850 the Lummis, who were primarily a fishing people, abandoned settlements in the San Juan Islands and established their main quarters on and adjacent to the mainland on the east. They moved because of smallpox and attacks of other tribes, especially those from present-day British Columbia. They also sought the lands and the fishing places of other peoples, for example, on the Nooksack River, where they defeated and assimilated the Hulhwaluqs and neighboring Skalakhans. Despite such conflicts the Lummis

and other Indians of northwestern Washington today have blood ties with northern tribesmen. After moving to and near the mainland, the Lummis built stockades, as did other area tribes, to protect themselves from northern tribes. Under their chief Chowitshoot, they were signatories to the Point Elliott Treaty, which concluded on January 22, 1855 (but not proclaimed until April 11, 1859). By its terms they and other northern Puget Sound Indians relinquished their rights to a large area west of the Cascade Mountains and north of present-day Seattle.

In 1857 one of the Lummi agents reported three Lummi bands, one at each of the three mouths of the Lummi, or Nooksack, River. All three bands acknowledged the headship of Chowitshoot. Four years earlier the ethnologist George Gibbs had stated that Chowitshoot led a southern band, while a chief named Chilleuk led a northern one. The Lummi Reservation was established by the Point Elliott Treaty. Originally 12,562.94 acres, it was enlarged by executive order on November 22, 1873, to approximately 13,600 acres. Although established for Lummi, Nooksacks, Samishes, and other local Indians, it was populated primarily by Lummis. Many of the Indians who were scheduled to go there never did, and some abandoned it after removing there.

Shortly after the treaty signing, Rev. Eugene Casimir Chirouse, O.M.I., and Rev. Louis J. D'Herbomez of the same order established a mission among the Lummis, introducing a Roman Catholic influence among them which remains at the present. At that time the Lummis came under the influence not only of missionaries but also of the military, who in 1856 established Fort Bellingham three and a half miles northeast of Whatcom Creek. The garrison was maintained until the spring of 1860, when it was vacated. It was officially abandoned in 1868. In 1858 the Lummis furnished goods and services to miners en route to the Fraser River goldfields in Canada. Gold seekers

111

and other whites often harmed the Lummi. In 1856 a Lummi chief had to canoe to Victoria on lower Vancouver Island to purchase blankets because those that his tribe had received from the government had been traded for liquor. After the Point Elliott Treaty the Lummis pleaded with government officials to send an agent to protect them from pernicious whites. They continued to fish for subsistence, but also began to work directly for whites. In 1871, for example, the monthly payroll for Indians working in the nearby Bellingham Bay coal mines was $700 in coin. For a long time the Lummis were embroiled with whites in fishing controversies that dated from around the turn of the century. At that time, among other problems, they had been unable to dislodge the Alaska Packers Association from one of their ancient tribal fisheries at Point Roberts near the Canadian border, because of an adverse legal decision in 1897 in *United States* v. *Alaska Packers' Association*. In 1974 some of the fishing rights of the Lummis and other treaty tribes were restored by the decision of federal judge George Boldt, which provided legal protections to them in their fishing.

Government and Claims: A new constitution adopted in 1970 by the Lummi Tribe, Lummi Reservation, Washington, gave broader powers to the tribe's business council. Eleven persons are elected to three-year terms on the council, which elects the principal tribal officers from among its own members and establishes committees to study and make recommendations pertaining to business and social services.

The Lummis filed a claim (Docket 110) to recover additional monies from the United States, claiming that the amount paid them for their lands under the Point Elliott Treaty was unconscionably low. On October 30, 1957, the Indian Claims Commission determined that a gross total of 107,500 acres had been taken from them. After the acreage of their reservation and the waters in the claimed territory were excluded, the net land area claimed amounted to 72,560 acres. On March 2, 1962, its fair market value was determined by the commission to be $52,067

in 1859. It was difficult to ascertain the amount of money that the Lummis had received, because the Point Elliott Treaty had not specified exact amounts for the twenty-three signatory tribes. Thus the Lummi case was combined with those of ten other tribes for the limited purpose of determining the amount due each petitioner (*Upper Skagit Tribe of Indians et al.* v. *United States,* 1964). In absence of proof of the amount paid each tribe, allocation of monies was determined by each tribe's proportion of the estimated tribal populations on the effective date of the treaty. It was determined that the Lummi Tribe had received $33,634.13. The difference between the amount paid the tribe and the fair market value of $52,067 was not considered unconscionable. Thus the commission made no additional award to the Lummis. The tribe appealed the commission's decision to the Court of Claims (197 C. C1. 789), which ruled in 1972 that the valuation that the commission had placed on the Lummi lands was the bare minimum fair-market value in 1859. It thus reversed the Claims Commission's decision and remanded the case for further proceedings. The commission then set the fair market value at $90,634.13 and on October 22, 1970, awarded the tribe $57,000.

Contemporary Life and Culture: The Lummi Reservation lands rise gently from Puget Sound. Most of them are timbered. There are some patches of fertile soil, but when the reservation was established, it was purposely separated from the rich Nooksook valley lands, which today are on the opposite side of Slater Road. By the summer of 1950, 10,162 acres of the reservation had been allotted, of which 2,040 were patented in fee, and 2 were reserved by the government. Sales of approximately 4,824 acres have reduced the allotted lands in trust to about 7,598 acres. There are about 20 acres of tribally owned trust lands. To help ease unemployment problems, the Lummi Business Council, in cooperation with other governmental agencies, in 1970 instituted its Aquacultural Project to cultivate and harvest food from nearby coastal waters. Pollution entering Puget Sound from the Nooksack River has posed a danger to the project. The tribe also operates fish hatcheries. Headstart and day-care centers have been developed, and medical-dental care is provided by the Indian Health Service. The formal education of Lummi children is provided by the schools at nearby Ferndale. Some children attend a Catholic parochial school in Bellingham. A home improvement program has been operating since 1969. The Nooksack River flooded out fifty-seven families in 1975, causing great need for reservation housing. The poor perking qualities of the reservation soils create sewage disposal problems that bring the tribe into conflict with Whatcom County officials.

Special Events: An important event is the annual Lummi Stommish Water Carnival featuring canoe racing between Lummi Island and the mainland. Coastal tribes, including those of British Columbia, compete in the eleven-man "war" canoes, which are fifty-odd feet long. The celebration is held near the middle of June. The date is contingent on the tides. It commemorates the end of hostilities between the Lummis and other tribes in 1821. Also included in the celebration are salmon barbecues and Indian games and dances, in which participants wear colorful costumes.

Suggested Readings: BIA Planning Support Group, Portland Area Office and the Western Washington Agency, *The Lummi Reservation: History, Present, Potential*, Report no. 220 (1974); Barbara Lane, "Anthropological Report on the Identity, Treaty Status, and Fisheries of the Lummi Tribe of Indians," submitted in *United States* v. *Washington*, May 10, 1973; Edmond S. Meany, "Legends, Traditions, and Present Condition of Lummi Indians," in Bagley Scrapbook no. 12 (1905), Pacific Northwest Collections, University of Washington; Ann Nugent, *The History of Lummi Fishing Rights* (Bellingham, Wash.: Lummi Communications, 1979); Ann Nugent, *Lummi Elders Speak* (Lynden, Wash.: Lynden Tribune, 1982); Ann Nugent, *Schooling of the Lummi Indians Between 1855–1956* (Bellingham, Wash.: Lummi Communications, 1981); Lottie Roeder Roth, *History of Whatcom County* (Chicago: Pioneer Historical Publishing Co., 1926); Bernhard J. Stern, *The Lummi Indians of Northwest Washington*, Co-

Lummi

A Lummi, circa 1920, in the warrior garb that the tribe wore in fights against tribesmen from as far away as northern British Columbia. As in the past, the Lummis are today a marine-oriented people. On their reservation, just west of Bellingham, Washington, they have an ambitious aquaculture program. Courtesy of the North Central Washington Museum Association.

113

lumbia University Contributions to Anthropology, No. 17 (1936; New York: AMS Press, 1969); John Stolpe, *A Look at the Lummis* (Bellingham, Wash.: Goliards Press, 1972); Wayne P. Suttles, *The Economic Life of the Coast Salish of Haro and Rosario Straits*, vol. 1 of *Coast Salish and Western Indians* (New York: Garland Publishing, Inc., 1974); Wayne P. Suttles, "Post-Contact Changes Among the Lummi Indians," *British Columbia Historical Quarterly* 18 nos. 1 and 2 (January–April, 1954); David G. Tremaine, *Indian and Pioneer Settlement of the Nooksack Lowland, Washington, to 1890*, Center for Pacific Northwest Studies Occasional Paper no. 4, (Bellingham, Wash.: Western Washington State College, 1975).

LUMMI TRIBE OF INDIANS

Under the Point Elliott Treaty on January 22, 1855, many tribes of northern Puget Sound were assigned to the Lummi Reservation. For an account of the ancestry of this group, known today as The Lummi Tribe of Indians, see **Lummi.**

LUMMI TRIBE OF INDIANS

Pauline Smith, 1989, of the Lummi Tribe of Indians. In the past several decades the tribe has revived the aboriginal Smokehouse religion in which some aspects of the once-secret society Black Tamanhous were practiced (youths were starved, bitten, and beaten until they hallucinated). In 1983 the state shut down a blackjack operation that the tribe had begun. The decree was lifted after the 1988 Federal Indian Gaming Regulator Act, as long as the tribe did not initiate a Class III gaming operation, which would require a state compact. The tribe declared its independence of BIA paternalism in 1991. The first tribal college established in the Pacific Northwest, the Northwest Indian College, is on the Lummi Reservation.

Maps

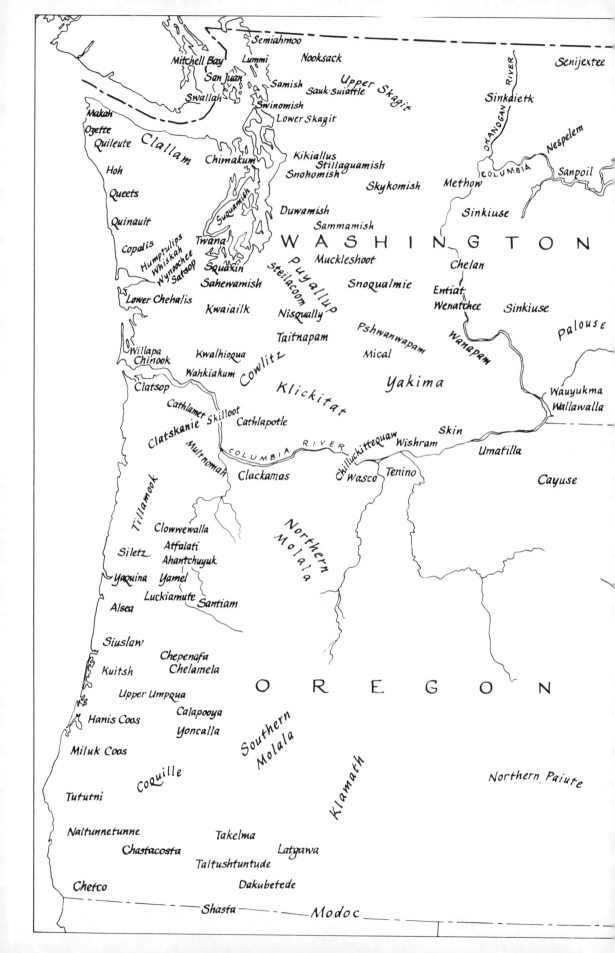

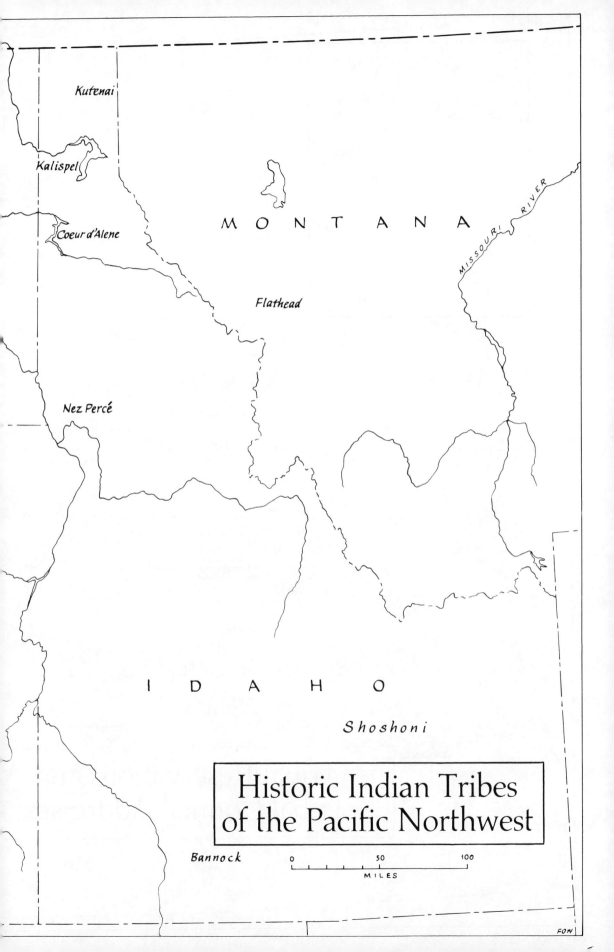

Kutenai

Kalispel

Coeur d'Alene

M O N T A N A

MISSOURI RIVER

Flathead

Nez Percé

I D A H O

Shoshoni

Historic Indian Tribes
of the Pacific Northwest

Bannock

0   50   100

MILES

FOW

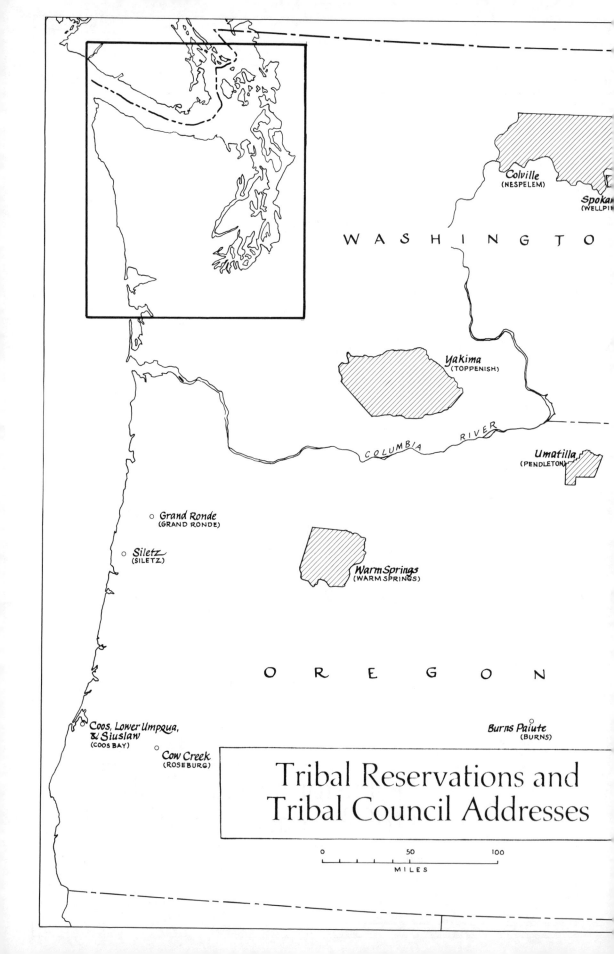

Colville
(NESPELEM)

Spoka[n]
(WELLPI[N]

W A S H I N G T O [N]

Yakima
(TOPPENISH)

COLUMBIA   RIVER

Umatilla
(PENDLETON)

○ Grand Ronde
(GRAND RONDE)

○ Siletz
(SILETZ)

Warm Springs
(WARM SPRINGS)

O R E G O N

Coos, Lower Umpqua,
& Siuslaw
(COOS BAY)

○ Cow Creek
(ROSEBURG)

Burns Paiute
(BURNS)

Tribal Reservations and
Tribal Council Addresses

0   50   100

MILES

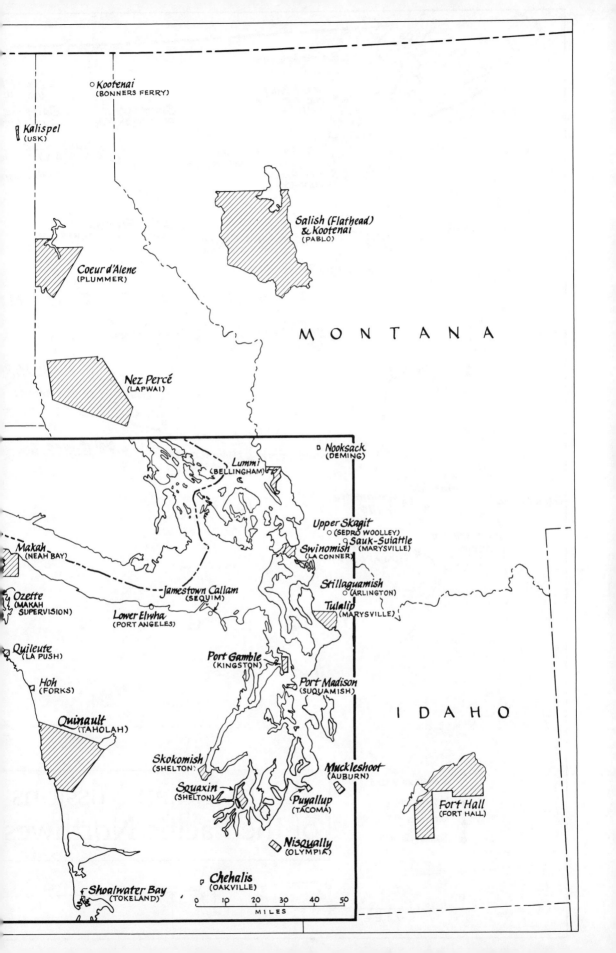

○ *Kootenai*
(BONNERS FERRY)

◘ *Kalispel*
(USK)

*Salish (Flathead)
& Kootenai*
(PABLO)

Coeur d'Alene
(PLUMMER)

M O N T A N A

Nez Percé
(LAPWAI)

□ *Nooksack*
(DEMING)

Lummi
(BELLINGHAM)

Upper Skagit
○ (SEDRO WOOLLEY)
○ *Sauk-Suiattle*
(MARYSVILLE)
Swinomish
(LA CONNER)

Makah
(NEAH BAY)

Stillaguamish
○ (ARLINGTON)

Ozette
(MAKAH
SUPERVISION)

— *Jamestown Callam*
(SEQUIM)

Tulalip
(MARYSVILLE)

Lower Elwha
(PORT ANGELES)

Quileute
(LA PUSH)

Port Gamble
(KINGSTON)

Hoh
(FORKS)

Port Madison
(SUQUAMISH)

I D A H O

Quinault
(TAHOLAH)

Skokomish
(SHELTON)

Muckleshoot
(AUBURN)

Squaxin
(SHELTON)

Puyallup
(TACOMA)

Fort Hall
(FORT HALL)

Nisqually
(OLYMPIA)

Chehalis
(OAKVILLE)

Shoalwater Bay
(TOKELAND)

0   10   20   30   40   50
M I L E S

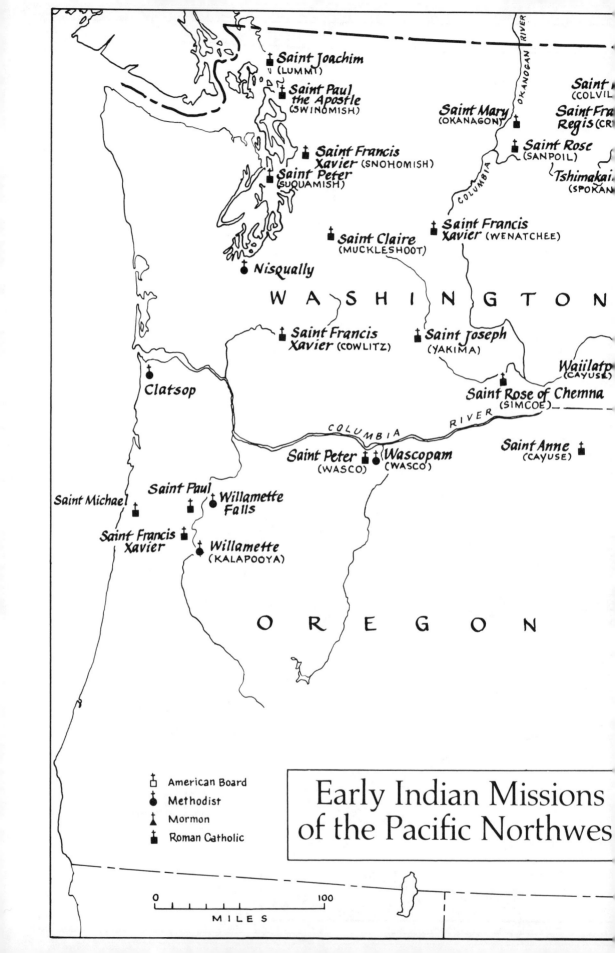

Saint Joachim
(LUMMI)

Saint Paul
the Apostle
(SWINOMISH)

Saint Mary
(OKANAGON)

Saint
(COLVIL...

Saint Fra...
Regis (CR...

Saint Rose
(SANPOIL)

Saint Francis
Xavier (SNOHOMISH)

Saint Peter
(SUQUAMISH)

Tshimakai...
(SPOKAN...

Saint Francis
Xavier (WENATCHEE)

Saint Claire
(MUCKLESHOOT)

Nisqually

W A S H I N G T O N

Saint Francis
Xavier (COWLITZ)

Saint Joseph
(YAKIMA)

Waiilatp...
(CAYUSE)

Clatsop

Saint Rose of Chemna
(SIMCOE)

COLUMBIA   RIVER

Saint Anne
(CAYUSE)

Saint Peter
(WASCO)

Wascopam
(WASCO)

Saint Paul

Willamette
Falls

Saint Michael

Saint Francis
Xavier

Willamette
(KALAPOOYA)

O R E G O N

† American Board
● Methodist
⚥ Mormon
◼ Roman Catholic

Early Indian Missions
of the Pacific Northwes...

0   100

M I L E S

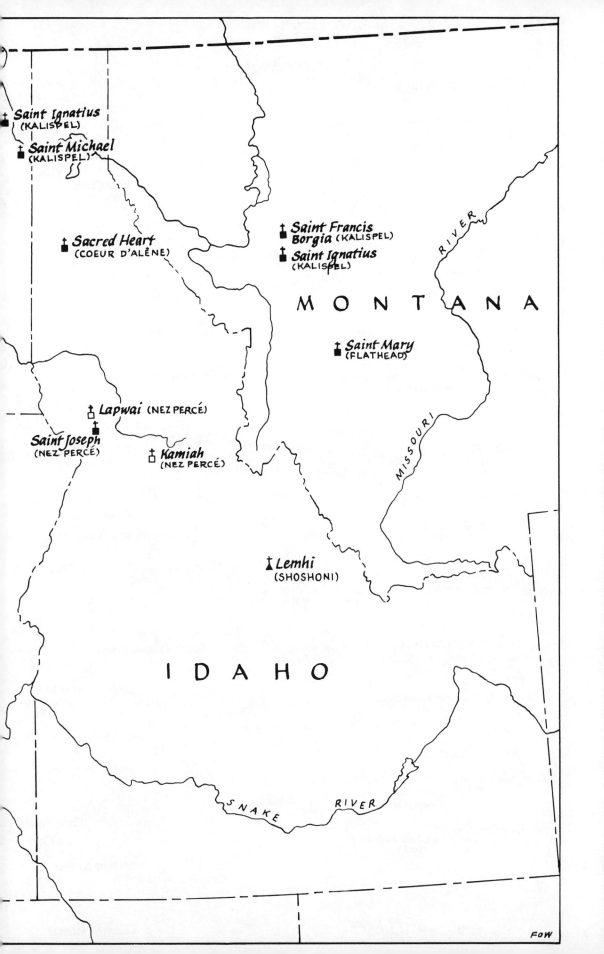

Saint Ignatius
(KALISPEL)

Saint Michael
(KALISPEL)

Saint Francis
Borgia (KALISPEL)

Saint Ignatius
(KALISPEL)

Sacred Heart
(COEUR D'ALÊNE)

M O N T A N A

Saint Mary
(FLATHEAD)

RIVER

Lapwai (NEZ PERCÉ)

Saint Joseph
(NEZ PERCÉ)

Kamiah
(NEZ PERCÉ)

MISSOURI

Lemhi
(SHOSHONI)

I D A H O

S N A K E   RIVER

FoW

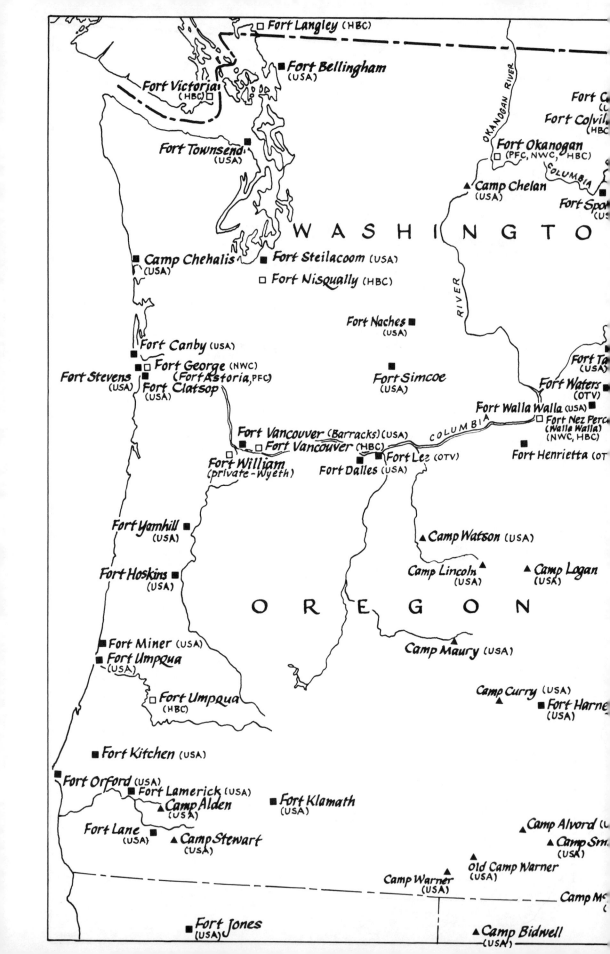

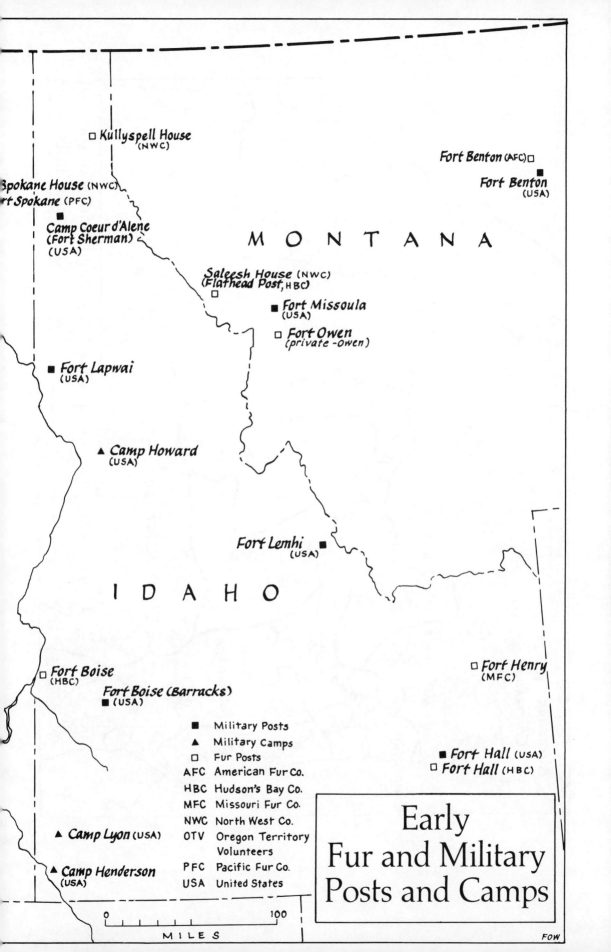

□ Kullyspell House
(NWC)

Fort Benton (AFC) □

Fort Benton
(USA) ■

Spokane House (NWC)
rt Spokane (PFC) ■

M O N T A N A

Camp Coeur d'Alene
(Fort Sherman)
(USA) ■

Saleesh House (NWC)
(Flathead Post, HBC) □

Fort Missoula ■
(USA)

Fort Owen □
(private - owen)

Fort Lapwai ■
(USA)

▲ Camp Howard
(USA)

Fort Lemhi ■
(USA)

I D A H O

Fort Boise □
(HBC)

Fort Henry □
(MFC)

Fort Boise (Barracks)
(USA) ■

■ Military Posts
▲ Military Camps
□ Fur Posts
AFC American Fur Co.
HBC Hudson's Bay Co.
MFC Missouri Fur Co.
NWC North West Co.
OTV Oregon Territory
      Volunteers
PFC Pacific Fur Co.
USA United States

Fort Hall (USA) ■
Fort Hall (HBC) □

▲ Camp Lyon (USA)

Early
Fur and Military
Posts and Camps

▲ Camp Henderson
(USA)

0   100

M I L E S

FOW

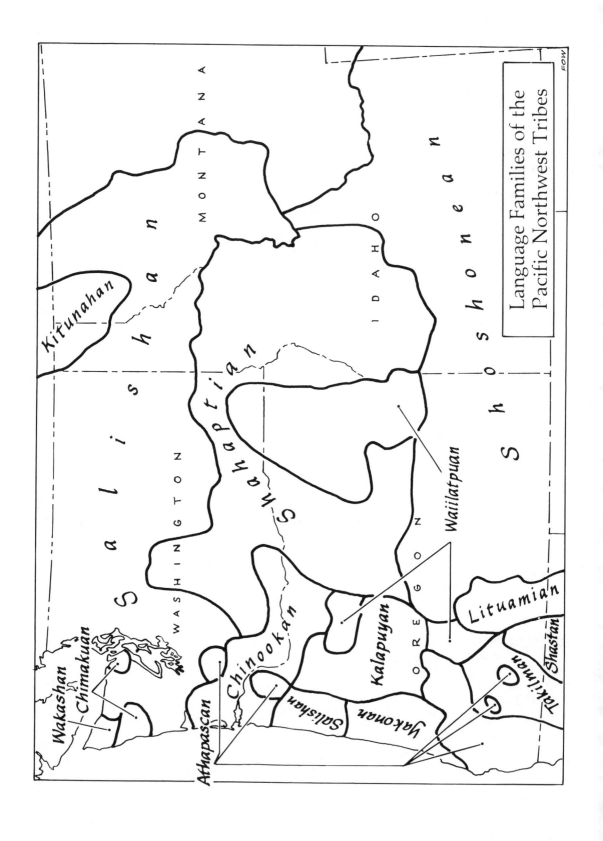

Language Families of the Pacific Northwest Tribes

MAKAH
(Wakashan)

With the exception of their southern branch, the Ozettes, the Makahs were the only people of Wakashan linguistic stock in the United States. Their name, originally a derisive Clallam word for them, derives from their location at Cape Flattery, the very tip of the continental United States in Washington state and means "the care people." They were also called by a name meaning "people who live on a point of land projecting into the sea" in the Wakashan tongue. The Makahs came to that area from Vancouver Island about five hundred years ago. Archaeological excavations and carbon-14 dating, however, indicate that the coastal village of the Ozette branch was occupied as long as 1,500 to 2,000 years ago. Another Makah village, Wa'atch, is believed to have been occupied 1,500 years ago, and its beach was used 1,000 years earlier.

The Makahs are remembered primarily for their intrepidity in hunting whales, which they canoed far out in the Pacific Ocean to harpoon. They buoyed up their prizes with skin floats and towed them ashore, where they processed and distributed them with much ceremony according to tribal custom. There was considerable interaction among the peoples of the five permanent Makah villages, leading some anthropologists to believe they were more truly a tribe than other native peoples of present-day Washington state. In historical times Makah villagers took slaves from other natives, but generally not from each other. Because they were isolated for so long from white settlement, the Makahs maintained a higher native blood quantum than did most other Pacific Northwestern peoples.

Location: Most Makahs today are of the Makah Tribe, Makah Reservation, Washington. Their reservation, lying at the north-west tip of the Olympic Peninsula, fronts both the Pacific Ocean and the Strait of Juan de Fuca.

Numbers: Tribal membership in 1985 was 919. In 1805–1806 they were estimated at 2,000. In 1853 the ethnologist George Gibbs placed their number at about 500. One cause of the severe decline in their population was the smallpox, which struck them in 1853. Some Makahs reportedly carried it home aboard ship from California. In 1861, the observer of Indians James Swan recorded 654 Makahs living in permanent villages. His figure was slightly higher than that given in government reports in 1870. The Makahs were numbered at 435 in 1905, 407 in 1937, and 550 in 1950.

History: The Makahs were similar in language and other cultural traits to the Nootkas, Wakashan speakers on Vancouver Island on the north. That suggests that the Makahs drifted south in precontact times, possibly five hundred years ago. Their early Nootkan association did not prevent them from joining their Ozette allies in conflicts with Nootkan peoples, such as the Nitinats on the southwest coast of Vancouver Island. The Makahs also fought tribes on the south, such as the Quileutes, the Hohs, the Quinaults, and the Queetses. In 1788, during the early contact period, the British sloop *Princess Royal*, commanded by Charles Duncan, anchored within the Strait of Juan de Fuca at the Makah village of Classet. On April 3, 1789, Neah Bay, whose name derives from that of the Makah village Deah, was visited and described by the Boston trader Robert Haswell. In 1790, under their chief, Tutusi, the Makahs traded at Neah Bay with some Spaniards under their commander Manuel Quimper. Impressed with a Spanish show of force after the natives wounded a soldier who had strayed from camp to molest a native woman, Tutusi kept on peaceful terms with his white visitors. In 1791 the Spanish explorer Francisco de Eliza visited Neah Bay, where for thirty-three sheets of copper he purchased twenty small boys and girls. In 1792 the Spaniards returned, aboard the brig *Princesa*, and established the colony of Núñez Gaona, primarily to check British moves across the strait. From these Spaniards the Makahs received what was perhaps their first major introduction to European culture. Conflict between them and the Spaniards caused the commander, Salvador Fidalgo to abandon the place to the natives, whom he described as "warlike, treacherous and thievish." Conflicts followed with other white mariners, such as the British Capt. George Vancouver in 1792. With the decline of the sea-otter trade in the early nineteenth century, Makah contacts with whites became less frequent. During the Hudson's Bay Company era they occasionally traded with personnel aboard the Bay Company's ships and at Fort Nisqually, which the company established in 1833 at the southern end of Puget Sound. Also in 1833, the Makahs enslaved three of the crew of a wrecked Japanese junk, holding them until they were ransomed by a Bay Company official. After the beaching of a Russian vessel on Makah shores around 1840, there was an infusion of Caucasion blood among these natives.

The Makahs were party to a treaty effected with Washington Territorial Governor and Superintendent of Indian Affairs Isaac Stevens at Neah Bay on January 31, 1855. Among its provisions was the establishment of the Makah Reservation, which was enlarged by executive orders on October 26, 1872, and January 2 and October 21, 1873. On their reservation the Makahs did not become agrarians that the government wished them to be. Not only was their land unsuited for such enterprises, but also elderly tribesmen, having faced the dangers of whaling and other kinds of hunting, ridiculed younger men for "digging in the earth like squaws."

Government officials pressured the unwilling Makahs to send their children to agency schools. At the same time the officials came to realize that it was almost impossible to alter the ways of the elderly tribesmen. The enrollment in an industrial school at the agency was seventy. A police force was established, and in 1882 an attempt made to establish an Indian court. There was friction not only between tribal members and agency officials but also among the officials themselves. In 1869, Makah agent Harry A. Webster traveled to Washington, D.C., to defend himself from the charge, among others, that he had traded with natives for dogfish oil and furs at his store on the edge of the reservation. Until the later nineteenth century the Makahs sent war parties against other American tribes, such as the Clallams, and against Canadian tribes, such as the Sookes and Nitinats of Vancouver Island.

The Makahs' economy continued to center around the sea. In the late 1880s they hunted seals from aboard ships owned by whites. By the end of the century they not only owned their own ships but also hired whites to work for them. By then many of the traditions and ceremonials attending their maritime pursuits had disappeared. Allotment of agricultural lands on the reservation was delayed until 1907, when each Indian received ten acres. Tracts were reserved for schools and other purposes on lands adjoining the townsite of Neah Bay. In 1931 the relative isolation of the reservation and its peoples was broken by the completion of an automobile road to Neah Bay.

Government and Claims: In 1934 the Makah Tribe, Makah Reservation, Washington, voted to accept the Indian Reorganization Act (48 Stat. 984). They received their constitution in 1936 and their tribal charter the next year. The first tribal chairman was Maquinna Jongie Claplanhoo, whose first name was that of a powerful eighteenth-century Nootka chief. At the time of the passage of the Indian Reorganization Act, the trust period for the Makah Reservation had not expired. The land, reconverted into a tribal trust, was protected from aliena-

METHOW
(Interior Division, Salishan)

The Methows (or Mitois) lived mainly on the river bearing their name, which enters the Columbia River in north-central Washington at the town of Pateros on U.S. Highway 97. Besides the river, a valley and a town in that valley bear the tribal name. The Methows spoke an Okanagon dialect of the Interior Salishan language. In earlier times, before they lost their old speech forms, their dialect belonged to the Columbia-Wenatchi dialect cluster.

Some have suggested that Methows inhabited the eleven scattered lodges of the Metcowwees that the American explorers Meriwether Lewis and William Clark found on the Columbia north bank a few miles above and across from the John Day River. That seems unlikely, though upper Columbia River peoples sometimes traveled as far south as the John Day River to trade. In 1811 the North West Company trader David Thompson visited the tribe at their salmon fisheries at the mouth of the Methow River. He called them Smeathhowes and wrote that they knew little of the Columbia River below their own lands. In 1814, Alexander Ross of the North West Company visited the Methows, whom he called the Battle-le-mule-emauhs, on the Salmon Falls (later the Methow) River. He described them as "in all respects exceedingly kind." Thompson had assessed them in a similar manner.

The Methows' 1780 numbers have been estimated at 800, including the Sinkiuses (Moses Columbias). In the early 1870s they were listed at 300, an equally misleading statistic because it included other bands between the Methow and Wenatchee rivers. Because of their low numbers, the Methows played a minor role in nineteenth-century conflicts between Indians and whites. In the later part of the century the tribe came under the jurisdiction of the Colville Agency. Wishing to retain their traditional independence, they kept aloof from agency officials. One Methow band, the Chilliwists, wintered on the Lower Okanogan River, wedged between two Sinkaietk bands.

Methow

Methow George and his wife, Jennie, circa 1910. One of the few bearded Indians, George drowned in the Methow River, a Columbia affluent in north-central Washington. At the time of his death he was a reported 104 years of age. Among the first white men to visit his people was the fur trader-explorer David Thompson in 1811. Courtesy of the North Central Washington Museum Association.

The Methows had small farms and enclosures in which they planted corn and potatoes after their contact with white men. Around 1870 a Methow band traveled to Walla Walla to purchase agricultural tools. The Methows also did considerable trading with whites in Ellensburg in the Kittitas valley on the south. Some Methows, whose tribal lands lay within the Moses, or Columbia, Reservation, accepted 640-acre allotments under provisions of the Moses Agreement of July 7, 1883. Accepting Chief Moses' leadership, other Methows settled with him and his people in the Nespelem valley of the Colville Reservation. Today there is no Methow tribe as such. From early times until the later nineteenth century, the Methow valley had been the tribe's domain and gathering place, where local Indians had gathered on their return from fall hop picking in the Yakima valley. Today the Methow valley is filled with orchards, small farms, towns, and tourist facilities. In an attempt to preserve the Methow language, courses in it have been offered in a nearby community college. See **Confederated Tribes of the Colville Reservation, Washington.**

Suggested Readings: James A. Teit, *The Middle Columbia Salish, University of Washington Publications in Anthropology* 2, no. 4 (1928); James A. Teit, "The Salishan Tribes of the Western Plateaus," *Forty-fifth Annual Report of the Bureau of American Ethnology* (Washington, D.C.: Government Printing Office, 1930).

MICAL
(Shahaptian)

The now-extinct Micals lived on the upper courses of the Nisqually River, a Puget Sound affluent in Washington state. Their dialect of the Shahaptian language closely resembled that of the Pshwanwapams, a Kittitas band of Upper Yakimas, who were just east of the Cascade Mountains in the upper watershed of the Yakima River, a Columbia River affluent. It also resembled that of the Shahaptian-speaking Klickitats and Taitnapams. Some anthropologists believe that the Micals were joined by some Pshwanwapams migrating west over the summit of the Cascade Mountains and by others of that cluster of tribes of similar dialect.

Suggested Readings: Melville Jacobs, "A Sketch of Northern Sahaptin Grammar," *University of Washington Publications in Anthropology* 4 no. 2 (1931), 85–292; Leslie Spier, *Tribal Distribution in Washington,* American Anthropological Association, General Series in Anthropology, no. 3 (Menasha, Wis.: George Banta Publishing Company, 1936).

MILUK COOS
(Yakonan)

The Miluk Coos (or Koweses) were also called Lower Coquilles. They formed the southern dialect division of the Kusan linguistic family, of which the Hanis Coos spoke the northern dialect. Both Coos tribes lived in what is now southwestern Oregon. The word *coos* is said to mean "on the south," "lagoon" or "lake," and "place of pines." The Miluk Coos had two villages. The Miluks proper lived on the north, up the Coos River estuary from the Pacific Ocean; and the Nasomahs lived on the south, as far as the estuary of the Coquille River, a Pacific Ocean affluent near present-day Bandon. Some authorities maintain, however, that there were two other Miluk Coos villages. A bay, county, and city in southwestern Oregon bear the Coos tribal name. The Miluk and Hanis Coos population was estimated to have been at 2,000 in 1780, about 500 more than were believed to exist in 1805–1806. In 1871 there were 136 Cooses at the Alsea Subagency of the Siletz Reservation. In 1910 the combined Coos numbers were given at 93; in 1930, at 107; and in 1937, at 55.

The Miluk Coos obtained subsistence from the sea, from which they gathered foods such as clams. From the land they gathered camas and other roots and berries. Wood was important not only for their housing but also for their transport in canoes dug out of logs. These craft were of the Klamath type. They were shorter and shallower than those of the Chinooks and had no distinct bows. The Miluks inhumed their dead in graves, which they often lined with cedar planks and accoutered with possessions of the deceased. Like other Oregon coastal peoples, they held slaves, and on occasion they were in turn enslaved by natives, such as the Coquilles, who raided them.

The Coos traded with white ships' crews at least from the time that Capt. George Vancouver visited them in 1792. They traded with Hudson's Bay Company fur men after 1826, when an employee of that company, Alexander McLeod, traveled overland to their country. Shortly after that contact, they were found with metal weapons, including an occasional gun, and European clothes, though generally they remained aloof, finding little value in the white man's money and other trade articles, such as clothing. A few Miluk Coos of the Nasomah branch and their relatives, the Upper Coquilles (Mishikhwutmetunnes), along with other Athapascan-speaking peoples of the area, signed a treaty with Oregon Superintendent of Indian Affairs Anson Dart on September 20, 1851.

After an Indian guide misled W. G. T'Vault and his party, as they searched for an overland route between the coast and the Willamette valley, some natives, most probably Miluks, on September 14, 1851, attacked the party at the mouth of the Coquille River. Their weapons—bows and arrows, war clubs, and knives—were made from iron from the vessel *William G. Hagstaff*, which previously had wrecked near present-

Miluk Coos

The ancestors of this Miluk Coos family of southwestern Oregon had traded with white mariners at least from the time of Capt. George Vancouver, who visited them in 1792. They accepted white ways slowly, but eventually made a rather complete surrender to them, as shown in this picture posed in a studio circa 1893. Courtesy Coos-Curry Museum and Historical Society.

day Port Orford. Wading into the water, the natives attacked before the T'Vault party could ready its rifles. It is said the Indians caused eight whites to be killed or drowned in the attack. By swimming to the opposite shore, T'Vault escaped. As a result of retaliatory attacks by whites, the natives in late November, 1851, lost fifteen killed and

131

many wounded. Their villages and stores were also destroyed. In the ensuing months the whites, mostly miners, continued their retaliation. With little provocation they shot and hanged the natives. In response to a message from whites, the chief Tie-John in early 1854 vowed to kill every white man coming against him. On the night of January 28, 1854, a group called Minute Men of the nearby town of Randolph surprised a Coquille village. Randolph, earlier called Whiskey Run, was six miles north of the mouth of the Coquille River, where gold had been discovered. In an ensuing attack the Minute Men killed sixteen men and wounded four others and many women and children. The vengeful miners also captured some elderly men and put their village, including the canoes, to the torch. Chief Tie-John and his braves escaped. Shortly after that the chief was forced to sue for peace. Three captured braves were hanged at Randolph. In another fight, in the spring of 1855, the Indians lost fifteen men killed and thirty-two women and children captured. In November of that year an Indian agent, Ben Wright, dissuaded an armed party of Coos Bay whites from destroying Coos camps, but later that month settlers, on rumors of a native attack, assaulted the Coos on the lower Coquille, killing four and hanging four others.

Aware that the gold diggings would soon be exhausted, whites saw opportunities for settlement in the fertile lands of the Coquille River valley. On August 11, 1855, Oregon Superintendent of Indian Affairs Joel Palmer made a treaty with several tribes of the Oregon coast, including Coos peoples. During the Rogue Wars, which ended in 1856, Coos were generally peacefully disposed to whites, despite harassment by them. During the war years they remained under the guard of the Coos County Volunteers at Empire City (Coos Bay). At the end of the war they were temporarily lodged under the guard of a subagent stationed on the north side of the mouth of the Umpqua River. They were also kept under surveillance by troops from nearby Fort Umpqua. With closure of the Umpqua Subagency on September 3, 1859, the Coos with Umpquas, numbering about 460 in all, were sent northward to Yachats on the Siletz Reservation (later the Alsea) to live with the Siuslaw Indians. Their mode of life there included the cultivation of gardens, but repeated crop failures reduced these nonfarmers to starvation. With the 1875 closure of the Alsea Reservation, the Coos and Kuitshes drifted down the coast to Coos Bay, where, after the beginning of the twentieth century, they purchased a 6.1-acre reservation on western Coos Bay.

With Kuitshes and Siuslaws the Coos met at Coos Bay in 1916-17 to organize and to plan a suit against the federal government to seek compensation for their lost lands. Their suit (Case No. K-345) was not decided until May 2, 1938, at which time the Court of Claims ruled the Indian testimony inadmissible because of inadequate documentation. The United States Supreme Court on November 14, 1938, refused to hear their subsequent appeal. Between 1947 and 1951, despite additional evidence based on the words of fur trappers, diarists, Indian agents, and others, the Indian Claims Commission refused to hear their case, maintaining that they had already had their day in court. The descendants of Miluk Coos who, until the midtwentieth century, had been members of the Coos Tribe of Indians and were able to prove Coquille (Mishikhwutmetunne) ancestry, shared in an award of $847,190.40 by the Court of Claims (Case No. 45230) for the Coquilles' land cession, after a Supreme Court ruling on April 6, 1951, that interest would be disallowed. This award immediately caused a schism in the Coos Tribe of Indians. Those sharing in the award became affiliated with the Coquille Indian Tribe, who are also based at Coos Bay (see **Coos Tribe of Indians** and **Coquille Indian Tribe**. For information on present-day Coos social programs, see **Hanis Coos**. For details of their reservation life and claims see **Siuslaw**.)

Suggested Readings: Stephen Dow Beckham, *The Indians of Western Oregon: This Land Was Theirs* (Coos Bay, Ore.: Arago Books, 1977); Leo J. Frachtenberg, *Coos Texts*, Columbia University Contributions to American Anthropology, no. 1, (New York, 1913); Leo J. Frachtenberg, *Lower Umpqua Texts and Notes on the Kusan Dialects*, Columbia University Contributions to American Anthropology, no. 4 (New York, 1914); Melville Jacobs, "Coos Myth Texts," *University of Washington Publications in Anthropology*, 8 no. 2 (Seattle, 1940); Melville Jacobs, "Coos Narrative and Ethnologic Texts," *University of Washington Publications in Anthropology* 8 no. 1 (Seattle, 1939); Henry Hull St. Clair and Leo Frachtenberg, "Traditions of the Coos Indians," *Journal of American Folklore* 13 (1909), 25–44.

MISHIKHWUTMETUNNE
(See **Coquille**)

MITCHELL BAY

The Mitchell Bay Indians are descendants of natives who for generations lived in the San Juan Islands of Washington state and on lower Vancouver Island in British Columbia. Their name, apparently given them by a special Indian agent in 1919, refers to a tribal settlement on Mitchell Bay on the northwestern shores of San Juan Island, the largest in the archipelago of that name.

The Mitchell Bays still live primarily in the San Juan Islands and at other places in the Puget Sound area. Their ancestors spoke a Lkungen dialect of the Coastal Salishan language. They claim that the ancestral village, Taleqamus, was composed of three Songish subdivisions. It lay on the western shore of San Juan Island. Archaeologists have found it to have been very populous. Other Songish villages were on Open Bay on Henry Island, on Garrison and Wescott bays on San Juan Island, and opposite Spieden Island on San Juan Island. In the 1850s and 1860s, during the controversy between Great Britain and the United States over location of the international boundary, the Pig War was "fought" mainly on San Juan Island. Ancestors of the Mitchell Bays remained friendly to representatives of both nations, trading with each. After the Fraser River gold discoveries in Canada in the late 1850s and early 1860s, whites settled in the San Juan Islands. Their presence contributed to the decline of the already dwindling native population. In 1919, 181 Mitchell Bays were reported. In 1980 the tribe numbered over 100.

Apparently the first governmental mention of a Mitchell Bay tribe was in a report for the Office of Indian Affairs by Charles Roblin, who conducted a survey between 1916 and 1918 of homeless and landless Indians. Operating under a five-member council, the tribe seeks federal acknowledgement and the accompanying fishing rights. The economy of the Mitchell Bays, like that of their ancestors, depends principally on fishing. In 1982 the Department of the Interior defined the Mitchell Bay Indians as a "group" of Indians who are similar to the "San Juan Island Indians." In 1957 the group filed a claim under the latter name with the Indian Claims Commission (Docket 214), which was denied on the grounds that the group was descended primarily from Lummis and Samishes and therefore the claim was covered under the claims of those tribes. Presumably the group is quite labile, having had members within it from Canadian tribes. See **San Juan Tribe of Indians.**

MODOC
(Lutuamian)

The name Modoc stems from the native word for "southerners," indicating that it may have been given the tribe by northern neighbors, such as the Klamaths. Today a county bears the name, as well as Modoc Point, Oregon. Formerly, Tule and Clear lakes were known as the Modoc Lakes. Several places in the central and southern United States bear the name Modoc.

The Modocs lived in what today are the Oregon-California borderlands, on Lower Klamath, Modoc, Tule, and Clear lakes and in the Lost River valley. At times their territory extended to Goose Lake. Historically, they were closely associated with the Klamaths and perhaps drifted with them into the lakes district of southern Oregon and northern California as early as the fifteenth century. The two peoples separated after the middle of the eighteenth century, but were later rejoined.

The Modocs are remembered for their stubborn but futile resistance to American troops and their Indian scouts in the Lava Beds of northern California in 1872 and 1873. Their 1780 numbers have been variously estimated at from 400 to 800. In 1905 there were 56 on the Quapaw Agency in Indian Territory (Oklahoma), where they were sent after their defeat except for 223 who remained on the Klamath Reservation. Of 282 Modocs in 1910, 212 lived in Oregon, 33 in Oklahoma, and 20 in California. The remainder were scattered among at least five other states. In 1937 there were a reported 329 Modocs. Today they are incorporated with other Indian tribes, especially the Klamaths, under whose standard Modoc descendants were involved in the mid-twentieth-century termination of the Klamath Reservation.

The Modocs hunted deer, antelope, and mountain sheep, as well as rabbit and squirrel. They also gathered roots and seeds, most commonly the *wocus*, a species of water lily that was sought by the Klamaths also. They also caught and dried fish. In aboriginal times they made their clothing of grass or tule fiber and animal skins decorated with shell beadwork, plus belts of braided grass. By the middle of the nineteenth century they had adopted European-style clothing. Before 1800 they set their lodges in excavations that were a half foot to four feet deep and from twelve to twenty feet wide. The frameworks of willow poles were covered with tule matting plus layers of earth. They traveled on their lakes in dugout log canoes or rafts of tule bundles. They did not acquire horses until about 1825.

The Modocs' initial contacts with whites were with fur traders around 1825 when Hudson's Bay Company brigades traversed their lands. For the next fifteen years the brigades, mostly en route to California, scarcely altered Modoc living patterns.

During a severe winter around 1830, tribal food caches were lost in deep snow drifts that obliterated natural landmarks. Consequently, many Modocs died from starvation huddling in their lodges. On one occasion some Modocs were saved from starvation when an antelope herd plunged into Tule Lake in front of their village.

Not until around 1835 did some Modocs travel northward to The Dalles of the Columbia River. Although impressed with the goods traded there, they initially had little to exchange for them. Later they discovered that female slaves brought good prices at that native market. In the following decade Modocs mercilessly raided neighboring California tribes, the Pit Rivers and the Shastas, for human spoils, from the sales of which they acquired horses. Usually they did not take their slaves to The Dalles, but traded them to middlemen, such as the Klamaths and the Teninos, who went there.

During the 1840s and 1850s the Modocs' contacts with whites were sporadic. Among the white travelers who interrupted their isolation was Capt. John C. Frémont, who entered their lands in December, 1843, and again in May, 1846. In 1846 Frémont's party traveled northward to around Klamath Marsh, where Klamaths attacked and killed four of its number. The noted western scout Kit Carson, who was with Frémont, returned to burn the Klamath village in retaliation. In July of that same year a fifteen-man party worked its way east from the Willamette valley through the Klamath and the Modoc lands, laying out the Scott-Applegate Road, which was a circuitous southern detour from the main Immigrant Road (the Oregon Trail) by which immigrants entered the Willamette valley. In the late summer and early fall of 1846 Modocs attacked immigrants traveling the route.

In 1847 and 1848 many Modocs succumbed to the measles carried by immigrants into their lands, but by 1849 these natives were strong enough to resume raiding white travelers. On one occasion they killed eighteen at a place, known to Oregon pioneers as Bloody Point, where the Applegate Road first strikes Tule Lake after its long descent from the highlands around Clear Lake. Equally upsetting to Modocs were the miners who traversed their lands en route to California after gold was discovered there in 1848. Two years later gold was discovered near Yreka, California, near the Modoc country, and more miners trespassed their lands. By summer, 1851, hundreds of whites had occupied Modoc lands, which many of them farmed. Confrontations with the natives caused the whites to organize vigilante groups, against which the Modocs retaliated by more attacks at Bloody Point. Despite provocations they kept out of the Rogue Wars of the 1850s. They were, however, harmed by them, because the whites, after defeating the Indians of the Rogue country, more easily imposed their culture on other tribes in southern Oregon. The Modocs abandoned the slave trade, but their women drifted into prostitution and performed domestic tasks for whites in exchange for money, much of which went for liquor.

When whites grew adamant about removing Indians to reservations, some Modocs, such as Old Schonchin and his band, were willing to remove; but not Captain Jack (Keintpoos) and his band, who knew that whites coveted their lands in the Lost River and Tule Lake countries on which to graze their stock. The upshot of the white pressures was a treaty effected October 14,

Modoc

Hooka (or Hooker) Jim, a Modoc prisoner taken in the war between his people and American troops in the Lava Beds, today a National Monument in north-central California. After eluding the troops, the Modocs, under Captain Jack, were forced to surrender, but unlike Captain Jack, Hooka Jim escaped trial and punishment after the war.

135

1864, with the Modocs, Klamaths, and Ya-huskins (Northern Paiutes), by which those tribes agreed to remove to a reservation in the Klamath country. Since the confine was outside their own lands, the Modocs and Yahuskins signed reluctantly. They were perhaps influenced to sign because the Wal-papis (Northern Paiutes) under Chief Paulina were attacking the Modocs and Klamaths, who saw a possible ally in the United States military. American officials preferred to deal with Chief Schonchin instead of his rival, Captain Jack, who repudiated his own signature on the treaty and left the Klamath Reservation in 1865. Despite pressures from the white community for his return, Jack kept aloof from the confine, while Schon-chin moved his people from the main Kla-math Agency to that at Yainax about thirty-five miles to the east, where they suffered starvation and opposition from the Kla-maths. In council on Lost River, December 23, 1869, Jack and 43 of his band agreed to remove to the Klamath Reservation, where they too suffered starvation and Klamath indignities. In April, 1870, Jack and nearly all the Modocs, about 375 in all, abandoned the reservation for the Lost River country. To survive in that bare-bone country, they demanded rent from area whites. When the latter refused to pay it, Jack and his men raided the stock of passing immigrants. He wished to avoid the Klamath Reservation and insisted on one in his own lands, a request that American officials refused.

Late in 1872 troops closed in on Jack's camp. Thus began the Modoc War, in which three Modoc bands of only 170 souls with-stood 1,000 American troops and settlers, who tried for several months to dislodge them from the fastness of what is now the Lava Beds National Monument in the Tule and Klamath lake basins. Worn down by attrition, the Modocs ended their war on June 1, 1873, when Jack and his chiefs were captured and confined at Fort Klamath. There he and three others were hanged, and two had death sentences commuted to life imprisonment on Alcatraz Island. In Octo-ber, 1873, 153 Modoc prisoners were set-tled on the Quapaw Agency in Indian Ter-ritory.

In 1902 the Modocs in Indian Territory sent representatives to the Klamaths, seek-ing their permission to return to the Kla-math Reservation. Twenty-one returned in 1903 to settle on the northeastern portion of that reservation. In 1909 the Modocs who had remained on the Quapaw were given the option of selling their lands and returning to Oregon to allot on the Klamath, or keeping and leasing their lands on the Quapaw. The present-day Modoc Tribe of Oklahoma, which has a government-to-government relationship with the United States, is descended from Modocs who re-mained in Oklahoma and some of the others who went west but returned to Oklahoma to join their fellow tribesmen.

After the return of forty-seven Modocs to the Klamath Reservation from Okla-homa, the Modocs and Klamaths in time became assimilated. In 1964 there were but seven or eight Modocs speaking their native language, and today, largely through inter-marriage, there are none of full blood. As people of the Klamath Reservation, Modoc descendants shared in the termination of the Klamath tribe's trust relationship with the United States in 1954. About 300 of them live today in the area of Chiloquin, about thirty miles north of Klamath Falls, Oregon. See **Klamath.**

Suggested Readings: S. A. Barrett, "The Material Culture of the Klamath and Modoc Indians," *University of California Publications In Ameri-can Archaeology and Ethnology* 5 (1907–1910); Jeremiah Curtin, *Myths of the Modocs* (New York: B. Bloom, 1912); Ivan Doig, "[Edward] Fox Among the Modocs," *Pacific Search about Nature and Man in the Pacific Northwest* 10, no. 7 (May, 1976); A. B. Meacham, *Wigwam and War-Path; Or The Royal Chief in Chains* (Boston: John P. Dale & Co., 1875); A. B. Mea-cham, *Wi-Ne-Ma (The Woman-Chief.) And Her People* (Hartford, Conn.: American Publishing Co., 1876); Keith A. Murray, *The Modocs and Their War* (Norman: University of Oklahoma Press, 1959); Verne F. Ray, *Primitive Pragma-tists: The Modoc Indians of Northern California* (Seattle: University of Washington Press, 1963); Jeff C. Riddle, *The Indian History of the Modoc War and the Causes that Led to It* (Eugene, Ore.: Urion Press, 1914).

MOLALA
(Waiilatpuan)

In early times the Molalas were neighbors of the Cayuses and were thought to have shared the same linguistic stock with them. Anthropologists now disagree with this contention. They lived near the eastern slopes of the Cascade Mountains of central Oregon near the Warm Springs River, a tributary of the Deschutes, which in turn flows into the Columbia. Less aggressive than the Cayuses, the Molalas were pushed westward sometime after 1780 by more aggressive tribes of the Oregon interior. Some anthropologists once believed those aggressors to be Northern Paiutes pushing north, but now it is believed that pressure came from even more aggressive Teninos pushing south on the horseless Paiutes.

The Molalas split into two groups. The Southern, or Lower, Molalas migrated to lands around headwaters of the Umpqua and Rogue rivers of southern Oregon. The Northern, or Upper, Molalas remained primarily in the Willamette watershed, west of Mount Hood in the Molalla River country and on the south in the Santiam River watershed. Even in their new homes, they were still occasionally raided by the Cayuses. Besides holding the northeastern slopes of the Willamette country, the Northern Molalas claimed its bottomland hunting grounds, which they left in the hands of the peacefully disposed Kalapuyan peoples. Today the river and city of Molalla in the region bear the tribal name.

The Molalas lived in mat houses in summer and in mud-covered semisubterranean houses in winter. Both the Northern and the Southern Molalas were closely related to the Klamaths, who called them a name meaning "people of the serviceberry tract," and in early times ridiculed them for their incorrect use of the Klamath language.

From the Molalas the Klamaths obtained elk-horn spoons in exchange for the *wocus* lily roots of the Klamath Marsh. In 1780 the Molalas and Cayuses combined numbered an estimated 500; and in 1848, 200. In 1851 there were 123 Northern Molalas. In 1870 there were 74 Molalas on the Grand Ronde Reservation, and in 1881, 55 on the Klamath Reservation. In 1910 there were but 31 Molalas, 6 of whom lived outside Oregon.

After a disturbance between whites and Molalas, in 1846, a volunteer company marched to a Molala settlement, where the troubles were resolved. In March, 1848, when some Klamaths traveled north along the Klamath Trail to the Silverton, Oregon, country to camp with some Molalas, frightened settlers wanting them removed engaged them in what was known as the Abiqua War. In the two days of fighting thirteen Klamaths were reported killed, and one was wounded, as was a white man.

Molala subsistence patterns were disrupted not only by encroaching whites but by laws, such as that passed by the Oregon Territorial Legislature in 1854 prohibiting sales of firearms to Indians. Such a ban forced Molalas and other Indians to resort to their aboriginal weapons to secure what little game remained.

On May 6 and 7, 1851, at Champoeg, Oregon Territory, two treaties were made with the Northern Molalas for cession of their lands to the United States. Effecting the treaty on behalf of the government was a commission under Superintendent of Indian Affairs Anson Dart, which, unbeknownst to its members, had been stripped of its authority by Congress two months earlier. Signing on May 6 for the 58-member "main band" of Molalas were their chiefs, Quai-eck-e-ete, Yal-kus, and Crooked Finger. The latter was killed in Clackamas County, Oregon, by a settler. Signing on May 7 for the 65 Santiam Molalas was their chief, Coast-no. It had been the original intent of Superintendent Dart to obtain the consent of Indians west of the Cascade Mountains to be moved east of that range, but the Molalas, like other Willamette Indians, refused to leave their homes. That they had originally lived east of the Cascade Mountains was of little importance to them. On January 9, 1855, with the Clackamases, Clowwewallas, and others, they signed a

137

Molala

Fred Yelkis, a Molala. The Molalas originally lived in central Oregon, but were pushed west of the Cascade Mountains by other tribesmen. Once there, they divided into northern and southern branches of the tribe. Courtesy of the Smithsonian Institution (photographer and date unknown).

treaty (10 Stat. 1143, ratified March 3, 1855) ceding all of the Willamette valley to the United States. They also agreed to remove to a reservation at such time and place that one should be established for them. Before they were removed, as war clouds were forming over the Yakima country in the interior on the northeast, Oregon Superintendent of Indian Affairs Joel Palmer issued a proclamation on October 13, 1855, ordering the Willamette valley Indians to remain in temporarily designated areas. Whites regarded their absence from those designated areas without permission as dangerous to the peace of the region. Indians who were unable to account for their presence outside those areas were to be arrested, retained in custody, and sent to county jails or to the military Fort Vancouver.

The temporary reservation of the main band of Northern Molalas was on Silver Creek at the base of the Cascade Mountains. The reservation of the Molalas in the Santiam area was quite mountainous with some agricultural lands, parts of which whites claimed as their own. When on October 8, 1855, the Rogue Wars flared anew, Superintendent Palmer persuaded the Southern Molala chief and about thirty of his tribe to go on the Umpqua Reservation in the Umpqua valley. The group arrived there on November 7, 1855. Because of actual and potential conflicts with whites, the Southern Molalas signed a treaty on December 21, 1855 (12 Stat. 981, ratified March 8,

1859 and proclaimed April 27, 1859), by which they were persuaded to cede their lands, confederate with the Yoncallas and the Upper Umpquas, and remove with those tribes to the headwaters of the Yamhill River, an area later known as the Grand Ronde. Having started on January 10, 1856, these peoples arrived on the Grand Ronde Reservation on February 2, 1856. Later they were moved to the reservation established on November 9, 1856, on the coast that was later called the Siletz. On April 3, 1950, descendants of the Southern Molalas were awarded $34,996.85 by the Court of Claims (Case No. 45231) for recovery of the Umpqua Reservation lands reserved for them by the December 21, 1855, treaty in which they had confederated with the Umpquas and the Yoncallas. That treaty had stated that they would share in the Umpqua Reservation, but they never occupied any portion of it. After only two months' residency there they were removed to the Grand Ronde.

No one today speaks the Molala language. Pacific Northwest newspapers used to carry stories of the last of various Oregon tribesmen. One such story appeared in the Portland *Journal* on July 3, 1957, reporting Fred Yelkis to be the last of the Molala tribe.

Suggested Reading: Albert S. Gatschet, "The Molale Tribe Raided by the Cayuses," Manuscript no. 2029, National Anthropological Archives Collection, Smithsonian Institution, Washington, D.C.

MOSES COLUMBIA
(See **Sinkiuse.**)

MUCKLESHOOT TRIBE, MUCKLESHOOT RESERVATION, WASHINGTON

The Muckleshoots' name stems from that of the Buklshuhls, a Puget Sound basin Salish people who lived in the White and Green river valleys of western Washington state. The Muckleshoot tribe was, in fact, an amalgam of several peoples. The tribal name

**Muckleshoot Tribe, Muckleshoot
Reservation, Washington**

*Eva Jerry, 1986, seventy-two years old. She was a
member of the Indian Shaker church and had
reared ten children. She had thirty grandchildren
and eleven great grandchildren. She taught tribal
language in the Auburn, Washington, school district and in the tribal school. She served as judge
for the tribal court. The Muckleshoot Reservation
southeast of Seattle, Washington, is characterized
by its highly irregular configuration. One must
have one-eighth degree Muckleshoot blood to be a
member. Photo courtesy of the Muckleshoot Tribe.*

first appeared in government records about
1868 as that of the Indians on the Muckleshoot Reservation. There was controversy
later whether the Muckleshoots were, in
fact, a treaty tribe, a controversy that had
significant implications in the tribe's contention with the state of Washington over
fishing rights.

One group from which the Muckleshoot

Tribe was formed was the Skopahmishes,
or Green River Indians, who had formerly
inhabited the central Green River valley and
later moved to the Muckleshoot Reservation. Another group, the Smulkamishes,
had inhabited the vicinity of present-day
Enumclaw before they moved to the Muckleshoot Reservation. Another group, the Skekomishes (Stakamishes), or White River Indians, moved to the Port Madison Reservation. Important Muckleshoot villages were
the Yelaco, of seventeen houses at the confluence of Green River and Suice Creek;
the Quiats, on the Green River; and the
Cublokum, which consisted of one large
building on Boise Creek. The present-day
Muckleshoots are known officially as the
Muckleshoot Tribe, Muckleshoot Reservation, Washington.

Unlike many Coastal Salish peoples, the
Muckleshoots did not live on the shores of
Puget Sound but a few miles inland. Nevertheless, salmon fishing was important in
their economy, which was based on other
types of fishing as well and on hunting and
gathering. They traveled eastward to the
Cascade Mountains to trap goats, from
whose wool they made blankets and burial
robes. Also hunting in that area were the
Klickitat Indians, to whom the Muckleshoots
were related, as they were to the Puyallups.

Location: The irregularly shaped 3,440-acre
Muckleshoot Reservation lies near the city
of Auburn, Washington, and along the White
River, which was formerly called the Sto-
kamish, or Smalhko, by natives.

Numbers: In 1984 tribal membership stood
at 425. An estimate of the 1780 numbers
of the natives who would later become
Muckleshoots was 1,200. No doubt included
were other natives of the Puget Sound area.
In 1854, Washington Territorial Governor
and Superintendent of Indian Affairs Isaac
Stevens listed the Smulkamishes at 50, the
Skopahmishes also at 50, and the Skekomishes at 30. At about that time the ethnologist George Gibbs listed the Smulkamishes at 8, the Skopahmishes at 50, and
the Skekomishes at 30. In 1937 the U.S.
Office of Indian Affairs reported 194 Muckleshoots. In 1989 they numbered 2,963.

History: The Muckleshoot Reservation, in essence, grew out of the Medicine Creek Treaty of December 26, 1854, when Governor Stevens effected a treaty with bands of Nisquallis, Puyallups, and other natives of lower Puget Sound. No mention was made in that treaty of the Muckleshoots as such, but the treaty scheduled tribes from the Green and White rivers to remove to the Nisqually Reservation. The treaty also provided that for their welfare they could be removed to a more suitable place, and on December 5, 1856, Stevens recommended the establishment of the Muckleshoot Reservation between the Green and White rivers on Muckleshoot Prairie. The president approved that recommendation on January 20, 1857. The reservation had formerly been a military tract. An executive order on April 9, 1874, gave definite metes and bounds to the reservation, which at that time consisted of 3,532.72 acres. Thirty-nine Muckleshoots were later allotted 3,191.97 acres of the reservation. During the Indian War of 1855–56, under their chiefs Kitsap and Nelson, the Muckleshoots joined the warring coalition against the Americans. They were involved in the so-called White River Massacre of October 28, 1855, in which eight Americans were killed. After the war a Roman Catholic church was built on the reservation, as on so many others. The Indians complained of the encroachments of whites, a problem that was particularly acute on the Muckleshoot Reservation because of its fragmented and irregular configuration, which caused its residents to contend with the government over its boundaries.

Government and Claims: The constitution of the Muckleshoot Tribe, Muckleshoot Reservation, Washington, since amended, was approved on May 13, 1936, under the Indian Reorganization Act (48 Stat. 984). Its charter was ratified on October 21, 1936. The governing body is the Muckleshoot Indian Tribal Council, to which three new members are elected annually. The Muckleshoot Reservation is one of several under the jurisdiction of the Western Washington Indian Agency located at Everett, Washington, which is staffed to provide professional and technical services in connection with reservation tribes and their economic development. The Muckleshoot Tribe is also a member of an intertribal court system formed in 1978 by several reservation tribes. The tribe levies taxes on liquor, which go into general funds for its members and into a fund for land acquisition. Tribal members also sponsor a fish-hatchery. The tribe has business licensing, zoning, a land-use ordinance, and a water code. They run a bingo operation.

The Muckleshoots were denied their land claim in the Court of Claims in their suit, *Duwamish Indians* v. *United States* (79 C.Cl. 530) (1934), on the grounds that the United States had no basis on which to award judgment because it had no treaty with them. The Indian Claims Commission, however, found (in Docket 98) that the tribe had 101,620 acres of aboriginal land valued at $86,377. Consequently, on March 8, 1959, the commission ordered that the Muckleshoot Tribe should be awarded that amount.

Contemporary Life and Culture: As of 1975 there were 1,201.26 acres of trust lands on the reservation. The allotments are covered with second-growth timber save for small cleared homesites interspersed with non-Indian farmlands. Some Muckleshoots are employed by industries in Auburn or by the tribal government in various state and federal programs. Some engage in fishing, logging, and agriculture. As mentioned above, the tribe operates fish-hatching facilities. It also has a community center, community housing, Headstart facilities, a library, a medical-dental clinic, educational training programs, a fisheries patrol, and a youth group program including foster care. It has a water system and various housing improvement programs, one of which is called House My People. Cooperation exists between the tribe and the public school system in Auburn. On the reservation there is a Pentecostal and an Indian Shaker church. In 1980 a Catholic church there was being restored.

Special Events: Discontinued is the formerly

held early-May event, the Skopbsh.

Suggested Readings: American Friends Service Committee, Uncommon Controversy: Fishing Rights of the Muckleshoot, Puyallup, and Nisqually Indians (Seattle: University of Washington, 1970); Barbara Lane, "Anthropological Report on the Identity and Treaty Status of the Muckleshoot Indians," Political and Economic Aspects of Indian-White Culture Contact in Western Washington in the Mid-19th Century, May 10, 1973. Photocopy in Washington State Library, Olympia, Wash.; "Muckleshoot Indians," Indians of North American Tribes: Oregon and Washington, n.d., pamphlet file, Northwest Collections, University of Washington, Seattle; Catherine Eileen Reaugh, Muckleshoot, Port Gamble, Puyallup and Tulalip: Four Puget Sound Indian Communities Today (1970); State of Washington Indian Task Force, Are You Listening Neighbor? . . . The People Speak. Will You Listen? (Olympia, Wash., 1978).

MULTNOMAH
(Upper Chinookan Division of Chinookan)

The Multnomahs, whose name means "down river," lived on Sauvies Island in the lower Columbia River. Portland lies on the south in the Oregon county that bears their name. The Multnomahs were of the Clackamas division of the Upper Chinookan linguistic stock. Early writers called the Willamette River the Multnomah. Tradition has it that in the distant past Kalapuyan peoples "from the south" displaced Multnomahs, presumably those of the Willamette valley, though it is also said that the two peoples fought a battle for possession of Sauvies Island. Some ethnologists have grouped lower Columbia River Multnomahs in ten bands, one of which was the Multnomahs proper. The American explorers Meriwether Lewis and William Clark observed one of those bands, the Clahnaquahas of Sauvies Island. Under the heading Wappatoo Indians the ethnologist James Mooney estimated the numbers of the Multnomahs and neighboring tribes at 3,600. In 1805–1806 they were listed by Lewis and Clark at 800. The Rev. Samuel Parker visited their homelands in 1834 and stated that they were extinct from the epidemic diseases that had raged along the Columbia River in the late eighteenth and early nineteenth centuries. Some ethnologists believe that they became extinct as late as 1910. In 1907, 10 were said to remain of the once-populous Wappatoo Indians. See **Clackamas**.

NALTUNNETUNNE
(Athapascan)

The Naltunnetunnes spoke an Athapascan dialect distinct from that spoken by the Tututnis (Coast Rogues). They lived along the Oregon coast between the Tututnis and another Athapascan peoples, the Chetcos, until they were rounded up and moved north to the Siletz Reservation. Like their neighbors, they experienced a decline in population, numbering 77 in 1877.

NESPELEM
(Interior Division, Salishan)

The Nespelems lived in what is now north-central Washington state, primarily on the Nespelem River (a Columbia River tributary), on which today is a town named Nespelem. They also lived downstream along the Columbia to its confluence with the Okanogan River. The tribe's name derived from their native word meaning "large open meadow," "barren hill," or "prairie of flat open country." The Nespelems were among the natives of the northern interior whose traditions told of an ash fall from an eruption of Mount Saint Helens in or about the year 1802. In their eagerness to appease the Great Spirit for that catastrophe, they neglected to gather food, and some starved to death.

The Nespelems were closely related to the Sanpoils, who lived primarily along the river bearing their name, which enters the Columbia a few miles upstream from the mouth of the Nespelem. Because of the cultural similarity of the two peoples, anthropologists grouped them together for study, as did government officials for purposes of enumeration. Like the Sanpoils, the Nespelems had no treaty with the United States and remained aloof from agency officials. Both tribes were angered when the government in the 1880s permitted other Indians to move onto the Colville Reservation, which was on the homelands of the two tribes. On the reservation the Nespelems and Sanpoils refused annuities and other government aids and would not tell their numbers. Their refusal to cooperate with government officials was to a considerable extent due to their nativist Dreamer religion, against which Roman Catholic missionaries contended in attempting to convert them. By the beginning of the twentieth century the Nespelems were recognized as a tribal entity separate from the Sanpoils. At that time their economies differed somewhat: where the Sanpoils sought to maintain their independence largely by hunting, fishing, and farming, the Nespelems, whom some whites characterized as industrious and thrifty, sought independence mainly by raising grain and other crops. The differing economies of the two tribes might help explain their separate enumeration. The Nespelems were said to number 62 in 1892 and 45 in 1910, by which date the Indians acknowledged that there were but few living. In 1959 statistics revealed only 17 Nespelems of full blood on the Colville Reservation, and 8 of that blood quantum outside it. See **Confederated Tribes of the Colville Reservation, Washington.**

Suggested Readings: Verne F. Ray, "The Sanpoil and Nespelem Salishan Peoples of Northeastern Washington," *University of Washington Publications in Anthropology* 5 (1933); Robert H. Ruby and John A. Brown, *Half-Sun on the Columbia: A Biography of Chief Moses* (Norman: University of Oklahoma Press, 1965); James A. Teit, "The Middle Columbia Salish," *University of Washington Publications in Anthropology* 2, no. 4 (1928); James A. Teit, "The Salishan Tribes of the Western Plateaus," *Forty-fifth Annual Report of the Bureau of American Ethnology* (Washington, D.C.: Government Printing Office, 1930).

Nespelem

Que-Que-tas-ka, a woman of the Nespelem Tribe of north-central Washington. Her husband, Nespelem George, had a reputation among government officials in the early twentieth century as a "progressive." By contrast, the Nespelems traditionally avoided accepting government aid or control. Photograph by Frank Avery.

NEZ PERCÉ
(Shahaptian)

Some scholars believe the name Nez Percé derived from *nez pres*, meaning "flat nose," a name given them by early-day French-Canadian trappers. The tribe's language consisted of two dialects, Upper and Lower Nez Percé, in the Shahaptian linguistic family. According to their tradition, they first heard their name applied to them when some of their number traveled to Saint Louis a quarter century after their 1805–1806 meeting with the American explorers Meriwether Lewis and William Clark, who called them the Chopunnish. They called themselves Nimipu (variously spelled), meaning "we the people" or "the real people." They were also called Tsoop-Nit-Pa-Loo, or "the walking out people."

According to the mythology of this most numerous branch of Shahaptian speakers, the Nez Percés were created at Kamiah on a branch of the Clearwater River, a Snake River affluent in central Idaho. Understandably, they believed that the ark of the Flood rested on a mountain in that vicinity. The Nez Percés lived in at least twenty-seven permanent villages on the Clearwater River and its branches. There were eleven villages on the Snake River between the mouths of the Clearwater and Imnaha rivers, three permanent villages on the Salmon River and its tributaries, six permanent villages south of the Grande Ronde River (the area of Oregon's Wallowa Mountains and river valley, where the famed Nez Percé Young Chief Joseph lived) and on the western Snake River and three permanent villages between the Grande Ronde and Snake rivers west of the Idaho-Washington border. There were several villages along the Snake between the Clearwater and Tucannon rivers.

The Nez Percés served as intermediaries in trade between the Flatheads on the northeast and the natives of the Columbia Plateau on the north and west. They were generally on good terms with those peoples, but they were much less friendly with tribes on the south, such as the Bannocks and Shoshonis, and with the Blackfeet on the east. A handsome, hardy people, the Nez Percés were noted for several things: their traditional friendship with Americans, a posture that some believe began with their meeting with Lewis and Clark; their horsemanship, which they developed after acquiring that animal around 1720; and finally, the poignant story of Young Joseph and a small Nez Percé band fleeing government troops in 1877.

Before they acquired horses, the Nez Percés lived in separate but ethnically and culturally related villages. With horses they tended to coalesce into larger and more cohesive settlements and in their sociopolitical patterns. Lapwai Creek, a Clearwater tributary, was considered the dividing line between the buffalo-hunting Nez Percés and their primarily fishing and hunting fellow tribesmen. With horses the buffalo hunters traveled mainly the ancient, well-known Lolo Trail through the Bitterroot Mountains that Lewis and Clark followed and that U.S. Highway 12 follows today. Sometimes the Nez Percés moved north through the Bitterroot valley into the country of the Flatheads, whom for a time they joined on buffalo hunts. From the peoples of the Great Plains, on which they hunted the buffalo, the Nez Percés acquired certain cultural traits. Their intratribal organization was especially strengthened by the use of horses in times of war, replacing the old village controls that prevailed in times of peace. For decision making, the Nez Percés acted in councils under rules of unanimity. Chiefs and headmen were elected on the basis of achievement.

Location: Formerly the Nez Percés lived in numerous scattered and independent communities in a wide area of present-day north-central Idaho, parts of southwestern Washington, and northeastern Oregon. Today most of their descendants are members of the Nez Percé Tribe of Idaho, Nez Perce Reservation, Idaho, and live on or near the reservation on farms and in towns and cities such as Lapwai, Spalding, Culdesac, Craigmont, Ferdinand, Ahsahka, Orofino, Kamiah, Kooskia, Stites, Nezperce, Winchester, Lewiston, Grangeville, and Cottonwood. The last three places are off the reservation.

Numbers: In 1805–1806, Lewis and Clark estimated the Nez Percé numbers at 6,000, 2,000 more than their estimated numbers of a quarter century earlier. In 1827 a Hudson's Bay Company official placed them at 1,450. In 1901 they numbered 1,567. The constancy of their numbers is partially a reflection of their relative isolation, which spared them from the epidemics that proved so disastrous to natives living on or near routes of white travel and settlement. Further evidence of that isolation was seen as late as 1950, when their census revealed 608 full-blooded Nez Percés in Idaho. That was a higher native blood quantum than existed in most other Pacific Northwestern tribes. Since 1950, however, there has been considerable intertribal and interracial mixture. Then there were 1,261 on their reservation. Fifteen were enrolled at that time on the Colville Reservation, and 115 on other reservations. In 1985 the Nez Percés numbered 2,015, and in 1989, 2,455.

History: During the precontact and early contact periods the Nez Percés were involved in conflicts with powerful Plains tribes on the buffalo ranges, which at one time extended west from the Rocky Mountains into the intermontane Nez Percé homelands. As the buffalo retreated eastward during the first half of the nineteenth century, the Nez Percés allied with other Shahaptian and Salish peoples and with them hunted buffalo east of the Rockies, where they were challenged by Blackfeet and other Plains tribes. On the south they traded with and fought against the Bannocks, the Paiutes, and the Shoshonis. At a very early time they were obtaining native goods from great distances. When Lewis and Clark were among them, they had goods obtained from the Spaniards far to the south and from white mariners along the Pacific Coast. At that time they had few firearms, but they procured more of them shortly after with the advent of the inland fur trade.

In 1831 the Nez Percés were among the native delegations who traveled to Saint Louis to receive the "White man's Book of Heaven," the Bible. Among those who responded to their plea were missionaries of the American Board of Commissioners for Foreign Missions, including the Reverend and Mrs. Henry H. Spalding, who in 1836 established a mission at Lapwai. Spalding introduced them to novelties such as domestic animals and a printing press. Another mission was established among them in 1839 at Kamiah under the Reverend Asa Bowen Smith. One of Spalding's first converts was Old Joseph, father of the Young Joseph who helped lead his band in retreat from army forces in 1877. In December, 1842, the Nez Percés met with Indian agent Dr. Elijah White to ratify his laws, which to a great extent imposed American legal mores on them. At that time the first head

chieftaincy of all the Nez Percés was established. The American Board mission was terminated shortly after the 1847 killing of the Reverend Dr. and Mrs. Marcus Whitman and others at their Waiilatpu Mission in the Walla Walla valley.

Not abandoned was the division of the Nez Percé peoples into Christian and nativist blocs. Intratribal conflict between pro-American Christians and the anti-American nativist faction came to light in the brief Cayuse War, which followed the Whitman killings, and in the Indian War of the later 1850s. At the 1855 Walla Walla Treaty Council dissatisfaction with the treaty, which precipitated the war, was evident among traditionalist Nez Percés, who were embittered by the pro-American faction who had secured tribal adherence to the treaty. The Nez Percés recorded the treaty council proceedings on paper in their own language. Under the treaty they yielded their vast homelands of about 11 million acres in Idaho and Oregon for a reservation of about 7,694,270 acres. After gold was discovered on the reservation in 1860, Americans were permitted to intrude on it, and the town of Lewiston was established. On April 10, 1861, government officials effected an unratified agreement whereby that portion of the reservation lying north of the Snake and Clearwater rivers was to be opened to Americans and Indians in common for mining, but Indian root grounds on the reservation were not to be occupied. No Americans were permitted residence on the reservation south of the above-mentioned line except on a right-of-way to the mining district. In keeping with a provision that a military patrol force could be stationed on the reservation, troops were sent there. Commissions sent by the government to negotiate with the Nez Percés for their reservation resulted in the cession of June 9, 1863 (14 Stat. 647, ratified April 17, 1867), which left the tribe with a reservation of only 1,182.76 square miles, one tenth of its original size.

The opposition of traditionalists to that land loss caused the Nez Percés to abandon the head chieftaincy that had been established by Dr. White. In the early 1870s the

Reverend Spalding, who returned among the Nez Percés after a long absence, conducted revival meetings, which strengthened the Protestant-Presbyterian Nez Percé community in the face of the Roman Catholic and native traditionalist presence. Presbyterian control was strengthened under the Ulysses S. Grant Peace Policy of the 1870s, which gave that church the management of the Nez Percé Agency. Unhappy with what he saw as differences between Christian American preachments and practices, Old Joseph tore up his New Testament, while Young Joseph, also embittered, tried unsuccessfully to retain his ancestral homelands in the Wallowa country. A reservation had been established there by executive order on June 16, 1873, but was withdrawn by another order on June 10, 1875. Such developments led to the involvement of Young Joseph and his band in the Nez Percé War with the United States. In 1877, during that conflict, the Indian chiefs with Young Joseph—Looking Glass and White Bird—engaged the army in several bloody fights, as they retreated about 1,800 miles generally to the northeast. Although a small number escaped to Canada, 375 others were captured and taken to the Indian Territory (Oklahoma). After great suffering there, some returned to Lapwai, and 118 adults with Young Joseph and Yellow Bull, his second-in-command (including 16 children and 14 infants), went to the Colville Reservation, where they settled under the aegis of Chief Moses.

Government and Claims: The Nez Perce Tribe of Idaho, Nez Perce Reservation, Idaho, has a constitution and bylaws, which were approved by the United States on April 2, 1948, and ratified by the tribe in general assembly on April 30, 1948. The governing body is the Nez Perce Tribal Executive Committee, whose members are elected at large by the General Council. The Executive Committee administers and guides tribal economic development, improvement of human and natural resources, and the investment of income and assets of the tribe.

In July, 1951, the Nez Percés filed three petitions with the Indian Claims Commis-

Nez Percé

Silas Whitman, 1977, at the White Bird (Idaho) battlefield, site of the 1877 confrontation of the Nez Percé with the U.S. military. Whitman comes from a strong Nez Percé Presbyterian church background but like other present-day Native Americans has turned to traditional native religion. Nez Percés had a reputation for friendliness to Americans from the time of Lewis and Clark's visit in 1805. The one physical conflict with the United States, in 1877, involved only a portion of the tribe, who were seeking to escape from army troops. Courtesy of Lewiston Morning Tribune, *Lewiston, Idaho.*

sion. One claim (Docket 175) was for additional compensation for the 1855 cession of their aboriginal lands. At the same time the Colville, or (Chief) Joseph, Nez Percés of the Colville Reservation filed a claim (Docket 180) for compensation for the loss of the same lands in the same cession. At the order of the commission the claims were combined in a new docket (175) on February

147

27, 1953. On August 25, 1971, the commission awarded the Nez Percés $3,550,000, of which 86.5854 percent went to the Nez Percés of Idaho. A third claim (Docket 179) filed in July, 1951, by the Confederated Tribes of the Colville on behalf of the Colville Nez Percés was for governmental mismanagement of tribal funds and assets. On November 5, 1968, those of Joseph's band living in Idaho filed an intervenor claim. On April 29, 1970, the commission made an award of $119,071.78, of which the Colville Nez Percés received two thirds, and the Idaho Nez Percés received the remainder. An additional claim (Docket 179-A) was filed by the Nez Percé Tribe of Idaho alone for mismanagement after June 30, 1951. Since the claim was not settled by September 30, 1978, when the life of the Indian Claims Commission had expired, it was transferred to the Court of Claims.

Another claim (Docket 186) was filed for compensation for the withdrawal of the reservation in the Wallowa country, which had resulted ultimately in the destruction of the Wallowa, or Joseph, band as a viable economic, social, and political entity. That band had originally brought a claim before the Court of Claims (95 C.Cl. 11) in 1941, but the court had held that they were not representative of the "roaming bands" for whom the reservation had been established and that the 1873 order establishing the reservation did not imply their exclusive aboriginal claim to the land because the reservation had been created for nonroaming Nez Percés as well as the Joseph Band. The Indian Claims Commission decided that the executive order of 1873 did give that Joseph Band a compensable interest on the Wallowa Reservation, even though the roaming bands under Joseph, Looking Glass, Big Thunder, White Bird, and Eagle from the Light had not accepted the 1873 order. On October 31, 1974, the commission awarded these Nez Percés $725,000 of which 150/268, or $406,542.07, went to the Joseph Band on the Colville Reservation, and the balance went to the Nez Percés of Idaho. A claim (Docket 175-A) was separated from Docket 175 and filed as such on December 4, 1957, for additional compensation for 6,932,270

acres of the Nez Percé Reservation ceded the United States on June 9, 1863. The consideration that the petitioners had received had been $352,394.94. From an award of $4,650,000, from which would be deducted that consideration plus a compromised value for offsets of $140,000, the Nez Percés received an award on June 17, 1960, of $4,157,605.06. On April 7, 1964, the Indian Claims Commission ordered dismissed a claim (Docket 175-B) for an additional payment for cession in 1894 of 549,559 acres from the 762,000-acre reservation after allotments agreed to on May 1, 1893. The commission decided that the consideration the Nez Percés had received for that cession was not unconscionable. The Nez Percés then took their case to the Court of Claims as Appeal No. 5-64 (decided July 15, 1966, 176 C. Cl. 815), wherein the court found that the compensation allowed for the cession was the minimum amount and referred the case back to the commission, which on November 14, 1969, made a final award of $3,022,575 minus the consideration of $1,634,664 paid after the 1894 cession. On the $1,387,911 due the tribe from 1894, the Claims Commission allowed it 5 percent interest. The defending United States then appealed to the Court of Claims, which ruled against payment of interest to the tribe. Of the remaining reservation lands 180,657 acres were allotted, and the other lands put in trust for the tribe.

A claim (Docket 180-A) separated from Docket 180 was for compensation for trespass on, and gold taken from, the reservation before the cession of a large part of it to the United States. The Nez Percés had previously litigated such a claim before the Court of Claims (95 C.Cl. 1). The decision on October 6, 1941, had been favorable to the tribe. The Claims Commission, accepting the petitioner's argument that the Court of Claims had no jurisdiction to determine equitable claims of Indians, on December 31, 1959, awarded the Nez Percés $3 million, of which the Idaho Nez Percés received $2,168,761 and the Colville Nez Percés received the balance. The tribe has also been awarded $2.8 million for loss of fishing rights at Celilo Falls on the Columbia River,

148

which are now covered by waters of Dalles Dam. The cash allotments of $1,400 to each tribal member were to be spent on home improvements, farm machinery and so on. The tribe, with twenty-four others throughout the western United States, filed claims (Dockets 523-71 and 524-71) that reached the Court of Claims for mismanagement of Indian Claims Commission judgment funds and for mismanagement of other funds, such as Individual Indian Money accounts held in trust by the United States. The Nez Percé Tribe was awarded $232,905.25 in 1980.

Contemporary Life and Culture: About two-thirds of the Nez Percé Reservation is in individual allotments, some of which have been sold to non-Indians. Trust lands as of 1975 totaled 87,015.39 acres. About 80 percent of the total reservation acreage is leased to non-Indians. Farm and timber lands produce most of the tribal income. Children attend public schools, and an increasing number are completing high school and pursuing advanced academic and vocational training. The tribe, like several others in the Pacific Northwest, administers a scholarship fund for the postsecondary education of worthy students. It operates a printing plant, which does job printing for it and others. It also operates a marina at Dvorshak Dam on the Snake River. There is a limestone quarry on the reservation. Among the tribe's cultural achievements was the completion in 1961 of a translation of *Webster's Collegiate Dictionary* into the Nez Percé language by Corbett Lawyer, a grandson of the famous Chief Lawyer. The Nez Percés were among Shahaptian speakers who in the later 1970s alphabetized their language. By 1980, linguist Haruo Aoki had completed the transcription of Nez Percé texts, a dictionary, and the first authoritative Nez Percé grammar. In 1977, as evidence of their newly found tribal identity, the Nez Percés commemorated the conflict between Chief Joseph's band and the United States in sacred rites on the battlefield at White Bird, Idaho. From that event they returned to their homes resolved to conduct their own affairs and fashion their own destiny in an atmosphere of revived spiritism and tribalism.

Special Events: On Lincoln's Birthday games and war-dance contests are held at Kamiah. In the first week of March the tribe holds the E-pah-tes championship Indian games and war dances at Lapwai. In the first week in May at Lapwai it holds the Spring Root Festival. In early summer at Craigmont is held the Talmaks, an annual camp meeting of religious services. Games and races are held in conjunction with Talmaks on the Fourth of July. In the second week in August at Lapwai is held the Pi-Nee-waus Days, featuring parades, war dances, Indian games, and tribal exhibits. In the third week of August at the Mud Spring Camp at Craigmont are held Indian games and feasts. In late November at Lapwai is held the Thanksgiving Day celebration, in which the tribe holds games and war dances. See also **Confederated Tribes of the Colville Reservation, Washington.**

Suggested Readings: Edward S. Curtis, *The North American Indian* (1912; New York: Johnson Reprint Corporation, 1970), vol. 7; Francis Haines, *The Nez Percés: Tribesmen of the Columbia Plateau* (Norman: University of Oklahoma Press, 1955); Alvin M. Josephy, Jr., *The Nez Perce Indians and the Opening of the Northwest* (New Haven: Yale University Press, 1965); Archie Phinney, *Nez Percé Texts*, Columbia University Contributions to American Anthropology, vol. 25 (New York, 1934); Robert H. Ruby, "Return of the Nez Perce," *Idaho Yesterdays* 12, no. 1 (Spring, 1968); Allen P. Slickpoo, *Noon nee-me-poo (We, the Nez Perces)* (Lapwai, Idaho: Nez Perce Tribe of Idaho, 1973); Herbert Joseph Spinden, *The Nez Perce Indians*, Memoirs of the American Anthropological Association, vol. 2, pt. 3 (Lancaster, Pa.: November, 1908); Deward Walker, *Conflict and Schism in Nez Perce Acculturation: A Study of Religion and Politics* (Pullman, Wash.: Washington State University Press, 1968); Deward Walker, *Indian Peoples in Idaho* (Moscow, Idaho: University of Idaho Press, 1978).

NISQUALLY
(Coastal Division, Salishan)

The name Nisqually is said to derive from that for the Nisqually River flowing into southern Puget Sound in western Washington. Some anthropologists suggest that there was no basis in fact for the name *nez quarrés*, meaning "square noses," which supposedly was given to the Nisquallis by French-Canadian fur men. The Nisquallis spoke the Nisqually dialect of the Coastal Salishan language. They believed, as did other Puget Sound natives, in the deity Dokibatt (variously spelled among the tribes), the Changer, who was the son of a woman and of a star. They believed that Dokibatt had much to do with the world as it existed. The trickster Coyote, who figures prominently in the mythology of natives east of the Cascade Mountains, appeared occasionally in Nisqually mythology also. Some scholars see in that a cultural link between the Nisquallis and the peoples of the interior, such as the Klickitats and their subdivisions west of the Cascade Mountains, and the Yakimas, with whom, like the Klickitats, the Nisquallis traded marine products and intermarried. From the Klickitats the Nisquallis purchased horses, which they pastured on their prairies, and they raised more of these animals than did most tribes west of the Cascades.

Location: In former times the Nisquallis occupied at least forty villages, which were on both banks of the Nisqually River and extended nearly thirty miles upstream from its delta. The modern-day Nisquallis of the Nisqually Indian Community, Nisqually Reservation, Washington, live on their reservation on the west side of the Nisqually River in Thurston County or in the lower Nisqually valley. Others live in the town of Yelm, which is about fifteen miles southeast of Washington's state capital, Olympia. Some tribal members have intermarried with Puyallups, Muckleshoots, and members of other tribes.

Numbers: The Nisqually tribal membership in 1989 was listed at 1,455. The Nisquallis were said to have numbered 258 in 1838–39

and 200 five years later. At the time of their treaty with the United States at Medicine Creek in 1854, they numbered less than 300. Some enumerations, not only in early times but also in early twentieth century, placed their numbers as high as 1,000, a figure that probably included other speakers of the Nisqually dialect of the Coastal Salishan language. As it did with those other speakers, disease played a major role in the Nisqually decline.

History: The first major contact between Nisquallis and whites occurred with the establishment of the Hudson's Bay Company's Fort Nisqually in their homelands in 1833. Besides purchasing furs from the Nisquallis and surrounding tribes, the post traders tried to instruct them in the doctrines of the Christian faith. In 1839 the Roman Catholic secular priest Modeste Demers met several tribesmen at Fort Nisqually, where he had gone to thwart the establishment of a Methodist mission. Two Methodist missionaries, John Richmond and William Wilson, came to Fort Nisqually in 1840, but they remained only two years. A Catholic priest, Pascal Richard, established an Indian mission north of present-day Olympia in 1848. Around 1825 the Nisquallis and other Coastal Salish peoples attacked Cowichans of the southwestern coast of Vancouver Island. In the attack the Nisquallis and their allies suffered heavy losses. At nearby Butlers Cove in 1855, Stikine Indian war parties from Canada raided Puget Sound settlers after a white man had murdered a Stikine chief in his employ.

The original Nisqually Reservation was established by the Medicine Creek Treaty of December 26, 1854, with Washington Territorial Governor and Superintendent of Indian Affairs Isaac Stevens. It consisted of 1,280 acres on Puget Sound near the mouth of Shenahnam Creek. By executive order on January 20, 1857, it was enlarged to 4,717 acres on both sides of the Nisqually River a few miles above its mouth. Since the Nisqually Reservation was on both sides of the river, the tribe claims the river, which comprises 210 additional acres, securing for its people the right to take fish, in the words of the treaty, "at usual and accustomed places." This provision has embroiled the Nisquallis and other tribes in controversy with state and federal governments.

A Nisqually chief, Leschi, was the leader of the Indian coalition against the Americans in the 1850s. To his death he declared that he had never signed the treaty. During the negotiations, when each chief was expected to make a map of his country in preparation for a composite one, Leschi reportedly refused to complete his and tore up a paper commissioning him as chief. He was angry that under the treaty his people were scheduled to settle at the mouth of McAllister Creek, a heavily wooded area, which was a poor place for them because they were accustomed to gathering marine foods at places such as the mouth of the Nisqually River. It also had been their practice to pasture their horses in the Nisqually valley, whose prairies they fired to prevent forest growth and to promote the growth of grasses. As a result of Leschi's anti-American activities, which whites called murder but Leschi called warfare, the chief was sentenced to hang at the end of the war on February 19, 1858. His people came to his defense, as did prominent members of the American community, but their support was to no avail. He was condemned in the white men's court and, as a white historian later recorded, "strangled according to the law." Not all of the Nisquallis were combatants during the war. Many were among the natives of lower Puget Sound whom an acting Indian agent, J. V. Weber, confined to Squaxin Island in 1855 to keep them from hostilities.

On September 30, 1884, the acreage set aside for the Nisqually Reservation was divided into thirty family allotments on both sides of the Nisqually River. The acreage did not include the river itself. After that the tribe lived in peace for some time, harvesting fish from the Nisqually River and growing potatoes on prairie tracts. Tribal members received few government rations and among other foods they consumed as

Nisqually

George Kalama, a Nisqually tribal chairman active in national Indian politics. The Nisquallis, who traditionally are a fishing people, engaged with state and federal officials in the conflicts known as the Fish Wars.

many as 500 salmon annually per family. In the winter of 1917 the U.S. Army, without warning, moved onto Nisqually lands and ordered them from their homes. The army later condemned about two-thirds (3,353 acres) of the Nisqually Reservation to expand its Camp (later Fort) Lewis base. Replacement lands were secured for the Nisquallis at points as distant as the Quinault River on the Olympic Peninsula. Other lands were purchased for displaced Nisquallis at such places as the Puyallup, Skokomish, and Chehalis reservations. The Nisquallis were also paid $75,840 for their lands and improvements. On April 28, 1924, Congress belatedly awarded them $85,000 as compensation for the hunting rights that they had lost with their lands, as well as for lost access to lakes and streams. In the post–World War II period the focus of Washington state action was at Franks Landing, a six-acre tract on the Nisqually River just below the reduced Nisqually Reservation, which Willie Frank had purchased to replace, in part, lands that he had lost in the government's Fort Lewis acquisition. In the 1960s, Frank's Landing was the scene of sometimes-violent confrontations between state police and game officials and the Nisquallis. Helping focus national attention on the conflict was the symbolic arrest there of actor Marlon Brando during a "fish-in" and the appearance of Dick Gregory, a well-known entertainer and civil-rights activist. (For an explanation of the background of the conflict, see **Puyallup**.)

Government and Claims: The Nisqually tribe was organized under provisions of the Indian Reorganization Act (48 Stat. 984) as the Nisqually Indian Community, Nisqually Reservation, Washington. Its constitution and bylaws were approved on September 9, 1946.

After filing a claim (Docket 197) with the Indian Claims Commission, the Nisquallis received a final award of $80,013.07 for which funds were appropriated on September 30, 1976. The monies awarded by the Claims Commission were set aside for land acquisition. This award did not include compensation for land within Fort Lewis Reservation for which Nisquallis later sought compensation. In 1991 the tribe dedicated a salmon hatchery on Clear Creek.

Contemporary Life and Culture: Reservation acreage is as follows, excluding, as noted, the Nisqually River of 210 acres: allotted lands in trust or in restricted status, 715 acres; alienated lands, 392 acres; tribally owned lands and those in trust, 247 acres (including a cemetery of 2.5 acres); and a recent addition, because of a reservation boundary change, 45 acres. In recent years the tribe has enlarged its on-reservation housing by forty-eight units and has erected a tribal center. The reservation is the focus of the Nisqually Community. The major source of tribal income is fishing, which is a major cultural and identity touchstone for tribal members. One tribal spokesman, writing of the favorable decision by Judge George Boldt in 1974 and the *U.S.* v. *Washington* fishing cases stated that they had gone far beyond the improvement of Nisqually fisheries by reinforcing and validating tribal members' knowledge of themselves as Nisqually Indians, their fishing way of life, and their community. The predominant religion in the Nisqually Community is Roman Catholic. There are also adherents of the Indian Shaker Church.

Suggested Readings: American Friends Service Committee, *Uncommon Controversy: Fishing Rights of the Muckleshoot, Puyallup, and Nisqually Indians* (Seattle: University of Washington Press, 1970); Della G. Emmons, *Leschi of the Nisquallies* (Minneapolis: T. S. Denison, 1965); Marian W. Smith, *The Puyallup-Nisqually* (Columbia University Contributions to Anthropology, vol. 32 (New York, 1940); Jamie Sanchez, "The Nisqually Indian Reservation," *The Indian Historian* 5, no. 1 (Spring, 1972).

NOOKSACK
(Coastal Division, Salishan)

Nooksack was the name of one of the tribe's villages. White men applied the name indiscriminately to all of the Indians in the valley of the Nooksack River, a Puget Sound affluent. The word means "bracken-fern roots." It is also said to be a corruption of Kunuhsaack, the name of one of the tribe's several bands.

In the middle of the nineteenth century the Nooksacks lived in three main villages northeast of present-day Bellingham in northwestern Washington. One of those villages was near present-day Deming; another was near present-day Goshen; and a third was near present-day Everson and Nooksack. Besides the town, a river bears the tribal name.

The Nooksacks are of mixed lineage, having been allied and intermarried with such tribes as the Lummis on the west, the Skagits on the south, and the Chilliwacks in British Columbia. Their dialect, but not their culture, was closely related to that of the Squawmishes of British Columbia.

The Nooksacks were a riverine people. Although they hunted game in the Cascade Mountains and gathered plant foods on natural prairies, it has been estimated that at least 50 percent of their food was obtained from fishing, especially during annual salmon runs on the Nooksack River and its branches in the area stretching upriver from Ferndale (once generally recognized as the Nooksack-Lummi boundary). They fished especially on the North and South forks of the Nooksack, but they were also active at the mouth of that river; around Bellingham and Chuckanut bays, as well as on the Sumas River and Sumas Lake; on the Samish, Fraser, and Skagit rivers; and on Lake Whatcom. They gathered sea foods from Bellingham Bay northward along the coast.

Location: Most of the successors of the Nooksacks are members of the Nooksack Indian Tribe of Washington, as the tribe is officially known, and they live in the general area of Deming, Nooksack, and Everson. They have no contiguous land base. Their reservation at Deming is only nine-tenths of an acre.

Numbers: In 1984 tribal membership stood at 453. In 1978 it stood at 425. In 1856 there were 376 Nooksacks by official count.

In 1864 an agent wrote that this "stubborn and desperate tribe of Savages" could field about sixty-five warriors. In 1906 there were 200 Nooksacks by official count. The ethnologist Charles Hill-Tout claimed that in the early twentieth century there were but a half dozen Nooksack males of full blood.

History: In the contact period the Nooksacks communicated but little with American settlers around Puget Sound, but as noted, they did not isolate themselves from native peoples. They made fishnets of cedar and nettle roots. To make their sinew-backed bows they obtained glue from the sturgeon in Canada's Fraser River, to which they traveled over three trails. Like many tribes during the fur-trade era, they traded with the Hudson's Bay Company at its Fort Langley, which was established in 1827 on the lower Fraser. There they purchased, among other goods, guns, powder, and lead. An early-day shifting of the Nooksack River cut them off from riverine travel to the mouth of that stream. Like other natives of the Puget Sound basin, the Nooksacks raised potatoes on the rich bottomlands in a culture that they probably had learned from Hudson's Bay Company personnel. In 1856 an American agent reported that they had a patriarchal government under chieftains who held considerable power. He noted the absence of slaves, an indication to him of the absence of the class structure common among the saltwater tribes.

Inclement weather kept the Nooksacks from attending the Point Elliott Treaty Council held near Mukilteo, Washington, on January 22, 1855. The treaty authorized the establishment of the Lummi Reservation, to which the Nooksacks had little wish to remove. Some of the tribe did settle on it, but they later left. The tribe was much dissatisfied by the establishment in 1858 of a ferry over the Nooksack River for miners en route to the newly discovered goldfields on the Fraser and Thompson rivers. Farther upstream, in the Mount Baker country, however, some Nooksacks served as guides and sold potatoes to the prospectors probing that region for gold. Among the ill effects of the Nooksacks' confronta-

153

Nooksack

Phyllis Roberts, 1987, at Deming, Washington, location of the Nooksack tribal headquarters. The Nooksacks live primarily in Whatcom County, Washington. Historically, they have been a fishing people, but since white contact they have supplemented their incomes by farming, logging, and other occupations. Tribal members have been especially active in the past several decades practicing their revived traditional Spirit Dancing.

tions with whites was the smallpox, or "Nooksack sickness," as the Skagit Indians called it. In the 1870s the Nooksacks along the lower and middle Nooksack River again clashed with whites, who settled both on tribal lands and on the lands of Nooksacks who had severed tribal relations.

Government and Claims: Business is conducted by the Tribal Council of the Nooksack Indian Tribe of Washington, which was established after the tribe was federally recognized in 1973.

With several Puget Sound tribes, most of whom were parties to the Point Elliott Treaty, the Nooksacks were party in 1934 to a suit (*Duwamish Indians* v. *United States*, 79 C.Cl. 530) in which they sought payment for lands taken by the government. Because they had not been party to the Point Elliott Treaty, the Nooksacks were not officially recognized as having original title to the lands involved. Because the Court of Claims took the position that it could not deal with them, the Nooksacks then filed a claim (Docket 46) with the Indian Claims Commission for the loss of their lands. The commission decided that the tribe did have aboriginal ownership of 80,590 acres. On October 20, 1958, it awarded the Nooksacks $52,383.50, the 1858 value of their lands, but finally, on February 9, 1962, the commission awarded the tribe $49,383.50, after deducting a $3,000 counter claim.

Contemporary Life and Culture: Virtually a landless tribe insofar as their reservation is concerned, the Nooksacks live on fragmented allotments totaling about 2,906 acres, which are mostly second-growth upland timber- and bottomlands, some of which are river-washed. Some holdings are non-trust homesteads that escaped jumping by non-Indians before the legal titles were obtained by Indian homesteaders. Much land is used for subsistence gardening. Small incomes are derived from rentals to non-Indians. Most of the income of tribal members comes from fishing, logging, and seasonal farm work. Tribal goals have been established, with much attention given to youth, land, housing, health, education, and fish-

154

ing. One goal, the establishment of a tribal center, was achieved by the construction of an impressive complex at Deming.

Suggested Readings: Pamela Amoss, Coast Salish Spirit Dancing: The Survival of an Ancestral Religion (Seattle: University of Washington Press, 1978); Robert Emmett Hawley, Skgee Mus or Pioneer Days on the Nooksack (Bellingham, Wash.: Miller and Sutherlen, 1945); P. R. Jeffcott, Nooksack Tales and Trails (Sedro-Woolley, Wash., Courier Times, 1949); Nooksack Tribal Council, Nooksack Tribal Planning Project Phase I: A Report to the Community (Sedro-Woolley, Wash., 1974); Allan S. Richardson, "Longhouses to Homesteads: Nooksack Indian Settlement, 1820 to 1895," American Indian Journal, August, 1979; Lottie Roeder Roth, History of Whatcom County (Chicago: Pioneer Historical Publishing Co., 1926); David G. Tremaine, Indian and Pioneer Settlement of the Nooksack Lowland, Washington to 1890, Center for Pacific Northwest Studies Occasional Paper no. 4 (Bellingham, Wash.: Western Washington State College, 1975).

NORTHERN PAIUTE
(Shoshonean)

The term Paiute, of uncertain origin, has been interpreted to mean "water Ute" or "true Ute." The Northern Paiutes were called the Paviotso by the scientist Maj. John Wesley Powell. Their language was called Mono-Paviotso by the anthropologist A. L. Kroeber. They were also designated as "digger" Indians to distinguish them from the horse-riding peoples of the plains. In scanty clothing of brush and willow bark, they struggled for subsistence, migrating to the mountain tops to gather nuts and berries and returning to the valleys to dig roots and to fish. They occupied lands in northwestern Nevada, in southwestern Idaho, in central and southeastern Oregon, and in California east of the Cascade and Sierra Nevada mountains and north of Owens Lake.

Some ethnologists have applied the term nation to collective Shoshonean linguistic groups and the term tribe to individual groups. In this guidebook, however, we follow those ethnologists who consider the Northern Paiutes to be a tribe and the groups to be bands. Geography influenced the organization and development of the twenty-one Northern Paiutes bands, which had political autonomy and internal organizations that were outwardly simple. Because of the vastness of their lands, the Northern Paiute population, though low per square mile, was large by Pacific Northwestern standards. With the Southern Shoshoneans (the Ute-Chemehuevis of western Utah, northwestern Arizona, southeastern Nevada, and parts of southeastern California), the Northern Paiutes numbered about 7,500 in 1845 and 5,400 in 1903. They have always been an independent people.

Before the eighteenth century the Paiutes of central and southeastern Oregon were encroached on by the Teninos and Wascos, who previously had lived on the north bank of the Columbia River for protection from them. The Northern Paiutes' conflicts with those tribes was noted by the American explorers Meriwether Lewis and William Clark in 1805. Lacking white men's weapons and horses, and lacking the war complex of their foes of the plains, the Paiutes were unable to retaliate against their Columbia River enemies. Thus around 1810 they accepted a buffer zone between themselves and Columbia River peoples.

The following subdivisions, or bands, of the Northern Paiute peoples in the Pacific Northwest were sometimes designated as "diggers" or "Snakes":

The Hunipuitokas (Walpapis) occupied about 7,000 square miles on streams that eventually enter the Pacific Ocean or that feed the Great Basin lakes with no drainage to the sea. Paulina and Weahwewa were important among their chiefs. In 1870 the Hunipuitokas numbered 98 on the Klamath Reservation.

155

The Goyatokas (Yahuskins), or "crawfish eaters," occupied a 5,000 square-mile region around the Silver, Summer, and Abert lakes in Oregon. Under Chief Moshenkosket they numbered about 100 on the Klamath Reservation in 1867.

The Wadatokas, or "seed eaters," occupied a 5,250-square-mile area around Burns, Oregon, in a land of streams flowing into Harney and Malheur lakes and the Malheur River. They were one of four bands living on streams in the Pacific watershed. Among their chiefs were Oytes and Egan, who was also the chief of the Weiser Indians.

The Koaagaitokas, or "salmon eaters," occupied lands in southern Idaho. Since numerous claims by Northern Paiutes and Western bands of Northern Shoshonis placed both tribes in southwestern Idaho, neither owned that area at the exclusion of others. The peoples of the Koaagaitoka subdivision intermixed and intermarried with some of the people from the sedentary Western bands of Northern Shoshonis, who were primarily fish eaters. By historic times, and certainly by the middle of the nineteenth century, the two peoples had banded together for mutual protection from the whites invading their lands. The Shoshonis were the Wararereekas and Wihinashts (Winnases). Combined, they were popularly called by the name of the local river, the Weiser, and were perhaps predominantly Northern Paiutes, and few Boise and Bruneau Shoshonis.

The homelands of the Tagotokas, or "tuber eaters," were roughly 7,500 square miles, mostly in the Owyhee River watershed of Oregon and Idaho. Among their chiefs were Paddy Cap and Leggins. The descendants of the band live on Nevada's Duck Valley Reservation, which was established on April 16, 1877.

The Tsosoodos tuviwarais, or "cold dwellers," of Oregon's Steens Mountain were possibly the "berry eaters" under Chief Winnemucca, by reason of his marriage to a woman of their group.

The Kidutokados, or "woodchuck eaters," occupied a territory of about 5,000 square miles including Surprise Valley on the border of northern California and Warner Valley in Oregon, as well as the valley along the eastern slopes of Oregon's Warner Range. Their chiefs were Ocheo and Howlark (Howlah). Howlark, who lived around the Sprague River, was one of those with whom the United States attempted to effect a treaty in 1865. Probably the Kidutokados were a band of 150 "Snakes" on the Klamath Reservation whose descendants live at Fort Bidwell, California, and in settlements around their homelands.

The Agaipaninadokados ("fish lake eaters"), or Moakokados ("wild onion eaters"), lived around Summit Lake, Nevada, and along the southern Idaho border east of the Kidutokado lands in a roughly 2,800-square-mile region. One of their chiefs, Sequimata (Chiquite, or Little Winnemucca), was noted for his leadership when miners attacked the Pyramid Reservation and precipitated the Pyramid Lake War of 1860.

The Atsakudokwa tuviwarais, or "red butte dwellers," occupied roughly 2,700 square miles in northwestern Nevada but did not extend above the southern Idaho border. Slated for removal to the Pyramid Reservation, their chief, Itsaahmah, in 1870 refused to lead his 140-member band to that place.

The Yamosopo tuviwarais, or "half-moon valley dwellers," occupied roughly 2,000 square miles east of the Atsakudokwas in the Little Humboldt River drainage area of Nevada's Paradise Valley.

The Hunipuitokas, more popularly known as Walpapis, were the most familiar to Oregon whites of all the Northern Paiute bands because they most often came into conflict with Americans during the latter nineteenth century. Also familiar to whites for the same reason were the Goyatokas, better known as Yahuskins (Yahooskins). The latter designation was of fairly recent, midnineteenth-century origin. The Goyatokas' name, meaning "people far off below," was perhaps given them by Klamaths. About 22 of them were present with 710 Klamaths and 339 Modocs at a treaty council with United States officials on October 14, 1864, when they ceded their lands (16 Stat. 407) and agreed to live on the Klamath Reservation. See **Klamath.**

The Walpapis' occupied lands encompassed the Crooked River valley and extended as far north in Oregon as the headwaters of the John Day River and as far south as Two Buttes. In 1864 the band numbered about 500. Those under Chief Chocktoot numbered 100 in 1872 and 128 the following year. Their head war chief, Paulina, signed a treaty with the United States on August 12, 1865 (14 Stat. 683), mainly to obtain release of several of his people held hostage by the military, including members of his own family. Paulina agreed to cede his lands and live on the Klamath Reservation, where he, four of his men, and eighteen women and children remained during the winter of 1865–66 on the reservation's upper reaches. They abandoned it at the urging of the Kidutokado chief, Howlark, to wage full-scale war against whites. They also agreed to cease skirmishing against other tribes. For some time Paulina eluded the troops sent to capture him and raided mines and miners, as well as immigrants and their trains, in a swath across south-central and eastern Oregon. In attempting to capture him, the military established several camps in the area, including Bidwell in Surprise Valley, Alvord east of Steens Mountain and the Old Camp Warner north of Lakeview, Oregon. Other Paiute bands of that Oregon region, as well as those of southwestern Idaho Territory, took to the warpath against Americans in the Snake War of 1866–68. Paulina also fought the Modocs under their chief, Schonchin, and swept down on the Klamath Agency.

During that time the Paiutes' ancient foes, the Teninos, were recruited from the Warm Springs Reservation in Oregon by the military as scouts in the fighting that had begun as early as 1854 when Paiute bands attacked the Ward party on the Immigrant Road (Oregon Trail) in southern Idaho. Having killed most of their horses for food, the Paiutes, starving and war-weary, finally surrendered. After the whites had killed Paulina in April, 1867, his people were led by Ocheo and by Weahwewa. During the Snake War the military conducted campaigns to round up the Oregon Paiutes and place them on the Klamath Reservation. In July, 1866, sixteen Walpapis were brought to that reser-

Northern Paiute

Winnemucca, sometimes called The Giver, was chief of one of the twenty-one Northern Paiute bands who roamed parts of Idaho, Oregon, California, and Nevada. A city in Nevada bears the chief's name. Courtesy of the Oregon Historical Society.

vation, and sixty more came there the following month. Most escaped its confines. In September, 1867, nineteen Walpapis were brought to the Klamath Reservation by the military, who in August, 1868, corraled a few more from the Silver Lake area, including Chocktoot and his band, making a total of 130 Walpapis on the reservation. Starvation subsequently drove the Walpapis to wander from the Klamath in search of subsistence (except for Chocktoot and about a hundred others). Ocheo moved to the Klamath in November, 1869. In March, 1870, twelve more Walpapis were brought there from the Silver Summer lakes area.

As a result of the Snake War campaigns and starvation, perhaps two-thirds of the Oregon Paiutes perished. A treaty that had been negotiated with three bands under Egan, Oytes, and Weahwewa on December 10, 1868, at Fort Harney was never ratified; consequently, the government made no treaty with them. An executive order on March 14, 1871, set aside lands in southeastern Oregon to keep them out of the public domain, and on September 12, 1872, the Malheur Reservation was established by executive order in eastern Oregon from those lands. At that reservation certain Walpapis (except for Chocktoot and those with him on the Klamath Reservation) were joined by other free-roaming Paiutes of southeastern Oregon. Because they had not been assigned to a reservation, the Paiutes were sent to the Malheur, whose 2,775 square miles was increased on May 15, 1875, to 1,778,580 acres. On January 28, 1876, a subsequent order diminished and redefined the reservation.

About 200 independent Paiutes and Shoshonis in the lower Weiser country of Idaho went to live on Miller Creek at the northern end of the Duck Valley Reservation on the Idaho-Nevada border. Most of them refused to remove to the Malheur when it was initially designated for them. Today their descendants are a fragmented amalgam of Egan's Weiser Paiutes and a few Shoshonis. With other Northern Paiutes the Weisers fought in the Bannock-Paiute War under Chief Paddy Cap. (For an account of Paiute participation in that war see **Bannock**.)

At the end of the war Paddy Cap's people scattered to the following reservations: the Malheur in Oregon, the Fort Hall in Idaho, the Yakima in south-central Washington, and the Warm Springs in Oregon. Separate from whites and from so-called "progressive" Shoshonis and Paiutes, they adhered longer to their traditional ways than did others. Paddy Cap and certain of his followers ended their roamings on the Duck Valley Reservation on lands that were withdrawn from the public domain and set apart as an addition to the Duck Valley by executive order on May 4, 1886. In 1887 there were 115 Paiutes on the Duck Valley Reservation. In the 1950s there were over 500 there.

On September 27, 1879, 38 Paiutes, after imprisonment at Fort Vancouver, Washington Territory, were taken to the Warm Springs Reservation, including the prophet and war instigator Oytes, who later left for the Yakima Reservation to visit Paiutes there. On February 2, 1879, 540 scattered combatants and noncombatant Paiutes who had been rounded up after the war, arrived on the Yakima after a long march from southern Oregon through deep winter snows under their leader Leggins, a noncombatant from western Nevada. Oytes was detained on the Yakima, as were others at Fort Harney, under the watchful eye of the military.

In 1960, 207 Paiutes of full or mixed blood were listed on the Warm Springs Reservation. In 1945, 145 were listed on the Umatilla Reservation. The noncombatant Paiutes under the western-Nevada Paiute chief Winnemucca clustered at Camp McDermit in Nevada. Winnemucca and the Kidutokado chief, Ocheo, kept their people mostly at Camp McDermit and Camp Bidwell. Many Paiutes drifted south from the Yakima after they were permitted to leave it in 1883. Of that group about 300 went to the Bend, Oregon, area. Certain of those soon moved to Nevada because the Malheur Reservation was being usurped by white farmers and stockmen. Executive orders on September 13, 1882, and May 21, 1883, restored the Malheur to the public domain except for 317.65 acres that were reserved from the reservation's North Half for the Camp Harney military post, which was restored to the public domain by executive order on March 2, 1889. The Paiutes had abandoned the reservation in June, 1878, during war time, and they did not reoccupy it until four and a half years later when it was restored to the public domain. The Malheur Agency office had been discontinued on December 23, 1880, though the reservation existed until September 13, 1882. In June, 1884, Paddy Cap and about fifty of his people moved from the Yakima to the Duck Valley Reservation. In August, 1884,

Oytes and about seventy of his people left the Yakima for the Warm Springs.

In 1969 a settlement was completed, with a per capita payment of $741 to nearly 850 Paiutes who were able to prove that they were related to tribesmen formerly located on the Malheur. That payment was the award from a claim (Docket 17) made on December 4, 1959, for Paiute descendants of former Malheur residents. The Indian Claims Commission determined that Paiutes held title to that reservation as described in the executive order of January 28, 1876, and that the area under consideration was 1,449,304.77 acres. That was the acreage after deduction of 120,019.43 acres for road grants across the confine, 17,541.96 acres in allotments to Indians after 1879, and 10,000 acres that were in question in the location of the southern boundary of the reservation. To the descendants of those who were party to the unratified treaty of December 10, 1868, the Claims Commission awarded $579,722, because those descendants had held original title to the Malheur.

Another claim (Docket 87) from petitioning Paiutes on six reservations in Nevada was decided on November 4, 1965. Among the petitioners from those reservations were Paiutes who (except for descendants of the Malheur Walpapis and Yahuskins) had shared in awards to the Paiutes of Owens Valley in California and Nevada of $935,000, the fair market value of their aboriginal lands as of March 3, 1953; plus an award to the Paviotsos of $16 million, the fair market value of their lands in Nevada and California as of December 31, 1962; and an award to Pacific Northwestern Paviotsos of $3,650,000 for the "Snake Tract" in Oregon, which also included lands in southwestern Idaho and northeastern California. The Walpapis and Yahuskins were recipients of an award to Klamath Reservation Indians covered under Docket 100 (see **Klamath**).

In 1897, 115 homeless Paiutes of Oregon had received individual allotments east of Burns. Three-quarters of a century passed before they had a reservation, the Burns-Paiute Indian Colony. Tribal government had evolved there through agreements from 1936 to 1938 between the Burns-Paiute Colony and the BIA. Three-fourths of the members live on or adjacent to the reservation. Operating under a business committee, the Colony generates income from a 110-acre tribally owned farm (see **Burns Paiute Indian Colony**).

On April 16, 1977, the governor of Nevada proclaimed Duck Valley Indian Reservation Day in commemoration of the hundredth birthday of the original 312,320-acre reservation, which was enlarged by executive order on May 4, 1886, to a half-million acres. In 1980 the main sources of revenue for about 1,200 tribal members were ranching and farming. There is also considerable fishing in reservoirs. Irrigation is made possible by the waters from reservoirs, such as the Wild Horse and Sheep Creek in Nevada and the Mountain View in Idaho. The reservation is administered by a council. With federal funds a tribal complex was constructed at the state line. Education is provided through the Elko, Nevada, school system, with grades one through twelve located in Owyhee, the only townsite on the reservation.

Suggested Readings: "An Interview with Thurman Welbourne," *Idaho Heritage* 1, no. 10 (October, 1977); Gae Canfield, *Sarah Winnemucca of the Northern Paiutes* (Norman: University of Oklahoma Press, 1981); Verne F. Ray et al., "Tribal Distribution in Eastern Oregon and Adjacent Regions," *American Anthropologist* 40, no. 3 (July–September, 1938); Omer C. Stewart, "Culture Element Distributions: XIV Northern Paiute," *Anthropological Records* 4, no. 3 (1941); Omer C. Stewart, "The Northern Paiute Bands," *Anthropological Records* 2, no. 3 (1939); Virginia Cole Trenholm and Maurine Carley, *The Shoshonis: Sentinels of the Rockies* (Norman: University of Oklahoma Press, 1964); Erminie Wheeler Voegelin, "The Northern Paiute of Central Oregon: A Chapter in Treaty-Making," *Ethnohistory* 2, nos. 2 and 3 (1955), and 3, no. 1 (1956); Robert H. Ruby and John A. Brown, *Indians of the Pacific Northwest: A History* (Norman: University of Oklahoma Press, 1981).

Northern Paiute

Old-style nobees alongside canvas tents in a Paiute encampment. Courtesy of Nevada Historical Society, Reno.

OKANAGON
See **Sinkaietk.**

OZETTE
(Wakashan)

The Ozettes (Hosetts) lived on the western Olympic peninsula of present-day Washington state on the lake and river that bear their name and at Flattery Rocks. Ozette Island, reportedly their burial grounds, was discovered on March 22, 1778, by the British naval explorer Captain James Cook.

The Ozettes were a Makah group who in early times, like other Makahs, migrated southward from the west coast of Vancouver Island. In their new home they sometimes fought peoples from the north, such as the Nitinats, a Nootkan people of southwestern Vancouver Island. Sometimes they fought Makah villagers, but often joined them in fighting their southern neighbors, particularly the Quileutes. With other Makah peoples, the Ozettes traded with their erstwhile Quileute foes such items as dentalia shells and Hudson's Bay Company blankets in exchange for whale oil and dried fish, which they in turn traded to the peoples of Vancouver Island. Archaeological excavations begun in the 1970s at Usaahluth (Usahl), the ancient Ozette village at the mouth of the Ozette River, revealed the importance to its inhabitants of whaling and other maritime pursuits. Many artifacts were unearthed that were used in hunting and processing game and in rituals associated with those activities. Several houses of the village were covered by mud slides from as long ago as 500 to 800 years to as recently as the middle of the nineteenth century. The village was reoccupied after each slide. In 1872 an Indian agent reported 200 natives living there. In August of that year they killed as many as nine whales.

An 1870 census reported 188 Ozettes. During the 1880s their population grew, mostly from an influx of families from Neah Bay whose elders opposed sending their children to boarding schools at that place. The excavated Ozette Village was the population center of the 640-acre Ozette Reservation along the Pacific Ocean at Cape Alava, about fifteen miles south of the tip of the Olympic Peninsula, established by executive order on April 12, 1893. Its population declined from 91 in 1888 to 44 in 1901 and 35 in 1906. In 1914, seventeen people were reported as living in the Ozette Village. On March 4, 1911, Congress passed an act (36 Stat. 1345) directing the secretary of the interior to make allotments to Ozettes, Hohs, and Quileutes on the Quinault Reservation as stipulated in an 1856 treaty. With the Makahs, the Ozettes had treated with the United States on January 31, 1855. Lack of farming and grazing land on the Quinault halted the allotting process there in 1913, but that did not halt the exodus from the Ozette Village. Among those abandoning it were some who had returned to Neah Bay and faced reluctantly the white influence there. In 1923 there were said to have been only eight Ozettes. In 1937 only one Ozette was reported living on the reservation, which was later abandoned. He moved to the Makah Reservation where, described by the press as the "last living Ozette," he applied for monies remaining in tribal funds. See **Makah.**

PAIUTE
(See **Northern Paiute**.)

PALOUSE
(Shahaptian)

The Palouses comprised three autonomous Shahaptian-speaking bands along the lower Snake River from Alpowa west to the Columbia-Snake confluence. Between those two points and in adjacent areas, usually on sandy terraces or in sheltered canyons, lay over forty Palouse winter villages. The Palouses called themselves the Nahaum, or Palous, after the "standing rock," a massive basaltic outcropping at the mouth of the Palouse River near the Middle Palouses' main village, which was also called Palus. The Palouses explained the rock variously as a remnant of a wicked woman whose defiance had led to her transformation into stone, the heart of a giant beaver, or the boat of the mythical trickster Coyote. In the nineteenth century the Palouse lands were divided into three general areas on the lower Snake. There were not only slight differences in the climates of the three areas, but also different dialects were spoken by the three Palouse (Upper, Middle, and Lower) bands who inhabited them. In the Upper Palouse villages, more food and animal resources supported larger populations. Besides the Palouse River, the spectacular Palouse Falls and a town bear the Palouse name. Possibly the name of the Apaloosa horse stems from that of the tribe.

The ethnologist James H. Teit held the opinion that the Palouses were a Yakima people, or closely related to the Yakimas, and that they once occupied the lower middle Columbia River, from which some of their number had moved to the lower Snake and Palouse rivers. In 1780 the Palouses numbered roughly 1,800. In 1805–1806 they were estimated at 1,600. In 1854 they numbered about 500. Besides villages on the Snake River upstream from the mouth of the Palouse, there were at that time several lodges farther downstream under a chief Quelaptip, others under So-ei on the Snake north bank thirty miles below its confluence with the Palouse, and yet others at the mouth of the Snake under Tilcoax. When visited by the American explorers Meriwether Lewis and William Clark, the Palouses lived in wooden houses, in contrast to the mat tipis of their neighbors. The explorers noted some neighboring Nez Percé wooden houses, of which the Nez Percés may have learned the construction from the Palouses. The Palouses were primarily a piscatory people, but migrated from their permanent salmon-fishing villages to gather roots and berries and to hunt. Early nineteenth-century fur traders en route to posts in the upper interior traversed the Palouse country and continued northward across the Columbia Plateau. For that part of their journey they often purchased horses from the Palouses, who managed their herds with a skill equal to that of the Nez Percés.

The Palouses were one of the tribes whom the white treaty makers designated as members of the Yakima Nation in the Walla Walla Treaty of 1855. During the 1855–58 war that followed the treaty signing, they fought against the Americans. The leader of the Indian coalition in the Yakima phase of the war (1855–56) was Kamiakin, who was of Palouse-Yakima ancestry. In September, 1858, U.S. Army Colonel George Wright invaded the Spokane–Coeur d'Alêne country in retaliation against the Palouses and other tribes who had participated in the war and for their part in the defeat of the army command of Col. Edward Steptoe in that country the previous May. To put his native adversaries afoot, Wright ordered the killing of about 800 horses, which were reported to have belonged to Tilcoax, but probably belonged to the Palouse chief Poyakin.

In the immediate postwar period the Britisher John Keast Lord wrote: "The Pelouse [sic] Indians were at one time numerous, predatory, and always at war, but this once-dreaded tribe has dwindled away to a mere remnant." Living at the center of a triangle at whose points lay the Nez Percé, Yakima, and Umatilla reservations, the Palouses were urged by government officials to remove to one of them. They not only avoided those confines but also refused government aid, and they would not give their numbers. They claimed that the United States had failed its treaty obligations by failing to evaluate and compensate them for their properties. Especially zealous in seeking their removal to the Yakima Reservation was its agent under the President Ulysses S. Grant Peace Policy, the Methodist Reverend James Wilbur. In 1872, at the beginnings of the Peace Policy era, the Palouses had numbered 150, a number large enough to cause white settlers to seek their removal so that they could appropriate their lands. Although some Palouses had agreed at a Spokane River council on August 18, 1877, to remove to either a proposed Spokane reservation or to the Coeur d'Alêne, they continued until the end of the nineteenth century subsisting on small farm patches in their homelands. Some Palouses of the Dreamer religious persuasion, called "renegades" by white men, fought alongside the Nez Percé Chief Joseph against American forces in 1877 and went with him into exile in Indian Territory (Oklahoma), from which they returned to settle on the Colville (Washington) Reservation in 1886. Traps and wheels on the Columbia River denied the Palouses the salmon so vital to their existence. Encroaching ranchers and farmers also denied them their native sources of

Palouse

Harlish Washshomake, or Wolf Necklace, also known as Tilcoax the Younger. Although small in numbers no Indian people resisted white influence more than did Washshomake's Palouses. Courtesy of Richard Scheuerman.

food. In 1919 they numbered only 82. Today they are virtually extinct, though Palouse blood flows in the veins of Indians on several reservations.

Suggested Readings: Angelo Anastasio, *Intergroup Relations in the Southern Plateau*, master's thesis, University of Chicago, 1955; Albert W. Thompson, "The Early History of the Palouse River and its Names," *Pacific Northwest Quarterly* 62, no. 2 (April, 1971); Richard D. Scheuerman and Clifford Trafzer, "The First People of the Palouse Country," *The Bunchgrass Historian* 8, no. 3 (Fall, 1980); Clifford Trafzer and Richard D. Scheuerman, *Renegade Tribe* (Pullman, Wash., 1986).

PEND d'OREILLE
(Interior Division, Salishan)

Anthropologists and ethnologists such as John R. Swanton, Frederick Webb Hodge, Leslie Spier and James Mooney classified the Upper Pend d'Oreilles, or Upper Kalispels, and the Lower Pend d'Oreilles, or Lower Kalispels, as one tribe, based on linguistic similarity. This classification is followed in this guide. Certain anthropologists, ethnologists, and field observers, such as Edward S. Curtis, Verne F. Ray, and James H. Teit, have considered the two groups to have always been two tribes with distinct cultural and political characteristics. The two groups lived contiguous to each other (see **Kalispel**); today, however, the groups are separated.

After the midnineteenth century the Upper group moved to Flathead Lake in the eastern part of their territory and became part of another tribe (see **Confederated Salish & Kootenai Tribes of the Flathead Reservation**). The Lower group, which was of a nontreaty, nonreservation status, moved to the western part of its area and refused to join any tribe on a reservation. Near the end of the century the United States government gave the Lower Pend d'Oreilles, or Lower Kalispels, a reservation in their own homeland area, and they achieved tribal status as a political entity in themselves. See **Kalispel Indian Community, Kalispel Reservation**.

PORT GAMBLE INDIAN COMMUNITY, PORT GAMBLE RESERVATION, WASHINGTON

The Port Gamble Indian Community, Port Gamble Reservation, Washington, was formerly one of three Clallam bands but has obtained tribal status. In the later nineteenth century some Clallams from the country around the Elwha River (a tributary to the Strait of Juan de Fuca) returned from fishing on Hood Canal and stopped to work at a sawmill at Port Gamble. They stayed to settle near the mill, which had been established in 1853. Their settlement became known as Little Boston. Under the Point-No-Point Treaty of 1855 they, like other Clallams, were scheduled to remove to the Skokomish Reservation, but remained instead in their Port Gamble settlement. They remained autonomous but were without a reservation until the 1930s when the government provided them one. The Port Gamble Reservation had been begun in 1936–37 when the government had purchased and put in trust 1,231.70 acres for them in the Little Boston area. The purchase, amounting to $15,000, was made pursuant to section 5 of the Indian Reorganization Act of June 18, 1934 (48 Stat. 984). Known as the Port Gamble Tract, it was located across a small inlet from the town of Port Gamble, approximately three miles from original Clallam lands.

Location: The center of the Port Gamble Indian Community is its Port Gamble Reservation on the northern Kitsap Peninsula of northwestern Washington state.

Numbers: In 1985 there were 534 Port Gamble Clallams enrolled in the Community. About 375 live on the reservation.

Government and Claims: A tribal constitution was adopted on September 7, 1939. It provided for a business council, which meets regularly and appoints standing committees to deal with education, health, planning, housing, and personnel. The Community also conducts a fisheries enhancement program coordinated through the Point-No-Point Treaty Council of January 26, 1855.

For the purpose of recovering additional compensation for lands ceded to the United States, the three Clallam bands consolidated their claims against the government (see **Clallam**).

Contemporary Life and Culture: All businesses on the reservation are owned by the Community. They include a store, smoke shop, gas station, and mobile-home park. There are also forestry, craftshop, and silk-screen enterprises. Fishing is done on an individual basis, but there are tribal fish hatchery facilities. Among the programs conducted for the benefit of the Community are those dealing with justice, fire prevention, education, foods service, and community and environmental health. There is a Young Adult Conservation Corps and a preschool. Most elementary students attend the David Wolfe School. Other students attend the North Kitsap middle and high schools in nearby Paulsbo. Tribal programs are administered by accounting, personnel, and planning departments housed in a beautiful complex encompassing about thirty offices and facilities. Several members of the Community are employed in a nearby sawmill. Members also work at government projects in the area and for the tribe. Law enforcement is largely in tribal hands, but the office of the Kitsap County sheriff is called in some emergency situations. Religious preference has been predominantly Protestant.

Special Events: The Port Gamble Klallam Derby, usually held late in September, features fish-catch prizes, children's games, and potluck foods. See **Clallam**.

PSHWANWAPAM
(Shahaptian)

The now extinct Pshwanwapams lived just east of the Cascade Mountains on the upper courses of the Yakima River, a Columbia River affluent in Washington. They gave themselves their name, which means "stony ground." Their language was speculated to have been in the Yakima dialectic division of the Shahaptian group. They were reported as closely related culturally and possibly politically to the Upper Yakimas (Kittitas). Some anthropologists believe that the language of the Pshwanwapams was similar to that of the Shahaptian-speaking Klickitats, Micals, and Taitnapams. At one time individuals from those tribes probably moved freely from one band to another and intermarried. Today they are generally accepted by anthropologists as having been a band of Kittitas.

Suggested Readings: Melville Jacobs, "A Sketch of Northern Sahaptin Grammar," *University of Washington Publications in Anthropology* 4 (1931) 85–292; Leslie Spier, *Tribal Distribution in Washington*, American Anthropological Association General Series in Anthropology, no. 3 (Menasha, Wis.: George Banta Publishing Co., 1936).

PUYALLUP
(Coastal Division, Salishan)

The derivation of the name Puyallup has been traced to a Nisqually Indian word for the mouth of the Puyallup River, along which the Puyallup villages extended for about fifteen miles east from Commencement Bay, on which lies the city of Tacoma, Washington. The name Puyallup has also been traced to a native word meaning "shadow," because of the dense forest shades of Puyallup lands. It is also said to mean "crooked stream." At certain seasons the Puyallups were found at various places besides the Puyallup River, such as Carr Inlet and southern Vashon Island in Puget Sound. A reservation, city, and a valley near Tacoma also bear the tribal name.

The Puyallups were primarily a piscatory people. They supplemented that diet with berries and roots and with potatoes after contact with fur traders. The original 1,280-acre Puyallup Reservation was established by the Medicine Creek Treaty of December 26, 1854. It was later enlarged to 18,062 acres by executive orders on January 20, 1857, and September 6, 1873. Some Nisquallis, Cowlitzes, Muckleshoots, Steilacooms, and Indians of other tribes also lived on the reservation. Although many of the Pacific Northwestern Indian reservations were located at some distances from large population centers, that was not true of the Puyallup. The city of Tacoma on its borders was at one time larger than Seattle farther north. The proximity of the reservation to an urban center affected not only its eventual size but also cultural developments among its inhabitants.

In the 1960s and 1970s the contemporary Puyallup Tribe, Puyallup Reservation, Washington, was in the forefront of the fish wars with the state of Washington over Indian off-reservation fishing on the Puyallup River, whose waters the state regulated for purposes of conservation. Once an abundant resource, salmon was the measure of wealth for many Pacific Northwestern Indians. By the early twentieth century this natural resource was diminished through overharvesting and the alteration of streams for power production and irrigation. The artificial means used to revive the runs were insufficient to meet the demands of white and Indian sport and commercial fishermen. Indians were losing out in the competition for fish, which led the Puyallups and other Indians of the Pacific Northwest Coast, Puget Sound, and the Columbia River, including the Nez Percés of Idaho, to assert their rights under their treaties with the United States. Major combatants in this new type of legal warfare were the Puyallups, who fished in defiance of state laws. The clash was publicized when Hollywood personalities joined them in the "war," which involved verbal, and sometimes physical confrontations with state officials on the Nisqually River south of the Puyallup Reservation. On October 13, 1965, at Franks Landing on the Nisqually River six Puyallups were the first Indians arrested and jailed for illegal fishing. Their trial was delayed until January 15, 1969. Other litigation involving fishing cases followed until the federal government sued the state of Washington on behalf of the Indians for their rights to fish. In 1974 a federal judge, George Boldt, ruled that federally recognized western-Washington Indian tribes were entitled to take from many western Washington streams 50 percent of the harvestable runs of salmon and steelhead trout (*United States* v. *State of Washington*, 384 F. Supp. 312, 1974).

Numbers: As of 1984 the Puyallup Tribe numbered 1,286. In 1853 the Puyallups had numbered 150. In 1854 they were reduced to 50, perhaps because of the ravages of smallpox. An official report in 1856 gave their numbers as 550, but that may have included tribesmen of other tribes. In 1929 the base tribal roll was 344. In 1937 they were listed at 322. In recent times their quest for tribal identity and the lowering of the native blood quantum have increased Puyallup numbers. In 1989 there were 7,987.

History: In Puyallup mythology, as in that

Puyallup

A Puyallup couple, Burnt Face Charley and his wife, photographed circa 1895. The Puyallups' country was on Puget Sound, primarily along the river bearing their tribal name. Much of their lands near Tacoma have been appropriated for commercial and industrial enterprises. Courtesy of the Washington State Historical Society.

of other nearby tribes, the figure Dokibatt the Changer, or Transformer, was believed to have created everything from language to roots and berries. It was believed that Dokibatt had removed life from stones, had rendered the insects small and less harmful, and had taught the people how to make fire, clothing, fish traps, and medicines. In reality, the greatest "changer" of the Puyallups was the white man, especially Americans. Attempting to interfere as little as possible with Indian mores, the British Hudson's Bay Company had been content simply to draw the Puyallups and other tribes of the region into its trading system, but from the time of their first settlement on southern Puget Sound in 1845, Americans had pressured their government to effect a treaty with these Indians. The result was the Medicine Creek Treaty of 1854, to which the Puyallups were a party. In the war that broke out the following year, the Upper Puyallups joined other Indian combatants in futile resistance of the Americans. In 1855 many Puyallups were among the 530 Indians whom an acting agent, J. V. Weber, confined to Squaxin Island in Puget Sound to separate them from the "hostiles" in the war.

The Puyallups first came under Roman Catholic influence in the 1840s, but under the Puyallup Agency they were supervised by Protestants because of the President Ulysses S. Grant Peace Policy of the 1870s. During this period the cultivated acreage on their reservation increased from 291 acres in 1871 to 1,200 in 1880, a significant increase considering the difficulty of clearing land. The Puyallups raised wheat, oats, and hay on natural meadows near tidal flats. An American traveler among them in 1884, on observing the efforts of their school children and other signs of Puyallup "progress," termed the Puyallups the "most creditable specimens of civilized Indians to be found in the West." Among the various schools established over the years on the Puyallup Reservation was the Puyallup Indian School, earmarked after 1906 as a trade school for Indians of all tribes. In 1910, as the Cushman Indian Trade School, it attracted Indian youth of various tribes.

Increasing white preemption of the Puyallups' marine food sources hastened the allotment process on their reservation, for which provision had been made in their Medicine Creek Treaty. Allotting and patenting were completed in 1886, one year before the enactment of the General Allotment, or Dawes Severalty, Act of 1887. The continued growth of Tacoma, which by 1890 had a population of 40,000, caused its citizens to seek removal of the restrictions on allotted reservation lands. Their first maneuver resulted in the establishment by Congress on August 19, 1890 (26 Stat. 354), of a commission to authorize sale of Puyallup Reservation tracts. An act of March 3, 1893 (27 Stat. 612, 633), provided for another commission to select and appraise portions of allotments not required for Indian homes and part of an agency tract that was not needed for school purposes, to arrange for their sale by public auction. The 1893 statute provided that the land not chosen for sale remain in Indian hands and not be sold for ten years. When that time expired in 1903, buyers were able to deal directly with the Indians. Before that time Indian signatures were required for sale of their lands. The sales, which began in May, 1895, were conducted by agency personnel and approximately half of the reservation was sold under the authorization of the commission. The Indians claimed that they were coerced into signing permissions for the sales. A railroad company that had located its western terminus near the Puyallup Reservation in 1873 was said to have obtained its lands by cunning. By congressional action on March 2, 1899 (30 Stat. 990), railroad companies received blanket approval from the secretary of the interior for rights-of-way through Indian lands. Among the Puyallup lands sold by the commission were valuable waterfront tracts which were concentrated in the possession of railroad, lumber, and land companies and other businesses and industries. In 1903, when the ten-year restriction against selling their lands had expired, the Indians had little choice but to succumb to whites and lose their lands, and by 1909 their losses were nearly complete. That year the Puyallups tried to regain their tidelands in a lawsuit, *U.S.* v. *Ashton* (170f. 509, 1909), and lost their case. But in another suit the United States Supreme Court on February 20, 1984, upheld a United States Circuit Court of Appeals ruling that twelve acres taken over by the Port of Tacoma in 1950 belonged to the Puyallups. This twelve acres was but a small part of exposed original 270 acres on the channel of the Puyallup River after it was diverted in 1918 and in the 1940's. The area involved extended southeast from Tacoma's Commencement Bay to the limits of the city of Puyallup, and it became occupied by homes and farms of non-Indians. In February 1989, President George Bush signed a bill settling Puyallup tribal claims against the federal government. The latter paid $77.25 million of a $162 million agreement. The balance consisted of $43 million from the Port of Tacoma, $21 million from the state of Washington, $11.4 million from private businesses, and $9 million from local governments. Each tribal member was paid $20,000, and the first government housing project was begun. A $5 million commercial marina with 298 moorings is planned.

Government and Claims: The Puyallup Tribe, Puyallup Reservation, Washington, owns 66.9 acres of land in several parcels. It maintains a tribal organization provided under its constitution, which was approved by the secretary of the interior on May 13, 1936. The Puyallup Tribal Council is the designated governing body.

The Puyallups submitted a claim for compensation for alienated lands before the Indian Claims Commission (Docket 203). Because of the poor recovery rates experienced by various tribes and the great amount of work in pressing their claims, all of which

would have yielded them but a small per capita payment, the Puyallups ceased their efforts before their case was even heard or acted upon.

Contemporary Life and Culture: Many tribal members are employed as skilled and semi-skilled workers in lumbering, fishing, and other industries. The tribe has begun a salmon business since its victory in the contest for fishing rights on its ancestral fishing grounds on the Puyallup River. The tribe also operates a fish hatchery. Work on a 350-bed hospital began in 1941. Later the facility became a diagnostic center run by the state of Washington, but after confrontations less violent than those attending the fish wars, the center was returned to the Indians in 1980.

Special Events: The Puyallups participate in a powwow held in Tacoma late in August or early in September.

Suggested Readings: American Friends Service Committee, *Uncommon Controversy: Fishing Rights of the Muckleshoot, Puyallup, and Nisqually Indians* (Seattle: University of Washington Press, 1970); Myron Eells, *History of Indian Missions on the Pacific Coast, Oregon, Washington and Idaho* (Philadelphia, 1882); Barbara Lane, "Anthropological Report on the Identity, Treaty Status, and Fisheries of the Puyallup Tribe of Indians," "Political and Economic Aspects of Indian-White Culture Contact in Western Washington in the Mid-19th Century, May 10, 1973," manuscript in Washington State Library, Olympia, Wash.; Marian Smith, *The Puyallup-Nisqually*, Columbia University Contributions to Anthropology, vol. 32 (New York, 1940); State of Washington Indian Affairs Task Force, *Are You Listening Neighbor? . . . The People Speak: Will You Listen?* (Olympia, Wash., 1978).

QUEETS
(Coastal Division, Salishan)

The name of the Queets (formerly also called the Quaitso) is said to stem from a word meaning "people made of dirt." The tribe lived on the Queets River and its branches on the Pacific side of Washington's Olympic Peninsula. They were closely related to their neighbors on the south, the Quinaults, who claimed the lands south of the Queets River. The Queets Indians were on poor terms often with the neighboring Quileutes to the north and also occasionally with the Quinaults. Informants told of an abortive Queets invasion of Quinault lands around 1800, at about the time the Queets Indians suffered attacks by the Chehalises, who burned several of their villages and killed many of their people. Often the Queets and the Quinault Indians would vent their aggressive feelings in a rough-and-tumble game of shinny. At other times the two peoples peacefully gathered roots at such places as Baker Prairie, halfway between Moclips and Point Grenville on the coast. Perhaps conflict was kept in check between the Queets Indians and the neighboring Quileutes, Hohs, and Quinaults because those tribes were in a confederation to oppose such tribes as the Clallams, Makahs, Ozettes, Satsops, plus others who lived farther south to the mouth of the Columbia River. The Queets Indians were geographically central in the confederation and in a trading complex that stretched from Vancouver Island south to the Columbia river and beyond.

During the contact period the Queets Indians were wary of white traders, having learned of the conflicts between whites and natives at various places along the coast. With guns and knives Queets Indians in 1854 prevented an Indian agent and his party from passing through their lands. At about that time one Howyatchi (Hoo-e-yas'lsee), or Sampson, received from a gov-ernment official a commission recognizing him as the Queets head chief. With Quinaults and others, the Queets Indians met with Washington Territorial Governor and Superintendent of Indian Affairs Isaac Stevens at the abortive Chehalis Treaty Council early in 1855. A white settler who attended the council, James Swan, stated that a Chehalis shaman with great bravado shot a young Queets chief because his people and the Quinaults had favored the treaty. Opposed to such violence were followers of the Indian Shaker faith, which was carried to the Queets peoples by Quinaults after its founding in 1882 by a Squaxin Indian, John Slocum.

With the Quinaults, the Queets Indians petitioned the Indian Claims Commission (Docket 242) for additional remuneration for the lands that they, along with the Quileutes and the Hohs, had yielded to the United States under their so-called Quinault River Treaty on July 1, 1855 (12 Stat. 971), signed January 25, 1856, and ratified March 8, 1859. The Quinault Reservation had originated under that treaty, but was subsequently enlarged by executive order on November 4, 1873. After an appeal to the Court of Claims, which that body dismissed, the Queets and Quinault petitioners finally received a compromise settlement from the Claims Commission, which on June 25, 1962, approved a judgment against the United States of $205,172.40. Both tribes shared in the settlement.

Descendants of the aboriginal Queets tribe live mainly in the towns of Queets and Taholah within the Quinault Reservation, where the Queets tribesmen received allotments. They have intermingled with the peoples of the Quinault, and today there is no Queets tribe as such. As a separate tribe in 1885 they numbered 85. In 1936 they numbered 82. Never a numerous people, they had been enumerated by the American explorers Meriwether Lewis and William Clark in 1805–1806 at 250 living in eighteen houses. See **Quinault**.

QUILEUTE
(Chimakuan)

The name Quileute (Quillayute) is said to mean simply "name." According to the photographer and observer of American Indians Edward S. Curtis, the tribal name was applied originally to natives of the village of Ziliyut (now La Push, Washington) at the mouth of the Quillayute River. Some scholars maintain that its meaning is unknown. Other names were given the Indian village at the mouth of the Quillayute River. Besides the Hohs, the only linguistic kin of the Quileutes south of Vancouver Island were the Chimakums, who were said to have fled eastward from huge tides in early times (see **Chimakum**). Quileute family-unit settlements extended for thirty miles up the Quillayute, which tumbles from the Olympic Mountains west to the Pacific Ocean in Washington.

The Quileutes believed that they had been created from wolves by Dokibatt the Changer, or Transformer, who looms large in Pacific Northwest coastal mythology. Among the Quileutes' myths, like those of other tribes of the region, was the story of the huge whale-snatching bird, Tistilal, whose flapping wings were thunder and whose yellow feathers were lightning. In early times there were six Quileute societies: for the fisherman, the elk hunter, the whale hunter, the weather predictor, the medicine man, and the warrior (the latter society performed the wolf dance). The societies reflected the nature of Quileute life. With the vast Olympic Peninsula at their backs, the Quileutes turned to the Pacific Ocean as the main source of their subsistence, becoming proficient seal and whale hunters. They never achieved the acclaim enjoyed by Makahs for whale hunting, and it was probably from them that they acquired the techniques of the hunt, which they in turn passed on to the Quinaults.

Location: The modern-day Quileute Tribe, Quileute Reservation, Washington, live on or near their 593.84-acre Quileute Reservation, which was originally 837 acres when established by executive order on February 19, 1889. It is situated on a beautiful stretch of ocean about fourteen miles west of the logging community of Forks on U.S. Highway 101 and about a hundred miles north of the Grays Harbor cities of Hoquiam and Aberdeen. The largest number of Quileutes live in the reservation town of La Push, which is on the south side of the Quillayute River about thirty-eight miles south of Cape Flattery at the northern tip of the Olympic Peninsula.

Numbers: The Quileutes numbered 383 in 1985. With the Hohs they were estimated to have been about 500 in 1780. In 1888, when the two tribes were enumerated separately, the Quileutes numbered 64. In 1962 their numbers were estimated variously from 10 to 100. Their population later increased, like that of many other Pacific Northwestern tribes.

History: More study is needed to ascertain the times and the routes of the early migrations that brought the Quileutes to their historic location, where they occasionally fought other tribes, such as the Makahs. When attacked by superior numbers, the villagers at the mouth of the Quillayute River took refuge on the impregnable James Island nearby, from which a Quileute village was moved to the mainland in the nineteenth century. The Quileutes fought nearly every saltwater tribe between Vancouver Island and the Columbia River. According to their tradition, their last big battle occurred on the Grays Harbor mud flats when they fought a Chinook-Clatsop coalition.

Petty intertribal strife, especially with the Makahs, continued into the latter half of the nineteenth century, but such conflicts did not prevent the intertribal trade by which the Quileutes obtained such goods as dentalia and blankets from the Makahs and the Ozettes. They in turn traded those goods to the Quinaults for that people's highly prized salmon. The Quileutes and their neighbors also traded whale products to the natives of Vancouver Island. Like other tribesmen of the region, the Quileutes held potlatch ceremonies, at which a man's wealth was measured not by what he possessed but by what he gave away.

Quileute tradition tells of shipwrecked Spaniards, the "drifting white people" who lived among them in early times. In May, 1792, they traded with the American Capt. Robert Gray at their main village, the present-day La Push. They were among the natives who attacked and for a time enslaved persons from a Russian vessel that wrecked near the mouth of the Quillayute River on November 1, 1808. In the 1840s the Quileutes survived a severe famine. From the time of Captain Gray's visit until 1855, when they were contacted by Americans seeking to effect a treaty with them, their dealings with whites appear to have been few. Indian Agent M. T. Simmons, representing Washington Territorial Governor and Superintendent of Indian Affairs Isaac Stevens, was among the first to break their relative isolation. On January 25, 1856, Chief How-yaks (How-yat'l) and two sub-chiefs whom Simmons appointed were in the territorial capital of Olympia to sign officially with Stevens the Quinault River Treaty, which they and others had informally signed on July 1, 1855. In 1863 an agency was established at the Makah Reservation, and in 1864 another was established on the Quinault. The Quileutes were administered variously from the town of Taholah on the Quinault Reservation and the town of Neah Bay on the Makah Reservation. According to their 1856 treaty, they were to live on the Quinault, but they chose not to, even after its establishment on November 4, 1873, After they refused to remove to the Quinault, they settled on their own Quileute Reservation, established in 1889.

In 1866 twenty soldiers were dispatched to the Quileute country to arrest three natives accused of killing a white man. Ten others were arrested for offenses that ranged from slave trading to the murder of another white man some years previously. The prisoners were incarcerated at the U.S. Army's Fort Steilacoom, from which they escaped in 1867. The Quileutes had much trouble from the invading white settlers, who in 1867 tried to establish a "Quilehuyte County" government and petitioned the American government to confine the Quileutes to a reservation. In 1882 whites requested that the Quileute shaman Obi, who had opposed them, be removed from the territory as a "troublemaker." Obi appears to have been at the root of violent quarrels over the Quileute chieftaincy. He was finally arrested by his son, an agency policeman. In 1889, while the Quileutes were away hop picking, a white man, seeking to appropriate their properties, burned down twenty-six of their houses at La Push. The Quileutes were forced to build new ones on the beach, which was flooded during storms and high water.

The establishment of the first school among the Quileutes in 1883 set poorly with them. One task of its first teacher was to give the children Christian, or what he called "civilized," names. The Quileutes were relatively free of white pressures during the first decade of the twentieth century. Until about then there were but two wagon roads in the entire western Olympic Peninsula. In 1912 whites established a salmon cannery on the Quillayute River and infringed on Indian fishing by appropriating their ancient fishing sites. Indians were treated as noncitizens and declared ineligible to obtain licenses. By an act on March 4, 1904 (36 Stat. 1346), the commissioner of Indian affairs declared the Quileutes eligible to obtain allotments on the Quinault Reservation as stipulated in their 1856 treaty (the first allotments had been made to Quinaults on the reservation in 1892). A reverse decision two years later denied the Quileutes their allotments. Again the decision was reversed on March 4, 1911, when by congressional action the secretary of the interior was directed to allot land to all Quileutes, Hohs, and Ozettes on the Quinault Reservation as stipulated in their 1856 treaty, though the various tribes had reservations of their own. Lack of farming and grazing land on the Quinault brought allotting there to a halt in 1913. The remaining 168,000 acres of the Quinault Reservation were timbered and were to be held by the Quinault Tribe as a whole. Finally, in 1928 the government completed the allotment by granting 165 Quileutes each an 80-acre timbered tract on the Quinault Reservation.

Government and Claims: The Quileute Tribe voted to organize under the Indian Reorganization Act (48 Stat. 984, 1934) and adopted a constitution and bylaws approved by the secretary of the interior in 1936. The governing body is the Quileute Tribal Council, which elects the principal tribal officers from among its members. A difference from former times is that the tribe does not recognize the chieftaincy, a position that nominally remains in several tribes. The Quileute Tribe has gained several important powers, including the power to veto any sales, disposition, lease, or other encumbrance of tribal lands; to advise on and approve of appropriations; to levy and collect taxes and license fees from nonmembers doing business on the reservation; to enforce ordinances dealing with visitors, trespassers, and tribal membership; to establish a tribal court; and to maintain law and order.

With the Hohs, the Quileutes claimed (Docket 155) additional compensation for lands that they had ceded to the United States under the Quinault River Treaty. With Quinault and Queets Indians, they and the Hohs had received $25,000 as stipulated by treaty, and they claimed that compensation was unconscionably small. The Indian Claims Commission determined that all four tribes had had aboriginal title to 688,000 acres as of March 8, 1858, and on April 17, 1963, awarded the Quileutes and Hohs $112,152.60 for their share. At the time of white contact the Quileutes had claimed about 900 square miles of land.

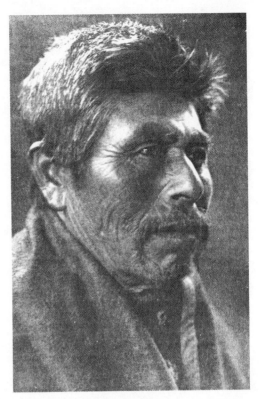

Quileute

Today members of the tribe of this early twentieth-century Quileute man live on their nearly 600-acre Quileute Reservation on the Pacific Coast in northwestern Washington, earning their livelihoods mainly by fishing and logging. Photograph by Edward S. Curtis, from Curtis's The North American Indian *(1907–1930), volume 9.*

Contemporary Life and Culture: Many Quileutes earn their living by fishing and logging. Some receive income from land and timber sales. As of 1975 there were 593.84 acres of trust lands on their tribally owned and unallotted reservation. As noted, reservation residents live primarily in the village of La Push on the Quillayute River, which provides a harbor for fishing boats, as it is sheltered by a breakwater permitting safe passage to and from the Pacific Ocean. The predominant religious orientation is Protestant. An Indian Shaker church was established shortly after the foundings of the faith in 1882. Social services are provided through local and federal agencies. The reservation is serviced by the Forks Consolidated School District, although there has been a move afoot to establish a tribal school at La Push. One was abandoned there in 1927. During World War II twenty-two Quileutes served in the American armed forces. A 14,000-word Quileute dictionary and study manual have been prepared. Considerable attention has also been given to preserving native crafts and culture. The Quileutes are one of few tribes requiring for membership a 50 percent native blood quantum and birth on the reservation.

Special Events: The Quileutes hold their annual Quileute Days usually on the first weekend of August.

Suggested Readings: Edward S. Curtis, *The North American Indian* (1912; New York: Johnson Reprint Corporation, 1970), vol. 10; Philip Drucker, *Indians of the Northwest Coast* (New York: McGraw-Hill, 1955); Harry Hobucket, "Quillayute Indian Tradition," *Washington Historical Quarterly* 25, no. 1 (January, 1934); Ronald L. Olson, *The Quinault Indians; Adze, Canoe, and House Types of the Northwest Coast* (Seattle: University of Washington Press, 1967); George A. Pettitt, "The Quileutes of La Push, 1775–1945," *Anthropological Records* 14, no. 1 (1950); J. V. Powell, et al., "Place Names of the Quileute Indians," *Pacific Northwest Quarterly* 63, no. 3 (July, 1972); Jay Powell and Vickie Jensen, *Quileute: An Introduction to the Indians of La Push* (Seattle: University of Washington Press, 1976); Albert B. Reagen, "Tradition of the Hoh and Quillayute Indians," *Washington Historical Quarterly* 20, no. 3 (July, 1929); *Seattle* (Wash.) *Times*, Pictorial, June 25, 1978; "Teacher 22 Years Among Quillutes," *Tacoma News Tribune*, February 17, 1963.

QUINAULT
(Coastal Division, Salishan)

The name Quinault (Quinaelt) derives from that of the tribe's largest settlement, which was on the site of present-day Taholah, Washington at the mouth of the Quinault River on the Pacific Coast of the Olympic Peninsula shores. The Quinaults' homelands were the Quinault River valley and the coast between Raft River and Joe Creek. Like their neighbors, they were intermediaries in the cultural flow between natives of the Strait of Juan de Fuca on the north and the tribes of the Columbia River on the south. The Quinaults were the southernmost peoples along the coast who hunted whales, but, they did so less extensively than the Makahs north of them. They secured the other items of their subsistence not only from the sea but also from the forests and rivers. Their most important food was the succulent salmon that they caught in the Quinault River. They also fished for salmon and sturgeon in the Columbia River and like other salmon-fishing peoples, they observed taboos attending the catching of that fish. Quinault mothers sent their daughters off to a village so that their menses would not frighten salmon away. Understandably, fish were also important in their mythology. Their ease in obtaining it and other foods caused some early-day whites to regard them as lazy. The customary flattening of the heads of high-born children and such practices as shamanism also encouraged the opinion among whites that Quinaults were a barbarous people.

Location: Today most Quinaults are members of the Quinault Tribe, Quinault Reservation, Washington, and live on the tribe's 189,621-acre reservation, which lies on a coastal plateau extending east from the Pacific Ocean to the foothills of the Olympic Mountains. Most residents of the reservation live in the towns of Taholah (on U.S. Highway 109) and Queets (on U.S. Highway 101). A few families live on allotments, and some live off the reservation.

Quinault

Johnnie Saux, a Quinault, holding a dog salmon in 1936 at Taholah on the Quinault Reservation on Washington's coast. The salmon caught by the Quinaults in their homelands were said to have been the most succulent of all Pacific Coast salmon. Courtesy of the National Archives.

Numbers: In 1984 the tribe numbered 1,623, about 440 more than the 1912 numbers. In 1989 there were 2,260. In the early contact period they were estimated conservatively at about 2,400. In 1885 they numbered 102.

History: The Quinaults usually kept on friendly terms with their neighbors, to whom they extended their hospitality. Sometimes, however, they engaged in conflicts with other Pacific Coast natives and with tribes to the east such as the Twanas, who traveled through the Olympic Mountains onto Quinault lands. The first recorded contact between Quinaults and whites took place on July 13, 1775, when they visited the Spanish vessel *Sonora* in their canoes. On the following day, emerging from the forest, they killed five Spaniards, but lost several of their own number in an ensuing fight. As late as 1854 the early white settler James Swan was of the opinion that there were Quinaults living farther up the Quinault River who had never seen white men. It is possible that Swan was the first white person to see Lake Quinault. It is an indication of the Quinaults' isolation that white settlers did not arrive among them in any appreciable numbers until the late 1880s. Whites also entered Quinault territory from the sea at Point Grenville to shoot sea otter, whose valuable furs they sold to others of their own race. The very existence of these animals was endangered by the guns in the hands of whites and their Indian employees. In the early 1860s troops were dispatched to the Quinault River, and a blockhouse was built, to restrain the natives, who were angry with white trespassers.

With Hoh, Queets, and Quileute Indians, the Quinaults signed the Quinault River Treaty with the Indian agent M. T. Simmons on July 1, 1855. The treaty was formalized in a signing with Washington Territorial Governor and Superintendent of Indian Affairs Isaac Stevens on January 25, 1856. The Quinault Reservation, which originated with the treaty, was enlarged by executive order on November 4, 1873. On February 17, 1892, the president authorized allotments to the Quinaults on the reservation. The reservations of some other tribes who were signatories of the Quinault Treaty were small and barren, and after some controversy the government in 1907 permitted allotments to Queets and Quileute Indians along with the Quinaults on the Quinault Reservation. On March 4, 1911, Congress passed an act directing that Hohs and Ozettes also be allotted on the Quinault Reservation, in hopes that they too would become agrarians. In 1932 the United States Supreme Court ruled that Chehalises, Chinooks, and Cowlitzes should also be allotted on the Quinault. By 1933 the last of the 2,340 allotments on the reservation had been made, leaving no tribally owned land remaining there.

Like other natives, the Quinaults resisted farming. They also resisted sending their children to school. One of their chiefs, Wakeenus, declaimed, "I would rather hang than send my children to school." It was a sign that the relentless white culture was beginning to rub off on the Quinaults when they established a tribally owned fish trap replete with ropes and pulleys near the mouth of the Quinault River at the end of the nineteenth century.

Government and Claims: The governing body of the tribe is the Quinault Tribe, Quinault Reservation, Washington. The tribe's Business Committee functions under bylaws adopted on August 24, 1922. The tribe voted to accept the Indian Reorganization Act of 1934 (48 Stat. 984), but did not reorganize under its terms. Indian personnel staff the reservation police force, and there is a tribal court including a chief judge and associate justices. Tribal leaders believe that their reservation would be better policed if the state of Washington were to recognize the tribe as sole governing body. In 1975 the Quinaults adopted a new constitution which assigned decision-making power to the eleven-member Business Committee instead of the traditional General Council of the tribe.

The Queets and Quinault Indians petitioned the Indian Claims Commission (Docket 242) for additional monetary compensation for the lands that both tribes had ceded to the United States under the Quinault River Treaty. The commission heard the case along with that of the Quileutes and Hohs (Docket 155) because both claims were for compensation above the $25,000 granted by the treaty for the overlapping lands. The commission found that the petitioners had had aboriginal title to approximately 688,000 acres of land as of March 8, 1858. After tribal appeals a Claims Commission order to the Court of Claims (Docket 6-61) was dismissed, and the commission in a compromise settlement with the Quinault and Queets tribes on June 25, 1962, ordered a judgment against the United States of $205,172.40. After the tribes were awarded the monies on April 17, 1973, the Quinaults voted to use their share of the awards for community projects. The two tribes had retained three lawyers.

Contemporary Life and Culture: Nearly a third of the Quinault Reservation has been alienated and is owned largely by timber and saw-milling companies. Having previously sold its timber rights, the Quinault Tribe is in the process of regaining them. There remain approximately 130,000 acres on the reservation which are in an allotted-trust or otherwise restricted status. Many tribesmen engage in logging, sawmilling, and allied industries. Besides a lumber mill, the Quinault Tribe has built a salmon hatchery and a fish-processing plant. It markets a considerable amount of such seafoods as clams. It also operates an arts-and-crafts manufacturing plant. The tribe planned to sue the government because forestry practices on the reservation were bad for the environment. At that point, however, the situation became complicated when members of about ten other tribes were allotted on the reservation. In 1968 those tribes organized the Quinault Allottees Association, and in 1971 filed suit in the Court of Claims, doing so without congressional authorization because they did not have tribal status. When the Court of Claims refused to dismiss the case, the Supreme Court on June 27, 1983, ruled that the Allottees Association could sue the United States for mismanagement of Quinault Indian resources on the reservation. There has been considerable contention between the tribe and the Allottees Association. Tribal officials fear interference from the latter group.

The tribe closed several miles of Pacific Ocean beach to the general public because of abuse of these tribal lands. In 1988 the tribe accepted 11,900 acres of Forest Service land for land omitted from the reservation in an erroneous 1892 survey by Public Law 100-638. Such land was added along both inland reservation borders. In 1989 the tribe also accepted $26.6 million offered to it to settle a timber lawsuit, filed in 1971, for careless timber cutting and for lower prices Indians received as compared with off-reservation sales. Contemporary Quinault art style incorporates South Pacific motifs, introduced by a returning Quinault soldier from World War II, with Quinault motifs. The Indian Shaker church has an active congregation as does the same church on the Queets Reservation. Most tribal members are Protestants.

Special Events: The Quinault Trout Derby is held annually, usually around Memorial Day. The main feature is a cedar dugout race. The tribe also holds Taholah Days, a Fourth of July celebration featuring Indian dances, canoe races, and salmon barbecue.

Suggested Readings: Pauline K. Capoeman, ed., *Land of the Quinault* (Taholah, Wash.: The Quinault Indian Nation, 1990); Philip Drucker, *Indians of the Northwest Coast* (New York: McGraw-Hill, 1955); George Gibbs, "Tribes of Western Washington and Northwestern Oregon," *Contributions to North American Ethnology*, 1 (Washington, 1877), part 2; Ronald L. Olson, *The Quinault Indians: Adze, Canoe, and House Types of the Northwest Coast* (Seattle: University of Washington Press, 1967); Charles Clark Willoughby, "Indians of the Quinault Agency, Washington Territory," *Annual Report of the Smithsonian Institution* (1886); Quinault Tribal Council, *Portrait of Our Land* (Taholah, Wash.: Quinault Tribal Press, 1978).

SAHEWAMISH
(Coastal Division, Salishan)

The Sahewamishes lived on the innermost fingerlike reaches of southern Puget Sound in Washington state. Some of their villages were located on the lower Nisqually River and McAllister (Medicine) Creek and on several bays and inlets, including Budd Inlet, Eld (Mud) Bay, Hammersley Inlet, Henderson (South) Bay, Shelton Inlet, and Totten (Oyster) Bay. The large Sahewamish village near Arcadia, Sahéwabc or Sahéwabsh, commanded outlets of Budd and Shelton inlets and Mud and Oyster bays. Because of its prominence, the name of the Sahéwabsh village, sounding like *sahewamish*, was extended to the natives of other villages. The Sahewamish numbers were estimated at 1,200 in 1780 and at 780 in 1907. After a severe smallpox plague in 1853, government officials counted 50 Sahewamishes living at Eld, Hammersley, and Totten inlets. The Sahewamishes were closely related to the neighboring Squaxins, for whom Squaxin Island was set aside as a reservation. Yet some Sahewamishes intermarried with natives from as far away as northern Puget Sound, and some settled on reservations, such as the Skokomish at the southern end of Hood Canal, on which lived other Sahewamish neighbors, the Twanas.

SALISH & KOOTENAI CONFEDERATED TRIBES
(See **Confederated Salish & Kootenai Tribes of the Flathead Reservation**)

SAMISH
(Coastal Division, Salishan)

The significance of the name Samish is unknown. The name is perpetuated in an island, a bay, a lake, and a river, all in northwestern Washington. The Samishes spoke the Lkungen dialect of the Coastal Salishan language. Their winter villages were on various islands: Samish (south of Bellingham), Guemes (north of Anacortes), and Fidalgo (on which Anacortes lies). From those sites they moved throughout the San Juan Islands to numerous fishing sites. Culturally they were closely linked with the Lummis. In the 1840s the Samishes were reduced to a single village by disease and the raids of more-powerful northern tribes. On Samish Bay and Samish Island, which is linked to the mainland by a natural landfill, the Samishes lived close to the once-powerful Nuwaha villagers grouped by anthropologists with the Skagits, many of whom joined with the Samishes at the beginning of the twentieth century. The Samishes were known for their canoe making and their gift-giving potlatches, which were attended by tribesmen from all over Puget Sound, Vancouver Island, and the Fraser River country. The Samishes' last large potlatch was held shortly after 1900.

Location: Most Samish tribal members live in such communities as Anacortes, Mount Vernon, Bellingham and Everett and in many smaller ones in northwestern Washington. A small number live on nearby reservations, such as the Lummi and the Swinomish.

Numbers: As of 1980, Samish tribal enrollment stood at 590. The aboriginal Samish population was estimated at 1,000, including Lummis and Nooksacks. In 1850, Samish numbers were approximately 150, the same as were reported by government sources at the time of the Point Elliott Treaty in 1855. In 1930 the tribe numbered 280; and in 1951, approximately 350.

History: A Nuwaha chief, Pateus (or Pattehus), was said to have signed the Point Elliott Treaty of January 22, 1855, for the Samishes. Other sources claim that the Lummi chief Chowitsoot signed for them. The nineteenth-century ethnologist George Gibbs, in government employ in the Pacific Northwest at the time, stated that 113 of the 150 Samishes attended the treaty council. The Samishes did not appear in the final draft of the treaty; yet present-day Samishes claim to have documentation showing that their ancestors were included in its initial draft, but were inadvertently omitted from a final one. After the treaty was ratified, the Samishes were sent to reservations such as the Lummi and the Swinomish. Refusing to leave their homelands, many left the reservations for the territory traditionally held by them. Samish informants maintain that as late as the end of the nineteenth century American soldiers drove their ancestors to the reservations and that some of those who refused to remove were put to death, while others escaped to Canada. Samish Indians of the lower classes and males suffered the most. Upper-class Samish women married to white men generally escaped such cruelties. Approximately forty-seven Samishes were on the Lummi Reservation, where they were often in conflict with the Lummi and Nooksack Indians. Most of the Samishes, except those who had intermarried with Lummis, returned to their tribe, which remained on Samish Island during the 1870s.

Samish

Ken Hansen, circa 1987, a Samish Indian of Northwestern Washington, was in the forefront of the Samishes' attempts to achieve federal recognition and regain fishing and other rights for their once-powerful tribe. He exemplified the many active tribal leaders of the Pacific Northwest in the 1970s and 1980s.

Under the Point Elliott Treaty the Samishes were to have had an area set aside for them on the Swinomish Reservation. The area was to have been the western half of March's Point on Fidalgo Island (just east of Anacortes). When the Swinomish Reservation boundaries were defined by executive order on September 9, 1873, most of the Samishes, the largest tribe scheduled for the reservation, found themselves outside its confines. Only a half dozen of the ninety-seven allotments on the reservation were for Samishes, who were often erroneously referred to in agency records as Skagits.

The Samishes found themselves outside the protection of the United States government and once again were forced to move, this time to Guemes Island, which is in an

179

area now called Potlatch Beach that was formerly referred to as New Guemes to distinguish it from earlier Samish villages on the island. The Samishes built a longhouse approximately 60 by 480 feet, in which over a hundred people lived. Each of nine principal family heads was a religious leader who kept alive traditional religious beliefs despite the ongoing governmental efforts to stamp them out on the reservations. Observers at the time referred to the Samish village on Guemes Island as the "Pagan capital." Two Samish headmen, Sam Watchoat and Bob Syithlanoch (Citizen Sam and Bob Edwards) filed for and received trust allotments for the Guemes Island property under a homestead act. In 1883 they received trust patents to the lands, which protected them for a twenty-year period. The patents expired in 1903. Because the Samishes had the only fresh spring water on the island, much pressure was exerted on them by their white neighbors, and by 1912 they had been forced off their lands, as they had been forced off Samish Island by whites about fifty years earlier. After the breakup of the Guemes Island village, some Salishes remained as squatters, and others removed to various communities in Samish country, such as Anacortes, Blanchard, Bay View, Edison, Bow Hill, and Summit Park. Throughout the 1890s and well into the 1900s the Samishes continued occupying fishing villages on Lopez and Cypress islands in the San Juans and traveled throughout those islands in large canoes, some of which were thirty-six feet long. Many took allotments on the Swinomish Reservation in 1885 and eventually (after 1900) moved onto the reservation. Other Samishes received allotments there in 1905.

Government and Claims: The Samishes developed a political organization as early as 1907 and met in their longhouse on Guemes Island and later in Anacortes. Later still, they held meetings on the Swinomish Reservation, strictly as their own tribe. Around 1918 the Lower (Samish Flat or Stick Samish) Nuwahas merged with the Samishes. In 1924, their tribal president was S. J. Kavanaugh, who had also been elected president of the Northwestern Federation of American Indians organized in Tacoma in 1914 to push for fulfillment of treaty claims. In 1926 the Samishes organized under a formal constitution and bylaws, which were replaced by new ones in 1951, 1965, and 1974. Today they are known as the Samish Indian Tribe. Although landless, they fought alongside their reservation allies for the greater self-government provided under the Indian Reorganization Act (48 Stat. 984) in the 1930s, against termination of the Indians' special relationship with the federal government in the 1950s, and against state jurisdiction. The federal government would not recognize or acknowledge them as a tribe despite all their efforts. In 1975 they filed a petition seeking recognition, but three years later the government, without acting on it, returned it to them. In 1979 the tribe developed and submitted a new petition under newly developed federal guidelines, but they were again denied acknowledgment in 1982.

Federal acknowledgment of the Samishes as a tribe would have given tribal members the rights enjoyed by the members of the several other treaty tribes of the region. One important right pertains to fishing. In 1974 the Samish Tribe intervened in *United States v. Washington*, a case pertaining to a decision by federal judge George Boldt that clarified treaty language by reserving half the harvestable salmon and steelhead trout in the waters of Washington state for federally recognized, land-based treaty tribes. After receiving an unfavorable decision by Judge Boldt in 1979, the Samish Tribe with four other landless tribes appealed its case to the Ninth Circuit Court of Appeals.

After filing its land claim (Docket 261) before the Indian Claims Commission in 1951, the Samish Tribe was awarded a settlement on October 6, 1971. The award of $5,754.96 was for lands alienated to the United States under the Point Elliott Treaty. The United States argued that of the $17,000 to which the Samishes were entitled for their lands, about $11,245.04 had already been provided them in blankets, food, and other governmental "services." The commission determined that the Samishes had exclusively used and occupied about 9,233 acres ceded under the Point Elliott Treaty. In 1979 the Bureau of Indian Affairs declared the tribe extinct. In 1992 a federal judge declared the Samish a viable entity. This left the door open to getting federal recognition.

Suggested Readings: Samish Tribal Press, *Petition for the Federal Acknowledgement of the Samish Indian Tribe* (Anacortes, Wash., 1979); Martin J. Sampson, *Indians of Skagit County* (Mount Vernon, Wash., 1972); Wayne P. Suttles, *The Economic Life of the Coast Salish of Haro and Rosario Straits,* vol. 1 of *Coast Salish and Western Washington Indians* (New York: Garland Publishing, Inc., 1974).

SAMMAMISH
(See **Duwamish.**)

SAN JUAN TRIBE OF INDIANS

The San Juan Tribe of Indians is descended from Lummis, Samishes, certain Canadian tribesmen, and even an Alaskan Indian family, all of whom have come together as a political organization.

Location: Tribal members live largely in the San Juan Islands and on the nearby mainland in northwestern Washington.

Numbers: In 1955 the tribe numbered 255.

Government and Claims: The San Juan Tribe of Indians claims aboriginal possession of approximately 120,000 acres of land in San Juan County, the county that comprises most of the San Juan Islands archipelago. The San Juans were one of several petitioning tribes of the Puget Sound area claiming that compensation was due

them from the United States for alienation of their aboriginal lands. In *Duwamish et al.* v. *United States* (79 C.Cls. 530) it was decided that the San Juans had no claim for compensation because they were not recognized by the United States as a tribe, having never treated with its government. The San Juan Tribe next petitioned the Indian Claims Commission for its claim (Docket 214). The Commission dismissed the case because the San Juans had no identifiable ancestry as a group. They could, however, recover from any award that the Lummis (Docket 110) or Samishes (Docket 261) might receive if they showed descendency from those two peoples. The San Juan Tribe today still seeks federal acknowledgment, which among other things, would permit its members fishing rights guaranteed under the 1855 Point Elliott Treaty with the United States. See **Lummi, Mitchell Bay,** and **Samish.**

SANPOIL
(Interior Division, Salishan)

The word Sanpoil is of native origin despite its Gallic form. The early nineteenth-century fur trader Alexander Henry wrote that the Sanpoils called themselves Spoil-Ehieh (Sin-

poelihuh). He also wrote that they seldom left their own lands, which were primarily along the Sanpoil River in present-day north-central Washington. Their main win-

Sanpoil

Joe James, elder brother of the early twen-tieth-century chief Jim James, who was known among whites as a progressive. Before the Jameses' time, like their close neighbors, the Nespelems, the Sanpoils had isolated them-selves from the federal government, increas-ing the influence of the tribe's most prom-inent nineteenth-century figure, the Dreamer prophet Skolaskin. Photograph from Cull White Collection, taken about 1910.

tering village was near the confluence of the Columbia and Sanpoil rivers. They hunted game and gathered roots and berries in their homelands and in those of their neighbors on the west, the Nespelems, as well as in lands bordering the Columbia River on the south. During salmon seasons they fished at the mouths of the Sanpoil and Spokane rivers (the latter enters the Columbia on the east of the Sanpoil coun-try). With the less-numerous Nespelems, the Sanpoils developed a reputation for inde-pendence among whites and Indians. Tra-dition has it that in precontact times San-poil villagers were attacked by Salish-speak-ing peoples, such as the Spokanes and Co-lumbia Sinkiuses, while tending to their own business, and also by Shahaptian-speak-ing Yakimas and their allies. Sanpoil inde-pendence was not absolute, for they married into other tribes and carried on some trade with them. They were among the natives who visited the Roman Catholic missionaries François Blanchet and Modeste Demers at Kettle Falls on the Columbia River in 1838.

After the Indian wars of the 1850s the Sanpoils, as a nontreaty tribe, remained aloof from the officials of the Colville Agency, under whose jurisdiction they fell. Among their nativist-isolationist responses was their refusal to provide government officials a census of their people. Enhancing their iso-lationism were the ministrations of their prophet-chief Skolaskin, who eschewed not only government aid but also the ministra-tions of Catholic priests. To control his people, he kept a pile of logs in front of his lodge, with which he claimed he would save them from a flood that he predicted would destroy those who did not yield to his authority. He was incarcerated for a time in Alcatraz and became a Catholic con-vert shortly before his death.

In the 1880s the Sanpoils opposed settle-ment on the Colville Reservation with other tribes, such as the Sinkiuses under Chief Moses and a Nez Percé remnant under Chief Joseph. The Sanpoil-Nespelem lands were in the southern part of the Colville Reser-vation, where many Indians coming onto that place settled. The Sanpoils refused gov-ernment aids, such as tools, preferring their traditional hunting, fishing, gathering, and small-patch farming for their subsistence.

Anthropologists have listed Sanpoil numbers as being from 800 to 1,700 immediately before their first contacts with whites. A fur trader in 1827 listed their numbers at 218. During the later nineteenth century various problems attending the census taking by federal officials rendered the accuracy of their numbers tenuous. The Sanpoils declined from 324 in 1905 to 202 in 1913, a downward trend that continued during the twentieth century. In 1959, 110 "fullblood" Sanpoils were reported on the Colville Reservation and 22 of "full blood" beyond its borders. Today their numbers are included with those of the Colville Confederated Tribes. See **Confederated Tribes of the Colville Reservation, Washington.**

Suggested Readings: Jessie A. Bloodworth, "Human Resources Survey of the Colville Confederated Tribes," Field Report of the Bureau of Indian Affairs, Portland Area Office, Colville Agency, Nespelem, Wash., 1959; Rickard D. Gwydir, "A Record of the San Poil Indians," *Washington Historical Quarterly* 8, no. 4 (October, 1917); Verne F. Ray, "The Sanpoil and Nespelem Salishan Peoples of Northeastern Washington," *University of Washington Publications in Anthropology* 5 (1932); Robert H. Ruby and John A. Brown, *Dreamer-Prophets of the Columbia Plateau* (Norman: University of Oklahoma Press, 1989); Robert H. Ruby and John A. Brown, *Half-Sun on the Columbia: A Biography of Chief Moses* (Norman: University of Oklahoma Press, 1965).

SANTIAM
(Kalapuyan)

The Santiams, or Ahalpams, comprised at least four bands on the Santiam River, which flows westward from the Cascade Mountains to the Willamette River in west-central Oregon. They spoke a dialect of the Central Kalapuyan language. At the time of white contact the Santiams and other local natives could not identify the builders of the numerous mounds on the Calapooya River and Muddy Creek and at other locations. The mounds had been built before these Kalapuyan peoples migrated into the Willamette valley, where the Kalapuyans were said to have replaced the tribes whom some scholars have called the Multnomahs.

Like so many native peoples of the Willamette valley, the Santiams dressed lightly in summer, but during other seasons they wore cloaks, buckskin shirts and short trousers, moccasins, and hats of grey fox and raccoon, which contrasted with the basket hats that they wore in summer. Early white visitors found them subsisting by hunting, fishing, and gathering. They harvested grasshoppers and caterpillars as well as plant foods. The natives who occupied the east side of the Willamette valley, from the Santiams' lands north to those of the Northern

Molalas, united in annual hunts, known as "surrounds."

At times the Santiams were subject to encroachments by the Molalas and other native peoples. They and others of the Willamette opposed the fur traders hunting game on their lands. It was probably between the Santiam lands and those of another Kalapuyan group, the Ahantchuyuks (Pudding Rivers), that the Reverend Jason Lee in 1834 established his Methodist mission near present-day Salem. The intermittent fever of the 1830s, by reducing native populations, frustrated missionary endeavors. By the 1840s white immigrants were entering western Oregon in increasing numbers. In 1846 some of them unjustly accused the Santiams of stealing cattle. At that time the Oregon Rangers of Salem were called out to recover the animals and punish the alleged thieves. In negotiations with government agents beginning April 11, 1851, the Santiams under their chiefs Tiacan, Alquema, and Sophan strenuously opposed removal east of the Cascade Mountains. During the negotiations a small band, the Hanshokes, who had formerly separated from the Santiams, rejoined the tribe. Under

Santiam

Abe Hudson, a Santiam. His tribe, one of several in the Kalapuyan linguistic family of western Oregon, was one of the native peoples who vigorously opposed government proposals to move them from the Willamette valley to eastern Oregon to make room for white settlers. The Santiams remained in western Oregon, but on the Grand Ronde Reservation.

pressure from white negotiators, the Santiams agreed on April 16, 1851, to cede their lands in exchange for goods, such as blankets, clothing, and calicos, and a small reserve in their homelands. At that time they numbered 155 souls. Aware of government opposition to Indian slavery, they denied having kept people in bondage. They, however, regarded white men's schools as a form of bondage. Their hopes of escaping further white encroachments were soon shattered, and in 1854 they were asked to renegotiate their treaty. In a pact with Oregon Superintendent of Indian Affairs Joel Palmer, dated January 22, 1855 (10 Stat. 1143, ratified March 3, 1855), they agreed to remain in the Willamette valley until a suitable reservation was designated as their permanent home. They agreed that they would remove to the reservation when the government established it. In 1856 they moved west to the headwaters of the Yamhill River, on which the Grand Ronde Agency was established in the following year. On its reservation the Santiam remnant was led by their chief, Jo Hutchins, who tried to help his people adjust to reservation life and the ways of white men. They numbered 125 on the reservation in 1870. In 1906 there were 23, but four years later, only 9. Today the Santiams are extinct.

Suggested Readings: Stephen Dow Beckham, The *Indians of Western Oregon: This Land Was Theirs* (Coos Bay, Ore.: Arago Books, 1977); S. A. Clarke, *Pioneer Days of Oregon History* (Portland, Ore., 1905); Leo J. Frachtenberg, "Ethnological Researches Among the Kalapuya Indians," *Smithsonian Miscellaneous Collections*, vol. 65, no. 6 (Washington, D. C., Government Printing Office, 1916, pp. 85–89); J. A. Hussey, *Champoeg: Place of Transition* (Portland: Oregon Historical Society, 1964); Melville Jacobs, "Santiam Kalapuya Ethnologic Texts," *University of Washington Publications in Anthropology* 11 (1945), pp. 3–82; Harold Mackey, *The Kalapuyans: A Sourcebook on the Indians of the Willamette Valley* (Salem, Ore.: Mission Mill Museum Association, 1974); W. W. Oglesby, "The Calapooyas Indians," [188?] Manuscript P-A 82, Bancroft Library, University of California, Berkeley; James L. Ratcliff, "What Happened to the Kalapuya? A Study of the Depletion of Their Economic Base," *The Indian Historian* 6, no. 3 (Summer, 1973).

SATSOP
(Coastal Division, Salishan)

The Satsops lived on the Satsop River, a tributary of the Chehalis River in southwestern Washington. Some anthropologists believe that the Satsops' dialect was distinct from other dialects in their area. Others maintain that it was a continuum of the dialect spoken by the Kwaiailks (Upper Chehalises) and other peoples as far west as the Lower Chehalises. The Satsops' political organization was like that of the Lower Chehalises and the Humptulipses and Hoquiams, who were their neighbors. Besides the Satsop River, a settlement and a nuclear plant were given the name Satsop. The Satsops occupied an intermediary position between the Twana peoples of Hood Canal on the north and the Chehalis peoples on the south. Through the Satsop lands ran the trail over which goods passed south along the Pacific Coast to Grays Harbor and from there down the coast to Willapa (Shoalwater) Bay. Through the Satsops the Twanas obtained hemp fiber and mountain-goat hair, which were traded from east of the Cascade Mountains. Cultural activities also followed the trade routes, such as intermarriages between Satsops and Chehalises. In early times the Satsops fought the natives of Willapa Bay and joined the Chinooks from near the mouth of the Columbia River in fighting the Quileutes, a Pacific Coast people of the Olympic Peninsula. After devastating epidemics, especially smallpox, reduced their numbers, a Satsop remnant was invited by the government to remove from their ancestral lands to the Chehalis Reservation at the confluence of the Chehalis and Black rivers. Those Satsops intermarried with persons of other tribes and settled on various reservations. With the Hoquiam band, the Whiskahs, and the Wynoochees, the Satsops numbered 350 in 1870. An 1885 census listed their numbers at 12, as did a census three years later. There is no Satsop tribe today. Indians of Satsop blood were among the Kwaiailks (Upper Chehalises) who on October 7, 1963, by an Indian Claims Commission decree, received a net sum of $754,380 for loss of ancestral lands and fishing rights. See **Confederated Tribes of the Chehalis Reservation, Washington.**

SAUK-SUIATTLE
(Coastal Division, Salishan)

The Sauk-Suiattles are the descendants of peoples of the upper Skagit River watershed in northwestern Washington. In the nineteenth century they were designated as Skagits by government treaty makers and other whites. Because their homelands were near the Cascade Mountains along the Suiattle River, a tributary of the Sauk (which is itself a tributary of the Skagit), their subsistence patterns and dialect varied from those of the other Skagit peoples of the lower Skagit River and Puget Sound. In aboriginal times, their ancestors were said to have occupied five winter houses, which were situated from the mouth of the Sauk upstream to Sauk Prairie, an important gathering place of several tribes. They lived farther upstream in summer.

Location: Members of the Sauk-Suiattle Indian Tribe of Washington live at various places in northwestern Washington. Like the Upper Skagits, some live on scattered public-domain allotments in Skagit County. Some of their ancestors moved to reservations, such as the Swinomish near the mouth of the Skagit.

Numbers: Tribal membership as of 1985 stood at 260.

Sauk-Suiattle

Martin Sherman of the Sauk-Suiattle Tribe, which bears the names of two streams in the upper Skagit River watershed of northwestern Washington. Although the tribe lived west of the Cascade Mountains, they and their neighbors had contacts not only with the coastal natives but also occasionally with peoples east of the Cascades. The Sauk-Suiattles are among the tribes who received federal recognition in the 1970s. This picture was taken in 1983.

History: At the time of the Point Elliott Treaty (1855), the Sauk villagers among the upper Skagits were known as the Sahkumehus and Sabbu-uqus. Their chief, Wawsitkin, refused to sign the treaty because he feared that under it his people would receive no reservation of their own. A subchief, Dahtldemin, however, did sign the document. The upriver location of Sauk-Suiattles did not prevent them from associating with other natives, some of whom visited them from east of the Cascade Mountains. Tradition has it that, when Roman Catholic priests first visited the Indians of

the upper Skagit River, its natives sent a delegation to near Walla Walla to visit a mission that had been recommended to them by natives from east of the Cascade Mountains. On the delegation's return, the Indians built a crude mission of their own. White settlers caused the Sauk-Suiattles to abandon their traditional subsistence patterns, which included hunts for such big game as elk in the Cascade Mountains. As early as 1870 surveyors entered their lands seeking a pass by which a railroad could cross the mountains. White settlers regarded not only the living Indians as obstacles to settlement but also the dead in the native graveyards, who had been sent there by white men's diseases such as smallpox. In the mid-1880s whites burned a native village of eight large cedar-board longhouses at the confluence of the Skagit and Sauk rivers. With the encroachments of whites, some Indians moved to the Swinomish and other reservations of the region.

Government and Claims: In 1946 the Sauk-Suiattles became a tribal entity separate from the Upper Skagits. Tribal affairs are handled by a seven-member council under a constitution and bylaws which were approved by the secretary of the interior September 17, 1975. In June, 1973, the tribe received federal recognition. They were helped in achieving that status, for which a land base is one qualification by their ownership of a small plot of land in common with the Upper Skagits. Because it has fishing rights recognized under the Point Elliott Treaty, the tribe is a member of the Skagit System Cooperative organized in 1976 to regulate and enhance fishing in the Skagit River system. Also participating in the cooperative are the Upper Skagits and the Swinomish Tribal Community.

To recover losses for lands taken under the Point Elliott Treaty, the Sauk-Suiattles brought suit against the United States in 1936. Their claims were submitted to the Court of Claims (82 C.Cl. 697). When they received no award, they submitted a claim (Docket 97) to the Indian Claims Commission, which dismissed it because the Sauk-Suiattles were not an identifiable tribal entity separate from the Upper Skagits at the time of the Point Elliott Treaty. As a federally acknowledged tribe, however, the Sauk-Suiattles were included in a claim with the Upper Skagits (Docket 92). For information on these claims see **Upper Skagit.**

Contemporary Life and Culture: Some tribal members work in the white community. As noted, the Sauk-Suiattle Tribe, jointly with the Upper Skagit Indian Tribe, owns lands in trust to the United States in Skagit County. Sauk-Suiattles also live on scattered individual public-domain allotments in Skagit County.

Suggested Readings: Nels Bruseth, *Indian Stories and Legends of the Stillaguamish, Sauks, and Allied Tribes* (Fairfield, Wash.: Ye Galleon Press, 1977); June McCormick Collins, *Valley of the Spirits: The Upper Skagit Indians of Western Washington* (Seattle: University of Washington Press, 1974); Barbara Lane, "Anthropological Report on the Identity, Treaty Status and Fisheries of the Sauk-Suiattle Tribe of Indians," *Political and Economic Aspects of Indian-White Culture Contact in Western Washington in the Mid-19th Century, May 10, 1973,* Manuscript in Washington State Library, Olympia, Wash.; Martin J. Sampson, *Indians of Skagit County* (Mount Vernon, Wash.: Skagit County Historical Society, 1972).

SEMIAHMOO
(Coastal Division, Salishan)

The Semiahmoos, like their neighbors the Lummis and Samishes and the Songishes of southern Vancouver Island, spoke the Straits, or Lkungen, dialect of the Coastal Salishan language. The Semiahmoos lived far up on the Northwest Coast of the continental United States, near present-day Blaine, Washington, which is on Interstate Highway 5. Their territory extended onto the southwestern British Columbia mainland. They have been called the Birch Bay Indians because some of them lived on Birch Bay. According to an Indian informant born around 1820, an ancient people, the Hulhwaluqs, lived on Birch Bay and southward to Lummi Island. The Hulhwaluqs had been attracted to that area from southern Vancouver Island by the abundant clams in Birch Bay and the elk in nearby hills. Deep middens at Birch Bay attest to the presence there of early villagers. Before the coming of white men, the Hulhwaluqs and the neighboring Skalakhans were defeated and assimilated by the Lummis, who were moving from the San Juan Islands to the mainland seeking lands and fishing places such as those on the Nooksack River.

The Semiahmoos may have been the natives whom Spanish explorers saw in 1791 at Point Roberts fishing for salmon at reef-net locations, although other peoples were also known to fish there. Those natives may not have seen white men before, but they at least had indirect contact with them, as evidenced in brass bracelets obtained through trade. The usually informed George Gibbs in 1853 could only write of the Semiahmoos: "The Shimishmoo inhabit the coast toward Frazier's river; nothing seems to be known of them whatever." He was at least aware of their numbers, which he reported as 250, about 50 less than those given a dozen years earlier by the American naval lieutenant Charles Wilkes. The Semiahmoos were drawn into the Hudson's Bay Company trading orbit, especially by the establishment of Fort Langley in 1827 on the lower Fraser River. A Semiahmoo chief, Kwetiseleq, was said to have become rich selling furs at the fort and purchasing slaves with his earnings. The Semiahmoos may have been among those who met the Roman Catholic missionary Modeste Demers at Fort Langley late in the summer of 1841. Demers wrote that natives had assembled there from great distances to meet him. The Semiahmoos appear not to have signed the Point Elliott Treaty in 1855. Some of them went on the Lummi Reservation and, like the Nooksacks, left it after a time. In the late 1850s, immediately after the treaty, most of the Semiahmoos in the United States moved north across the Canadian border. A small remnant lived in Canada into the twentieth century. A bay bordering the Washington state–British Columbia mainland bears the tribal name as does a small Indian reserve in the latter province.

SENIJEXTEE
(Interior Division, Salishan)

Senijextee

Albert Louie, a Senijextee, or Lake Indian, who served in the American armed forces in World War II. In the nineteenth century Indians scouted for American forces in the Pacific Northwest. They also served in World War I, but they fought in much greater numbers in World War II.

The Senijextees are commonly referred to as the Lake Indians. French-Canadian furmen called them *gens des lacs* ("peoples of the lakes"). They lived along the Columbia River in present-day Washington state from Kettle Falls north to the Canadian border. They also lived along the lower Kettle River, a Columbia tributary, and in Canada in the Arrow Lakes region of the Columbia and along its tributary, the lower Kootenay. They were closely related to the Colvilles and often gathered with them at Kettle Falls during the summer and fall fishing seasons. In the nineteenth century they traded furs at the Hudson's Bay Company's Fort Colvile and worshiped at nearby Roman Catholic missions. On one occasion a Senijextee band arrived at Fort Colvile in a fleet of about thirty canoes and offered to exchange forty prime beaver pelts for the prayers of the fort traders. Their chief, Gregoire, or Gregory, remained on good terms with white men. By protecting them from unfriendly tribesmen, he gained a wide reputation as a peacemaker among whites and Indians.

Like the Colvilles, the Senijextees below the Canadian border were reluctant to leave the Colville Reservation, which was established east of the Columbia River in 1872 and replaced that same year by another west of that stream. On May 23, 1891, Senijextee and Colville chiefs signed an agreement to cede the North Half of the Colville Reservation, where many of them subsequently went to live. One of the stipulations of the agreement had allowed them to take 80-acre allotments on the North Half. Some Senijextees moved to the South Half of the reservation to live with a Colville band there. The 1780 Senijextee population has been estimated at 500. Their official numbers were 239 in 1870, 300 in 1882, and 294 in 1910. The last figure perhaps included some Colvilles, with whom the Senijextees were closely related culturally. The tribesmen are divided into two groups by the 49th parallel. They are also divided spiritually into activists and conservatives among them. There is disagreement over who is the hereditary leader. They united temporarily, however, in Canada, in 1991, to rebury remains of tribesmen returned to them by the Royal British Columbia Museum. See also **Confederated Tribes of the Colville Reservation, Washington.**

Suggested Readings: David H. Chance and Jennifer V. Chance, *Kettle Falls: 1971 and 1974 Salvage Archaeology in Lake Roosevelt,* University of Idaho Anthropological Research Manuscript Series, no. 69 (Moscow, Idaho: University of Idaho, 1982); David H. Chance and Jennifer V. Chance, *Kettle Falls: 1976 Salvage Archaeology in Lake Roosevelt,* University of Idaho Anthropological Manuscript Series, no. 39 (Moscow, Idaho: University of Idaho, 1977); Ruth Lakin, *Kettle River Country* (Colville, Wash.: Statesman Examiner, Inc., 1976); Andrew M. Perkins, "The Lake Indians," Manuscript in possession of authors.

SHASTA
(Hokan)

The Shastas lived primarily in northern California along the middle of the Klamath River in the drainage area of two tributaries, the Scott and Shasta rivers. A small portion of the tribe lived across the California border in Oregon. The name Shasta is believed to be derived from a well-known tribe living near the site of Yreka, California, around 1874. One ethnologist, Roland B. Dixon, gives Kaho'sadi as the Shastan name for the smaller portion of the tribe in Oregon. Others say it is the name for the tribal language. Some Shasta villages in Oregon were south of present-day Ashland and Jacksonville on the northern borders of the Siskiyou Mountains and perhaps between Ashland and Table Rock in the Rogue River drainage area. The Oregon Shastas and two other Oregon tribes, the Takelmas and Latgawas (Rogues), had a common bond in opposing encroaching miners and settlers in the Rogue River country. On one occasion, while escaping a posse of whites the Shastas hid out in the lands of the Rogues. On July 21, 1852, the Rogues signed a tenuous peace treaty with American officials, by which they agreed not to communicate with the Shastas, whose warriors continued to join the Rogues to avenge Shastan blood spilled by miners. In their lust for gold the miners often ignored that some of their victims were friendly to whites. The Oregon Shastas were included in the treaties that the United States effected with the Indians of the Rogue River valley in the mid-1850s, and they were eventually removed with those Indians to the Grand Ronde and Siletz reservations of Oregon. On the Grand Ronde in 1871 they numbered 51. On the Siletz Reservation that same year, along with Chastacostas and Umpquas, they numbered 57.

Suggested Readings: Stephen Dow Beckham, *The Indians of Western Oregon: This Land Was Theirs* (Coos Bay, Ore.: Arago Books, 1977); Edward S. Curtis, *The North American Indian* (1912; New York: Johnson Reprint Corporation, 1970), vol. 13; Roland B. Dixon, *The Shasta* (New York: AMS Press, 1983); Frederick Webb Hodge, *Handbook of American Indians North of Mexico,* pt. 2 (Washington, D. C.: Government Printing Office, 1910); C. Hart Merriam, "Source of the Name Shasta," *Journal of the Washington Academy of Sciences* 16, no. 19 (1926).

Shasta

The Shasta Tribe, to which this woman belonged, lived in northern California and southern Oregon. The Oregon Shastas were included in treaties with the United States in the mid-1850s and were removed north to the Grand Ronde and Siletz reservations. Courtesy of the American Museum of Natural History.

SHOALWATER BAY TRIBE, SHOALWATER BAY RESERVATION

The Shoalwater Bay Tribe, Shoalwater Bay Reservation, Washington, had its inception in the establishment by executive order on September 22, 1866, of the 334.75-acre Shoalwater Bay Reservation for about thirty or forty Indian families of Willapa (formerly, Shoalwater) Bay in southwestern Washington. Members of the tribe are also commonly referred to as Georgetown Indians. Their ancestors were primarily Chinook and Chehalis peoples. Like other Northwest Coast Indians, the Shoalwater Bays are rich in tradition. They told of a canoe from a "far, cold country" that carried a hundred warriors and their families south to the Columbia River. When strong winds forced them back from the Columbia estuary, they abandoned their craft. When they returned later, they discovered that it had "grown" not only Shoalwater Bay and its environs but also its peoples. An early people of Willapa Bay were the Willapas (Willopahs), whom some ethnologists claim were a Chinookan peoples living on the lower course of the Willapa River flowing into the bay. Others maintain that, since the northern limit of Chinookan speakers was the Nemah River, which lies south of the Willapa River, the Willapas were not Chinookan but possibly a branch of a nearby Athapascan people, the Kwalhioquas. When the natives of Willapa Bay succumbed to the devastating plagues of the nineteenth century, the Lower Chehalises moved onto their lands.

The Willapa Bay Indians favored the marine location of the Shoalwater Reservation, but since it was agriculturally unproductive, many other tribes stayed away from it who were scheduled to be removed there. Some of them worked for whites in the logging and oystering industries. Some who were entitled to allotments on the reservation were alloted instead on the Quinault Reservation on the coast farther north. Among the last of the oldtime Indians was Light-House Charley Ma-tote, or Toke, who was appointed head chief of the Shoalwater Bay people. His son George A. Charley (chief of the Shoalwater Bay Tribe from 1889 to 1936) was one of the last of the Pacific

Northwest Indians to have a flattened skull, an indication of his royal lineage. By 1879, Indians of the Shoalwater Bay Reservation spoke the Lower Chehalis dialect of the Coastal Division of the Salish language.

Shoalwater Bay Tribe, Shoalwater Bay Reservation

Rachel Whitish Brignone, age seventy-five in 1986, a member of the Shoalwater Bay Tribe. Historically, Shoalwater Bay tribesmen depended to a great extent on seafoods for subsistence and worked for white entrepreneurs harvesting oysters from the bay for sale in San Francisco and elsewhere. Today there is marked unemployment, and members are moving back to the shy square-mile reservation where they are looking forward to establishing fishing rights and an aquaculture program. In 1981 they built a multipurpose tribal center, and in 1980 six new HUD houses were built, and in 1984, eight more. Photo courtesy Lucinda Shipman, Tokeland, Washington.

Location: About a half-dozen Indian families reside on the Shoalwater Bay Reservation, which fronts the northern end of Willapa Bay and the Pacific Ocean.

Numbers: Tribal membership as of 1985 stood at 64. In 1992 enrollment was 134.

Government: The forerunners of the Shoalwater Bay Tribe, Shoalwater Bay Reservation, Washington, rejected the Indian Reorganization Act in 1934 (48 Stat. 984), but adopted a constitution and became formally organized on May 22, 1971. The tribe's executive body, the Shoalwater Bay Tribal Council, was elected shortly thereafter. In 1984 the tribe, in exchange for $1 million, renounced its claim to eight acres in Tokeland, Washington, which the government conveyed to a citizen in 1872.

Contemporary Life and Culture: Among the businesses on the reservation is a restaurant at Tokeland featuring Indian fry bread and seafoods. The non-Indian community surrounding the reservation provides work for tribal members in the cranberry bogs, fishing, crabbing, and other industries. Children attend public schools off the reservation in the town of Ocosta. Tribal services are provided by local, state, and federal jurisdictions.

Suggested Readings: George A. Charley, "The Indian," *The Sou'wester* (Pacific County Historical Society) 11, no. 3 (Autumn, 1976); Har Plumb, "A Happy Summer on Peacock Spit," *The Sou'wester* 13, nos. 2 and 3 (Summer–Autumn, 1978); Robert H. Ruby and John A. Brown, *The Chinook Indians: Traders of the Lower Columbia River* (Norman: University of Oklahoma Press, 1976); *Seattle* (Wash.) *Times*, Pictorial for January 26, 1975, and April 22, 1979; James G. Swan, *The Northwest Coast; or, Three Years' Residence in Washington Territory* (1857; Fairfield, Wash.: Ye Galleon Press, 1966); Isaac H. Whealdon, "Stories and Sketches from Pacific County [Washington]," *Washington Historical Quarterly* 4, no. 3 (July, 1913).

SHOSHONE–BANNOCK TRIBES OF THE FORT HALL RESERVATION, IDAHO

The members of the Shoshone–Bannock Tribes of the Fort Hall Reservation, Idaho, are descendants of the two tribes, who developed close ties during the nineteenth century and finally settled together on the Fort Hall Reservation.

Location: Most Shoshone–Bannocks live on the Fort Hall Reservation in southeastern Idaho.

Numbers: The combined tribal membership was 3,921 in 1984. In 1989 it was 6,617.

History: In the second Fort Bridger Treaty of July 3, 1868 (15 Stat. 673), the Bannocks were promised a reservation on Idaho's Portneuf and Kansas (Camas) Prairie just southeast of Fort Hall. Instead they were given the Fort Hall Reservation by an executive order on July 30, 1869. By an executive order of June 14, 1867, that reservation had also been set aside for the Shoshonis

of southern Idaho. The Boise Shoshonis and Bruneau Shoshonis moved there between March 12 and April 13, 1869. A total of 1,150 Indians lived on the reservation at that time. Other bands who signed peace treaties with the United States were also removed to Fort Hall: the Pohogues, the Bannock Creeks, the Cache Valleys, and a few Weber Utes (of Northwestern Shoshonis) and Bear Lake Indians. It was also expected that the Lemhi Shoshonis, Bannocks, Tukuarikas (Sheepeaters) and other Shoshonis would move to the reservation as had been agreed on May 14, 1880 (12 Stat. 687, ratified February 23, 1889). Those groups would have been leaving their 64,000-acre Lemhi Reservation (established by executive order on February 12, 1875). After a September 24, 1868, treaty went unratified, thirty-two Lemhi Reservation Indians moved to the Fort Hall. The others at first refused to move, but after their chief, Tendoy, died in May, 1907, 474 did remove there. Absent from the Fort Hall Reservation were a few Bannocks and certain Shoshonis, particularly many of the aforementioned Weber Utes, who remained in Utah, and about six families in the vicinity of Salmon, Idaho, who owned no land and received no government aid.

In August and September, 1877, fifty Bannock scouts were enlisted by the United States military to fight Nez Percés led by Joseph and other chiefs. On May 30, 1878, the Bannock War began at Camas Prairie, Idaho (see **Bannock**). Due to an influx of citizens into southern Idaho Territory and consequent railroad developments, the government on May 14, 1880, made an agreement, with the Shoshone–Bannocks of the Fort Hall Reservations and the Lemhis on their reservation on the north, for removal of the latter to the Fort Hall Reservation with the Shoshone–Bannocks. The government also made an agreement with the Shoshone–Bannocks for cession of 325,000 acres of the southern portion of their reservation in exchange for annuities and allotments on lands remaining on the confine. Congress was reluctant to approve the agreement, and the Lemhis eventually refused to remove. In the meantime, the Utah and Northern Railroad Company sought an east-west right-of-way across the Fort Hall for what was to become the Oregon Short-line Railway, which, like the Utah and Northern, was a subsidiary of the Union Pacific. On July 8, 1881, the Shoshone–Bannocks agree to cede 772 acres to the Utah and Northern. Congress ratified the agreement on July 3, 1881, but legislation for cession of reservation lands for white settlers was stalled in Congress. In the meantime, many settlers flocked to the site that became Pocatello, Idaho. On May 27, 1887, the government made an agreement with the Shoshone–Bannocks under which the two tribes ceded 1,840 acres for the Pocatello townsite. The agreement was amended and approved by Congress on September 1, 1888, Pocatello citizens were allowed rights to water from a reservation source. After citizens agitated for cession of the south half of the Fort Hall Reservation, Congress on June 6, 1900, finally approved a 416,000-acre cession

Shoshone-Bannock Reservation Tribes of the Fort Hall Reservation, Idaho

This man, photographed about 1890, was a forebear of the modern-day Shoshone-Bannocks of the Fort Hall Reservation in southeastern Idaho. The close ties between the Shoshones and the Bannocks during the nineteenth century led to their settlement on the same reservation. Despite their traditional aloofness from white society, the Shoshone-Bannocks have modern irrigation and other projects on their reservation. Courtesy Idaho State Historical Society.

from the reservation, an area much larger than that originally sought.

Seventy-nine Indians were permitted to remain and received allotments of 6,298.72 acres on the latter cession. The remainder of the 409,701.28 acres was opened to white settlement on June 17, 1902. A total of 1,863 Indians received allotments on 338,909 acres of the diminished reservation by congressional approval on October 28, 1914. By the twentieth century the Fort Hall Reservation, formerly of 1.8 million acres, had been reduced to 525,000 acres. About 45,594 acres were set aside as a timber reserve, and 36,263 were reserved for grazing, as approved on October 28, 1914, under the authority of an act dated March 3, 1911 (26 Stat. 1058-64).

Among later nineteenth-century developments on the Fort Hall was the February, 1880, establishment of the reservation's first boarding school. Three years later an industrial boarding school opened. Day schools had begun operating in the 1870s. In 1881 an eight-man police force was organized, as was a tribal police court in 1888. Important early-twentieth-century developments included the building of a hospital in 1902. In 1907 the government established the Fort Hall Irrigation Project. Similar projects followed, including the establishment of the Minidoka Project in the 1920s, construction of the American Falls Reservoir, and the development of 30,000 irrigated farmland acres at Michaud Flats in the 1930s.

Government and Claims: The Indians of the Fort Hall Reservation adopted their constitution and bylaws in 1936. On April 17, 1937, they ratified their corporate charter. Their governing body is the Fort Hall Business Council, whose members are elected by secret ballot for two-year terms.

An aboriginal land claim (Docket 326-H) was filed with the Indian Claims Commission by the Shoshone Tribe of the Wind River Reservation, Wyoming, on behalf of all Eastern, Northern, and Western Shoshonis and Bannocks for the lands used and occupied by those tribes. They had occupied approximately 38,300,000 acres in Wyoming, Colorado, Utah, Nevada, and Idaho.

The claim, which was first litigated in the Court of Claims, resulted in an adverse decision for the petitioning tribes. The decision, which was upheld by the United States Supreme Court (324 U.S. 335, 1945), denied a motion for a rehearing (324 U.S. 890, 1945). A recall amendment of the Supreme Court's mandate was also denied (325 U.S. 840, 1945). All of the Shoshoni, Bannock, and Shoshone–Bannock groups petitioned the Indian Claims Commission (Docket 326) to recover for multiple claims. The commission separated the various claims into separate dockets on July 5, 1957. The following tribes outside the Pacific Northwest were petitioners: the Western Shoshones of Nevada and Utah (Docket 326-A) for United States mismanagement of funds; the Gosiutes (Western Shoshones of Utah) (Docket 326-B), also for mismanagement of funds; the Gosiutes (Docket 326-J), for recovery of their lands; and the Western Shoshones (Docket 326-K), for recovery for their lands.

The Northern, Western, and Northwestern Shoshoni petitioners included the following Pacific Northwest peoples: the Pohogwes (or Fort Halls), the Cache Valleys, the Bear Lakes, the Bannock Creeks, the Lemhis, the Boises, and the Bruneaus, along with Eastern (Washakie) Shoshonis. Their Claims were in Docket 326-C, which was divided into 326-C1 and 326-C2. Those dockets were transferred to the Court of Claims after dissolution of the Indian Claims Commission. The Docket 326-C1 was for grazing, timber, and fiscal mismanagement and was settled for $1.6 million on October 8, 1982. Docket 326-C2 was for the government's failure to protect water rights of the tribes. A claim by the Shoshone-Bannocks of the Fort Hall (Docket 326-D) was for government mishandling of $99,323.80 for irrigation projects. A consideration in Docket 326-E was for compensation to the Fort Hall Shoshone–Bannocks for a 1900 cession of 406,864 acres of the reservation in return for the unconscionably low sum of $525,000. The Shoshone–Bannocks' Docket 326-F was for $120,000 in additional compensation for an 1889 cession of approximately 297,000 acres of the Fort Hall Reservation. Yet another claim (Docket 326-G) by the Fort Hall Tribes was on behalf of the Bannocks for the failure of the United States to provide them a reservation as promised in the Eastern Shoshoni and Bannock Treaty of July 3, 1868 (ratified February 26, 1869). An identical claim, filed by individual Bannocks as an alternate representative-action claim (Docket 366), was combined with Docket 326-G. The Fort Hall tribes also placed a claim (Docket 326-H), with the Wind River tribes and the Northwest Bands of Shoshone Indians of Washakie, Utah, for loss of aboriginally owned, used, and occupied land (the Northwest Bands were a nonreservation group that included the Weber Utes and a few other Northwestern Shoshones). A separate but identical claim (Docket 367) was filed by a group of individuals calling themselves the "Shoshone Nation or Tribe of Indians" and was combined with Dockets 326-H. Dockets 326-D, E, F, G, and H and Dockets 366 and 367 were consolidated for the purpose of entering a single judgment. The Indian Claims Commission on February 13, 1968, approved a total judgment amounting to $15.7 million. In Docket 326-D, E, F, and G an all-claims payment of $500,000 went to the petitioners of the Fort Hall Reservation. For Docket 326-H the payment to the Indians of the Wind River Reservation was $7,259,699.39; the payment to the nonreservation Northwest Bands of Shoshone Indians of Washakie, Utah, was $1,375,000.00; and the payment to the Fort Hall tribes was $6,565,300.61.

A separate claim (Docket 326-I) was also heard by the commission. In 1980 the Northwest Bands of Shoshone Indians were federally recognized but without a federally approved constitution. Government services for that band were administered through the Fort Hall Agency. The Shoshone-Bannocks of Fort Hall, on behalf of Lemhi bands, sought additional monies for loss of aboriginal lands and were awarded $4.5 million by Docket 326-I.

The Wind River Shoshones filed a claim (Docket 63) for additional monies for 700,642 acres that had been ceded from their original 3,054,182-acre reservation by agreement on September 26, 1872 (18 Stat. 291) and for gold taken from those 700,642 acres between July 3, 1868, when the reservation was set aside by treaty, and the date of that cession and for offsets erroneously adjudged against the petitioner by the Court of Claims in prior action on the same issues (H-219, 82 C.Cls. 23 and 85 C.Cls. 331, 1937). The Claims Commission decided that the $27,500 paid for the cession was an unconscionably low amount and awarded the Wind River Shoshones the sum of $533,013.60 on August 20, 1954, less an offset of $100,000. That award was approved by Congress on April 22, 1957. The gold claim and the claim for offsets deducted prior to the Court of Claims' decision of June 1, 1937, were put in a separate claim (Docket 157). Decisions by the Court of Claims and the Supreme Court (304 U.S. 111, 82 L. ed. 1212, 58 S.C. 794) had established the Shoshonis as the owners of underground minerals. The defending United States asked that those two causes of action be barred by *res judicata*. The Claims Commission found that the gold claim had not been barred, but dismissed the action pertaining to the offsets as established by the Court of Claims. By a compromise settlement the Wind River Shoshones on February 24, 1965, were awarded $195,000 less the $75,000 offset for the lost gold.

The Shoshonean-speaking peoples, including Paiutes as well as Shoshonis, with twenty-four other tribes throughout the western United States filed a claim (Docket 342-70) with the Claims Commission. The case, which was transferred to the Court of Claims, was for mismanagement of Indian Claims Commission judgment funds and for other funds, such as Individual Indian Money accounts, held in trust by the United States. The Shoshonean peoples were awarded $221,012.98 in 1980.

Contemporary Life and Culture: Among industries on the Fort Hall Reservation are a tribal trading post, a construction enterprise, and a 1,500-acre farm and agricultural enterprise. An open-pit phosphate mine has operated on the reservation for some time. Indians and non-Indians engage in farming, livestock raising, and other agriculturally related enterprises. An important economic hub of southeastern Idaho is the 20,000-acre Fort Hall Reservation Irrigation Project. A zoning ordinance seeks to ensure clean air, water, and orderly economic growth. An active employment program was instituted in 1975. Important developments in tribal education include an alternate school where students work at their own individual pace. There is a learning lab designed for adult education. The Shoshone-Bannock Tribes also have a library and media center. There is a Fort Hall recreation department and teen center. Tribal health is advanced through the Shoshone-Bannock Tribal health department. As on other reservations, alcoholism has been a major health problem. Another related problem, as on other reservations, has been suicide, the rate among Shoshone–Bannocks being 14 percent above the national average. The idea of tribal members leaving the reservation to join the mainstream of American society has not taken hold on the Fort Hall Reservation. Yet it is one of many signs of white acculturation that over half the people identify themselves with a Christian church. Among those present are Baptist, Episcopal, Roman Catholic, and Mormon denominations. Some are members of the Native American Church for which they worked in 1991 for legislation legalizing peyote use in the state. The same year the tribe negotiated the Fort Hall Water Rights Agreement with Idaho state and private persons over Snake River water rights. In March 1991 the BIA approved for the tribe a tax code that had created a tribal tax commission in October 1989 to tax Indian and non-Indian businesses on the reservation, including utility companies and mining operations.

Special Events: In the second and fourth weeks of July, the Sun War Dances and Indian games are held in the Ross Fork and Bannock Creek districts. Around mid-August the Shoshone-Bannock Indian Festival and Rodeo is held at Fort Hall. In the latter part of September Indian Day is held at Fort Hall, featuring war dances, Indian games, and an all-Indian rodeo.

Suggested Readings: Clyde Hall, "A Visit with Rose Koops," *Idaho Heritage* 1, no. 10 (October, 1977); Sven Liljeblad, "Epilogue: Indian Policy and the Fort Hall Reservation," *Idaho Yesterdays* 2, no. 2 (Summer, 1958); Sven Liljeblad, "Some Observations on the Fort Hall Indian Reservation," *The Indian Historian* 7, no. 4 (Fall, 1974); Brigham Madsen, *The Bannock of Idaho* (Caldwell, Idaho: Caxton Printers, Ltd., 1958); Brigham Madsen, *The Lemhi: Sacajawea's People* (Caldwell, Idaho: Caxton Printers, Ltd., 1980); Brigham Madsen, *The Northern Shoshoni* (Caldwell, Idaho: Caxton Printers, Ltd., 1980; Omer C. Stewart, "The Western Shoshone of Nevada and the U.S. Government, 1863–1950," in Donald R. Tuohy, ed., *Selected Papers from the 14th Great Basin Anthropological Conference*, Ballena Press Publications in Archaeology, Ethnology and History, no. 11 (Socorro, N.M., 1978); Anna Lee Townsend, "Shoshone–Bannock Legend," *Idaho Heritage* 1, no. 10 (October, 1977); Mark N. Trahant, "The Invisible Line," *Idaho Heritage* 1, no. 10 (October, 1977); Virginia Cole Trenholm and Maurine Carley, *The Shoshonis: Sentinels of the Rockies* (Norman: University of Oklahoma Press, 1964).

SHOSHONI
(Shoshonean of the Uto-Aztecan)

The Shoshonis were popularly known as the Snake Indians, among not only whites but also Plains tribes, presumably because they painted snakes on sticks to frighten their foes. The origin of the word Shoshoni is unknown, but it is believed to have stemmed from some English name given them by whites. What has been referred to as the Shoshoni Nation did not exist. The Shoshonean peoples had no composite organization or commonality of lands. In the mideighteenth century they dominated a consider-

Shoshoni

A Shoshoni warrior, circa 1890. The Shoshonis, popularly called the Snake Indians, occupied vast portions of the montane, intermontane, and plains areas of the American West. In the middle of the eighteenth century they dominated a considerable portion of the northern Great Plains. Courtesy of the Idaho State Historical Society.

able portion of the Great Plains, ranging north to the Saskatchewan River country (later Alberta Province). After a smallpox epidemic in 1782 and pressure from their Blackfeet foes, who had obtained firearms from white trappers, the Shoshonis abandoned the Great Plains and much of the upper Missouri River watershed, but they still occupied a vast mountain and intermontaine territory in the north-central American West. In that region they comprised diverse cultural groups, though all were of the same linguistic family.

Some Shoshonean bands were highly mobile; others were not. Differences in their economic activities also militated against formation of a pan-Shoshonean political unit and pan-Shoshonean land ownership. Because of common economic activities, the mounted Shoshoni bands and their Bannock (Paiute) neighbors had developed a loose tribal organization and land-owning complex by the middle of the nineteenth century. Before they acquired horses, the Shoshoni peoples were confined to smaller areas where they subsisted on small game and seeds. Some scholars believe that the horse-riding Shoshonis formed a special class who owned these animals as hallmarks of wealth. Those with fewer horses, the scholars believe, formed another less-mobile class who participated only partially in the nomadic life of the horse-owning Shoshonis. To a considerable extent this less-mobile class depended on fishing for subsistence. A third poorer, horseless class depended on the generosity of the wealthy for their subsistence, which they augmented by consuming rodents, seeds, and insects. The Shoshoni pre-horse political structure was adapted to the changes occasioned by the coming of that animal.

The Shoshonis have been classified in four major divisions: Southern, Western, Eastern, and Northern. We are not concerned here with the Southern division (the Utes), since they were entirely outside the Pacific Northwest. We are concerned with only the northernmost bands of Western Shoshonis, who roamed north from Utah into the southwestern corner of Idaho. In the latter half of the nineteenth century they became cul-turally mixed and blended with western groups of the Northern Shoshonis and with the Northern Paiutes in that region.

The Eastern (Wind River) Shoshonis roamed over a small part of southeastern Idaho, but for the most part they were active in Wyoming. The Eastern Shoshoni chief Washakie became the most powerful leader of the migratory horse-owning Shoshonis at the time when his people were under the greatest stress from whites late in the nineteenth century. He exerted great influence over the Northern Shoshonis and was temporarily allied with Shoshoni chiefs, such as the noted Bannock Creek leader Pocatello (Pocataro), for whom a city in southeastern Idaho is named. For a time Pocatello competed with Washakie for pan-Shoshonean leadership during the stressful period of white immigration. Also giving allegiance to Washakie was the Bannock chief Tahgee (Taghee) of the Northern Paiute upper class, who were affiliated with Shoshonis of similar status. He later became the Northern Shoshoni-Bannock head chief of the roughly 1.8-million-acre Fort Hall Reservation of southeastern Idaho, established June 14, 1867. Washakie later held a similar position on the Wind River Reservation, which was established by treaty in western Wyoming on July 3, 1868.

The most diverse of the Pacific Northwest Shoshonean-speakers were the Northern Shoshonis of Idaho. They were divided into four branches: Western, Mountain, Northwestern, and Pohogwe, or Fort Hall. The Western bands of Northern Shoshonis occupied the general area of southern Idaho. They included the historic Wararereekas—the sedentary fish-catching Boises and Bruneaus—who broke away from their horse-riding tribesmen. In the early nineteenth century the fur man Alexander Ross described them as being under the leadership of Peim (or Pee-eye-em, as Ross called him). In an October 10, 1864, treaty effected with Idaho Superintendent of Indian Affairs and Territorial Governor Caleb Lyon, the Shoshonis of Boise valley agreed to remove to an as-yet-undesignated reservation. On April 10, 1866, the Shoshonis of the Bruneau valley south of the Snake

River made a similar treaty for their removal to an undesignated reservation. (In the 1980s the descendants of both would attempt to receive compensation for their lost lands: see **Shoshone-Bannock Tribes of the Fort Hall Reservation**.) Peiem's successors, Captain Jim and Bannock John, led the Boise-Bruneaus to the Fort Hall Reservation between March 12 and April 13, 1869. To survive the pressures of white immigration a band of the Weiser Shoshonis (who were predominately Northern Paiutes) intermarried and banded together with the Western Shoshonis, sharing territory with them. They refused to leave their mountain homelands above the Payette River of western Idaho to remove to the Malheur Reservation in southeastern Oregon. Finally they were settled on the Fort Hall Reservation and the Duck Valley Reservation (which was established by executive order on April 16, 1877, on the Oregon-Nevada border).

This Western group of Northern Shoshonis of the Boise Basin along Snake River in southwestern Idaho were of that group called salmon fishers. Their semiarid country permitted them but few technical cultural items. Before whites threatened their existence, their largest unit was the village. The Bruneau Shoshonis did not take to horses or mingle with horse-riding peoples, but traveled south and adopted a Western Shoshoni dialect. The Boises had close ties with the Northern-Paiute Weisers, frequently mingling and eventually intermarrying with them.

The peoples who are grouped as Northwestern Shoshonis had roamed to southeastern Idaho from their Utah homelands. They formerly had been part of the mounted Northern Shoshoni bands, but in historic times they avoided the ambitious seasonal migratory rounds of that branch and of the mounted Bannocks. They were joined by others who shared more conservative life patterns, as various branches of the Northwestern Shoshoni tribe developed from shifting alliances. During the stressful midnineteenth century the Northwestern Shoshonis came under the leadership of the Bannock Creek band chief, Pocatello. In 1850 they numbered about 1,800 and occupied lands stretching northward from Salt Lake valley and the northern shores of the Great Salt and Bear lakes, and the Weber, Cache, and Malad valleys. As late as 1875, when they numbered about 600, they still lived near where the Bear River empties into the Great Salt Lake. By the turn of the century most of these Northwestern Shoshonis were on the Fort Hall Reservation.

The Bear Lakes, the Weber Utes, the Cache Valleys, and the Bannock Creeks were four of the ten Northwestern bands of Northern Shoshonis. The Bear Lakes eventually allied with the Wind River Shoshonis and ranged in southeastern Idaho along the river and lake bearing their name. The Weber Utes were overlooked in treaty making with the United States and were not assigned to a reservation. The Cache Valleys, ranging the upper Bear River (Idaho and Utah), were those suffering many casualties in the Battle of Bear River (southeast Idaho), January 29, 1863. The Bannock Creeks under Pocatello ranged from the Raft River to the Portneuf River in Idaho, claiming an area that encompassed the Fort Hall Reservation at the time of its establishment. Like other bands, they suffered during the fur trade era from the devastating rendezvous, when whites and Indians combined liquor with trading and funmaking to create mayhem. The three major Bannock Creek villages included Pocatello's 101 followers, Sam Pitch's 124, and Sagwitch's 158, all of whom were removed to the Fort Hall.

The Lemhis, the Agaidikas (or "salmon eaters"), and the Tukuarikas (or Sheepeaters), were among the Mountain Shoshonis who lived in the mountainous country of central Idaho, where wild sheep ranged. Historically, they were more conservative than other Northern Shoshoni bands. Their archaeological remains may be traced back several thousand years. Some have mistakenly suggested that they were renegades from other bands and tribes. Impoverished and disorganized in early times, with a disintegrating tribal entity, most of them became mobile after they acquired horses. Many of the Sheepeaters, for example, joined the Lemhi Shoshonis; few preferred the seclusion of the mountains. In time some

Bannocks also joined the Lemhis, with whom they traveled to Camas Prairie in south-central Idaho to trade buffalo meat for horses. On horseback they also went with the Eastern Shoshonis to the Great Plains of Montana and Wyoming. From natives of that region they acquired elements of the Plains culture, but they always returned to their homelands near present-day Tendoy in east-central Idaho.

The Lemhis were named for Limhi, a Nephite Mormon king, after members of the Church of Jesus Christ of Latter-day Saints established a mission among them on the Salmon River at Lemhi near Tendoy, Idaho, on June 12, 1855. A Lemhi Shoshoni girl, Sacajawea, after being captured by Plains Indians in 1800, accompanied the American explorers Meriwether Lewis and William Clark on their westward trek in 1805. She persuaded her people to provide the explorers horses for their crossing of the Lolo Trail in the mountains that lay before them. The Lemhi chief at that time was her "brother," Cameahwait. Succeeding Lemhi chiefs were Snag and Tendoy ("The Climber"), for whom a town is named. Tendoy managed to keep his people on their 64,000-acre Lemhi Reservation, which was established on the Lemhi River by executive order, February 12, 1875. On that confine in 1878 were 300 Tukuarikas, 190 Bannocks, and 450 Shoshonis. An attempt was made to force them onto the Fort Hall Reservation by an executive order on January 7, 1879. Their resistance to removal led to a conference in Washington, D.C., from which came the agreement of May 14, 1880, mandating their removal and the cession of their reservation to the United States. After protestations from the reservation's angry Indians, a commission recommended withdrawal of that part of the agreement calling for their removal. In 1882 thirty-two Lemhis voluntarily moved to the Fort Hall Reservation, and after Tendoy died in May, 1907, 474 more Lemhis moved to that reservation.

Preferring a more sedentary existence, the Tukuarikas, joining the Lemhis, continued living in the mountains, gaining their subsistence from gathering and from hunting game, such as mountain sheep. They processed mountain-sheep wool into clothing and coverings, and they received their name from those animals as consumers of their meat. White miners and settlers blamed the Tukuarikas for the massacre of some Chinese on February 13, 1879, and called on the military to round them up. After a series of desultory campaigns and skirmishes, the military netted but twelve combatants from their band, which numbered only fifty-two souls.

Another Northern Shoshoni band was the Pohogwes, or Fort Hall Indians, a mounted people. In the nineteenth century they became allied culturally with other Northern Shoshoni bands and migratory Bannocks, with whom they roamed from the Wind River Range of Wyoming to the Salmon Falls of the Snake River in Idaho and into northern Utah. They also assumed elements of Plains Indian culture. The Pohogwes signed the Soda Springs Treaty of October 14, 1863 (see below).

White travelers crossing Shoshoni lands over the Immigrant Road (the Oregon Trail) were attacked by dissident warriors, who in one year, 1851, claimed to have stolen $18 million worth of their properties. Shoshoni braves were free to attack the immigrants because their ancient Blackfeet foes were at last avoiding their lands after suffering defeats at the Shoshonis' hands. For many years after they had acquired horses and guns from white traders, the Blackfeet had held the upper hand over the Shoshonis, whose attacks on immigrants had usually been small-scale enterprises by splinter groups. In the 1850s, Shoshoni-Bannock combinations attacked at places as diverse as the Lemhi Mormon Mission (February, 1857) and the Immigrant Road. Americans responded to the attacks by sending out volunteers to patrol the road. The absence of regular army troops during the Civil War (1861–65) made it difficult to police this part of the American frontier. A volunteer force under Col. Patrick E. Conner, after several skirmishes with the Indians, inflicted the most damage on them. Four hundred Shoshonis were reported dead after Connor attacked Pocatello's Bannock Creeks and other Shoshoni bands, including the Cache

Valleys of the upper Bear River at Battle Creek, a Bear River tributary of southeastern Idaho. The Indian losses in that engagement on January 29, 1863, were said to be the largest suffered in any engagement between Indians and United States forces. Conner's victory caused white frontiersmen to breathe more easily. Pocatello was regarded as a leader of the antiwhite Shoshoni factions among the Northwestern Shoshonis. Whites were also relieved when he failed to wrest the Shoshoni leadership from Washakie, who was peacefully disposed to Americans.

When shortly after the Battle of Bear River other Shoshonis suffered defeat at Salmon Falls on the Snake River, the United States effected several peace treaties with Shoshoni bands both within and outside the Pacific Northwest. One of these was the Fort Bridger (Wyoming) Treaty of July 2, 1863 (18 Stat. 685) with head men of the Eastern, or Wind River, Shoshonis under Washakie, who at the time led 1,200 people. The treaty provided Americans safe passage through that chief's lands. American officials effected a peace pact (13 Stat. 663) at Box Elder, Utah, on July 30, 1863, with Pocatello's Bannock Creeks and nine other bands of southeastern Idaho and northern Utah. On October 1, 1863, another peace treaty (18 Stat. 689) was effected with Western Shoshoni bands at Ruby Valley in northeastern Nevada, guaranteeing their friendship with the United States and safe passage for the Americans. On October 12, 1863, a treaty (13 Stat. 681) was effected with the Gosiute band of Western Shoshonis of the Tuilla valley in northeastern Nevada, guaranteeing their friendship with the United States and safe passage through their lands for immigrants. A treaty of peace and friendship that went unratified was consummated on October 14, 1863, at Soda Springs in southeastern Idaho with the Bannocks and Pohogwes under Bannock chiefs Le Grand Coquin and Tahgee and with the chiefs of various bands of Northern Shoshonis.

Government officials estimated that the United States had treated with a thousand Indians at Soda Springs. It was estimated

that the parties to the various Shoshoni and Bannock peace treaties, represented 8,650 Shoshonean speakers. A second Fort Bridger Treaty (15 Stat. 673) was effected with the Eastern Shoshonis under Washakie on July 3, 1868, and stipulated their removal to the 3,059,182-acre Wind River Reservation. The Bannocks had been promised a reservation by their treaty but because the president had failed to establish the reservation, they were removed to the Fort Hall, which they shared with the Shoshonis. See **Shoshone-Bannock Tribes of the Fort Hall Reservation.**

Suggested Readings: W. A. Allen, *The Sheep Eaters* (1989); Merrill D. Beal and Merle W. Wells, *History of Idaho* (New York, 1959), 3 vols.; W. C. Brown, "The Sheepeater Campaign," *Tenth Biennial Report of the Board of Trustees of the State Historical Society of Idaho for the Years 1925–1926* (Boise, Idaho, 1926); Sven Liljeblad, *The Indians of Idaho* (Boise: Idaho Historical Society, 1960); Robert H. Lowie, *The Northern Shoshone,* Anthropological Papers of the American Museum of Natural History, vol. 2, pt. 2 (New York, 1909); Merle W. Wells, "Caleb Lyon's Bruneau Treaty," *Idaho Yesterdays* 13, no. 1 (Spring, 1969); Brigham D. Madsen, *The Lemhi: Sacajawea's People* (Caldwell, Idaho: Caxton Printers, Ltd., 1980); Brigham D. Madsen, *The Northern Shoshoni* (Caldwell, Idaho: Caxton Printers, Ltd., 1980); Julian H. Steward, *Basin-Plateau Aboriginal Sociopolitical Groups,* Bureau of American Ethnology Bulletin no. 120 (Washington, D.C.: Government Printing Office, 1938); Omer C. Stewart, "The Western Shoshone of Nevada and the U.S. Government, 1863–1950," in Donald R. Tuohy, ed., *Selected Papers from the 14th Great Basin Anthropological Conference,* Ballena Press Publications in Archaeology, Ethnology, and History, no. 11 (Socorro, N.M., 1978); Omer C. Stewart, "The Shoshoni: Their History and Social Organization," *Idaho Yesterdays* 9, no. 3 (Fall, 1965); Virginia Cole Trenholm and Maurine Carley, *The Shoshonis: Sentinels of the Rockies* (Norman: University of Oklahoma Press, 1964); Deward Walker, *The Indians of Idaho* (Moscow, Idaho: University Press of Idaho, 1978).

SILETZ
(Coastal Division, Salishan)

The Siletzes of the northwestern Oregon coast were the southernmost peoples of Salishan linguistic stock. A town, a river, and the reservation on which the tribe lived all bear the Siletz name, the significance of of which is unknown. In aboriginal times the tribe used the Chinook type of canoe for traveling and food gathering. They dip-netted for smelt, gathered crabs and clams, speared flounder, and gathered mussels for drying. Each spring they set large basket pots and traps near river estuaries to snare lamprey eels, which they smoked and sun-dried. Their hunters used sinew-backed bows, preferably of yew wood, and trapped big game, such as elk, in pitfalls. Their women dug roots and gathered berries, bracken fern, lupine, skunk cabbage, and salal. In bone, die, and shinny games the Siletzes sometimes wagered and lost all their possessions.

On their 225,000-acre reservation the Si-letzes lived among tribes of six other linguistic stocks. Like the others, they found it difficult to become the farmers that the government wished them to be. Before and during the reservation era, the relentless diseases and other consequences of white contact reduced their numbers. When officials began enumerating the peoples of the Siletz Reservation in 1857, they listed only 21 Siletzes. Perhaps because they were relatively isolated from whites in aboriginal times, estimates of their populations during that period appear to be nonexistent. One source states that in 1890 the Siletzes no longer existed as a tribe. In 1930 no more than seventy-two Siletzes remained. They were plaintiffs in a suit before the Court of Claims (Case No. 45230) seeking payment for alienated ancestral lands. (See **Confederated Tribes of the Siletz Indians of Oregon, Tillamook,** and **Yaquina.**)

SILETZ CONFEDERATED TRIBES
(See **Confederated Tribes of the Siletz Indians of Oregon.**)

SINKAIETK
(Interior Division, Salishan)

The Sinkaietks lived from around the confluence of the Columbia and Okanogan rivers north to the confluence of the Okanogan with the Similkameen River a short distance below the Canadian border. The Sinkaietks are also called the Southern (or Lower) Okanagons, a name that is said to derive from a native place-name for the area near the mouth of the Similkameen River. The Sinkaietks called themselves "people of the water that does not freeze." They were closely related to the Methows, Sanpoils, Nespelems, Colvilles, and Senijextees. Among their subdivisions were the Kartars, Tonas-kets, and Konkonelps.

According to elderly Sinkaietk informants, their ancestors suffered attacks by other Salish speakers, such as the Spokanes and Columbia Sinkiuses. The early nineteenth-century explorer-trader David Thompson dissuaded some Spokanes and Kalispels (Pend d'Oreilles) from attacking the Sin-kaietks. Like other horse tribes of the interior, the Sinkaietks hunted, fished, and gathered for their subsistence. Sometimes they joined other Salish and Shahaptian peoples on buffalo hunts on the Great Plains. Another early nineteenth-century fur trader, Alexander Ross, lived among them at Fort Okanogan (established August 31, 1811) at the confluence of the Columbia and Okanogan rivers. Ross wrote that polygamy was "the greatest source of evil existing among this otherwise happy people." Other Columbia Plateau peoples also practiced polygamy and, like the Sinkaietks believed in good and evil forces. The Sinkaietks were among the Salish peoples who met the Roman Catholic missionaries François Blanchet and Modeste Demers at Fort Colvile in November, 1838. Their introduction to the Christian faith had no doubt come earlier through contact with other Salishan peoples, such as the Flatheads, who had been introduced to Christianity by Iroquois Indians in the beginning of the nineteenth century. About the time of their meeting with the two Catholic missionaries, the Sinkaietks visited the Lapwai (Idaho) mission of the Reverend Henry Spalding of the American Board of Commissioners for Foreign Missions.

The Sinkaietks were not party to the 1855 Walla Walla Treaty with Washington Territorial Governor and Superintendent of Indian Affairs Isaac Stevens, nor did they participate in the ensuing Yakima War (1855–56) against Americans, which broke out because of the natives' dissatisfaction with the treaty. The Sinkaietks were influenced by one of their chiefs, Walking Grizzly-bear, to refrain from the hostilities. They were, however, among those at McLoughlin Canyon near the Okanogan River south of present-day Tonasket, Washington, where in the summer of 1858, Indians attacked and reportedly killed six men of a party of miners en route to Canadian goldfields. Some Sinkaietks were among those who unsuccessfully engaged U.S. Army Colonel George Wright and his command in two fights in the Spokane country in September, 1858. In the postwar period the tribe was angered by the establishment of the Moses, or Columbia, Reservation in their lands and especially angered with the chief for whom it was named, whom they did not recognize as their leader. It was especially galling to them that Chief Moses collected grazing fees

Sinkaietk

Many Indians bore the name Eneas, from the French Ignace. This Eneas, photographed in 1905, was a Sinkaietk, or Southern Okanagon. On his tribal lands lay portions of the Colville Reservation in north-central Washington. His clothing was suitable to the rigorous climate of the reservation, where winters were cold and summer frosts were common. Photograph by Frank Avery.

203

from white cattlemen running herds on Sinkaietk lands. When the Moses Reservation
was terminated in 1884, some Sinkaietks
remained in their homelands west of the
Okanogan River, and others (for example,
those under the influence of the pro-American chief Tonasket) remained on their own
lands in the Colville Reservation east of the
Okanogan River.

Sinkaietk numbers, excluding the Northern (Upper) Okanagons in Canada, have
been estimated at 1,000 in 1780 and 348
in 1906. The 1906 figure was about 187
higher than that given by a Colville Reservation agent in 1870. In 1959 there were
91 Sinkaietks of full blood on their reservation and 34 outside of it. Like other Indians on reservations east of the Cascade
Mountains, those on the Colville retained a
higher quantum of Indian blood than the
tribes west of the Cascades, where contacts

with whites were more frequent. Today the
Sinkaietks are amalgamated with the tribesmen of the Confederated Tribes of the Colville Reservation, Washington. See **Confederated Tribes of the Colville Reservation,
Washington**.

Suggested Readings: Walter Cline et al., *The Sinkaietk or Southern Okanagon of Washington,*
ed. Leslie Spier, American Anthropological Association, General Series in Anthropology, no. 6
(Menasha, Wis.: George Banta Publishing Co.,
1938); Alexander Ross, *Adventures of the First
Settlers on the Oregon or Columbia River* (Lon-
don, 1849); Alexander Ross, *The Fur Hunters
of the Far West* (Norman: University of Oklahoma Press, 1956); Robert H. Ruby and John A.
Brown, *Half-Sun on the Columbia: A Biography
of Chief Moses* (Norman: University of Oklahoma Press, 1965); James Teit, "The Middle Columbia Salish," *University of Washington Publications in Anthropology* 2, no. 4 (1928).

SINKIUSE
(Interior Division, Salishan)

The name Sinkiuse is said to mean "between
people." The Sinkiuses of the Rock Island
area of the Columbia River near Wenatchee,
Washington, were called by early French-
Canadian fur traders *Isle des Pierres* ("[peo-
ple of] the island of rocks"). They called
themselves Kawachens, or those "living on
the banks." Another of their villages, known
as "roasting place," was along the Columbia
in desert country near present-day Beverly,
Washington.

Sinkiuse origins are shrouded in controversy. Some anthropologists claim that with
the introduction of horse culture in the southern Pacific Northwest interior, the Sinkiuses
and other Salishan peoples were pressured
northward from the lower Columbia River
by Shahaptian peoples, such as the Yakimas
and the Klickitats. Other scholars dispute
those origins. Elderly Sinkiuses—or Moses
Columbias, as they were called in the later
nineteenth century—claimed that their ancestors had come "from the north" in the

distant past. Although the tribe lived primarily along the Columbia, its members
roamed a 5,000-square-mile area, mostly
on the Columbia Plateau south and east of
the Columbia River. The northern boundary of their lands (in present-day Washington state) ran along Badger Mountain
just east of the Columbia and south of
Waterville, Washington; and northeast to
the Grand Coulee Dam, from which the
territory extended southwest a few miles,
following the eastern slopes of the Grand
Coulee and then south to include Soap Lake,
Ephrata, and Moses Lake. From Moses Lake
the boundary ran south to approximately
the forty-seventh parallel and from that line
southwest to the Columbia at Beverly.

In July, 1811, a band of Indians, whom
the Northwester David Thompson recorded
as the Sinkowarsin (Sinkiuse-Kawachen?),
met the fur man at Rock Island of the Columbia below present-day East Wenatchee.
Thompson was on his "Journey of the Sum-

mer Moon" searching for wider trading opportunities for the North West Company.

In the early nineteenth century the Sinkiuses were led by the powerful Sulktalthscosum, or Half-Sun, who was killed on a buffalo hunt by Plains Indians sometime around 1850. After the death of his eldest son, Quiltenenock (Quiltomee), at the hands of white miners below the mouth of the Wenatchee River in 1858, tribal leadership passed to Quiltenenock's brother, Moses, who had received his biblical name as a lad in the school run by the American Board of Commissioners for Foreign Missions at present-day Lapwai, Idaho. Today a coulee, a lake, and the city of Moses Lake, Washington, on Interstate 90 bear his name. Moses fought Americans in the 1850s, but assumed a peaceful posture in the postwar period, withholding his braves from hostilities. He also assumed the leadership of the nontreaty peoples on the mid-Columbia. The Columbia, or Moses, Reservation was established for him and his followers by executive order on April 19, 1879. It was enlarged to the south by executive order on May 6, 1880, so that it stretched from Lake Chelan north to the Canadian border and from the crest of the Cascade Mountains to the Okanogan River. The fifteen-mile strip across the reservation's northern end was withdrawn at the insistence of miners by an executive order of February 23, 1883. Then the diminished reservation was relinquished by an agreement with Moses on July 7, 1883 (ratified by Congress on July 4, 1884). The land was restored to the public domain on May 1, 1886. Moses and his band never occupied the reservation, though the chief collected rent from its white cattlemen. He and his people were removed to the Colville Reservation, which had been established July 2, 1872, across the Okanogan River east of the Columbia Reservation.

In 1851, the Sinkiuses numbered roughly 300. The 1870 number of Sinkiuse Columbias has been estimated at roughly 1,000. The increase was due to the accretion of nontreaty peoples seeking the leadership of Moses. In 1900 their numbers were listed at around 300 to 400. A 1910 census listed

Sinkiuse

Sinkiuse Chief Moses, in 1890. The Sinkiuses were sometimes called the Columbia-Sinkiuses because of their location on the mid-Columbia River and the adjoining Columbia Plateau. Moses assumed leadership of the nontreaty tribesman along the Columbia in the latter part of the nineteenth century. He and his people were removed to the Colville Reservation in north-central Washington.

them at 52. Tabulations as late as 1959 listed 94 of full blood living on the Colville Reservation and 52 of full blood living outside its confines. Today a small remnant proudly stresses its Sinkiuse-Moses Columbia roots. See also **Confederated Tribes of the Colville Reservation, Washington.**

Suggested Readings: Walter Cline, et al., *The Sinkaietk, or Southern Okanagon of Washington,* ed. Leslie Spier, American Anthropological Association, General Series in Anthropology, no. 6 (Menasha, Wis.: George Banta Publishing Co.,

1938); Grace Christiansen Gardner, "Life Among North Central Washington First Families," *Wenatchee* (Wash.) *Daily World,* May 31–December 20, 1935; Robert H. Ruby and John A. Brown, *Half-Sun on the Columbia: A Biography of Chief Moses* (Norman: University of Oklahoma Press, 1965); James A. Teit, "The Middle Columbia Salish," *University of Washington Publications in Anthropology* 2, no. 4 (June, 1928); James A. Teit, "The Salishan Tribes of the Western Plateaus," *Forty-fifth Annual Report of the Bureau of American Ethnology* (Washington, D.C.: Government Printing Office, 1930).

SIUSLAW
(Yakonan)

The Siuslaws lived on and near the Siuslaw River along the Oregon coast, in an area of sand dunes south of the rocky cliffs of Sea Lion Caves and Heceta Head. The houses of their roughly thirty-four villages consisted of excavations beneath frame-board structures covered with earth. Two or more of these houses were sometimes joined together. Passage in and out was by ladders. Siuslaw subsistence patterns included gathering foods from the sea and hunting game. A small tribe numerically, the Siuslaws on occasion were encroached upon by peoples from as far north as the Columbia River. In 1835 the latter captured and enslaved some Siuslaw women and children. To replace their lost women, Siuslaw men reportedly went south seeking wives among the Umpquas, because that tribe was "most like the Siuslaws." It was also said that at sometime before the middle of the nineteenth century Siuslaw women introduced the practice of flattening the heads of their infants. Not knowing the precise pressure needed for the head-molding process, they watched helplessly as their babies died, whereupon Siuslaw men killed some of the women for their negligence, ending the practice.

The Siuslaw homelands lay within the southern portion of the Coast Reservation, which was established by executive order on November 9, 1855. Before the Alsea Sub-

agency was established on that southern portion, the Siuslaws were under the Umpqua Subagency (which was off the reservation at the mouth of the Umpqua River). The Umpqua Subagency supervised the Hanis and Miluk Coos Indians and the Kuitshes (or Lower Umpquas). There were 690 Indians under the subagency. After it closed on September 3, 1859, the Siuslaws were marched northward from their homelands to the Yachats River, where the Alsea Subagency was established in 1861. The Cooses and Umpquas were also moved there. In 1862 the military Fort Umpqua was abandoned because the Indians had become less inclined to escape their reservation confine. When a central strip was taken from the reservation on December 21, 1865, the northern half became the Siletz Reservation. The 620-square-mile southern portion was then named the Alsea Reservation, containing 525 Indians. The removed strip, encompassing Yaquina Bay and Yaquina River, was opened to whites. The Alseas were living in their own homelands on the Alsea Reservation. They did not ally themselves with the Siuslaws, Kuitshes, and Coos who lived there also. An example of the friction among the tribes occurred on September 17, 1864, when the military settled an intertribal squabble over a beached whale by dividing the animal and apportioning half of it to

Alseas and the other half to other tribes. The Coos, Kuitshes, and Siuslaws were invited to a congressionally ordered council to secure their consent to closure of the entire Alsea Reservation. Despite their opposition to the closure, the reservation was restored to the public domain by an act of Congress on March 3, 1875 (18 Stat. 420, 446). The Alsea Reservation Indians, most of whom were Siuslaws, Kuitshes, or Coos, had the option of removing to the Siletz Reservation or resettling along the coast. Those who removed to the Siletz were to be provided allotments and subsistence in the Salmon River area in order not to overcrowd the Siletz valley. In 1881 a small number, 67 in all, representing fifteen families, took advantage of that option and moved to the Siletz. In 1876 the government granted 160-acre homesteads to those who had not removed to the Siletz. The Siuslaws among the latter group settled along the Siuslaw River in the Florence, Oregon, area. The Kuitshes went to the estuary of the Umpqua River, and the Coos went down to Coos Bay. Failing to adjust to white society in their former homelands, many Indians had drifted from the Alsea Reservation. Some went to the Siletz Reservation, only to starve because its agent, lacking funds, could not feed, clothe, or otherwise provide for them. Those who had organized gravitated in time to Coos Bay, where they purchased a 6.1 acre reservation, which is in nontrust status.

In 1916 a few Siuslaws joined the Kuitshes and the Hanis and Miluk Coos to form an extension of the Coos who had organized on their own at Coos Bay. Without a reservation or treaty, the four tribes in 1917 began pressing claims for the lands that had been taken from them. They formed a new council with a chief and legal counsel. In 1929 Congress passed an act permitting them to sue the United States for their alienated lands (Case No. K-345), but on May 2, 1938, the Court of Claims ruled that by their oral testimony they had not proved ownership or title to any large acreage. The Claims Court declared that, as nontreaty Indians (the treaties made with their ancestors had never been ratified), they were unable to establish titles to the lands that they claimed. One judge of the court went so far as to state that, since they had been a relatively peaceful people, it was difficult to establish with any certainty their location before 1855. On November 14, 1938, the United States Supreme Court refused to consider their appeal. In 1947, recognizing that the Bureau of Indian Affairs had constructed a large meeting hall and food-processing center a decade earlier on their 6.1-acre reservation, the Siuslaws, the Kuitshes, and the Coos, in conjunction with the Lower Chinooks, filed a claim against the United States. Three years later four petitioners—the Siuslaws, the Kuitshes, and the Hanis and Miluk Coos—were eliminated from the suit. The Indian claims commissioners told them that they had already had their day in court. On August 8, 1956, they filed a petition with the United Nations to renew their land claim. The international body declined to act in the matter, stating that the claim was an internal matter of the United States.

Today no one speaks the Siuslaw language. For recent cultural developments among the Siuslaws, see **Confederated Tribes of Coos, Lower Umpqua & Siuslaw Indians, Inc.**, and **Hanis Coos.**

Suggested Readings: Stephen Dow Beckham, *The Indians of Western Oregon: This Land Was Theirs* (Coos Bay, Ore.: Arago Books, 1977); *Indian Education,* a continuing publication of Coos County, Oregon, Intermediate Education District.

SKAGIT
(See **Lower Skagit** and **Upper Skagit.**)

SKILLOOT
(Upper Chinookan Division of Chinookan)

The Skilloots spoke the Clackamas dialect of the Chinookan language. In 1805 the American explorers Meriwether Lewis and William Clark found them on both the north and the south bank of the Columbia River above and below the entrance of the Cowlitz River, in present-day Oregon and Washington. The tribe numbered about 2,500 at that time. They were among the many lower Columbia River peoples who were virtually depopulated by plagues in the late eighteenth and early nineteenth centuries. Their 1780 numbers have been estimated at 3,200.

On the Oregon shore of the Columbia was the Conniac (Konnaack) Skilloot village. Its natives may have been the Chilwitses (or Hellwitses) who lived near Oak Point on the Columbia south bank, about forty miles upstream from where the river enters the Pacific Ocean. They hunted and came to the river to fish. They numbered roughly 200 in 1810, when the American Winship brothers (Abiel, Jonathan, and Nathan) attempted to build a fur post among them at Oak Point. If the post had been successful, it would have been the first such land-based establishment in the Pacific Northwest. It failed because of the hostility of the Chilwitses and other natives, and also because the Columbia River, nearing its seasonal June crest, flooded out the post that the Winships were building. In 1811 men of John Jacob Astor's Pacific Fur Company established Fort Astoria downstream from the Winship site. On August 8, 1851, Oregon Superintendent of Indian Affairs Anson Dart effected a treaty with what he called the "Kon-naack Band of the Chinook Tribe of Indians." In the treaty the Skilloots ceded lands on both sides of the Columbia River north and west of the lower Cowlitz River and across the Columbia from that stream on the south and west. In exchange, they were given goods, the privilege of occupying their place of residence at Oak Point, and the right to hunt on their ceded lands near Oak Point. See **Clackamas**.

SKIN
(Shahaptian)

The Skins (Skeens), or Skinpahs, lived on the north bank of the Columbia River east of the Wishram peoples, in what is present-day south-central Washington state. Their name derived from a word in the Tenino dialect meaning "cradle" or "cradle place." The tribal village was later named Wishram for the Skins' neighbors of that name. Later it was called Fallbridge. The Skins were believed to be the tribe whom the American explorers Meriwether Lewis and William Clark identified as the Eneeshurs in 1805–1806. At that time they were said to number 1,200, a tenuous estimate since it was difficult to separate them from the large native groups who gathered with them to fish and trade. It is some evidence of Skin ethnic identity that they were among the fourteen peoples who, at the time of their 1855 Walla Walla Treaty with the United States, formed what white officials then called the Yakima Nation. As such they were scheduled for removal to the Yakima Reservation. Because of their location at a key passage on the Columbia River, they engaged in considerable trading and fishing for their subsistence. Like others along the Columbia, they occasionally left the river to gather roots and berries. They were one of several native peoples of the Pacific Northwest who lost their tribal identities in the nineteenth century.

The Skokomish Tribe, Skokomish Reservation, had its beginning on January 26, 1855, at the Treaty of Point-No-Point when government officials treated with the Twana, Clallam, and Chimakum Indians. The reservation to which they were to remove was the Skokomish on the lower Skokomish River, an affluent of Hood Canal. The Skokomish name derives from one of the three Twana bands.

Location: Tribal members live not only on the Skokomish Reservation but also adjacent to it in such places as the city of Shelton, Washington.

Numbers: In 1984 tribal numbers stood at 507, and in 1989 at 829.

History: The Twana, Clallam, and Chimakum peoples were designated under the Point-No-Point Treaty to remove to the 3,840-acre Skokomish Reservation. By executive order on February 25, 1874, the reservation boundaries were established, and the acreage was increased to 4,986.97. Also in 1874, the Twanas, under the Medicine Creek Treaty, received allotments from their agent, Edwin Eells, thirteen years before the passage of the General Allotment Act, known as the Dawes Act. As was often the case, government officials soon called all the Indians on the reservation by the name of one tribal group, the Skokomish, for whom, in this case, the river in their aboriginal homeland was also named. Later in the nineteenth century an agent noted that only one-sixth of the Indians scheduled to go on the reservation ever did. Most of those who stayed away, primarily Clallams and a few Chimakums, remained in small villages along Hood Canal, Puget Sound, and the Strait of Juan de Fuca at distances of 50 to 150 miles from the reservation. Some of the Clallams who did remove to the Skokomish later abandoned it for their old haunts. The scarcity of good reservation land kept them from it, as did off-reservation employment in logging, milling, and canoeing. In 1870 the Clallam chief

Chitsamakkan (Chetzamokha), dubbed the Duke of York, was induced to come to the Skokomish. His bones at least came to rest in his homelands. On June 23, 1888, he was buried in the Masonic cemetery in Port Townsend.

The many works of missionary Myron Eells (who was the brother of Edwin Eells) reveal Skokomish Reservation Indians living in two cultural worlds, the native and the white—a state that one official termed "half-civilization." Native women set aside government-introduced spinning wheels in favor of their own whorls. They wove socks and other clothing for whites and for their own men, who worked in the logging camps and mills. As it had to other local Indian groups, the Shaker faith spread to the Skokomish from the nearby Squaxin Indians, among whom it had originated in 1882. Some Squaxins moved to the Skokomish Reservation, as did their neighbors the Sahewamishes. As late as the last quarter of the nineteenth century, Indians of the Skokomish held potlatches, which were often attended by as many as ten tribes. By the end of the century such holidays as the Fourth of July had begun to replace the traditional potlatch ceremonies.

Government and Claims: The Skokomish Tribe, Skokomish Reservation, is fully organized under the Indian Reorganization Act (48 Stat. 984). On May 3, 1938, the secretary of the interior approved the tribal constitution and bylaws. Its charter was ratified July 22, 1939. The Skokomish Tribal Council is the governing body. The tribe has established its own court to enforce its ordinances and to regulate hunting and fishing. Several kinds of services are provided by the federal government, and some law enforcement is by the state through the office of the Mason County sheriff.

The tribe submitted a claim to the Indian Claims Commission (Docket 296) for compensation for the 1855 cession of Twana lands to the United States. The commission determined that the tribe originally held 355,800 acres, which on March 8, 1859, had a value of $426,960, for which the tribe had already received an unconscionably low payment of $53,383. On June 30, 1961, the commission ordered an award to the tribe minus the amount already paid for the cession of their lands. The award approved on October 14, 1966, amounted to $373,577. In 1973 the tribe spent $104,000 of the claims money on payments of $250 per capita to its members. The remainder of the monies went into tribal development programs.

Contemporary Life and Culture: Of the enlarged Skokomish Reservation of 4,986.97 acres, nearly all of which were allotted, about 3,000 remain in Indian ownership as trust land. About 1,000 acres of bottomlands are subject to periodic flooding. Employment is available to tribesmen in traditional industries, such as logging, lumbering, and fishing. Some engage in farming and cattle grazing. Like their ancestors, a few trap and hunt deer and wild fowl to supplement their diets. A program of fisheries enhancement and management is coordinated with that of the Port Gamble Indian Community and the Lower Elwha Tribal Community, both of which are descended from the Clallam tribe of the Point-No-Point Treaty Council. The fish hatcheries installed in 1976 have been expanded. The tribe operates a fish processing plant and in 1980 owned two fishing boats. Many tribesmen, however, fish on their own. With the Chehalis, Squaxin, and Nisqually tribes, the Skokomishes belong to the Southern Puget Intertribal Planning Commission, which deals with economic problems and housing. Skokomish youth attend high school in nearby Shelton. Children attend a grade school operated by the Hood Canal School District. There is also a tribal school, called Kiikpahl, for children from kindergarten through grade four. The tribe retained the services of a resident anthropologist. In the 1970s, under his direction, it launched native language and curriculum projects for school children. Dictionaries of the Twana language have been prepared. In 1980 a basketry project was begun in cooperation with the Chehalis, Suquamish, and Nisqually Indians. On the

Skokomish Tribe, Skokomish Reservation

Mary Adams, of the Skokomish Tribe, Skokomish Reservation, circa 1880. Her people came under the influence of missionaries and mercantilists in the late nineteenth and the early twentieth century. Her people lived along the shores of Hood Canal in northwestern Washington, where their reservation, the Skokomish, was established at the southern end of the canal. Tribal members today are known as Skokomishes. In October 1989, Seattle University returned to the Skokomishes remains of their ancestors that the university had obtained from the University of Washington in 1974. Courtesy of Whitman College.

reservation are Indian Pentecostal and Shaker churches. Some tribal members are affiliated with a secret society that practices the traditional native *tamanawas* religion. In the pursuit of this ancient religion, its adherents, many of them young people, blacken their faces as part of their ritual.

Special Events: On the weekend nearest January 26 the tribe annually observes Treaty Days, which originated in the Point-No-Point Treaty made on that day in 1855. First salmon runs are also observed on the reservation, and the intertribal bone game, the Slahal, is played during the summer. A naming ceremony, in which tribesmen take ancestral names, is held in winter. The public is not invited to this event. See **Twana, Clallam** and **Chimakum.**

Suggested Readings: George P. Castile, "Edwin Eells, U.S. Indian Agent, 1871–1895," *Pacific Northwest Quarterly* 72, no. 2 (April, 1981); George Pierre Castile, *The Indians of Puget Sound* (Seattle, 1985); W. W. Elmendorf, *The Structure of Twana Society*, Monograph Supplement no. 2 (Pullman, Wash.: Washington State University, 1960); Myron Eells, *The Twana, Chemakum, and Klallam Indians of Washington Territory* (1887); Seattle: Shorey Book Store, 1971); Myron Eells, "The Twana Indians of the Skokomish Reservation in Washington Territory," *United States Geological and Geographical Survey* (a bulletin of the U.S. Department of the Interior), vol. 3, no. 1 (April 9, 1877); Robert H. Ruby and John A. Brown, *Myron Eells and the Puget Sound Indians* (Seattle: Superior Publishing Company, 1976), in which is contained a list of the published works of Eells; Nile Thompson, *What is Twana?* (Shelton, Wash.: Skokomish Indian Tribe, 1979)

SKYKOMISH
(Coastal Division, Salishan)

The Skykomishes, who originated as a subdivision of the Snoqualmies, lived in what is present-day Washington state. Their primary villages were on the Skykomish River, formerly called the North Fork of the Snohomish River. They also lived in the drainage area of the Snoqualmie River. Their land base at the time of the first white contacts comprised about 974,822 acres, of which roughly 538,048 were drained by the Skykomish River and about 436,744 by the Snoqualmie. In the Point Elliott Treaty of 1855, which two Skykomish subchiefs signed, the tribe appeared as the Skai-wha-mishes. They had been mentioned earlier in the journals of white men, such as the Hudson's Bay Company traders at Fort Nisqually, which was established in 1833 on southern Puget Sound. The Skykomishes traded at that fort, as did their neighbors and allies the Snoqualmies. Today the river along U.S. Highway 2 bears the Skykomish name, as does a Cascade Mountain town along that route.

A riverine mountain people, the Skykomishes subsisted mainly from the land. They hunted, fished, and gathered roots and berries on the western slopes of the Cascade Mountains. They were also found at times on the shores of Puget Sound on the west, where they went to trade. From the Snohomishes and the Clallams they obtained dog hair, which with goat wool, feathers, and fireweed, they wove into blankets. On occasion, they fought other tribes, such as the Klickitats and the Clallams. In May, 1849, some of their braves, with those of the Snoqualmies, attacked Fort Nisqually. In the Indian war of 1855–56, in which some Puget Sound Indians fought Americans, they remained neutral under their pro-American (though anti-British) Snoqualmie chief, Patkanin, who at an earlier time had opposed all whites. The close Skykomish ties with the Snoqualmies caused anthropologists to disagree whether or not the Skykomishes were a Snoqualmie subdivision. On June 30, 1960, the Indian Claims Commission handed down its decision in a claim (Docket 93) that had been filed by the Snoqualmies on behalf of the Skykomishes. Contrary to the Snoqualmie position, the commission ruled that the Skykomishes had been a separate identifiable people. The Snoqualmies appealed to the commission to modify its order in hopes that the commission would look further into the matter after consulting Indians of Skykomish descent in the Snoqualmie tribe. The commission denied the petitioners' claims to recover compensation on behalf of the Skykomishes. The Snoqualmies then appealed to the Court of Claims on August 27, 1965 (178 C.Cls. 570, 372 F. 2d 951). That court then reversed the commission decision on the issue. On September 23, 1968, the commission entered the final judgment in favor of the Snoqualmies for a settlement of $257,698.29 for themselves and the Skykomishes.

In 1849 the Skykomish numbers were listed at 410, and in 1852 at 175. In the 1860s many Skykomishes were living on the Tulalip Reservation on Puget Sound near the mouth of the Snohomish River. On that reservation, their last reported census listed them under their chief, William Stechlech, at 49 men, 44 women, and 51 children, for a total of 144. After 1871, statistical reports from the reservation did not list them as a separate people, because of the individual-allotment process there and because of their intermarriage with other native peoples and assimilation with whites. Thus the Skykomishes no longer exist as an identifiable tribe. See **Tulalip Tribes of the Tulalip Reservation** and **Snoqualmie.**

SNOHOMISH
(Coastal Division, Salishan)

The Snohomishes were sometimes called the Sinahomishes (or Sneomuses). Their name is said to mean "a large number of people" and has also been rendered as "a warrior tribe." They lived near the mouth of the Snohomish River, a Puget Sound affluent in northwestern Washington state north of present-day Marysville; on the southern tip of Camano Island; on Whidbey Island opposite the present-day city of Mukilteo; and up the Snohomish River as far east as present-day Monroe. Among the Snohomish subdivisions in those locations, besides the Snohomishes proper, were the Sdohobcs of the lower Snohomish River and Whidbey Island and the Sdocohobcs on the Snohomish River between Snohomish and Monroe. Other Snohomish subdivisions were the N'Quentlamamishes (or Kwehtlamamishes) of the Pilchuck River. Besides the river and the city, a county bears the tribal name.

Location: About 93 percent of the enrolled members of the Snohomish Tribe of Indians live within seventy-five miles of their ancestral lands. About 4 percent live out of state. The residences of the other 3 percent are unknown.

Numbers: In 1980 the Snohomishes numbered about 700. In 1844 they had numbered 322. A decade later their population stood at 350, indicating perhaps that a smallpox plague of that time did not strike them as severely as it did other natives of the region.

History: When the Snohomishes met the Hudson's Bay Company trader John Work in their country in December, 1824, they believed his party had come to attack them. They had long been in conflict with tribes such as the Clallams of the Strait of Juan de Fuca and the Cowichans of southeastern Vancouver Island. One Snohomish warrior demonstrated for Work's party how to kill the Cowichans if that tribe were to attack. The Snohomishes were among the various peoples who traded at the Hudson's Bay Company's Fort Nisqually, which was established in 1833 at the southern end of Puget Sound. They were also among those who met the Roman Catholic missionaries in their lands in the early 1840s. At the time of those contacts the Snohomishes were governed by chieftains, with one chief ruling several villages.

Nine Snohomish headmen signed the Point

Elliott Treaty, for which the council was held in 1855 in the Snohomish country near present-day Mukilteo. At the council about 350 Snohomishes and their allies, the Snoqualmies, were represented by Chief Patkanin, who had been hostile to Americans in pretreaty times but had become impressed with their potential power. With a small band, Patkanin was allied with the Americans during the Indian war of 1855–56. During that conflict most of the other Snohomishes remained neutral, which prompted an Indian agent in February, 1856, to recommend to Washington Territorial Governor and Superintendent of Indian Affairs Isaac Stevens that the tribe be disbanded, since they were "doing nothing for us." They were among the neutral Indians who were removed by government officials to such places in Puget Sound as Fox and Whidbey islands and Port Gamble on the Kitsap Peninsula.

The Tulalip (formerly the Snohomish) Reservation had been authorized under the Point Elliott Treaty and was enlarged by executive order on December 23, 1873, from 22,489.91 acres to 24,320 acres. It lay in Snohomish lands but was also intended for occupancy by the Skykomishes, the Snoqualmies, and the Stillaguamishes. Early in the reservation period the agent, Rev. Eugene Casimir Chirouse, O.M.I., employed various means to help the Indians survive the difficult transition that they were experiencing. During this time, because of their limited numbers, the natives' retaliations against the whites' encroachments took the form of isolated, unorganized attacks. Many Snohomishes left the reservation because of severe overcrowding which taxed their ability to subsist there. In the 1870s many more left because of oppressive government policies that hampered their native religious practices and the use of their language. Out-migration continued during the allotment period, 1883 to 1901, when it became evident that the reservation lands were too limited for individual occupancy.

Government and Claims: The Snohomish Tribe of Indians claims to have had continuous political authority over the cen-

Snohomish

Charles Jules, a Snohomish Indian, circa 1905. His people occupied the vicinity of present-day Everett, Washington, and the watershed of their namesake river, the Snohomish.

turies. Its members are descendants of those Snohomishes who refused to move or to return to the Tulalip Reservation as agreed in the Point Elliott Treaty. Since the 1920s the tribe has used the committee system of governance and has operated under councils and chairpersons. It was first incorporated under state law in 1927 and again in 1974. It functions under bylaws written in 1928 and a constitution written in 1934.

213

Although the federal government recognizes the Snohomish tribe as a political entity, because the forebears of tribal members signed the Point Elliott Treaty, it has not acknowledged the Snohomishes as a tribal entity. In October, 1977, the tribe adopted a comprehensive plan for restoration, and they continue to seek acknowledgment and a land base in the form of a reservation in the Snohomish River valley between Snohomish and Monroe, Washington. The Snohomishes filed a claim (Docket 125) with the Indian Claims Commission for the lands that they ceded to the United States in 1855, including the southern ends of Whidbey and Camano islands, all of Gedney (Hat) Island, and a portion of the mainland that confronts Puget Sound and stretches from Mukilteo north to Warm Beach. The east boundary extended from Granite City (Falls) south to the intersections of the Snohomish, Snoqualmie, and Skykomish rivers, and to Granite City on the north. It was within this 164,000-acre tract that the Tulalip Reservation was established. The commission determined the 1859 value of the land at $180,700 and made an award after considering offsets. On August 13, 1964, the commission determined that the total consideration paid to the Snohomishes for their aboriginal lands had been $44,534.21. The tribe therefore had $136,165.79 coming to it. See **Tulalip Tribes of the Tulalip Reservation.**

Suggested Readings: Rick Carter, "The Invisible Indians," *Snohomish County Tribune*, June 8, 1972; Gustaf B. Joergenson, *History of the Twin Cities* [of Stanwood and East Stanwood, Washington], *Twin City News*, April 1, 1948–October 27, 1949 (70 issues); Colin Ellidge Tweddell, "A Historical and Ethnological Study of the Snohomish Indian People," in *Coast Salish and Western Washington Indians*, vol. 2 (New York: Garland Publishing, Inc., 1974), pp. 475–694; William Whitfield, *History of Snohomish County, Washington*, 2 vols. (Evansville, Ind.: Unigraphic, 1979).

SNOQUALMIE
(Coastal Division, Salishan)

The Snoqualmies lived in two main villages in the Snoqualmie River valley, which is between Puget Sound and the Cascade Mountains in western Washington state. One of their villages was at the mouth of the Tolt River, and the other was about a mile below the spectacular Snoqualmie Falls. The Snoqualmie name is also perpetuated in a town near Interstate 90 and in a mountain pass that is traversed by Interstate 90. The Snoqualmies are said to have carried the designation "people of the moon," and also "crowned with snow." They believed themselves to have been transformed from the mythical Beaver. Unlike most other natives of the Puget Sound Basin, they were well organized, but such a degree of organization allowed less individual freedom for their people. Like their neighbors the Skykomishes, they hunted in the Cascade Mountains. Among their quarry were goats, whose wool their women wove into blankets, along with fireweed, feathers, and dogs' wool, which they obtained from peoples such as the Clallams and the Snohomishes. The Snoqualmies intermarried with the Yakimas (who lived just east of the Cascade Mountains), and they obtained horses from them. Snoqualmie summer houses were constructed of poles and mats, with one side open to an outside fireplace.

Location: Today most individuals of the Snoqualmie Tribe live on non-Indian land in the Snoqualmie River valley and at other places in the Puget Sound basin.

Numbers: As of 1982, Snoqualmie tribal membership stood at 505. Estimates of mid-nineteenth-century Snoqualmie numbers

Snoqualmie

The woven blanket worn here by David Delgard was typical of the Snoqualmies and their neighbors in the hills and Cascade Mountains of western Washington. Courtesy of the Everett Public Library.

varied from 225 to 350. Persons may become tribal members by proving at least one-eighth Snoqualmie parentage.

History: The Snoqualmies' usually peaceful routines were interrupted by conflicts with other tribes such as the Cowichans of southeastern Vancouver Island in Canada, the Clallams, and the Nisquallis. The Snoqualmies' chief, Patkanin, was initially hostile to Americans. After an attack on the Hudson's Bay Company's Fort Nisqually on May 1, 1849, in which an American was killed, six men under Patkanin's leadership were brought to trial in the white men's court, and two of them were hanged (including, reportedly, Patkanin's brother, a Skykomish). One who escaped punishment was an innocent slave, whom the Indians had tried to substitute for one of the guilty in keeping with an ancient practice. Changing his disposition toward Americans, Patkanin signed the Point Elliott Treaty of 1855. Although at the treaty council he said, "Our hearts are with the whites," he did not mean all whites, for he was said to have remained anti-British. He proved his loyalty to Americans by leading sixty warriors as American allies in the Indian war that broke out shortly after the signing of the Point Elliott Treaty. For delivering the slain bodies of their foes to government officials, he and his followers received money, blankets, and other goods. At the end of the war there were several homicides by younger Snoqualmies who had been inflamed by liquor obtained from whites. Patkanin was buried on the Tulalip Reservation, to which his people had been removed. They numbered 301 on that reservation in 1870 under their chief, Sanawa. In succeeding years they intermarried with Tulalip peoples and others and were slowly assimilated into neighboring white communities. After the Point Elliott Treaty the Snoqualmies tried unsuccessfully to secure a reservation in their ancestral lands in the vicinity of the Tolt River.

Since there was no longer an identifiable Skykomish tribe, the Snoqualmies filed a claim on their own behalf and that of the Skykomishes (Docket 93) to recover for lands ceded to the United States under the Point Elliott Treaty. On June 30, 1961, the Indian Claims Commission ruled against the petitioners. The Snoqualmies had maintained that the Skykomishes had been absorbed within their own tribe and thus that the Skykomish lands belonged to the Snoqualmies. The Snoqualmies subsequently appealed to the commission to modify its order, in hopes that it would look further into the matter after consulting Indians of Skykomish descent in the Snoqualmie Tribe, but the commission denied the petitioners' claim to recover compensation on behalf of Skykomishes. The Snoqualmies then appealed to the Court of Claims on August 27, 1965 (178 C.Cls. 570, 372 F. 2d 951), and the court reversed the commission's decision on the issue. On September 23, 1968, the commission entered a final judgment in favor of the Snoqualmies and the Skykomishes and offered a settlement of $257,698.29. As one of the tribes signatory to the Point Elliott Treaty, the Snoqualmies had already received $25,889.75 as a consideration for the loss of their lands. The tribe seeks to prevent power and other development on or near Snoqualmie Falls, which it regards as sacred.

Contemporary Life and Culture: As noted, most members of the Snoqualmie Tribe live on non-Indian lands. Yet assimilation of the tribe with non-Indians has been slow, because the past and present generations have married primarily Indians of their own and other tribes. Only a few speak the Snoqualmie tongue.

Suggested Readings: Edmond S. Meany, "Chief Patkanin," *Washington Historical Quarterly* 15, no. 3 (July, 1924); Robert H. Ruby and John A. Brown, *Indians of the Pacific Northwest: A History* (Norman: University of Oklahoma Press, 1981).

SPOKANE
(Interior Division, Salishan)

The Spokanes (Spokans) maintain that their name originated when a native beat on a hollow tree inside of which a serpent made a noise that sounded like "Spukcane." One day, they say, as their chief pondered the noise, vibrations radiated from his head, which gave the word the vague meaning "power from the brain." In early times the Spokanes called themselves the Spukanees, which is translated "sun peoples," or more freely, "children of the sun." Others maintain that the tribal name derived from that of one of their chiefs and from nothing else. The tribe lived on in the general area of the Spokane River in three primary bands: the Upper Spokanes, whose general area extended from Spokane Falls east to around the present-day Washington-Idaho border; the Middle Spokanes, who were west of Spokane Falls in the vicinity of the Little Spokane River; and the Lower Spokanes, whose territory was farther west as far as the confluence of the Columbia and Spokane rivers. A city and county are but two of the many things bearing the Spokane name. Although they comprised three groups, the Spokane peoples coalesced during times of emergency. No native people of the Pacific Northwest had stronger family ties than the Spokanes did. Their successors are known officially today as the Spokane Tribe of the Spokane Reservation, Washington.

Location: Among the various locations where Spokane Indians may be found are the 133,344-acre Spokane Reservation, established by executive order on January 18, 1881, northwest of the city of Spokane (on which live the greatest number of the tribe); other reservations, such as the Flathead (formerly the Jocko) and the Coeur D'Alene; and off-reservation locations, among which the city of Spokane is important.

Numbers: The Spokane Reservation tribal membership was 1,961 in 1985. Authorities disagree in their estimates of the Spokane population in the immediate precontact period. Their estimates vary from 1,400 to

Spokane

A Spokane couple, Alex and Margaret Sherwood, circa 1967. The Spokane Tribal Cultural Center on the Spokane Reservation at Wellpinit, Washington, bears his name. The reservation lies northwest of Spokane, which is named for the tribe. Customarily Indians were shunted onto unwanted lands. Ironically, rich uranium deposits were discovered on the Spokane Reservation.

2,500. A Hudson's Bay Company trader reported their number at 704 in 1827. A United States census in 1910 placed them at 643. In 1989 there were 1,248.

History: The Spokanes generally lived at peace with their Interior Salish neighbors, but were known to fight them at times. Conflicts were usually of short duration, lasting only until grievances were settled. With the acquisition of horses in the eighteenth century, the Spokanes, especially the Upper Spokanes, joined the Flatheads, the Kalispels, the Nez Percés, and other tribesmen in trading and buffalo-hunting expeditions across the Rocky Mountains on the Great Plains.

The Spokanes' association with the Kalispels was so close that in the middle of the nineteenth century a government official stated that the Kalispels were an amalgam of Kalispels, Spokanes, and Flatheads. Occasionally conflicts erupted between the tribes from west of the Rocky Mountains and the Blackfeet and other Plains tribes, who regarded the former as poachers on their lands.

The Spokanes made their first major entry into the white man's fur-trading complex in 1810 with the establishment of the North West Company's Spokane House, which was followed the next year by the rival Pacific Fur Company's Fort Spokane. After the failure of the Pacific Fur Company and the merger of the North West and Hudson's Bay companies in 1821, the Spokanes had a trading post in their lands until 1826, when the post was removed north to Fort Colvile. The Spokane tribe's first major confrontation with Christianity came around 1830 with the return of Spokane Garry (later Chief Garry) to his people, from an Anglican mission school at Red River (later Winnipeg). Between 1838 and 1848, missionaries, the Reverends Elkanah Walker and Cushing Eells were active among the Spokanes, having been sent by the American Board of Commissioners for Foreign Missions. The presence also of Roman Catholic missionaries, including Rev. Pierre De Smet, S.J., and his successors, further widened the divisions among the Spokane peoples. The Spokanes became involved in wars with whites by joining the Coeur d'Alênes and other Salish speakers, along with the Shahaptian-speaking Palouses, in fighting American troops under Maj. Edward Steptoe in May and Col. George Wright in September, 1858. The defeat of those tribesmen in two key fights with Wright's troops opened the interior of the Pacific Northwest to American settlement. Despite pleas by the younger Chief Joseph that the Spokanes enter the Nez Percé War of 1877 against the United States, the Spokanes remained neutral, like their Coeur d'Alêne neighbors.

There were two major agreements between the Spokanes and the federal government. On August 18, 1877, the Lower Spokanes agreed to move by November 1, 1877, to a tract of land that was established as the Spokane Reservation by executive order on January 18, 1881. Then on March 18, 1887, the Upper and Middle Spokanes agreed to remove to one of the following reservations: the Colville, the Flathead, or the Coeur d'Alene. That agreement was ratified July 13, 1892, and Congress later extended its benefits to the many Upper and Middle Spokanes who had removed to the Spokane Reservation. In 1897 there were 145 Spokanes on the Coeur d'Alene Reservation and 91 on the Flathead. In the meantime, trouble had broken out between the white citizenry of the rapidly growing city of Spokane and its Indians who had not removed to reservations. Several Spokanes, including Chief Garry, were involved with whites in wrangles over land titles.

Among various acts pertaining to the Spokane Reservation was a joint congressional resolution of June 19, 1902, providing that the secretary of the interior make allotments in severalty to Indians. In 1906 a total of 651 members of the Spokane tribe were allotted 64,750 acres. Among subsequent acts was that authorizing the secretary of the interior to sell surplus unallotted and agricultural reservation lands.

In its earlier period the Spokane Reservation retained its primarily Protestant orientation. After the removal there of Chief Enoch and his Catholic followers in 1896, the religious picture altered greatly; of an estimated 600 reservation inhabitants, about half were of the Catholic faith. Helping Spokanes to adjust to the white men's ways was Chief Lot, who favored white teachers for reservation children. After Fort Spokane, at the confluence of the Columbia and Spokane rivers, was abandoned in 1898 by the military, a government boarding school was established there. In the early twentieth century, when the reservation was under the Colville Agency, its chief executive, Capt. John McA. Webster, worked diligently on behalf of the Spokanes to prepare their entry into the modern world. Ironically, many of the technical advances that he sought for them benefited the white community. Traditionalism remained strong among the Spokanes. The termination movement of the

1950s never gained much support among them. A 1961 study of Spokane assimilation patterns indicated that there was closer assimilation with white culture in the later nineteenth century than there was a half century later.

Government and Claims: After the passage of the Indian Reorganization Act in 1934 (48 Stat. 984), it was not until May 12, 1951, that the Spokane Tribe of the Spokane Reservation, Washington, approved its formal organization by a vote of 95 to 34. Its constitution and bylaws were approved by the commissioner of Indian affairs on June 27, 1951.

On August 10, 1951, the tribe filed a petition with two claims (Docket 331) with the Indian Claims Commission. One claim alleged that the cession of the tribe's land to the United States under the agreement of March 18, 1887 (27 Stat. 120, 139; ratified July 13, 1892) had been for an unconscionably small consideration. A second, separate claim, filed by amended petitions for accounting purposes became Docket 331-A. The tribe alleged that the United States, which, as the tribe's guardian and trustee, held certain of its monies and properties in trust, had failed to account for their management, handling, and disposition. On February 3, 1969, the tribe and the United States filed a joint motion with the Indian Claims Commission, requesting that the two dockets (331 and 331-A) be consolidated. The commission approved a settlement of $6.7 million for both dockets. The final judgment was rendered on February 21, 1967, after the tribe in December, 1966, had voted 155 to 3 to accept the compromise offer. About half the monies received were distributed to the approximately 1,600 tribal members, with shares for minors placed in trust. The other half of the monies was spent for various tribal programs, such as land acquisition, scholarships, resource development, credit, and financing. Later the Spokanes filed claims (Dockets 523-71 and 524-71) that were transferred to the Court of Claims, for mismanagement of the Indian Claims Commission judgment funds and for other funds, such as Individual Indian Money accounts held in trust by the United States. The tribe in 1981 was awarded $271,431.23.

Contemporary Life and Culture: The tribe, as well as some individual Spokanes, has benefited from sales of the uranium ore that was discovered on the reservation in 1954. When the Midnight Mine from which the ore came became exhausted, its operator, the Dawn Mining Company, began processing low-grade ore. Another mine, the Sherwood, which is completely on tribal land, has been operated since 1966 by Western Nuclear. It too processes low-grade ore. From its operations the tribe receives a small dividend. The tribe has investigated the possibility of establishing a nuclear plant. A wood-veneer plant near the town of Ford on the eastern edge of the reservation was closed down in 1979. Spokanes on the reservation also engage in logging, stock raising, and farming. After a projected fruit-raising project failed to materialize, the tribe maintained that previous agreements for the construction of Grand Coulee Dam on the Columbia (completed, 1940) had provided for rehabilitation of Spokane lands. Thus the tribe was able to water 2,000 acres by a $6 million irrigation system for production of crops. The lands are on benches along the Spokane River on the southern edge of the reservation.

Like other tribes, the Spokanes have been involved in conflicts with state and federal agencies over jurisdictions on the reservation. They seek compensation for the water stored behind Grand Coulee Dam and other dams on the Spokane River. From Little Falls Dam on the Spokane they also seek a percentage of the revenues from power production. The tribe won its fight for the waters of Chamokane Creek on the eastern edge of the reservation when the state of Washington was forbidden to approve the tapping of new wells in the aquifer of that creek.

Initially the Spokane Agency was a subagency under the Colville Agency and was located at Chewelah. In 1887 it was moved to the Spokane Reservation, which is across the Spokane River from Fort Spokane. In

1902 the subagency moved to Fort Spokane across the river into abandoned buildings next to the boarding school. In 1912 the Spokane Subagency became a full agency. At that time it moved to the city of Spokane, but in the same year was returned to the old agency grounds on the Spokane Reservation. Because its facilities were run-down, the agency returned in November, 1913, to Spokane, where it remained until 1915, when it was moved to Wellpinit on the Spokane Reservation. In 1925 the agency was reduced once more to the status of a subagency under the Colville Agency until 1970 the Spokanes again had their own agency at Wellpinit. In 1973 the administration of the Kalispel Reservation, formerly under the Northern Idaho Agency at Lapwai, was transferred to the Spokane Agency.

With reestablishment of the Spokane Agency on the Spokane Reservation in 1970, health facilities were greatly expanded. Alcohol and drug-abuse programs were put in operation. Under BIA funding the tribe sponsored a summer work-experience program for its youth, who made trails and did cleanup work on the reservation. Under BIA control an Indian Action program trained tribal members in carpentry, heavy-equipment operation, electrical installation, clerical work, and other fields. On the reservation there have been Roman Catholic, Presbyterian, and Assemblies of God churches, which attempt to harmonize as much as possible the Christian faith with native traditions and ceremonials, such as root festivals. Among the classes offered in the Wellpinit school was a class on the Spokane language. The schools in the city of Spokane, which has a sizable Indian population, conducted classes which included Indian culture. The Alex Sherwood Memorial Center, dedicated June 7, 1975, fosters Spokane Indian culture. It is a large two-story stone structure housing tribal offices, a short-order food service, a library, and a museum. In 1979 a longhouse was dedicated near Wellpinit.

Noted historically for their conservatism, the Spokanes in the 1960s and 1970s opposed termination of their reservation and of their relationship with the federal government. In 1973, when militants of the American Indian Movement came on the reservation, they made little headway with its Indians.

As part of a land purchase program the tribe in August, 1982, purchased from heirs of an allottee a quarter section of land near Colville, Washington, for commercial development. Held in trust for the tribe, it is known as the Chewelah Homestead Allotment.

In 1992 the tribe considered a state order for a nuclear clean up of the abandoned Dawn mine and the twenty-eight-acre, seventy-foot-deep tailings pond of its mill, eighteen miles away at Ford, Washington. The mill had closed down in 1892. The clean-up project is a twenty-year project estimated to cost up to $40 million. The tribe was to be part of a study of health effects caused by emissions at mid-century from an off-reservation nuclear facility at the Hanford Nuclear Reservation. Seven other tribes were to take part. In June 1991 the tribe dedicated their $2.5 million salmon hatchery. One source of income is the Spokane Indian Reservation Timber Products Enterprise. Another is the casino, the first reservation-established casino in Washington.

Special Events: During a weekend in mid-May the Smoo-kee-shin Powwow is held at the Community Center in Spokane. Near mid-June the Reservation Day Celebration is held at Wellpinit. In early August a WRA-approved rodeo is held at Wellpinit. On Labor Day weekend the Spokane Indian Days celebration, featuring games, dances, and exhibits, is held at Wellpinit.

Suggested Readings: Clifford M. Drury, Nine Years With the Spokane Indians: The Diary, 1838–1848, of Elkanah Walker (Glendale, Calif.: Arthur H. Clarke Co., 1976); Prodipto Roy and Della M. Walker, Assimilation of the Spokane Indians, Washington Agricultural Experiment Station Bulletin no. 628 (Pullman: Washington State University, Institute of Agricultural Science, 1961); Robert H. Ruby and John A. Brown, The Spokane Indians: Children of the Sun (Norman: University of Oklahoma Press, 1970); David C. Wynecoop, Children of the Sun: A History of the Spokane Indians (Wellpinit, Wash.: David C. Wynecoop, 1969).

SQUAXIN
(Coastal Division, Salishan)

The Squaxins, or Squaxons, lived between Hood Canal and Case Inlet on the southern reaches of Puget Sound in Washington state. Their name is said to stem from a word meaning "alone." The Squaxins had ties with neighboring peoples (such as the Twanas of Hood Canal) with whom they intermarried. Successors of the original Squaxins are known officially today as the Squaxin Island Tribe, Squaxin Island Reservation, Washington.

Location: Under the December 26, 1854, Medicine Creek Treaty, Squaxin Island in southern Puget Sound was set aside as the Squaxin Reservation, which originally totaled 1,494.15 acres (the island is five miles long and three-quarters of a mile wide). Today, however, the Squaxins live off their island reservation, primarily in the area of Kamilche and Shelton.

Numbers: With their neighbors on Hood Canal the Squaxins were estimated to have been 1,000 in 1780. In 1856 they were listed officially at 375; in 1901, at 98; and in 1937, at 32. In 1984 tribal membership was 302.

History: After the Medicine Creek Treaty and the establishment of the Squaxin Island Reservation, government officials tried to adapt the Squaxins to an agrarian mode of subsistence. The task was difficult, partly because the island was largely timbered and did not lend itself to that type of economy. During the Puget Sound Indian War (1855–56) the Squaxins were confined on Squaxin Island, but at the end of the war they scattered to various places around southern Puget Sound. By then most of them had abandoned their traditional dress. Yet in the early 1860s they refused to live in small houses that the government built for them, and many continued such practices as shamanism and head flattening. In 1874 the reservation was patented in severalty to twenty-three Indians. The difficulty of obtaining subsistence there continued to keep many Squaxins

Squaxin

Calvin Peters, a Squaxin tribal chairman, photographed at the dedication of the Yakima Indian Nation cultural complex, in 1980. Squaxin Island in lower Puget Sound is a reservation for the tribe.

away. After the Skokomish Reservation was set aside on February 25, 1874, about thirty Squaxins went there and became assimilated into the Twana community. Although each spoke their own dialects, the Squaxins and the Twanas could understand one another. Some Squaxins were allotted on the Quinault Reservation, and many Squaxins have inherited interests there.

In 1882 the Squaxin John Slocum, on becoming ill, believed that he had died. Failing to enter heaven, he believed that he was told to go either to Hell or back to earth and preach to the Indians. Returning to earth—as it seemed to him—he discovered that his soul had returned to his body, and he began the Indian Shaker Church, which stressed strict morality, sobriety, and honesty. Shaker services were implemented by paraphernalia derived from Roman Catholic and Protestant churches and the native religions. Slocum was stimulated in his drive for moral living by his own and his people's exposure to immoral lumberjacks and whiskey peddlers. The Shaker faith spread throughout the Pacific Northwest and has had many Indian adherents down to the present. Within the Shaker ranks a division developed between those who emphasized the importance of the Bible and those who, in native fashion, believed that faith and inspiration come through nonwritten means.

Government and Claims: The governing body of the Squaxin Island Tribe, Squaxin Island Reservation, Washington, is the tribal council. The tribe voted to accept the Indian Reorganization Act of 1934 and adopted a constitution, which was approved by the secretary of the Interior on July 8, 1965.

After filing a claim (Docket 206) with the Indian Claims Commission, the tribe was awarded $7,661.82 on July 31, 1974.

Contemporary Life and Culture: The Squaxin tribe is predominantly Protestant, possibly because of its ancestors' opposition to Catholic priests, and because of the Protestant influence in the Puyallup Agency, under which the Squaxins came during the President Ulysses S. Grant Peace Policy era of

the 1870s. The income of tribal members is derived from lumbering, fishing, and other industries. Because of the salt-water environment of Squaxin Island, the state of Washington has established a park there, near which it leases tidelands. A third of the island is in non-Indian ownership. The tribe is reluctant to subdivide its roughly 827.89 acres of remaining trust lands on the island. Just off the Kamilche exit on U.S. Highway 101 is the tribal center, which serves as a recreation center and meeting place. Aided by the Economic Development Administration, the tribe, as part of its aquaculture program, operates its Harstine Oyster Company on an island adjacent to Squaxin Island. The tribe also operates a chum and coho salmon hatchery on a creek behind Taylor Towne. Marine scientists from the University of Washington advise and assist the tribe in clam raising on the Squaxin Island beaches. On the western shores of the island there is a salmon farm consisting of a series of holding pens. In the early 1970s the Squaxins bought, and the Department of the Interior accepted to hold in trust status, lands including the school district of Kamilche. Squaxins had moved into the Kamilche valley many years before.

Suggested Readings: Susan Olsen and Mary Randlett, *An Illustrated History of Mason County, Washington* (Shelton, Wash., 1978); Archie Satterfield, "The Squaxin Tribe: 'This is Our Home,'" *Seattle Times,* pictorial, June 7, 1970.

STEILACOOM
(Coastal Division, Salishan)

The Steilacoom, or Steilacoomamish, were a Salish-speaking tribe on Steilacoom (now Chambers) Creek in the southern Puget Sound region of Washington. Their name derives from a flower growing near the creek mouth. Some ethnologists claim that they were once part of the Nisqually tribe; others that they were a subdivision of the Puyallups. Their homeland was a 10,900-acre strip approximately two miles wide and eight miles long. Descendants claim that their original

tribal territory included that set out by Washington Territorial Governor and Superintendent of Indian Affairs Isaac Stevens in the Medicine Creek Treaty of 1854, to which the Steilacoom were a party. The area was on the southern shores of Puget Sound and its adjacent inlets, specifically from the Nisqually Flats north to Commencement Bay. Although the Steilacoom did travel with neighboring peoples over the area of the treaty, their homelands were confined to the environs of

Steilacoom Creek, especially the lower parts of that stream, which flowed through their village of Tchtelcab. Today a city bears the tribal name. Oriented toward the waters of Puget Sound, the Steilacoom fished with other natives around Anderson, Fox, and McNeil islands in southern Puget Sound. They hunted but little and never adopted horses as did the Nisquallis, who had close ties with the horseriding Yakimas and Klickitats. The Steilacoom political and land-holding units were autonomous villages, which were mainly exogamous and for the most part patrilocal. Winter social and economic activities united them. In summer their families drifted off to join natives of other villages with whom they had kinship and friendship ties. Because the institutions of the whites were established in their midst at an early date, some anthropologists believe that the Steilacoom culture was suppressed sooner than that of many other native peoples of the Pacific Northwest. Today many of the tribe's members trace their lineage to the Steilacoom of the 1850s.

Location: The Steilacoom thought to have numbered 500 in aboriginal times are a non-reservation tribe. Many live in the area occupied or visited by their ancestors in Pierce, Kitsap, and Thurston counties, where they have been assimilated with the communities.

Numbers: In 1853 the Steilacoom population was 175. In 1854 they were reported to number only 25. The reduction may have been due to the smallpox that was sweeping the region in 1853. In 1986 tribal numbers were 615.

History: The Steilacoom followed a pattern similar to that of other Pacific Northwest natives in their relations with whites. In the contact period they met explorers and traders. Among places where they met fur traders was Fort Nisqually, the Hudson's Bay Company post that was established in 1833 on the southern shores of Puget Sound. It was because of Indian-white friction in that area that the United States in August, 1849, established Fort Steilacoom about six miles north of Fort Nisqually. Dr. William F. Tolmie, who was in charge of the Puget Sound

Joan Ortez, a Steilacoom tribal chairperson, circa 1978. Contrary to popular belief, women have always played important roles in Pacific Northwest tribes, in addition to performing domestic chores. Among the important programs in which Ms. Ortez's people are engaged is the establishment of an activities center near Tacoma, Washington. Photo courtesy of N.E.W.S. Photo N.W.

Agricultural Company, a Hudson's Bay Company subsidiary, demanded and received $600,000 for fifteen years as rent for the Fort Steilacoom area, claiming that the land belonged to his firm. The lands included in this claim belonged not only to the Steilacoom but also to the Nisquallis, Puyallups, and Squaxins. The Indians again felt the presence of white men when Port Steilacoom was built at the main Steilacoom village in 1850, and when Steilacoom City was built in 1851. The two cities became known as Upper and

Lower Steilacoom. By 1853 enough whites had settled among the Steilacoom to support the construction of a store and hotel and, shortly thereafter, a school and a church, which were followed by the saw- and gristmills built by Thomas Chambers on Steilacoom Creek, which he renamed Chambers Creek. Steilacoom were among the thirty Indians whom Acting Agent J. V. Weber removed to Fox Island to separate them from the Indians who were hostile to Americans during the Puget Sound phase of the 1855–56 Indian War.

Government and Claims: The Steilacoom Indian Tribe has a constitution and bylaws which evolved from its original government organized in the 1930s. The governing body is a nine-member council under the direction of a chairperson, secretary, and treasurer. There is also an honorary chieftain. When the government closed down the Fox Island reserve, the Steilacoom refused to move to the Puyallup or Nisqually reservations as the government had planned. The Steilacoom Indian Tribe has not yet received official acknowledgment from the federal government. It has been estimated that payments to the tribe for lands alienated under the Medicine Creek Treaty have amounted to $10,727.57. The Steilacoom submitted a claim (Docket 208) to the Indian Claims Commission for additional compensation for their ceded lands. The commission decided that their value in the middle of the nineteenth century was $20,000. With the previous estimated payment deducted and an offset of $126.11, there remained $9,146.32, and that amount was awarded to the tribe in a final order on July 31, 1974. The tribe prepared a resolution asking the BIA to hold those funds in a trust to be used for a land-replacement program.

Contemporary Life and Culture: In June, 1981, the tribe signed an agreement to lease from the Pierce County government five acres in Fort Steilacoom Park that are on aboriginal Steilacoom grounds near the city of Steilacoom and fifteen miles from Tacoma. On that land the tribe is creating an activities learning center dedicated not only to the Steilacoom but to the general public. An important part of the center is the Steilacoom Institute of Appropriate Technology, featuring not only traditional Indian technology but also modern scientific endeavors developments such as energy conservation. The educational programs are emphasized and coordinated with those of Fort Steilacoom Community College. The institute is also geared to fulfill economic and social needs of the tribe. Some of its services will be available to the general public.

STILLAGUAMISH
(Coastal Division, Salishan)

The name Stillaguamish, or Stillaquamish, stems from a word meaning "river people." The tribe lived in about twenty-nine villages, which were mainly on the river bearing their name in present-day northwestern Washington but also on its branches between the Skagit River on the north and the Snohomish River on the south. An important gathering place for the Upper Stillaguamishes was southwest of present-day Darrington. The Lower Stillaguamishes often gathered near the modern-day settlements of Silvana, Trafton, Milltown, Hazel, and Florence. Descendants of the Stillaguamishes claim that their ancestral lands exceeded 300,000 acres along the Stillaguamish River from Stanwood east to Darrington. They were closely related to the Snohomishes, the Sauk-Suiattles, and the Skagits. They also intermarried with natives from points as far distant as Oregon and California. Their tribal identity has been acknowledged by the Indian Claims Commission. The successors of the original Stillaguamishes are known officially as The Stillaguamish Tribe of Washington.

Location: The Stillaguamish Tribe of Washington lives mostly in Snohomish County, but some live as far away as Arizona and Alaska.

Numbers: In 1984 the Stillaquamish Tribe numbered 156. In 1853 their numbers were officially given as 150 and 200, though there is evidence that their numbers were larger before a smallpox plague in that year.

History: At the time of the first white contacts the Stillaguamishes were apparently an independent people with no more than subtribal status. The observations in 1850 of Samuel Hancock, who is believed to have been the first white man to follow the course of the Stillaguamish River, reveal much about these people. It was clear that they were involved in intertribal conflict, for they believed that he and his party of native canoemen were on an expedition against them. Like other northern Puget Sound natives, they were occasionally attacked by other peoples, such as the Clallams. At the time of Hancock's journey they had had some contact with Christianity, for a chief in one of their villages of about 300 made the sign of the cross. The Reverend Eugene Casimir Chirouse, O.M.I., who established a mission in the lower Snohomish River country in 1857 and later supervised the nearby Tulalip Indian Agency, exerted considerable influence on the Stillaguamishes. At the time when Hancock visited them, they had few firearms and had never seen a revolver. Their women wore cedar-bark girdles. Their men and children were without "burthen of dress," but would have worn more clothing in winter. In the nearby Cascade Mountains they hunted goats, and they traded the skins to other natives or to whites for groceries and other items in such places as Victoria on lower Vancouver Island. Dogs, which they kept for their fur, were the measure of a woman's wealth. They buried the bones of animals, in the belief that their spirits would return, make new bodies, and roam in the hills. They ate salmon and other seafoods, roots, and berries. After the coming of the whites, they raised potatoes in small patches on bottomlands. Later they worked for whites at such tasks as clearing land and harvesting crops. Their winter houses were built with cedar planks supported by large poles and housed several families. Their portable summer dwellings were often made of cattail matting placed over wooden frames. They fished mainly with two-pronged spears or with nets. Sometimes they bobbed with pronged spears across the river currents.

Government and Claims: The Stillaguamish Tribe has no trust land and no land base, yet on October 27, 1976, it achieved a status very much like that of a federally acknowledged tribe, and it enjoys the benefits of acknowledgment. On July 4, 1975, Stillaguamish tribesmen had created a considerable stir by marching in parades with the American flag upside down to call attention to their drive for federal acknowledgment. Chief Esther Ross was one of the Stillaguamishes who for many years had worked diligently to obtain such status.

The Stillaguamishes filed a claim (Docket 207) with the Indian Claims Commission for payment for lands ceded to the United States under the Point Elliott Treaty of 1855. On January 8, 1970, pursuant to a settlement between the parties, the commission entered a final judgment in the amount of $64,460 for the tribe's 58,600 acres of aboriginal lands, less the consideration that had been paid it under the treaty. The net award was $48,570.

Contemporary Life and Culture: Tribal members are employed in various communities, especially in Snohomish County. The tribe operates fish-hatching facilities on Jim Creek. Tribal members are deeply interested in their tribal heritage and have cooperated with those assembling a tribal history.

Suggested Readings: Nels Bruseth, *Indian Stories and Legends of the Stillaguamish, Sauks, and Allied Tribes* (Fairfield, Wash.: Ye Galleon Press, 1977); Samuel Hancock, *The Narrative of Samuel Hancock, 1845–1860* (New York: R. M. McBride,

1927); Gustaf B. Joergenson, *History of the Twin Cities* (Stanwood and East Stanwood, Washington), published in 70 issues of the *Twin City News*, April 1, 1948–October 27, 1949; Barbara Lane, "Anthropological Report on the Identity, Treaty Status and Fisheries of the Stillaguamish Indians," in *Political and Economic Aspects of Indian-White Culture Contact in Western Washington in the Mid-19th Century*, May 10, 1973, manuscript in Washington State Library, Olympia, Wash.; Marian Smith, "The Coast Salish of Puget Sound," *American Anthropologist*, n.s., 43, no. 2, pt. 1 (April, 1941): 197–211; William Whitfield, *History of Snohomish County, Washington* (Evansville, Ind.: Unigraphic, 1979), 2 vols.

SUQUAMISH
(Coastal Division, Salishan)

The Suquamish name is derived from that of the ancient native village which lay along the shores of Agate Passage, near the town of Suquamish, on the eastern Kitsap Peninsula of western Washington state. The Snohomishes, who lived across Puget Sound from the Suquamishes on the east, called them "mixed people."

The Suquamishes lived from Gig Harbor north to Appletree Cove, between Hood Canal and Admiralty Inlet as far south as Case and Carr inlets, and on Black, Bainbridge, and Whidbey islands. Between Hood Canal and Admiralty Inlet they occupied at least three autonomous villages. It was in the village of Suqua that the famed "Ole Man House" stood. It was about 500 feet long and 60 feet wide and housed several families. In the 1870s a federal agent ordered the burning of this physical and spiritual center of the Suquamish community.

Suquamish life revolved around the seasonal harvests of fish, shell-fish, roots, and berries. As fall neared, the Suquamishes traded with neighboring tribes for such items as whale oil, razor clams, salmon, basketry, and beadwork. During the winter they repaired their utensils, tools, and weapons. In that season they also carried on carving, weaving, and basket making in their longhouses. Winter was a time when tribal elders taught the young through song, dance, story, and ceremony. Today the succesors of the aboriginal Suquamishes are known officially as the Suquamish Tribe, Port Madison Reservation, Washington.

Location: Roughly 200 tribal members live on or adjacent to the Port Madison Reservation, which was established under the Point Elliott Treaty of 1855 for the Suquamish, Duwamish, and Skekomish (Muckleshoot) Indians. Other tribal members live primarily in nearby communities, such as Sequim, Bremerton, Port Orchard, Seattle, and Tacoma.

Numbers: In 1985 the Suquamish tribal membership stood roughly at 577. In 1844 they were listed at 525; in 1856 at 509 and, by another listing, 441; and in 1909 at 180.

History: The Suquamishes remained mostly at peace with whites but not always with other tribes. Their famous chief Sealth, or Seattle (after whom the city was named), reportedly was born on Blake Island around 1786. According to Suquamish tradition, Sealth's father, Schweabe, was involved in wars with the Chimakums, who tried to encroach on Suquamish lands. The Suquamishes were also involved in conflicts with the Duwamishes, on whose lands they sought to encroach. The numbers of the two tribes were reduced partly because of Suquamish aggressions. Schweabe encouraged activities such as wood carving and the building of canoes, in which the Suquamishes journeyed to places as far distant as Vancouver Island. Seattle was born from the marriage of Schweabe to a Duwamish woman. The Suquamishes traded with surround-

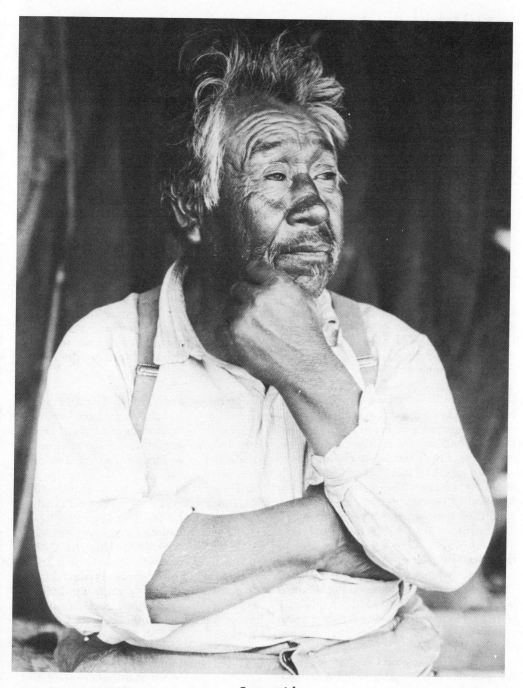

Suquamish

Jack Adams, a Suquamish of the Kitsap Peninsula in western Washington. Important developments among his people included the completion in 1980 of a beautiful tribal center, which houses, among other things, tribal heritage facilities. Courtesy of the Smithsonian Institution.

ing tribes and with the Hudson's Bay Company at Fort Nisqually, which the Bay Company established in 1833. The Suquamishes came under the influence of Roman Catholic missionaries in the late 1830s and early 1840s, and they remain predominately Catholic to the present day. They were, as noted, party to the Point Elliott Treaty, which was signed by their chief and six subchiefs. According to the treaty, they were scheduled to live on the 7,284.48-acre Port Madison Reservation, which was also at times called the Suquamish, Seattle, or Fort Kitsap reservation. Their chief, Kitsap, had disagreed with the terms of the treaty and chose not to live on the reservation.

Of the total acreage of the Port Madison Reservation, 5,909.48 acres were allotted to thirty-nine Indians. The remaining 1,375 acres went unallotted. Despite some government assistance, its natives were forced to leave the reservation in order to subsist. Complicating their problems were the continuing encroachments of Canadian tribesmen. For example, in 1859 the Suquamishes attacked a party of Haidas on the western shores of Bainbridge Island in retaliation for Haida attacks on Puget Sound. Living in the midst of hundreds of miles of poorly policed Puget Sound shorelines, the Suquamishes were especially vulnerable to the inroads of whiskey peddlers. In October, 1862, while attending a large Indian gathering at Port Madison to receive presents from the Duwamishes, the Suquamish headmen seized and burned a boat belonging to whiskey peddlers who were selling their wares to the assembled tribesmen. The Suquamishes worked for whites, especially the owners of the mills that sprang up around Puget Sound in the 1850s. At one Port Madison mill they were paid in inch-square brass pieces representing 25 and 50 cents, with which they could purchase goods at a store.

By act of Congress on October 24, 1864, the reservation was enlarged and redefined. Its lands lay on two projections separated by a body of water. On one of these is the Suquamish Reservation proper, on which today is located the tribal center. The other, referred to as the Indianola Tract, was added to the original reservation. Indians were often coerced into selling their reservation lands, until over half of the reservation had passed into non-Indian hands. In 1980 over 800 non-Indians lived on the reservation, and three times that number lived adjacent to it. In the early twentieth century the village of Suqua was acquired for a military post. The villagers were uprooted, as families were required to settle on individual allotments scattered across the reservation. On their allotments the Suquamishes, contrary to the government's wishes, farmed very little. They retained their fishing and hunting life-styles. Some families moved off the reservation rather than send their children to government boarding schools, thus relinquishing claims to its lands. By 1920 non-Indian fishing and canning industries were threatening the salmon runs not only in Suquamish waters but all over Puget Sound. Some indication of the American influence among the Suquamishes was the 1923 visit of their baseball team to Japan, where they sought to introduce the American game.

Government and Claims: The Suquamish Tribe, Port Madison Reservation, Washington, by the constitution and bylaws that it adopted on May 23, 1965, operates under an elected seven-member council. The large number of non-Indians on the Port Madison Reservation has posed some problems for the tribe. The tribe received little satisfaction from the United States Supreme Court ruling in *Oliphant* v. *Suquamish Tribe, et al.* (Case No. 76-5729, decided March 6, 1978), in which the court ruled that "Indian Tribal Courts do not have inherent criminal jurisdiction to try and to punish non-Indians, and hence may not assume such jurisdiction unless specifically authorized by Congress to do so."

The Suquamishes filed a claim (Docket 132) for additional compensation for lands ceded to the United States under the Point Elliott Treaty of 1855. The Indian Claims Commission found that the tribe had ceded 87,130 acres, exclusive of the 1,280 acres that were set aside for the reservation under the treaty, and that the fair market value of that land was $78,500 in 1859, the year that the treaty was ratified. To determine what sums were due the tribe, it was necessary, however, to ascertain how much of the consideration that it had received from the treaty was chargeable against the $78,500. The Suquamishes were one of eleven tribes that petitioned the commission (*Upper Skagit Tribe of Indians et al. v. U.S.*, 1964) to determine the amount that had already been paid to the Suquamishes. The Point Elliott Treaty had provided a consideration for the entire cession, but had failed to stipulate that the payment be made in specific proportionate amounts to the respective tribes. In final judgment dated October 22, 1970, the commission ruled that the Suquamishes should have received a total consideration of $36,329.51 for the aboriginal lands that they ceded to the United States, or 46 percent of the fair market value. Consequently, the commission decided on January 21, 1966, that they were entitled to an additional $42,170.49.

Contemporary Life and Culture: Of the original 7,284.48 acres of the Port Madison Reservation there remain but 2,849.42 acres in trust or in Indian ownership. The remaining acreage has gone into fee status. Several tribesmen work in reservation management. Some engage in logging, and some receive income from trust lands. Some are employed in the nearby Trident nuclear submarine base, on which construction began in 1975. Others engage in seasonal farm work and in fishing. The tribe operates hatcheries as part of its fisheries enhancement program. Besides fishing, clamming is an important activity of tribal members. The revenues derived from the sale of cigarettes have been reduced by federal court decisions requiring the payment of state taxes on reservation sales. Suquamish children attend local public schools. Welfare services are provided by federal and local governments. In 1977 the Suquamish Tribal Council established its Office of Cultural Programs to preserve and utilize Suquamish cultural and historical resources. In 1980 a beautiful tribal center was built after a fire the previous year had destroyed a nearly completed one.

Special Events: In August the tribe holds its annual Chief Seattle Days, featuring canoe races, baked salmon and clams, and a pageant portraying the history of local Indians, including the lives of chiefs Seattle and Kitsap. The celebration is held with help of the American Legion, which sets the date. See **Suquamish Tribe, Port Madison Reservation.**

Suggested Reading: Hermann Haeberlin and Erna Gunther, "The Indians of Puget Sound," *University of Washington Publications in Anthropology* 4, no. 1 (1930).

SUQUAMISH TRIBE, PORT MADISON RESERVATION

The Suquamishes and the Duwamashes were assigned to the Suquamish, or Port Madison, Reservation under the Point Elliott Treaty of 1856. Its Indians are known today as Suquamish Tribe, Port Madison Reservation. See **Suquamish** and **Duwamish.**

SWALLAH
(Coastal Division, Salishan)

Some ethnologists have grouped the Swallahs (or Swalishes) with the Lummis of present-day northwestern Washington, because both peoples spoke the Lkungen dialect of their Salishan language. The Reverend Myron Eells, who in the late nineteenth and early twentieth centuries wrote voluminously about the Indians of the Hood Canal and the Strait of Juan de Fuca, listed the Swallahs as living in the San Juan Islands, which lie between Vancouver Island and the United States mainland. The ethnologist John R. Swanton lists them as having lived in four villages in the San Juan Islands, located as follows: on the southeastern shores of Orcas Island; on the east side of San Juan Island; and in two villages on Waldron Island. They are also listed as having lived on Orcas Island, on which stands Mount Constitution, which bore the name Swelax, from which the name Swallah possibly derives.

SWINOMISH
(Coastal Division, Salsihan)

According to their tradition, the Swinomish tribe originated when a chief's son wandered from camp with his dog and suffered many hardships. Through purification of the spirit, he obtained great powers that enabled him to convert his dog into a beautiful princess, who became the wife and mother of the peoples whom he created by sowing (or throwing) rocks on the earth. In early days whites tended to group the Swinomishes with the Lower Skagits, but they were a separate people claiming occupancy of separate territory in present-day northwestern Washington. Their lands included portions of northern Whidbey Island and all of the islands in Similk Bay and northern Skagit Bay, including Hope, Skagit, Kiket, Goat, and Ika, as well as Smith Island on the west coast of Whidbey and Hat Island in Padilla Bay. A small, related band, the Squinomishes, occupied the mouth, estuary, and delta of the Skagit River on the north, forming a buffer zone between the Swinomishes and the Lower Skagits. The Swinomishes spoke the northern Lushootsled dialect of Coastal Salish.

The Swinomishes were a marine-oriented people. As much as 70 percent of their subsistence came from fish and other marine life. They also gathered berries, and after contact with white fur traders they raised potatoes. They maintained permanent villages during the winter months. At other seasons they roamed within reasonable distances of those villages to outlying fishing

Swinomish

Robert Joe, 1987, chairman of the Swinomish Indian Tribal Community, Swinomish Reservation, Washington, is of Swinomish descent. He is an example of a modern-day Native American administrator who is equally comfortable with the activities of his own culture or in the boardroom of the white culture.

and camping sites of varying degrees of permanency. From aboriginal times well into the nineteenth century, the more-or-less contiguous Swinomish villages, which were not totally autonomous in a political sense, enjoyed a certain measure of independence from each other. These villages were composed of several families under leaders whose positions were determined by material wealth and standing. None of them had complete control over all of the villages. There were strong kinship ties among the villages because they shared a common culture and language. Social contacts with natives living at some distance came through such ceremonies as the potlatch. This gift-giving feast, so common among Pacific Northwest coastal peoples, enabled its hosts to achieve social status.

Epidemics are believed to have struck around 1800, seriously reducing the Swinomish populations. In some areas deaths ran as high as 80 percent. Government officials in 1855 placed the Swinomish num-bers between 150 and 200. The Swinomishes were among the tribes who located on the Swinomish Reservation, which was set aside near the mouth of the Skagit River under the Point Elliott Treaty in 1855, which their head men signed. The reservation's northern boundaries were clarified by an executive order dated September 9, 1873, which in essence permanently established the 7,448.80-acre reservation. The Indian Claims Commission determined that the Swinomishes were an identifiable tribe, when they presented a claim (Docket 233) for compensation for the aboriginal lands that they had ceded under the Point Elliott Treaty, for which the United States had paid them an unconscionably low consideration. The Swinomishes requested the difference between the amount already paid them and the fair market value of the land. On July 6, 1972 they were awarded $29,000. See **Swinomish Indian Tribal Community, Swinomish Reservation, Washington.**

SWINOMISH INDIAN TRIBAL COMMUNITY, SWINOMISH RESERVATION, WASHINGTON

Most members of the Swinomish Indian Tribal Community, Swinomish Reservation, Washington, are descendants of the Swinomishes proper, the Skagits, and the Samishes.

Location: Tribal members live primarily on the Swinomish Reservation in Skagit County, near the mouth of the Skagit River on northern Puget Sound. The reservation lies adjacent to the Swinomish Slough, a channel forming the eastern boundary of the reservation. Across from the slough is the town of La Conner. Other members live in the farming, fishing, and lumbering region surrounding the reservation.

Numbers: In 1909 the tribe numbered 268. In 1937 they numbered 285. In 1985 they numbered 624.

History: The Swinomish Reservation was created as a consequence of the Point Elliott Treaty of 1855, which Swinomish headmen signed. An executive order of September 9, 1873, clarified the ill-defined northern boundary and added 59.73 acres, in essence, permanently establishing the 7,448.80-acre reservation. Having come under Roman Catholic missionary influences, the ancestors of the Swinomish Indian Tribal Community were under the Tulalip Agency, which was assigned to Catholics under the President Ulysses S. Grant Peace Policy. Under that policy, it was hoped that the Swinomishes would become agrarians, but they took to such pursuits reluctantly. During the 1860s they scattered to various points around Puget Sound, seeking employment. They clashed with white settlers over lands until the reservation boundaries were de-

Swinomish Indian Tribal Community, Swinomish Reservation

Annie McLeod, of the Swinomish Indian Tribal Community, Swinomish Reservation, circa 1900. Her people came under the influence of Roman Catholics during the Ulysses S. Grant Peace Policy, which got underway in the 1870's after the government stopped recognizing the Indian tribes as sovereign in 1871. Courtesy of the Skagit County Historical Museum.

fined. In 1884 about three-fourths of the Indians on the Swinomish Reservation were engaged in farming, logging, and milling. The remainder followed traditional pursuits, such as hunting and fishing.

Government and Claims: The Swinomish Indian Tribal Community operates under a constitution that was adopted by its members after they accepted the Indian Reorganization Act (48 Stat. 984) on November 16, 1935. They approved their constitution on January 27, 1936, and their charter, which was ratified on July 25 of that same year and later amended. Their governing body is the Swinomish Indian Senate, from which the principal tribal officers are elected. A Swinomish agent, O. G. Upchurch, believed that the introduction of formal democratic government among them simply reduced to written form a traditional expression of the will of the people.

232

The Swinomish Indian Tribal Community is composed of Swinomish, Kikiallus, Suquamish, Samish, and Upper and Lower Skagit peoples. The Community filed a claim (Docket 293) for an alteration in its reservation, claiming it was not as promised to them during the Point Elliott Treaty negotiations in 1855, though it had been enlarged. On June 21, 1971, the Indian Claims Commission ordered that the petition be dismissed.

Contemporary Life and Culture: On the Swinomish Reservation in 1950 there were 5,395 acres of allotted land, 40 acres of unallotted land, and 85 acres reserved by the federal government. In 1978 there remained 3,430.76 acres of allotted land in trust or otherwise restricted and about 263 acres of tribally owned land in trust. Since 1934–35, when the Swinomishes installed modern fish traps, they have engaged in commercial fishing, despite conflicts with the state of Washington over fishing jurisdictions. Among other enterprises, the Tribal Community operates the Swinomish Fish Company, whose facilities were installed in 1973. Its operations provide not only revenues but also employment for the Community's members. The Community is a member of the Skagit System Cooperative, which was organized in 1976 to regulate and enhance fishing in the Skagit River system. Also involved in the cooperative are the Upper Skagit and Sauk-Suiattle tribes. The income of most members of the Community is from fishing, farm labor, and lumbering. Some supplement their incomes by the sale of native goods that are woven, knitted, or carved. A center dedicated in August, 1964, injected new spirit into the Community. Socioeconomic services are provided through local, state, and federal agencies. After closure of the Tulalip school in 1932, Swinomish children attended school in nearby La Conner, where cooperation exists between school and tribal officials. Much-needed improvements in housing have been made. The Community's religous preference is Roman Catholic.

Special Events: On Memorial Day the Tribal Community holds the Swinomish Festival. Activities include ball and stick games, dances, and a salmon bake. Tribal members also observe Treaty Days the weekend nearest January 22, on which date in 1855 their Point Elliott Treaty was signed.

Suggested Readings: Herman Haeberlin and Erna Gunther, "The Indians of Puget Sound," *University of Washington Publications in Anthropology* 4, no. 1 (1930); Martin J. Sampson, *Indians of Skagit County* (Mount Vernon, Wash.: Skagit County Historical Society, 1972); O. C. Upchurch, "The Swinomish People and Their State," *Pacific Northwest Quarterly* 27, no. 4 (October, 1936).

TAITNAPAM
(Shahaptian)

The Taitnapams (Titon-nap-pams) were a Shahaptian group speaking the Klickitat dialect, or one very closely related to it. By the middle of the nineteenth century they had moved west of Washington's Cascade Mountains into the upper Cowlitz valley, where their women often married into Salish-speaking Cowlitz Indian families. Some ethnologists identify the Taitnapams as Upper Cowlitzes whose original band had absorbed sufficient numbers of Western Klickitats to form a new group (the Eastern Klickitats lived east of the Cascade Mountains). The Taitnapams retained much of the Cowlitzes' culture and the Klickitats' Shahaptian language.

The name Taitnapam derives from the Tieton River, a Yakima River tributary, which was probably their home before migrating west. One of their bands lived at what is today Mossyrock on the Cowlitz River, and their lands extended eastward up the Cowlitz watershed on the southern flank of Mount Rainier. Another band lived south of Mount Saint Helens in the Lewis River watershed. Both the Cowlitz and the Lewis River are tributaries of the Columbia. In their hilly and mountain homelands the Taitnapams hunted such game as elk, deer, and sheep. They also raised horses. Taitnapams on the upper Lewis River were perhaps the band that a North West Company fur trader in 1814 noted as living near Mount Saint Helens, from which they descended to hunt in the Willamette valley of Oregon. The ethnologist George Gibbs noted that the Taitnapams had a certain mystique among lower Cowlitz River Indians, who circulated tales that the Taitnapams stole and ate children and traveled invisibly. Eastern Klickitats called them "wild," or "wood," Indians. In 1853, Gibbs listed their numbers at around 75. With some Klickitats they were estimated at 600

in 1780. They joined Puyallups and Nisquallis in combat against Americans in the Puget Sound Indian War of 1855–56. In 1907 a Tacoma newspaperman wrote an article, entitled "Whole Tribe of Indians is Dead," on the passing of what he termed the "Peniyah" Indians, sometimes identified as Klickitats who had formerly lived in the lonely foothills southwest of Mount Ranier. Some Taitnapams were eventually driven back east over the Cascade Mountains to the upper Kittitas valley, where they joined a tribe of similar dialect, the Pshwanwapams, a Kittitas band of Upper Yakimas. Their descendants lived among not only the Pshwanapams but also the Micals of the upper Nisqually River on the west below Mount Rainier. There were still Taitnapams living off-reservation in their traditional territory in the 1970s. See **Cowlitz** and **Klickitat.**

Suggested Reading: Melville Jacobs, "A Sketch of Northern Sahaptin Grammar," *University of Washington Publications in Anthropology* 4, no. 2 (1931): 87–98; Leslie Spier, *Tribal Distribution in Washington*, American Anthropological Association, General Series in Anthropology, no. 3 (Menasha, Wis.: George Banta Publishing Co., 1936).

TAKELMA
(Takilman)

The Takelmas (or Dagelmas) were one of the Rogue River tribes who inhabited the Rogue River watershed on the east side of the Coast Range in southwestern Oregon. They were one of two major Takilman-speaking tribes in that area. The western, or Lowland Takelmas lived in villages along the middle Rogue River and its southern tributary, the Illinois River. Their name meant "those living alongside [the Rogue] river." The other Takelman-speaking tribe, the Latgawas, lived farther east on the upper Rogue River in the foothills of the Cascade Mountains. Their name meant "those living in the uplands." The two tribes spoke virtually the same language, but with dialect differences. Some linguists believe that Takilman speakers and those of Kalapuyan linguistic stock stemmed from a common language family. The name Rogue was applied to all people of the Rogue River valley by the early fur and mountain men, who regarded as unprincipled the natives' hostile acts against the strangers on their lands. The Takelmas were said to be larger in stature than the Latgawas, but less warlike and less accustomed to raiding other tribes for food and other valuables. The Takelmas were sold as slaves by the Latgawas to the Klamaths on the east. The Latgawas, much to the disgust of the Takelmas, ate crows, ants' eggs, lice, and insect larvae. Among the staple foods eaten by the Takilman peoples were acorns, manzanita berries (which they made into a drink by adding mashed pine nuts), and several varieties of seeds. They hunted deer and elk, often approaching the former with dogs in surrounds. The Takelmas also caught eels and fish in the Rogue River and fish in other streams. Their housing included small brush shelters at their mountain fishing places and permanent winter homes of split sugar-pine boards. They were said to have traded wives to the Shastas for basket hats. They traversed their watercourses in canoes. To protect themselves from their foes, they wore double-layered elk-skin armor fastened at the sides with sticks. Although sleeveless, these cuirasses were resistant to arrows. Their wearers believed that the symbolic designs on them also provided protection from enemy missiles. They used dentalia shells for ornamentation, and both men and women tattooed themselves. The women often accompanied the men to war.

The Takelmas believed that a person would die if a rattlesnake struck his or her shadow and that eagle cries heralded death by arrows. They prized very highly obsidian, which they secured in trade and used in weaponry. Their culture is enigmatic because they had traits of northern Californian Indians as well as those of Northwest Coast tribes. They appear to have had no concept of the guardian spirit that was so common in the traditions of the Pacific Northwest peoples. Some ethnologists classify the Rogue River peoples as members of the Lower Klamath cultural complex. Their village units were virtually autonomous units.

As noted, the Takelmas resented intrusions on their lands by strangers, such as the Hudson's Bay Company fur brigades who in 1829 began traversing their country en route to California. For several years thereafter, as travel through the Takelmas' land increased, they and the Latgawas tried to run off intruders by firing arrows into their parties. The cattle drovers en route to the Willamette valley from California in the 1830s were among those who came under the attacks of these natives. In 1846 they harassed the Scott-Applegate road-building party, as they also did immigrant parties. Their greatest hostility to travelers came after the 1848 gold discovery at Sutter's Mill in the Sacramento valley of California. Rogue bands attempted to match the firepower of these travelers by various means and built up a considerable arsenal of firearms by theft, depredation, and murder, as well as by extending favors and providing services to strangers.

In May, 1850, Oregon Territorial Governor Joseph Lane, in company with fifteen Klickitats under their chief, Quatley (Quart-

Takelma

Princess (or Lady) Oscharwasha, also known as Jennie, was one of the last of her tribe of Rogue River Indians. She died in May, 1893, in Jacksonville, Oregon, where she performed domestic work. She was buried in the robe shown here, which she had made of buckskin many years earlier. It weighed nearly fifty pounds and was rimmed in the most costly, elaborate manner. It appears to be fashioned in the manner of the Plains Indians and is atypical of the clothes worn by Indians of the Rogue River. Courtesy of the Southern Oregon Historical Society.

erly), set out to the south to effect a treaty with the Rogues. During their meeting the natives tried to attack Lane, but were repulsed by the Klickitat chief and his men. One Rogue River chieftain, impressed with Lane's bravery, asked to take the governor's name and subsequently called himself Joe (or Jo). Despite the ensuing treaty, conflict continued between the Rogue Indians and settlers. On June 17, 1851, Maj. Philip Kearney, U.S.A., with a detachment of mounted regulars en route to California, engaged the Rogues in battle near Table Rock in Takelma country. In that encounter the troops lost a captain, and the Rogues lost eleven killed and several wounded. The conflict resumed on June 23, and the Indians sustained several more casualties in a four-hour skirmish with the troops. Refusing to make a peace treaty the Rogues fled. Some of their captured women and children were eventually delivered to the new Oregon Territorial governor, John P. Gaines. In order to retrieve their families, the Rogues signed a treaty. According to its terms, they were to keep the peace and restore stolen properties, but again they reneged on the agreement. Their plight was made more acute by discovery of gold in their valley in 1851 when they were increasing their attacks on immigrants. After one attack by the volunteers Rogue chief Sam and his people, who were wintering in the Big Bar area, were surrounded and forced to sue for peace. In a July 21, 1852, treaty the Rogues agreed not to communicate with the Shastas on the south, whom whites blamed for numerous depredations. The Rogues also agreed to respect the property of whites in their valley. These agreements were difficult to accept because the gold miners muddied the streams, ruined the salmon runs, destroyed game, and committed numerous other depredations on the lands where they settled and cattle ran.

New towns, such as Jacksonville, Oregon, meant more trouble for the Rogues. After they had been attacked by regulars and volunteers from the towns and had lost thirty women and children to the troops of Major Kearney, the government moved Alonzo Skinner into the Rogue valley to serve as

Indian agent. In the meantime, miners continued to pour into the Rogue, Illinois, and Applegate river valleys. After a year's lull conflict resumed. The Rogues, Shastas, and Klamaths formed a coalition, but were decisively defeated in August, 1853. They lost eight killed and twenty wounded, though their coalition had been better armed than that of their foes. Typical of the American groups hostile to Indians was the Crescent City, California, Guard, who carried a banner bearing the word "EXTERMINATION." Because they respected former Governor Lane, who led the troops, the native combatants requested a council at Table Rock after the signing of a peace treaty on September 4. At the council about 700 armed Indians faced troops and Oregon Superintendent of Indian Affairs Joel Palmer, who was charged with the responsibility of effecting a long-term treaty with the Indians. The document signed on September 10, 1853 (ratified April 12, 1854), preserved the peace for about two years. Under its terms a reservation was established at Table Rock, to which chiefs Sam, Jim, and Jo moved their people. Opposite the reservation on the Rogue south bank was a military post, which operated until 1856, when the Indians were removed to a reservation. By the treaty the Rogue bands ceded to the United States about 2,500 square miles of their valley above Applegate Creek. In exchange they received $60,000, of which $15,000 were retained to pay whites for properties that Indians had destroyed. Before leaving the area, Lane made an informal peace arrangement with Shasta chief Tipsu. On November 18, 1854, Palmer treated with the Chastacostas (Shasta Scotons) and Grave Creek Umpquas. The latter ceded lands from south of Cow Creek to the Oregon-California border.

The Oregon-California border was relatively peaceful despite occasional conflicts between nonreservation Indians and whites, including so-called squawmen who fought the Shastas and spread rumors of Indian outbreaks. Reprisals and counter reprisals continued into 1855, however, involving Indians and posses out to revenge the killing of miners. In July, after Indians had slain eleven white miners along the Klamath River between Humbug and Horse creeks in California, whites fired indiscriminately at the Indians and hanged twenty-five of them in what was known as the Humbug War. These conflicts between Shastas and miners on the Klamath River spread to the Rogue valley, because whites blamed the Indians on the Table Rock Reservation for their troubles. White volunteers, ignoring the army and agency personnel among the Rogues, stormed Indian camps, killing women and children. On October 8, twenty-three Rogues were killed by volunteers near the mouth of Butte Creek. The next morning, roving Indians killed sixteen miners and settlers. Several Indians of a large force were killed in an October 17 fight with volunteers on Galice Creek.

By the fall of 1855, the Takelmas were no longer fighting to defend their homes but to survive. On October 31 and into November they fought a combined force of volunteers and regulars at Hungry Hill in the Grave Creek watershed. This last battle of the year, from which the white attackers withdrew, did little to help the Takelmas, who were without food, clothing, and shelter. With hope gone, 314 of the Indians turned themselves into the U.S. Army at Fort Lane for protection, while 300 others waited on the Umpqua for a decision about their fate. Superintendent Palmer decided to send the Umpqua valley Yoncallas and Southern Molalas to the future Grand Ronde Reservation on the Yamhill River, to which they departed in January, 1856. On February 22, 1856, the Takelmas and Latgawas from Table Rock also set out for that same reservation. Most traveled afoot except for thirty-four of the aged and infirm. Several orphans were, in the party, which lost several of its number along the way. Most of those who died were children or elderly.

Skirmishes between whites and Takelmas and Latgawas continued in the aftermath of that exodus. Most of this later fighting was on the coast and in mountainous stretches of the Rogue valley, where regulars did most of the fighting for the whites. In the interior volunteer forces did most of the fighting. After Rogues, Shastas, and a few Umpquas engaged volunteer troops in March, 1856, near Eight Dollar Mountain in the Umpqua valley, the Indians escaped to regroup on a bar below Little Meadows on the Rogue River. Forced to flee in mid-April, most of them escaped into woods ahead of the troops. After several Indian prisoners were sent to lure in the holdouts, the chiefs on May 21, 1856, met at the camp of Col. Robert Buchanan at Oak Flat on the Illinois right bank. On May 27 the Indians arrived a day late at a proposed council, and surrounded a small military force. In the ensuing Big Bend fight, which continued until May 29, the Indians, led by chiefs John and George, were defeated by a regular army-volunteer combination. After that defeat the Indians began their march downriver on June 10, 1856. Ten days later, at Port Orford, they boarded the steamer *Columbia*, which held about 600 Rogues, including Takelmas and Tututnis, along with Chetcos, Chastacostas, and Mishikhwutme-tunnes. They were shipped up the Pacific Coast and the Columbia and Willamette rivers to Oregon City, from which they were sent to the settlement of Dayton and then to what was supposed to be their new home, the Grand Ronde Reservation. A November, 1856, census revealed that those who were congregated there numbered 1,925, of whom 909 were of the Rogue and Shasta bands. By May, 1857, nearly all of the Rogues and Shastas had been moved again, this time to the Siletz Reservation. Only Chief Sam, a neutral during the war, remained on the Grand Ronde, with fifty-eight followers.

The Umpqua-valley Kalapuyan speakers on the Grand Ronde numbered 262 in 1857. The Kalapuyan peoples from the Willamette valley numbered 600 on that reserva-tion. Population figures for the Siletz Reservation in 1857 showed 554 Rogues and Shastas whose treaties had not been ratified. With other tribes of their area the Takelmas in 1852 numbered 1,154. Two years later they numbered but 523, and indication of the devastating effects of their war and the confinement of reservation life, which further decreased their numbers and their culture. In 1884 they numbered no more than twenty-seven. In 1905 there were reportedly only three or four elderly women on the Siletz who spoke the Takelman language, and but two women on the Grand Ronde, who spoke its upland dialect. By the early twentieth century any evidence of Takelma tribal entity had disappeared. Until then the few survivors had communicated mainly in the Chinook jargon, broken English or some Athapascan dialect. In the late 1970s archaeologists excavated Takelma village sites before they were covered by the waters behind a dam on the Applegate, a Rogue Tributary.

Suggested Readings: Stephen Dow Beckham, *Requiem For a People: The Rogue Indians and the Frontiersmen* (Norman: University of Oklahoma Press, 1971); Frederick Webb Hodge, *Handbook of American Indians North of Mexico*, vol. 2 (Washington, D.C.: Government Printing Office, 1910); Edward Sapir, "Notes on the Takelma Indians of Southwestern Oregon," *American Anthropologist*, n.s., 9, no. 2 (April–June, 1907); Edward Sapir, "Religious Ideas of the Takelma Indians," *Journal of American Folklore* 20 (1907): 33–49; Edward Sapir, "Takelma Texts," *University of Pennsylvania Museum of Anthropology Publications* 2 (1909): 1–263; Dorothy Sutton and Jack Sutton, eds., *Indian Wars of the Rogue River* (Grants Pass, Ore.: Josephine County Historical Society, 1969); Frank K. Walsh, *Indian Battles along the Rogue River, 1855–56* (Grants Pass, Ore.: Te-cum-tom Publications, 1972).

TALTUSHTUNTUDE
(Athapascan)

The Taltushtuntudes lived along Galice Creek, an upper-middle Rogue River tributary that enters that stream from the south in southwestern Oregon. Because of their location, the Taltushtuntudes were also known as the Galice Creek Indians. They spoke a dialect similar to that of the Dakubetedes, another Athapascan people who inhabited another Rogue tributary, the Applegate River, on the east. Culturally the Taltushtuntudes became assimilated with the Takilman-speaking Takelmas. They were with them at the middle of the century, and shortly thereafter both tribes failed to expel the white intruders from their lands. On the Siletz Reservation, under the classification Galice Creeks, the Taltushtuntudes were reported to number 18 in 1856 and 42 in 1937. For an account of their confrontations with whites and their treaties, wars and removal to the Siletz Reservation, see **Takelma.**

TENINO
(Shahaptian)

The Teninos were composed of four bands: the Teninos proper; the Tukspushes (Dockspuses), commonly called the John Day Indians for the river of that name; the Wyams (Waims); and the Tyighs (Tyghs). A valley in north-central Oregon bears the name Tygh. When the American explorers Meriwether Lewis and William Clark visited the Teninos in 1805–1806, the tribe's villages were on the north bank of the Columbia River, but they hunted and fished on the south side. The first Tenino village on the south side was believed to have been established in 1815 near the mouth of the Deschutes River, a Columbia River tributary. South of the Columbia, the Teninos appropriated the Tygh valley and a fishery (Sherar's Bridge), which was about thirty miles up the Deschutes from its mouth. Around 1820 they drove the Molalas westward across the Cascade Mountains and appropriated lands from the Columbia south to the Mutton Mountains. They shared lands with the Paiutes in a buffer zone between the two peoples. They then established two villages on the south side of the Columbia. One was about two miles east of what was later known as Big Eddy and two miles east of the main Wasco Indian village. The other was six miles inland on what today is known as Fifteen Mile Creek. The Wyams established a village on the Columbia south bank near present-day Celilo, and another a few miles up the Deschutes. A few miles up the John Day River, on opposite shores, were two villages of Tukspushes. In treaty times (circa 1855) the Wyams extended up the

Tenino

A Tenino brave from a long line of warriors who waged wars against such tribes as the Klamaths, the Molalas, and the Northern Paiutes.

239

John Day River as far south as present-day Clarno, Oregon.

Individuals and families of one Tenino village would freely affiliate with those of another village, though they tended to marry within their own bands. Each band owned its own fishing grounds. Besides being fishermen, the Teninos were mercantilists. They controlled vital places at Celilo Falls on the Columbia, where they exacted tolls of passersby and portaged their goods. In the 1840s they demanded "dollars" of Oregon-bound white travelers passing their stretch of river.

Lewis and Clark observed that the Tenino peoples, more than others whom they met on their trek, demanded more for their horses, which they acquired by raiding other tribes. They were not skilled horsemen like the Cayuses and Nez Percés on the east, and they did not geld their animals; yet they too regarded them as symbols of wealth and a means by which to exploit large areas. In 1780 the Tenino bands numbered an estimated 1,400 souls. In 1854 they numbered 500, and in 1858, 450. In 1962, 250 of their descendants were reported in Oregon. Formerly, the Teninos were sufficiently populous to substantiate their boast that they had killed 500 Paiutes and Klamaths and had captured 40 Paiute women and young girls. During the Cayuse War of 1848 the Cayuses attempted to pressure the Teninos into fighting volunteers of the Oregon provisional government. Two Tenino bands rendered half-hearted support to the Cayuses, but others went into hiding in the Yakima country. The Teninos temporized their support of the Cayuses even to the point of meeting with the commissioners sent out to negotiate with the Cayuses. They also returned livestock stolen from the whites.

On June 25, 1855, the Tenino bands signed a treaty (12 Stat. 963, ratified March 8, 1858, and proclaimed April 18, 1858) with Oregon Superintendent of Indian Affairs Joel Palmer. By its terms they alienated their lands in return for assignment to the Warm Springs Reservation in north-central Oregon. Some Tukspushes avoided the Warm Springs until 1878, when they left their homes in the area of Clarno. During the Yakima War (1855–56) some Teninos burned agency buildings on the Umatilla River, but in an attack on The Dalles they were unable to get aid from the preoccupied Cayuses. During the winter of 1855–56 some Teninos broke away from their combatant fellows. The Paiutes raided the Teninos and their allies on the Warm Springs Reservation until well past the middle of the century. Aware of intertribal animosities, the United States military in the 1860s recruited Tenino scouts from the Warm Springs Reservation in its war against the Paiutes, and it also recruited them in a war against the Modocs in 1873. On the Warm Springs the Teninos became incorporated within the Warm Springs Confederated Tribes. For additional information and suggested readings, see **Confederated Tribes of the Warm Springs Reservation of Oregon.**

TILLAMOOK
(Coastal Division, Salishan)

The Tillamooks were formerly called by other names, such as the Calamoxes. They lived on the Pacific Coast of Oregon between Nehalem and the Salmon River and from the crest of the Coast Range to the Pacific Ocean. The Tillamooks had been separated in precontact times from other Salish peoples to their north by Chinookan peoples around the mouth of the Columbia River. Consequently, their cultural traits varied somewhat from those of other coastal Salish peoples, showing Californian tribal influences. The word *tillamook* is said to mean "land of many waters." The anthropologist Franz Boas said it means "people of Nekelim, or Nehalem." An Oregon county and a city

240

on U.S. Highway 101 bear the tribal name. Some ethnologists have identified four groups within the Tillamook tribe: the Nehalems, the Tillamooks proper, the Nestuccas, and the Nechesnes (of whom the latter are often called the Salmon River Indians). In the middle of the nineteenth century government officials referred to the Nehalems and the Tillamooks proper as Northern Tillamooks, as opposed to the Nechesnes, who were misnamed Southern Tillamooks along with the Alseas, Yaquinas, and Siletzes. Recent linguistic studies have not confirmed the classification of the four Tillamook groups as a single tribe, though their dialects are similar. Until recently the Nehalems and Tillamooks proper were regarded as bands of a single tribe because they had banded together to petition the federal government for claims awards since the late nineteenth century. At the time of the first white contacts each of the four groups may have been composed of multiple villages. Subsequently the Tillamook peoples were generally reduced to a single village by diseases, such as syphilis and smallpox, and abuse of liquor and firearms. Each group was a tribal entity only in that it was autonomous.

The Tillamook peoples tended to be short of stature with broad, thick, flat feet, thick ankles, and crooked legs. They flattened the heads of their aristocracy by applying pressure to them in infancy. Before the nineteenth century the Tillamooks practiced tattooing. They had slaves in the manner of most Northwest Coast peoples. They subsisted on waterfowl, such as ducks and geese, which they caught by wading into the water wearing pitch-and-feather-covered baskets as decoys over their heads. With great dexterity they also hunted game in the nearby hills with bows and arrows. They caught fish and gathered shellfish, some of which they carried over the Coast Range into the Willamette valley to trade to natives of the Tualatin country for goods, such as the wappato root, which they also dug for themselves at Wapato Lake in the Tualatin country. Sometimes the Tillamooks canoed up the coast and the Columbia River to trade. Among the goods that reached them from great distances were the highly prized dentalia shells from Vancouver Island. At the time of the first white contacts Tillamook men wore animal skins, and their women wore petticoats or skirts of cedar bark, silk grass, plant flags, and rushes. The Tillamooks adopted Euro-American dress at an early date. They lived in plank-and-mat houses, many of which had pitched, shed-like roofs.

It is uncertain when the Tillamooks first met white maritime traders. Some Nehalems had Caucasian features indicating white contacts before 1775, when Spanish explorers were along their coasts. Beeswax found on Nehalem shores is believed to have been washed up from a wrecked Spanish ship, such as those that, beginning in 1560, sailed between Manila and Acapulco. On August 10 and 11, the Nestuccas traded warily with the American Capt. Robert Gray. On August 15 in Tillamook Bay, in exchange for sea otter and boiled and roasted crab, they received from Gray and his crew knives, axes, and adzes. They knew the value of metal knives, which they already possessed. When Gray's crew came ashore, the natives offered them food, but when one crewman grabbed a cutlass that another had carelessly left sticking in the sand, a skirmish over it ensued, leaving three natives and a crewman dead. In their canoes the natives failed to head off Gray's ship, *Lady Washington*. After firing her guns on the natives and their plank houses ashore, the ship sailed out of what Gray called "Murderers Harbour." Meriwether Lewis and William Clark were probably the first Americans to reach Tillamook country overland. When Clark visited the Tillamooks in January, 1806, they had just processed the flesh and meat of a 105-foot whale washed up on their beaches. Soon the Tillamooks had contact with traders of John Jacob Astor's Pacific Fur Company and their successors of the North West Company. Duncan McDougall, a North West Company trader from headquarters at Fort George (Astoria, Oregon), called the Tillamooks the "most roguish" people of the region.

Guns, liquor, and disease took their toll on the Tillamook peoples as outsiders con-

Tillamook

Maggie Adams and her daughter, Lizzie Adams, circa 1890. The people of these Tillamook women had contact with Meriwether Lewis and William Clark at the end of the American explorers' trek to the Pacific Coast of northwestern Oregon. The basket in Lizzie's hands was for carrying various goods, but sometimes the Tillamooks also wore feather-covered baskets over their heads as decoys to snare waterfowl. Courtesy of the Pioneer Museum, Tillamook, Oregon.

tinued to encroach on their country by land and sea. The passage of Hudson's Bay Company men and their trade goods along their coasts to their villages further broke down their society. On one occasion they were punished by company officials, even though in 1828 they had befriended and escorted to Fort Vancouver the American Jedediah Smith after the attack on his party by Kuitsh (Lower Umpqua) Indians. The greatest encroachment on Tillamook lands was by American settlers stimulated by the Donation Land Act of September 29, 1850. In the ensuing years whites literally crowded Tillamooks off their beaches. Kilchis, the chief of the Tillamooks proper and a friend of whites helped minimize racial confrontations. Yet, he was a bitter foe of Chief Kotata of the neighboring Clatsops on the north. Oregon Superintendent of Indian Affairs Anson Dart dealt with Kilchis in the unratified treaty of August 7, 1851. On the previous day the Nehalems had also signed a treaty to cede their lands. All of the tribes and groups south of the Tillamooks along the Oregon coast, misnamed Southern Tillamooks, on August 11, 1855, treated with Oregon Superintendent of Indian Affairs Joel Palmer. During the Indian wars of the 1850s, when pressured by Klickitat Indians to enter hostilities, the Tillamooks obeyed Kilchis's order that they bring in their guns to prove to whites their peaceful disposition. Kilchis also sought to maintain some semblance of the Tillamook tribal identity, which had been threatened by their losses of numbers. Lewis and Clark had estimated the Tillamooks at 2,200. By 1841 their numbers had fallen to 400.

Thirty years later there were but 28 Nehalems, 55 Nestuccas, and 83 of Kilchis's Tillamooks proper. In 1950 between 200 and 300 were able to prove Tillamook descent.

By act of Congress on June 7, 1897 (30 Stat. 67), the Nehalems were awarded a $10,500 settlement for their unratified 1851 treaty. On August 24, 1912 (37 Stat. 578), the Tillamooks proper were also awarded $10,500 for settlement of their claims. On August 27, 1962, they and the Nehalems shared an Indian Claims Commission award of $169,187.50 ($620 for each eligible recipient) after offsets for another claim (Docket 240). After their award the scattered Tillamooks were without organization. The Nechesnes received an award by the Court of Claims (Case No. 45230) as Alcea Band of Tillamooks et al. See **Yaquina.**

Suggested Readings: Franz Boas, "Notes on the Tillamook," *University of California Publications in American Archaeology and Ethnology* 33 (1923): 3–16; Franz Boas, "Traditions of the Tillamook Indians," *Journal of American Folklore* 11 (1898): 23–28; Elizabeth Derr Jacobs, *Nehalem Tillamook Tales* (Eugene, Ore.: University of Oregon, 1959); Ada M. Orcutt, *Tillamook: Land of Many Waters* (Portland, Ore.: Binfords and Mort, 1951); John Sauter, "History of Tillamook Indians," *Tillamook Times*, 5, Issue 1, n.d.; John Sauter and Bruce Johnson, *Tillamook Indians of the Oregon Coast* (Portland, Ore.: Binfords and Mort, 1974); Herbert C. Taylor, Jr., "Anthropological Investigation of the Tillamook Indians Relative to Tribal Identity and Aboriginal Possession of Lands," 1953, photocopy of manuscript in Tillamook County Pioneer Museum, Tillamook, Oregon.

TUKUARIKA (SHEEPEATER)
(See **Shoshone-Bannock Tribes of the Fort Hall Reservation** and **Shoshoni.**)

TULALIP TRIBES OF THE TULALIP RESERVATION

Tulalip Tribes of the Tulalip Reservation

Stanley Jones, Sr., a Tulalip chairman, circa 1980. The Tulalip Reservation, where most of the tribe live, is just west of Marysville, Washington.

The name Tulalip stems from a native word meaning "almost land-locked bay," referring to Tulalip Bay just north of present-day Everett, Washington. The name came to be applied to the nearby Tulalip Reservation, as well as to its Indians, who came to be known as The Tulalip Tribes of the Tulalip Reservation. They were Coastal Salish peoples, mostly Snohomish, Stillaguamish, Snoqualmie, Skyomish, Skagit, and Samish Indians (see also the entries for those tribes).

Location: Members of the Tulalip Tribes live on their reservation and in its environs in northwestern Washington. The reservation is located just north of Everett and west of Marysville and is bounded on the south and west by Puget Sound. Reservation roads connect with Interstate 5, which is along the reservation's eastern boundary along with the main north-south line of the Burlington Northern Railway.

Numbers: In 1985 the Tulalip Tribes had 1,099 members, most of whom lived on the reservation. About 1,000 non-Indians live on alienated lands within the reservation.

History: The beginnings of the Tulalip Tribes were at the Point Elliott Treaty of January 22, 1855, under which provision was made for the establishment of the 22,489.91-acre Tulalip Reservation (formerly called the Snohomish), which by executive order was enlarged to 24,300 acres on December 23, 1873, when its boundaries were defined. It was intended for the Snohomish, Snoqualmie, Stillaguamish, and Skykomish tribes and remnants of others. During the 1840s and 1850s, Indians of the Tulalip area came under the influence of Roman Catholic missionaries, some of whom, such as the Reverend Eugene Casimir Chirouse, O.M.I., actively ministered to the reservation's peoples. During the President Ulysses S. Grant Peace Policy era of the 1870s, during which religious denominations managed the various Indian agencies, the Tulalip was administered by Catholics, of whom the foremost was Father Chirouse, who served as agent. In his efforts to create a Paraguayan reduction for the Tulalip Indians, Chirouse faced innumerable problems. The Indians did not quickly adapt to agriculture as the federal government had hoped they would. The

244

heavily timbered reservation was poorly suited to agriculture; moreover, the Indians did not wish to alter their ancient means of livelihood: fishing, hunting, and gathering. Many were forced from the reservation to find subsistence elsewhere. Several farmed small patches, and some engaged in logging and in other tribe-related enterprises, to supply not only their own needs but also an expanding market among whites. At the same time the Tulalip Indians became victims of white men's diseases and the omnipresent liquor. The dream of Chirouse, like that of other agents in the same situation, was frustrated by a growing secularism, which eventually produced government control of the agencies in the post-Peace Policy era. Allotting was conducted on the Tulalip between 1883 and 1909. Since the reservation's acreage was limited and the land poorly suited to agriculture, some Indians failed to obtain allotments.

Government and Claims: The Tulalip Tribes of the Tulalip Reservation operate under a constitution and bylaws that were approved January 24, 1936, and a charter that was ratified on October 3, 1936. Both documents have since been modernized. Tribal affairs are supervised by a board of directors, which employs a business manager and other officials. Active committees administer lands and leasing, loans, education, enrollment, water resources and roads, hunting and fishing, and recreation.

The Tulalip Tribes did not file a petition with the Indian Claims Commission for any claim as the successor of any of the tribes sent to the reservation.

Contemporary Life and Culture: By the 1970s more than half the Tulalip Reservation (13,995 acres) had been sold to non-Indians. Of the Indian-owned lands at that time, 4,571 acres remained in trust or some other restricted status; 3,845 were tribally owned in trust; and 80 owned by the Tulalip Tribes in fee-patent status. Tribal members continue to live on allotments throughout the reservation. Since the virgin timber has been logged, the Tulalip Tribes have shifted to other sources of income, such as

the leasing of waterfront sites. The tribes own an industrial site and manage and operate a fish hatchery to generate income for Indian and non-Indian alike. Children in the upper grades attend schools in nearby Marysville. Three buildings on the Tulalip are on the National Registry of Historic Places: the Tulalip Shaker Church, Saint Anne's Catholic Church, and the Tulalip Agency building. The following faiths are represented on the reservation: Catholic, Mormon, Indian Shaker, Church of God, and Pentecostal. As part of the tribes' efforts to perpetuate ancient crafts a man has been employed to teach wood carving. Seeking to increase its funds, the tribe in June, 1983, opened its Entertainment Center featuring computerized bingo games. The 2,500-member tribe made the first state-tribe casino gaming compact in June 1991. They built a 12,000-square-foot casino near their 1,400-seat bingo parlor.

Special Events: Like other tribes under the Point Elliott Treaty, the Tulalip Indians observe Treaty Days on the weekend nearest January 22. On the Tulalip Reservation the event is also attended by other tribes who lack adequate facilities for Smokehouse (religious) ceremonies. During these ceremonies tribal elders remind younger members of the lands that once belonged to their ancestors, exhorting them to protect those that remain. A smoked-salmon feast is also held. Non-Indians may attend the event, and artists may portray it, but cameras and other recording devices are not permitted.

Suggested Readings: Gustaf B. Joergenson, *History of the Twin Cities* (Stanwood and East Stanwood, Washington), in 70 issues of *Twin City News*, April 1, 1948–October 27, 1949; Colin Ellidge Tweddell, "A Historical and Ethnological Study of the Snohomish Indian People," in *Coast Salish and Western Washington Indians*, vol. 2 (New York: Garland Publishing, Inc., 1974), pp. 475–694; William Whitfield, *History of Snohomish County, Washington* (Evansville, Ind.: Unigraphic, 1979), 2 vols.

TUTUTNI
(Athapascan)

The Tututnis (or Tututnnes), the meaning of whose name is unknown, were popularly called the Coast Rogues. Their several bands lived in what is now southwestern Oregon along the Illinois and the lower Rogue rivers and near the Pacific Coast between the Coquille River on the north and the Chetco River on the south. There were as many as seven Tututni groups, who were culturally related and had kinship ties. They did not, however, constitute a typical tribe because the usual sociopolitical organization, involving chiefs and governmental authority, was lacking. Their houses were twelve-to-sixteen-foot excavations, on the sides of which stood eight-foot puncheons beneath board-and-thatch roofs. Round holes at the gable ends served as entryways, and descent was made down notched poles. The Tututnis burned grassy headlands near river mouths in the belief that the practice ensured the return of salmon from the sea. They also harvested acorns, which they sometimes traded. From peoples of the Oregon interior they obtained highly prized obsidian, which, as evidence of wealth, they fashioned into blades that were as much as twenty centimeters in length.

In the spring of 1792, unadorned by the grease and paint so commonly used by other natives, the Tututnis paddled their canoes out to meet the British explorer Capt. George Vancouver. A quarter century later they met a white fur trader, Peter Corney, who recorded them as wearing dressed-deer-skin garments and small tight-fitting hats. To his North West Company ship they brought baskets, fish, and berries to trade. On June 27, 1828, they fled their villages on both sides of the Rogue River at the approach of a northbound American party under Jedediah Smith. Two years later, after a storm beached a Russian whaling ship, the Tututnis succumbed to some disease that they blamed on the Russians, unaware of the presence of the intermittent fever that some Indians believed had been brought by American maritime traders.

During the 1850s, Tututni game trails and hunting grounds were destroyed by whites clearing lands for farms. The Tututni women were corrupted by trappers and miners, and white ferrymen preempted their river-crossing businesses. In September, 1849, after the *William G. Hagstaff* went aground near the mouth of the Rogue River, Indians stormed and burned her and salvaged her chain plates to fashion into knives. Her captain, Charles White, and eighteen men wandered along the coast for three weeks. In June, 1851, some Tututnis were killed and wounded by shots from a small cannon that had been fired by men coming ashore from the steamer *Seagull*. White men established a beachhead on the Tututni lands, on which they laid out the town of Port Orford, which in August already numbered sixty souls. The security of the town was strengthened that month by the arrival of Lt. August V. Kautz, U.S.A., with twenty troops, and by the arrival of other soldiers from Fort Orford. The Tututnis were further pressured when more settlers came to Port Orford after the gold discoveries in the Rogue River valley in 1852.

In November, 1855, the Tututnis threatened the whites at Port Orford, while other Tututnis up the Rogue River urged the lower-valley natives to join them in war against the whites. On February 22, 1856, the Tututnis attacked the Gold Beach Guards, who were encamped opposite the large Tututni village at Port Orford. Moving through the forests, the Indians fired the cabins of miners and others who were attending a George Washington's Birthday celebration at Gold Beach, and they killed a number of whites. Prominent among a reported twenty-six killed was an Indian agent, named Ben Wright, who had been betrayed, it was said, by his common-law Indian wife, Chetco Jennie. He was felled by an axe wielded by one Enos, a "half-blood" Indian from the East, who urged the Indians to destroy white men. The conflict continued as the Tututnis burned most of the settlers' homes between Port Orford and Smith River. About 130 settlers escaped to Fort Miner, which was on the Rogue north bank near its mouth. From the Rogue south bank the Tututnis attacked for ten miles down the coast. It was a help to them that Major John F. Reynolds, U.S.A., was needed to protect Port Orford and therefore unable to dispatch an expedition to help the beleaguered whites. They were rescued five weeks later by army regulars from Fort Humboldt, California.

The Tututni resistance was both the cause and the effect of their treaties with the United States. By an unratified September, 1851, treaty various Tututni bands had surrendered 2.5 million acres in return for $28,500. They were caused further anguish by the treaties that they had made in August and September, 1855, with Oregon Superintendent of Indian Affairs Joel Palmer, and by Congress's failure to ratify those documents. In the final phase of what was known as the Rogue Wars, many Tututnis fled upriver to join Takelmas, the Latgawas, and their allies. By June, 1856, those Tututnis who had remained and other tribesmen of the Rogue valley had been rounded up at Port Orford. The moaning and the wailing of these nearly naked unfortunates and of those who were resisting capture could not have escaped the ears of their foes. In February, 1857, 152 more were rounded up. On June 20 about 600 Tututni, Chetco, Coquille, Chastacosta, Takelma, and Latgawa tribesmen and a few Shastas were herded aboard a steamer, as were nearly 600 more shortly thereafter. The captives were shipped up the coast and up the Columbia and Willamette rivers to Dayton, Oregon. From there they were marched over the Coast Range to an alien home on the Grand Ronde Reservation. They remained there for a year and then moved to the Siletz (first called the Coast Reservation), which was established by executive order on November 9, 1855. That they had no treaty with the United States made little difference to their captors. Because of the harshness and the strangeness of reservation life, only 141 Tututnis remained in 1930. By 1964 only 6 remained who spoke the native tongue. In 1854, during the turbulent decade of their demise, they had numbered roughly 1,311.

With certain other western Oregon tribes,

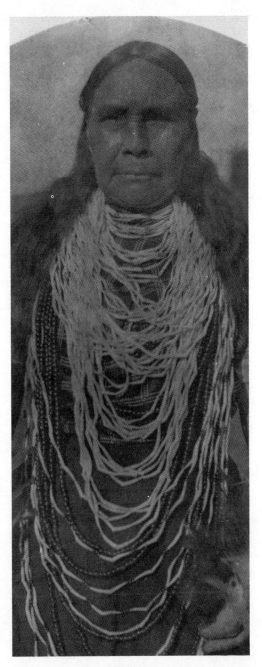

Tututni

Martha Johnson, a member of the Tututni tribe of southwestern Oregon, popularly known as Coast Rogues. Such beadwork was valuable not only for adornment but also for trading purposes.

the Tututnis were plaintiffs in a case (No. 45230) tried in the Court of Claims, in which the tribe sued for the loss of lands that were taken from the Coast Reservation by executive order on December 21, 1865, and by act of Congress on March 3, 1875. For details of the case see **Yaquina.** They appealed their award to the United States Supreme Court, which on November 25, 1946, upheld the April 2, 1945, ruling of the Court of Claims. The final award was $465,225.60 for the Tututnis.

Suggested Readings: Stephen Dow Beckham, *Requiem for a People: The Rogue Indians and the Frontiersmen* (Norman: University of Oklahoma Press, 1971); Percy T. Booth, *Valley of the Rogues* (Grants Pass, Ore.: Josephine County Historical Society, 1970); Edward S. Curtis, *The North American Indian* (1912; New York: Johnson Reprint Corporation, 1970), vol. 13; Cora DuBois, "The Wealth Concept as an Integrative Factor in Tolowa-Tututni Culture," in *Essays in Anthropology, Presented to A. L. Kroeber* (Berkeley: University of California Press, 1936).

TWANA
(Coastal Division, Salishan)

The name Twana is said to mean "people from below." In the Point-No-Point Treaty with the United States of 1855, they appear as the Toanhooches. Today a state park at the southern end of Hood Canal near U.S. Highway 101 bears the name Twanoh. The Twanas originally occupied both sides of Hood Canal in Washington state. In the nineteenth century the missionary Myron Eells divided them into three bands: Duhlelips, Skokomishes, and Kolsids (or Quilceeds). The largest of these bands were the Skokomishes, whose name is based on a Twana word meaning "people of the large river," referring to the Skokomish River, an affluent of Hood Canal. Others have identified five permanent Twana villages. The anthropologist William Elmendorf located them in nine permanent villages, most of which were at the mouths of salmon streams along Hood Canal. The modern-day descendants of these Twana peoples are members of the Skokomish Tribe, Skokomish Reservation.

Location: Tribal members live not only on the Skokomish Reservation but also adjacent to it in such places as the city of Shelton.

Numbers: Two hundred years ago with the neighboring Squaxins, the tribe was said to have numbered about 1,000. Official estimates in the 1850s placed the Twana numbers between 200 and 300.

History: Socially the Twanas had three classes: a high and a low free class and slaves. Although the village structure was informal and lacked true governing offices, considerable prestige and influence adhered to the high-ranking men of each village. As among other Salish speakers, religion played a major role in the Twanas' lives. Individuals acquired guardian spirits, which were ceremoniously revealed in winter dances. The Twanas sought peace despite attacks on them by natives of the Olympic Peninsula and Puget Sound. They had commercial ties with the Clallams and the Makahs on the north and west and with the Kwaiailks and Satsops on the south. They rarely undertook extensive trading expeditions, but did obtain such items as hemp fiber and mountain-goat hair from the east through intermediaries, such as the Satsops. From the Makahs and the Vancouver Island tribes they obtained, often through Clallam intermediaries, implements and ornaments of shell, bone, stone, fiber, wood, and, later, metal. In 1792 they presented members of Capt. George Vancouver's British expedition with bows and arrows. Some of the latter were iron-tipped, indicating that the Twanas had had contact with white mariners other than Vancouver or had traded with natives who had obtained metals directly or indirectly from whites. The metals may have come from wrecked ships, possibly from the Orient. The Twanas were among those who traded at the Hudson's Bay Company's Fort Nisqually, which was established in 1833 on the southern reaches of Puget Sound.

Today the Twanas belong to the Skokomish Tribe, Skokomish Reservation. That tribe may be said to have originated when Twana, Clallam, and Chimakum headmen signed the Point-No-Point Treaty on January 26, 1855. At the treaty council some Twanas opposed selling their lands. They were aware of their commercial value because whites were logging them for poles and lumber. They also opposed removal to any reservation that might be established on Clallam lands instead of on theirs. Eventually the three tribes were designated to remove to a 3,840-acre reservation carved from Twana lands along the lower Skokomish River. See **Skokomish Tribe, Skokomish Reservation.**

Suggested Reading: W. W. Elmendorf, *The Structure of Twana Society*, Monograph Supplement no. 2 (Pullman, Wash.: Washington State University, 1960).

Twana

A young full-blood Twana man, circa 1880. His short hair and clothing show the influence of missionaries. His ancestors lived in a society with strong class distinctions. When Capt. George Vancouver visited Puget Sound in 1792, the Twanas presented the British explorer with bows and arrows. Courtesy of Whitman College.

UMATILLA
(Shahaptian)

The Umatillas lived on the lower reaches of the Umatilla River, a Columbia River tributary in northeastern Oregon, and, along both banks of the Columbia from present-day Arlington, Oregon, east to the mouth of the Walla Walla River of southeastern Washington. The tribal name derives from a village name meaning "many rocks." It is also the name of a county and a town in Oregon. The Umatillas were estimated to have been 1,500 in 1780, 272 in 1910, 145 in 1923, and 124 in 1937. One estimate of the number of Umatillas in Oregon in 1962 varied from between 10 and 100. Before acquiring horses early in the eighteenth century, the Umatillas depended primarily on salmon and other fish for survival. Like many Columbia River peoples, they caught the salmon with an assortment of spears, nets, traps, and weirs. They sought bountiful catches by performing strict first-salmon ceremonies before the catches began. They also gathered mussels from the river. Away from the river, they gathered camas, berries, pine nuts, seeds, bark, and sap. They roasted food in earthen ovens and boiled it in water heated by hot stones. They lived in multifamily lodges constructed of poles and mats over shallow excavations. Some of their houses were as big as sixteen by sixty feet. Like other natives of the interior, they used sweat lodges for body conditioning. Their horses made them mobile, which facilitated their hunting of game.

The Umatilla had few intertribal political ties; yet, under threats by their most feared enemy, the Paiutes, they formed a war alliance with the Nez Percés on the east. When McNary Dam was built on the Columbia River, its backwaters covered Blalock Island, which was their stronghold against mounted Paiute raiders. In 1848 they sent warriors to join their Cayuse neighbors after the Whitman Massacre of the previous year. These Umatilla warriors remained with the combatants throughout most of the Cayuse War, which was fought against a volunteer army of whites from the Willamette valley. Living along the Immigrant Road (the Oregon Trail), as it broke westward to the Columbia, the Umatillas, like their Cayuse neighbors, were alarmed at the increasing numbers of immigrants passing over that route in the 1840s. Aware of the restiveness that white immigration had induced among the Indians, Congress passed the Donation Land law on September 29, 1850, allowing whites to homestead lands in Oregon not yet ceded by the Indians. Aware that the local tribes were restive, the government in 1851 established the Utilla (Umatilla) Agency on the Lower Crossing of the Umatilla River near present-day Echo, Oregon. The Roman Catholic mission of Saint Anne (later named for Saint Joseph and today for Saint Andrew) had been established in 1847 near Pendleton, Oregon, and had been abandoned in 1848 after the killing of Marcus and Narcissa Whitman and the Cayuse War. In 1851 it was reestablished. Like the Cayuses, the Umatillas frequented the Utilla Agency to obtain not only food but also intelligence concerning the activities of whites. They suffered at the hands of incompetent agents, one of whom encouraged them to steal immigrant cattle which he later purchased from them.

Fearing war, white cattlemen fled the Umatilla valley in October, 1855, the year that the Tenino Indians burned the agency building. The Yakima War of 1855–56 broke out in that same month. In May and June, 1855, the Umatillas met the Washington and Oregon superintendents of Indian affairs, Isaac Stevens and Joel Palmer, in the Walla Walla Treaty Council. Along with the Cayuses and the Wallawallas, they signed a treaty on June 9 (12 Stat. 945, ratified

250

Umatilla

Amy and Saul Webb, photographed in 1968 at Thornhollow, Oregon, on the eastern half of the Umatilla Reservation.

March 8, 1859, and proclaimed April 11, 1859), yielding their lands to the United States in return for a reservation north and south of the middle Umatilla River. Early in the Yakima War volunteer forces had manned Fort Henrietta on the Umatilla River at Lower Crossing, as they tried to control the hostile Umatilla and Cayuse elements. At that time those two tribes faced war against not only the whites but also their ancient Paiute foes. On one occasion at the height of the Yakima War, when the Umatillas were in council with the Cayuses and the Yakimas in the Grande Ronde valley, they were attacked by Paiutes and forced to flee, abandoning their old, young, and crippled. As noted, the Umatillas' numbers were given variously from 10 to 100 in 1962, but like their reservation allies, the Cayuses and Wallawallas, they had then lost most semblances of independent tribal identity. See **Confederated Tribes of the Umatilla Indian Reservation.**

Suggested Readings: Robert H. Ruby and John A. Brown, *The Cayuse Indians: Imperial Tribesmen of Old Oregon* (Norman: University of Oklahoma Press, 1972); Joel L. Shiner, "The McNary Reservoir: A Study in Plateau Archaeology," *Bureau of American Ethnology Bulletin no. 179* (Washington, D.C.: Government Printing Office, 1961).

UMATILLA CONFEDERATED TRIBES
(See **Confederated Tribes of the Umatilla Indian Reservation.**)

UPPER CHEHALIS
(See **Kwaiailk.**)

UPPER SKAGIT
(Coastal Division, Salishan)

The Upper Skagit Tribe of Washington comprises four of the eleven aboriginal bands of the Skagit River in northwestern Washington, where a river and a county also bear the tribal name. The meaning of the name Skagit seems to have been lost. The ancestors of the Upper Skagits were hunting, fishing, and gathering peoples. Among the neighbors with whom they had close cultural ties were the Sauks of the river of that name, a Skagit tributary. They also had close ties with the Suiattles of the Suiattle River, a Sauk tributary. On occasion, the Skagits traveled east of the Cascade Mountains to visit the natives there, and the latter traveled west of that range to visit them. Their relative remoteness from the peoples of the lower Skagit River is reflected in differences in their dialects. The secret society that was so important among the natives of Puget Sound appears to have been much weaker among the Upper Skagits.

Location: Upper Skagit tribal members live throughout northwestern Washington, but mainly in Skagit County.

Numbers: In 1984 there were 223 Upper Skagits. Around 1855 the natives of the upper Skagit River numbered about 300.

History: Headmen of the upper Skagit Basin were among the signatories to the Point Elliott Treaty of 1855. One who attended the treaty council but did not sign the document was the prophet-cultist Slaybebtkud, who came from east of the Cascade Mountains to join the Skagits. After the treaty he exerted great authority by uniting about ten extended and autonomous village bands of the upper Skagit River and its tributaries. For sixty years after the treaty the government claimed that the Indians of the upper Skagit River did not constitute a single tribe because they lived in villages as bands. Their lands were crossed by the surveyors of the Northern Pacific Railroad in 1870 and shortly thereafter were crossed by white

Upper Skagit

Knuckle Boome, former leader and chairman of the Upper Skagit Tribe of Indians, circa 1980. Leaders such as Boome led the tribe to recognition by the federal government. As a member of the Skagit System Cooperative, the Upper Skagit Tribe sought to restore and maintain fish runs in the Skagit River system.

settlers. The Indians were angered when the whites encroached on lands that held the graves of their dead. On one occasion settlers burned a village of eight large cedar-board houses at the confluence of the Skagit and Sauk rivers. Natives of the upper Skagit suffered the inevitable diseases that were a consequence of white contact. In 1889, for example, the bodies of the dead lay unburied after a smallpox epidemic. Initially the natives of the upper Skagit River were suspicious of Roman Catholic priests, but later the friendly disposition of Slaybebtkud to missionaries of that faith helped them to minister to his people.

Government and Claims: The Upper Skagits claimed that they had a right to federal acknowledgment as a tribe stemming from a 1913 congressional appropriation to them and to the Sauk-Suiattles for the purchase of a piece of land for a cemetery. This was proof, they claimed, of congressional recognition of the Indians of the upper Skagit valley as a single tribal unit. The Upper Skagits operate under a constitution and bylaws approved by the secretary of the interior on December 4, 1974. Their governing body is the seven-member Upper Skagit Tribal Council. Its chairperson is elected annually from among the tribal members by popular vote.

In January, 1951 the tribe filed a claim (Docket 92) alleging that the consideration it had received for lands acquired by the United States under the Point Elliott Treaty was unconscionably low. The 1,769,804 acres that the tribe claimed from Mount Vernon (county seat of Skagit County) to the Canadian border overlapped with the acreage claimed by the Lower Skagit Tribe (Docket 294). An amended petition filed on October 17, 1958, modified the boundaries of the Upper Skagits' land claim and also changed their name from Skagit Tribe of Indians to Upper Skagit Tribe of Indians. On September 23, 1968, a final judgment was ordered for the tribe, by which it was awarded $385,471.42.

Contemporary Life and Culture: During the period from 1977 to 1982, the tribe applied for and received several federally funded grants and contracts, which it utilized to purchase land. A 25-acre tract on Bow Hill north of the former tribal headquarters in Burlington was purchased over a four-year period, partly from tribal members who owned individual allotments in that area. Tribal members live in numerous scattered public-domain allotments in Skagit County. In 1981 a 74-acre parcel east of Sedro Woolley was purchased from a local resident, taken into trust status by the government, and declared reservation land (along with the Bow Hill holding). With the Swinomish Indian Tribal Community and the Sauk-Suiattles, the Upper Skagit Tribe is a member of the Skagit System Cooperative, which was organized in 1976 to regulate and enhance fishing in the Skagit River system. The Upper Skagit Tribe is also a member of the Northwest Washington service unit of the Indian Health Service, along with the Lummi, Nooksack, and Swinomish tribes. Tribal members are employed in the surrounding community.

In December 1990 the tribe signed a pact with the state Wildlife Department to adopt "comprehensive internal hunting regulations, sharing them with the state in a timely fashion," by which the tribe would set seasons, report kills, and issue hunting and identification requirements, much to the displeasure of non-Indian sportsmen. The tribe was joined by the Suquamish, Stillaguamish, and Sauk-Suiattle in this pact.

Suggested Readings: June McCormick Collins, *Valley of the Spirits: The Upper Skagit Indians of Western Washington* (Seattle: University of Washington Press, 1974); Martin J. Sampson, *Indians of Skagit County* (Mount Vernon, Wash.: Skagit County Historical Society, 1972).

UPPER UMPQUA
(Athapascan)

The Upper Umpquas lived in what is now southwestern Oregon in the valley of the south fork of the Umpqua River, an affluent of the Pacific Ocean. The name Umpqua has been variously interpreted to mean "high and low water," "thunder," and a native call, "A-i-e! Ump-sa-qua!" meaning "Boat, bring over the water!" In the middle of the nineteenth century the Upper Umpquas were divided into five bands: Miwaletas, Augunsahs, Quintiousas, Targunsans, and Wartahoos. The Miwaletas, who lived on Cow Creek, an Umpqua tributary, have also been called the Nahankhuotanas. The Upper Umpquas numbered about 200 to 400 in the middle of the nineteenth century. On the 60,000-acre Grand Ronde Reservation (established by executive order on June 30, 1857, in the Yamhill country north of the Upper Umpqua lands), the Upper Umpquas numbered 84 in 1902, 109 in 1910, and 43 in 1937.

Incarceration on the reservation was traumatic for the Upper Umpquas, who had been a fiercely independent people. In historic times their men had entered combat wearing thick, almost impregnable two-piece elk-skin cuirasses, which were laced at the sides and ornamented with figures and designs. Other ceremonial elements in their battle dress were single white eagle tail feathers. Among the first whites whom they met were the Astorian fur hunters, who entered the Umpqua homelands from the Willamette valley. These were the southernmost Astorian fur probes. Late in the fall of 1818, the Upper Umpquas were visited by the Nor'Wester Alexander Roderick McLeod leading a party of sixty, who crossed from the Willamette to the Umpqua and proceeded to the coast. The Upper Umpquas opposed trafficking with whites. Their disposition changed none with the killing of about fourteen natives on the Umpqua River in 1818, a deed that was believed to have been perpetrated by Iroquois in the employ of the North West Company. When the Hudson's Bay Company pushed its fur trade into the upper Willamette and Ump-

qua valleys in 1826, the Kuitshes (Lower Umpquas), remembering the 1818 killings, repulsed a free trapper who was working his way down the Umpqua. Ten years later the Hudson's Bay Company established a fur-gathering station, Fort Umpqua, near present-day Elkton, Oregon, about fifty miles from the coast on the Umpqua south bank, which was the western boundary of Upper Umpqua country. At that post Umpqua natives saw fur traders cultivate the land and raise stock before the post was abandoned in 1852. Since 1829, Bay Company brigades had traversed Umpqua country, hunting, trapping, and trading en route to the Sacramento River. They followed a route that was roughly that of present-day Interstate 5.

Abandonment by fur-trading brigades after 1843 did not reduce the number of immigrants crossing the Umpqua lands. The opening of the Scott-Applegate Trail in 1846 facilitated their passage. On the heels of those early immigrants came gold seekers traveling to and from California and other white settlers. Restive under such trespasses, the natives on the south (most likely the Takelmas, a Rogue people) sought to recruit the Upper Umpquas to help repulse the invaders, but the latter refused. With the outbreak of the Rogue Wars in the early 1850s, an Upper Umpqua chief, Napesa (Nez-zac), or Louis (who lived near where the Little River joins the North Umpqua River, near Glide, Oregon) moved his bands, in fear that soldiers, believing them warlike, would kill them. In 1855 a peaceful Umpqua band, moving to Flournoy valley (two miles west of Lookingglass, Oregon) to encamp, was killed by panicky whites.

On November 29, 1854, a treaty (10 Stat. 1125, ratified March 3, 1855) was signed between the Upper Umpquas of the middle Umpqua valley and Oregon Superintendent of Indian Affairs Joel Palmer. By this treaty the Umpquas and the Yoncallas of the Umpqua valley ceded their lands. In exchange they were given a temporary 67,820-acre reservation in their valley near the mouth of Calapooya Creek on lands that they had ceded about twelve miles downstream from the fork of the Umpqua River. They were to reside there until the October 8, 1855, renewal of the Rogue Wars when the government decided that they should be removed to the Grand Ronde valley.

In rounding up the Indians in southwestern Oregon Territory during the Rogue Wars, Superintendent Palmer made a treaty with several villages of the nomadic natives of Cow Creek, a tributary of the south fork of the Umpqua River. In the treaty making, Palmer lumped together some Miwaletas and Targunsans with some Takelmas and a few other Indians who were thought to be Southern Molalas. He called these combined peoples the Cow Creek Band of the Umpqua Tribe of Indians and made a treaty with them on September 19, 1853 (10 Stat. 1027, ratified April 1, 1854), by which they surrendered all claims to the Umpqua valley for a small temporary reservation on lands that they ceded. They stayed on that reservation until moved elsewhere by the government. For their cession the government promised them $12,000 and houses.

Seventeen of that Cow Creek Band and about thirty Southern Molalas signed a treaty on December 21, 1855 (12 Stat. 981), ceding their claims to the Umpqua valley and agreeing, with Upper Umpqua and Yoncalla approval, to remove with the latter two tribes to the Yamhill country on the north, where the Grand Ronde Reservation was to be established. The three tribes were first moved with the main body of the Upper Umpquas to the latter's temporary reservation, where roughly thirty Molalas and

Upper Umpqua

Tirzah Trask, an Upper Umpqua Indian, photographed by the well-known photographer Lee Moorhouse about 1900. Her people lived in southwestern Oregon in the valley of the south fork of the Umpqua River. In the fashion of the Indians of that region, she is seen here in the elaborate garb that evolved from the simpler clothes of earlier times. Courtesy of the Smithsonian Institution.

Yoncallas were put in one camp with Upper Umpquas. When the Cow Creeks were rounded up in November, 1855, many fled to the hills, where they were joined by others leaving the Yamhill country, to which they had been removed from the south fork of the Umpqua River. When the time came for the Umpquas to leave their temporary reservation for the Grand Ronde Reservation, Chief Napesa refused to leave the Umpqua valley. He and twenty of his band were permitted to remain in their homeland. With Napesa's death early in 1856 and burial in that land, one known as The Captain assumed leadership of the band.

On January 10, 1856, a total of 337 Cow Creeks, Yoncallas, and Upper Umpquas began their trek northward with a funeral chant and then trudged through snow and freezing weather to the Yamhill country, where they arrived on February 2. En route many lacked food and clothing, and many were too ill to travel. With but eight teams and wagons to transport them, many were forced to walk to their place of confinement. Once there, troubles continued to plague them as they tried to adjust to a new way of life in an alien land. The many deaths revealed how unsuccessful they were. The survivors were later moved to the 225,000-acre Siletz Reservation (established by executive order on November 9, 1855). Others made their way back to the Umpqua valley to join The Captain. Authorities made several attempts to round up his elusive band.

The Cow Creeks were plaintiffs in Case No. 45231 tried before the Court of Claims, in which that court decided on April 3, 1950, that they were not to be allowed recovery of money for their ceded lands. They were not so entitled, the court ruled, because an award would not have exceeded the $12,000 in installments already paid them under the treaty. Descendants of other Umpqua bands, along with descendants of twenty Yoncallas whose ancestors had lived in the Umpqua valley, were on April 3, 1950, awarded a judgment of $377,177.16 for the loss of the reserved area in the Umpqua valley from which they were removed in 1856. The award represented the principal of $67,820 plus interest and deductions for offsets. See **Cow Creek Band of the Umpqua Tribe of Indians.**

Suggested Readings: Lavola J. Bakken, *Land of the North Umpquas: Peaceful Indians of the West* (Grants Pass, Ore.: Te-cum-tom Publications, 1973); Stephen Dow Beckham, *Requiem for a People: The Rogue Indians and the Frontiersmen* (Norman: University of Oklahoma Press, 1971); Joel V. Berreman, *Tribal Distribution in Oregon*, Memoirs of the American Anthropological Association, no. 47 (Menasha, Wis.: George Banta Publishing Co., 1937); Leo J. Frachtenberg, *Lower Umpqua Texts and Notes on the Kusan Dialect*, Columbia University Contributions to American Anthropology, no. 4 (New York, 1914); Leslie Spier, "Tribal Distribution in Southwestern Oregon," *Oregon Historical Quarterly* 28 (December, 1927).

WAHKIAKUM
(Upper Chinookan Division of Chinookan)

According to the anthropologist Franz Boas, the Wahkiakums spoke the Cathlamet dialect of Upper Chinookan. Yet, living on the lower Columbia River, they were culturally related to two Lower Chinookan peoples, the Chinooks proper and Clatsops, whose culture was primarily that of the coastal Pacific Northwest peoples but modified by contacts with peoples east of the Cascade Mountains. Washington Irving had access to Astorian fur-trader notes of about 1811 that have since been lost. In writing his *Astoria* (1837), he stated that Wahkiakums and the Chinooks were initially one and the same people and that, about two generations before whites entered their lands, a quarrel erupted between their ruling chief and his brother, Wahkiacu, who then seceded with his people to form the Wahkiakus, or Wask-i-cums. In a similar vein, Abbé Domenech, in *Seven Years' Residence in the Great Deserts of North America* (1860), stated that the Wahkiakums were one of four "clans." The others were the Cathlamets, Chinooks, and Clatsops, who separated off around the middle of the eighteenth century because of quarreling among village chiefs. After the separation, the Wahkiakums visited and intermarried with other tribes in the lands where they went to fish, gather seafoods and berries, and hunt.

The principal Wahkiakum village lay in present-day Washington state on the Columbia north bank east of the Chinook lands, which they bordered at Grays River, an affluent of Grays Bay on the Columbia north bank. Boas stated that the Wahkiakums lived in two main villages, of which one, called Tlalegak, was located a little below Pillar Rock, a short distance above Grays Bay and the other, called Chakwayalham, was farther down the Columbia. At least one of the important Wahkiakum villages lay near present-day Cathlamet, Washington, in Wahkiakum County.

Although they fished off islands in the Columbia River opposite Grays Bay and upstream, the Wahkiakums lived primarily by the chase. Their hunting territory extended north from the Columbia to the Chehalis River watershed and west and south to the western end of Grays Bay.

Irving stated that there were sixty-six Wahkiakum warriors, a figure that supports the estimate of the American explorers Meriwether Lewis and William Clark of a total of 200 Wahkiakums in 1805–1806. En route down the Columbia in 1805, the explorers purchased fish and dogs from the Wahkiakums whom they called the "best canoe navigators." In 1841 the American naval explorer Lt. Charles Wilkes noted that the Wahkiakum chief, Skamakowa (Skumahqueah), had formerly ruled a large tribe which had become very small since the intermittent fever outbreak of 1829–30 had nearly destroyed it. Government officials estimated that there were 185 Wahkiakums, Cathlamets, and Chinooks living in thirty-seven houses at the time of those tribes' treaties with the United States. The ethnologist George Gibbs, writing shortly thereafter, stated that the chief was almost the last survivor of those peoples.

One provision of the treaty that the Wahkiakums signed August 8, 1851, was that in exchange for their lands, they were to receive a $700 annuity for ten years. The short period of time was dictated by their fears of becoming extinct. They were to be given $100 in cash and the remainder in goods. They retained rights to occupy their places of residence, fish in the Columbia and two small streams, cut timber for building and for fuel, and hunt. They also received the usual clothing, hardware, and miscellaneous items. Chief Skamakowa was to receive a fifty-dollar rifle. The treaty was similar to those concluded with other natives of the area at that time, but was never ratified by the United States Senate.

On August 24, 1912, Congress passed legislation to compensate the Wahkiakums, Chinooks, Clatsops, and Cathlamets for the loss of their lands in accordance with the decision of the Court of Claims. The Wahkiakums' share of the award was $7,000. The Chinook tribes, including the Wahkiakums, petitioned the government for additional compensation for the loss of aboriginal lands, in the case of *Duwamish et al. v. The United States* (79 C.Cls. 530). The Court of Claims dismissed the case on grounds that compensation had already been made to the tribes with whom the government had treated. Descendants of the Wahkiakums who were assimilated within other tribes, were among petitioners bringing claims before the Indian Claims Commission and sharing in any awards made. The Wahkiakums also filed suit in federal court, along with the Lower Chinooks and the Cowlitzes, seeking protection of their fishing rights in southwestern Washington, but they were excluded in *United States* v. *Washington* (384 F. Supp. 312, 1974) because they had tried too late to enter that litigation. It is unlikely that the Wahkiakums could be successful in any such case against Washington state, since they are not a federally acknowledged tribe, a prerequisite for the guarantee of fishing rights.

In January, 1979, descendants of the Wahkiakums, as the Wahkiakum Indian Tribe, having been excluded from earlier landmark treaty-rights cases, filed in the United States District Court of Oregon, asking that their "federally guaranteed right to take fish" in the Columbia River be recognized. The Wahkiakums acted separately from the Chinook Indian Tribe of Chinook, Washington, in initiating the fishing rights litigation, though the descent of the two groups is intermixed, and both were identified as Chinooks for allotment purposes on the Quinault Reservation. The Chinooks, nevertheless, maintain a separate tribal identity from the Quinaults, as do the Wahkiakums who are included on the membership rolls of the Chinook Indian Tribe. In May, 1980, a ruling by the United States District Court, which was upheld in September, 1981, by a United States Circuit Court of Appeals, denied the claim of about 50 Wahkiakums that their Columbia River fishing rights were guaranteed by the 1855–56 Quinault Treaty. Nonreservation Wahkiakums had also shared in a November 4, 1971, award to the Chinook Nation (see **Chinook**). Some Indians of Wahkiakum descent have joined a conglomerate including Kwalhioquas, Lower Chinooks, Cathlamets, Clatsops, Tillamooks, the Conniac Band of Upper Chinookan Skilloots, and Willapas. This conglomerate is organized under the name Confederated Treaty Tribes of Tansey Point.

Suggested Readings: Melville Jacobs, "Historic Perspectives in Indian Languages of Oregon and Washington," *Pacific Northwest Quarterly* 28, no. 1 (January, 1937); Albert Buell Lewis, "Tribes of the Columbia Valley and the Coast of Washington and Oregon," *Memoirs of the American Anthropological Association* (1906), vol. 2, pt. 2; Fred Lockley, *History of the Columbia River Valley from The Dalles to the Sea* (Chicago, 1928), 2 vols.; Verne F. Ray, "Lower Chinook Ethnographic Notes," *University of Washington Publications in Anthropology* 2, no. 2 (1938); Verne Ray "The Historical Position of the Lower Chinook in the Native Culture of the Pacific Northwest," *Pacific Northwest Quarterly* 28, no. 4 (October, 1937).

WALLAWALLA
(Shahaptian)

The Wallawallas lived along the Columbia River in the area of its confluence with the Walla Walla River, and east along the Walla Walla to its junction with the Touchet River.

There is a difference of opinion about

the meaning of the name Wallawalla. Linguist Bruce J. Rigsby says that the name, meaning "flow" and "stream," was used by a neighboring tribe, the Umatillas, to refer to the Wallawallas, and that from that source it became the name that the Wallawallas use for themselves. The ethnologist John R. Swanton stated that it meant "little river." John Keast Lord, a naturalist with the British Boundary Commission who visited the Walla Walla country around 1860, stated that it meant "ever-bright and sparkling." Because of their proximity and repeated exposure to their traditional foes the Shoshonis, the Wallawallas had close ties with other Shahaptian-speakers, such as the Nez Percés and the Umatillas, as well as with the Waiilatpuan-speaking Cayuses.

In 1805–1806 the Wallawallas met Meriwether Lewis and William Clark. Five years later and for several years thereafter, they met personnel of the fur-trading companies traveling up and down the Columbia River. In 1818, Fort Nez Percés, later Fort Walla Walla, was built in their lands near the confluence of the Columbia and Walla Walla rivers. Later a military post in the Walla Walla valley also bore the Wallawalla name. In 1836 the Wallawallas came under the ministrations of the Reverend Marcus Whitman and his wife, Narcissa, of the American Board of Commissioners for Foreign Missions. In 1838 they met two Roman Catholic missionaries, Rev. François Blanchet and Rev. Modeste Demers. Because the resident Cayuses were too proud to do so, Wallawalla women worked at the Whitman Mission, which was established in 1836 in the Walla Walla valley. The Cayuses regarded the Wallawallas as an inferior people descended from slaves. In 1844, when the son of Wallawalla chief Peopeomoxmox was killed by a white man at Sutter's Mill in the Sacramento country of California, the Americans there geared up for defense, fearing that a "thousand Walla Walla" would return to wreak vengeance on them. In that figure the Californians included Cayuses and Umatillas, as well as Wallawallas. A band of those northern Indians did return to California two years later, but they were too weak from disease and too few in number to wreak any kind of vengeance. Some Wallawallas were said to be among those who joined Capt. John C. Frémont's California Battalion in the fighting that led to the annexation of California by the United States. The Wallawallas did not participate in the November 29, 1847, Whitman Massacre, which was perpetrated by their Cayuse neighbors and by "half-bloods" married to Cayuse women. Some Wallawallas joined the Cayuses in their ensuing war against the Americans in 1848.

The Wallawallas attended the treaty council in the valley that bears their name. Un-

Wallawalla

This Wallawalla brave, photographed in the early 1900s, bore the name Piopio-Maksmaks. He was a relative of the famous Wallawalla chief, Peopeomoxmox, who was slain in an engagement with white volunteers in the late 1850s. Photograph by Edward S. Curtis from Curtis's "List of Large Plates Supplementing Volume 8," The North American Indian (Plate 267).

der provisions of the treaty that they signed on June 9, 1855, they, the Cayuses, and the Umatillas were scheduled to remove to the Umatilla Reservation in present-day northeastern Oregon. During the Yakima Indian war in the fall of 1855, after the Wallawallas had pillaged the fort that bore their name, Chief Peopeomoxmox was shot and killed, and his body was mutilated by white volunteer troops. There was no rush of Wallawallas to the Umatilla Reservation after that, but they slowly began drifting onto that confine as whites occupied their former lands. Prereservation estimates of Wallawalla numbers ranged from 500 in 1836 to 1,100 in 1841 and 2,000 in 1848. In 1962 their descendants in Oregon numbered between 100 and 200. On the Umatilla Reservation, where the Cayuses' ties were with the Nez Percés, the Wallawallas associated more with the Umatillas and the peoples of the Warm Springs Reservation farther west in north-central Oregon. By the early twentieth century tribal distinctions on the Umatilla had blurred. Today descendants of the Wallawallas, along with those of Cayuses and Umatillas, form the Umatilla Confederated Tribes. Yet their original tribal name is perpetuated in many things, including a river and its valley, a city, and a county. See **Confederated Tribes of the Umatilla Reservation.**

Suggested Readings: Angelo Anastasio, *Intergroup Relations in the Southern Plateau*, master's thesis, University of Chicago, 1955; T. W. Davenport, "Recollections of an Indian Agent," *Oregon Historical Quarterly* 8 (March-December, 1907); Robert H. Ruby and John A. Brown, *The Cayuse Indians: Imperial Tribesmen of Old Oregon* (Norman: University of Oklahoma Press, 1972); J. F. Santee, "Pio-Pio-Mox-Mox," *Oregon Historical Quarterly* 34 (March-December, 1933).

WANAPAM
(Shahaptian)

The Wanapams were composed of groups, one of which was called "Sokulks" by the American explorers Meriwether Lewis and William Clark. They lived along the Columbia River, or "Enche Wana," as they called it, in the area of the Priest Rapids, which today have been obliterated by the backwaters of the dam bearing that name in central Washington state. About fifteen miles upstream from Priest Rapids Dam, the Wanapum Dam bears the name of these peoples. Priest Rapids was named by fur traders, who on August 18, 1811, encountered a native priest there. A strong priestly influence remained among the Wanapams especially that exerted by the prophet Smohalla, whose Dreamer religion gained momentum around 1860. Smohalla is said to have been badly hurt in a fight with another Columbia River chief, Moses; to have wandered for a time; and then to have returned to his people a greater prophet than ever. He preached the sacredness of the earth and its final restoration to aboriginal purity. Through his ceremonials, which included flags, drums, and certain nativist and Christian forms, he was able to attract to his rush-mat lodge in P'na ("fish weir") village those traditionalists avoiding reservations whom the whites called "renegades." Under Smohalla's influence and leadership, the Wanapams maintained their independence despite the efforts of Indian agents to confine them to reservations. The Wanapams were successful partly because of the conflicts between Indian agents and army officials, who disagreed on the proper distribution of the tribe, and partly because of the barrenness of their Priest Rapids homelands, which did not invite white settlement. After his death in March 1895, Smohalla was succeeded by his son, Little Smohalla, who froze to death in 1917. A direct descendant, Puck Hyah Toot (Johnny Buck), was a Wanapam leader until his death on September 11, 1956. A Washington state law of 1939 allowed a tribal remnant to take fish for personal and ceremonial use, not for commercial purposes. When the laws were recodified in 1949, the one permitting the Wanapams to so fish was taken from the books. Therefore in 1981 the state enacted another law permitting them to obtain permits to take fish for ceremonial and subsistence purposes.

During World War II the Wanapams living in mat dwellings as they always had were removed to the foot of the Priest Rapids, from the area set aside for the Atomic Energy Reservation at Hanford, Washington. The Wanapams maintain that they have never signed any treaty with the government. The only "treaty" they have signed with whites is an agreement dated January 15, 1957, which four of their men made with the Washington's Grant County Public Utility District. The Federal Power Commission required such a pact to protect the utility from future claims on the site of the Priest Rapids Dam. By the terms of the agreement the utility agreed to pay the tribe a $20,000 cash settlement, most of which was to be divided among the surviving Wanapams. The utility retained $1,300 to finance feasts and religious ceremonies for the tribal remnant and their guests at the damsite. The Wanapams were also assured the right to hunt and fish on the lands and waters of the project and were assured lifelong housing in individual houses, electricity and water for the houses and yards, a longhouse, and employment on the dam. The utility agreed to move some petroglyphs from Whale Island in the Columbia River to the Wanapam burial grounds and a recreation area. The utility also agreed to provide a livelihood in coming years for the three families remaining at Priest Rapids.

Today remnants of Wanapam culture may be seen in the museum at the Wanapum Dam and in springtime first-roots festivals ("feasts of the new food"). In 1980 only two Wanapams remained of the four who had effected the 1957 agreement. Only four Wanapam families remained in 1980. In 1870 they numbered about 300. A hundred years earlier the Wanapams had numbered an estimated 1,800.

Wanapam

This Wanapam woman, photographed in the 1960s, was one of the last of her tribe remaining. The salmon she holds represented her people's chief source of food. Special laws passed by the Washington state legislature permitted the Wanapams to catch fish for ceremonial and noncommercial purposes.

Suggested Readings: E. L. Huggins, "Smohalla, the Prophet of Priest Rapids," *Overland Monthly*, 2d ser., vol. 17 (January-June, 1891); Maj. J. W. MacMurray, "The 'Dreamers' of the Columbia River Valley in Washington Territory," *Transactions of the Albany Institute* 11 (1887): 241–

48; James Mooney, "The Ghost-Dance Religion and the Sioux Outbreak of 1890," *Fourteenth Annual Report of the Bureau of American Ethnology* (Washington, D.C.: Government Printing Office, 1896); Click Relander, *Drummers and Dreamers* (Caldwell, Idaho: Caxton Printers, Ltd., 1956); Robert H. Ruby and John A. Brown, *Half-Sun on the Columbia: A Biography of Chief Moses* (Norman: University of Oklahoma Press, 1965); Robert H. Ruby and John A. Brown, *Dreamer Prophets of the Columbia Plateau* (Norman: University of Oklahoma Press, 1989); Margery Ann Beach Sharkey, "Revitalization And Change: A History of the Wanapum Indians, Their Prophet Smowhala, And the Washani Religion," dissertation, Washington State University, 1984.

WARM SPRINGS FEDERATED TRIBES
(See **Confederated Tribes of the Warm Springs Reservation of Oregon**)

WASCO
(Upper Chinookan Division of Chinookan)

The word Wasco stems from that tribe's own word meaning "cup" or "small horn bowl," a reference to a cup-shaped rock near The Dalles, Oregon. The Astorian Robert Stuart called the Wascos the Cathlascos, of which a variation is Calascos. Another fur man, Alexander Ross, called them the Wisscopams. They have also been called Wascos proper and Dalles Wascos. Among the places bearing their name are a county and a town in north-central Oregon, where they occupied the south bank of the Columbia River from The Dalles downstream to Hood River. In 1822, about seven years before the outbreak of the intermittent fever, the Wascos numbered about 900. In 1853 a United States military census placed their numbers at 300. By 1855 their numbers had dropped to 252, possibly because of the smallpox plague of 1853. Once the strongest of the Upper Chinookan peoples, they, like others of their linguistic family, declined in numbers, as well as in power, under pressure from the whites and their diseases.

Historically, the Wascos' power was to a great extent due to their geographic position along a key stretch of the Columbia River, where they became the foremost traders among the Upper Chinookan peoples. Their primary village, Winquatt, was the gathering place for many tribes. They owned and traded slaves and horses, but their main trade item was the several species of salmon that they caught and processed between May and October, sometimes in baskets that held as much as a hundred pounds. After processing, some of the fish were consumed locally, not only by the Wascos but also by tribesmen who gathered from hundreds of miles around. The Wasco country was possibly the most important locus of aboriginal trade in the Pacific Northwest interior. Fishing stations were individually controlled, and they were allotted first to family members, then to neighboring villagers, and finally to friendly visitors from farther away. In the later part of October the Wascos often journeyed downstream to the mouth of the Willamette River to dig wappato roots. They also dug camas roots in the valley of the White Salmon River, a Columbia affluent from the north. By the 1840s, when white travelers en route to the Willamette valley were entering the Wasco lands, the Wascos and their neighbors wanted "dollars" for the goods that they traded to the immigrants and for the portaging services that they provided them.

Wasco culture somewhat resembled that of the peoples of the Northwest Coast. For example, they lived in plank houses of the coastal type. Although they were also exposed to the cultures of the Columbia Plateau in the interior, they were not influenced by them to the same extent that the

Wasco

These Wasco Indians photographed in the early 1900s were, from left to right, Da-wa-da-tha (Peter Jackson), Wa-bi-ga, and Wa-lik-sma (Susan Seymour). The Wascos lived at The Dalles of the Columbia River, one of the Pacific Northwest's most important native fishing and trading places.

nearby Upper Chinookan Wishrams were. Except for brief intervals, the Wascos warred against the Northern Paiutes of the interior on the south. In one skirmish in 1811 the Paiutes attacked some Wascos in their canoes on the Columbia River. The conflicts between the two peoples were aggravated by the barrenness of the Paiute lands, on which the Chinookan speakers encroached seeking to improve their own means of subsistence.

263

During conflicts the Wascos imprisoned Paiute women and children and then sold them in village marts.

In 1838, Methodist missionaries began their Wascopam Mission at The Dalles in Wasco country. Later they sold out to the Roman Catholics, who began Saint Peter's Mission there in 1848. After the Whitman massacre on November 29, 1847, the Cayuse Indians threatened some Wascos into joining them in their war against the Oregon provisional government, but most Wascos refrained from hostilities. After 1850 The Dalles area was a center of American military operations against the Indians in the war that broke out in 1855. The war was precipitated by dissatisfaction with the June 25, 1855, treaty with the United States, which was signed by Wascos and other Upper Chinookans from the Columbia River and its Cascades and Hood River, as well as Shahaptian-speaking Teninos. Under the treaty these peoples relinquished about ten million acres for the Warm Springs Reservation, which was 464,000 acres before boundary adjustments in the Indians' favor. Removal from their homes to the soil-poor Warm Springs rankled that reservation's Indians for many years to come. Fortunately for them, Congress did not ratify a treaty (14 Stat. 751) signed on November 15, 1865, which would have rescinded their rights to fish in their traditional places along the Columbia River, which had been guaranteed by the 1855 treaty. On February 9, 1929 (45 Stat. 1158), about seven acres were set aside for a village at the old tribal fishing campsite near Celilo Falls on the Columbia for a small band of Indians living there who had been assigned to the Warm Springs. The vagueness of that reservation's northern and western boundaries also rankled the Wascos and other Warm Springs Indians.

After occupying multiple-family dwellings, sometimes called longhouses, the Wascos moved onto small plots on the Warm Springs Reservation between the agency headquarters and the Deschutes River. There they began clearing and farming the land. In 1866 they and the Teninos were recruited by the American military as scouts in a war with the Paiutes. The Wascos also served as scouts in the Modoc War of 1872–73. A Paiute remnant, who were victims of the Bannock-Paiute War of 1878, were eventually removed to the Warm Springs, where they were located about fifteen miles south of agency headquarters. Unlike the Wascos, who assumed tribal leadership roles on the reservation, the Paiutes remained aloof. In the 1870s the Wascos and other Warm Springs peoples came under the influence of the Presbyterians who managed the reservation during the President Ulysses S. Grant Peace Policy era under the agent, Capt. John Smith. The captain tried zealously to raise what he believed were poor moral standards brought on by previous military governance of the reservation. He also tried to eliminate native healings, polygamy, and other practices, such as slaveholding. On the reservation in 1869 the Wascos held some Achomawis and Atsugewis, or Pit River Indians, whom they had bought from Klamaths several years before. Under the General Allotment Act of February 8, 1887 (24 Stat. 388), 140,529 acres were allotted to 968 Indians on the Warm Springs Reservation, and 1,195 acres were set aside for agency, school, and church purposes. Today the Wascos are largely integrated with the other peoples of the Warm Springs Reservation. In 1946 there remained only twenty who spoke their native language. See **Confederated Tribes of the Warm Springs Reservation of Oregon.**

Suggested Readings: David French, "Wasco-Wishram," in Edward H. Spicer, ed., *Perspectives in American Culture Change* (Chicago: University of Chicago Press, 1961); Frederick Webb Hodge, *Handbook of American Indians North of Mexico,* pt. 2 (Washington, D.C.: Government Printing Office, 1910); Gordon MacNab, *A History of the McQuinn Strip* (Portland, Ore., 1972); Ralph M. Shane and Ruby D. Leno, *A History of the Warm Springs Reservation, Oregon* (Portland, Ore., 1949); Robert H. Suphan, "Ethnological Report on the Wasco and Tenino Indians," *Oregon Indians,* vol. 2 (New York: Garland Publishing, Inc., 1974), pp. 9–85.

WATLALA
(Upper Chinookan Division of Chinookan)

The Watlalas (or Wahlalas), also known as the Cascade Indians, were called the Shalala Nation by the American explorers Meriwether Lewis and William Clark, who met them in 1805–1806. Lewis and Clark described them as living in three subdivisions: the Yhehuhs, above The Cascades of the Columbia River; the Clahclellahs, below those rapids; and the Wahclellahs, on the Columbia at Beacon Rock, a few miles upstream from present-day Skamania, Washington. In fact, there were as many as six subdivisions of the Watlalas living where the Columbia breaks through the Cascade Mountains. Their dialect originally differed but slightly from that of the more dominant Wascos upstream with whom the Watlala remnant joined after the ravages of the intermittent fever in the 1830s. The tribe then became known by the name of one of its subdivisions, the Watlalas. Sometimes they were called the Cascade Wascos. Their villages lay on both the north and the south banks of the Columbia near present-day Cascade Locks, Oregon.

At the beginning of the nineteenth century like the Wascos and the Chilluckittequaws (Hood Rivers), who were also Upper Chinookan speakers, the Watlalas were a sedentary people who combined a basically northwest Coast culture with elements from the Columbia Plateau of the interior. Like other Upper Chinookans, they fished and traded. During the fishing seasons, from May to October, they caught several species of salmon. Fishing stations were controlled and were allotted first to family members, then to neighboring villagers, and finally to friendly peoples from farther distances. When Lewis and Clark met them, they had

no horses. In the early nineteenth century white travelers feared passage around The Cascades of the Columbia, where the native mausoleums and steep bluffs hiding the sun added to the gloom of the place. The natives of The Cascades had a reputation for thievery because they appropriated the goods of travelers along that vital stretch of the river, where they exacted tolls from passersby and served as their porters.

Under the designation Wahlalas, the Watlalas signed with Kalapuyan tribes a treaty with Oregon Superintendent of Indian Affairs Joel Palmer on January 22, 1855 (10 Stat. 1143, ratified March 3, 1855), ceding to the United States their lands west of the Middle Cascades of the Columbia. Under the designation "Kigaltwallas," they ceded their lands east of the Middle Cascades in a treaty of June 25, 1855, that the United States effected with the tribes of "Middle Oregon."

In 1855 the Watlalas numbered about 70, nearly twice as many as in the 1830s, when the epidemic had raged. In March, 1865, they were lured into anti-American hostilities, apparently by a Klickitat-Yakima Indian coalition. Ironically, despite their pleas of innocence, some Watlalas were subsequently hanged by the victorious American military. With the Wascos they were estimated to have been 3,200 in 1780, 2,800 in 1805–1806, and 1,400 in 1812. Today no one speaks their language, and the tribe is extinct.

Suggested Reading: Frederick Webb Hodge, *Handbook of American Indians North of Mexico*, pt. 2 (Washington, D.C.: Government Printing Office, 1910).

WAUYUKMA
(Shahaptian)

The Wauyukmas lived on the Snake River below the mouth of the Palouse River in modern-day Washington state. They are believed by some to be closely related to the

Palouse Indians of that region, and by others to be a band of the Palouse tribe. The name Wauyukma, meaning "old salmon trap," is appropriate for them, since salmon fishing provided much of their subsistence. The Wauyukmas' 1780 population, apparently including the Palouses, has been estimated at 1,800. It seems that they occupied a single village.

Suggested Readings: Melville Jacobs, "A Sketch of Northern Sahaptin Grammar," *University of Washington Publications in Anthropology,* 4, no.2 (1931); Verne F. Ray, "Native Villages and Groupings of the Columbia Basin," *Pacific Northwest Quarterly* 27, no. 2 (April, 1936).

WENATCHEE
(Interior Division, Salishan)

The name Wenatchee (or Wenatchi) is derived from a Shahaptian word loosely meaning "water coming out." The opening from which the water came was possibly Tumwater Canyon on the Wenatchee River near present-day Leavenworth, Washington, on U.S. Highway 2. In the early nineteenth century the Wenatchees comprised five bands, who lived primarily in the Wenatchee River watershed and the area near its mouth and for a short distance up and down the Columbia River, to which the Wenatchee is a tributary. Some anthropologists maintain that other Wenatchees lived in early times in the Kittitas valley of the upper Yakima River country, across the Wenatchee Mountains from the Wenatchee River country. The natives of the Kittitas valley, the Kittitas band of Upper Yakimas, were, according to these anthropologists, absorbed by Shahaptian peoples who imposed their language upon them. These Upper Yakima peoples camped with the Wenatchees at fisheries on the Wenatchees' lands about twenty-five to thirty miles up the Wenatchee River from its Columbia confluence. The Wenatchees first appeared in print as "Wahnaachee" in the maps and journals of Meriwether Lewis and William Clark. The Wenatchees called themselves the Pisquows (Pisquoses), the name by which early-day fur men referred to them and their river. They depended more on their river valley and its environs for subsistence than did the Sinkiuses (Moses Co-

lumbias), who were their neighbors across the Columbia River. Yet the Wenatchees were known to travel as far away as The Dalles and across the Cascade Mountains to the Puget Sound to trade.

In 1841 the Wenatchees met Lt. Robert Johnson of Lt. Charles Wilkes's United States Navy expedition near the mouth of the Wenatchee. Johnson reported that the natives were growing potatoes in turf enclosures, an evidence of fur-trader influence. A dozen years later natives there entertained Capt. George McClellan of the Pacific Railroad Survey and later of Civil War fame by racing horses.

Wenatchee chief Tecolekun was one of fourteen signers of the Yakima Treaty at the Walla Walla Council in 1855. Some Wenatchees joined the Yakimas in their war against the Americans, which broke out that fall. During the war troops attacked and killed innocent villagers on White River, a Lake Wenatchee tributary. Also during the war, troops on a punitive expedition to the Wenatchee River in August, 1858, without any semblance of a trial, hanged four natives, in the belief they had attacked white miners. Earlier that summer miners en route to the Canadian goldfields, after skirmishing with Wenatchee Indians at the mouth of their river, killed a brave, Quiltenenock (Quiltomee), whose brother, Moses, assumed leadership of the scattered mid-Columbia bands. Tecolekun was reportedly killed that May during fighting between Indians and the troops of U.S. Army Col. Edward Steptoe near present-day Rosalia, Washington, south of Spokane Falls.

The Wenatchees experienced the missionary efforts of Roman Catholic priests, such as Rev. Urban Grassi, S.J., whose journey to the Wenatchee River in the summer of 1873 led to the establishment of the Saint Francis Xavier Mission near present-day Cashmere (formerly, Mission), about ten miles from the mouth of the Wenatchee River. After a major earthquake in 1872, Grassi sought to convert to his faith the powerful Wenatchee, prophet Patoi, who was attracting many followers by his nativist preachings. During the reservation era the Wenatchees refused to take allotments on the Yakima Reservation. Because of their associations with the Upper Yakimas at such places as the Wenatshapam Fishery, which were reserved for Indian use under the Yakima Treaty, the Wenatchees were grouped by government officials with the Yakimas. They were angered when their fisheries were sold for $20,000, on January 8, 1894, because of the urging of the Yakima agent, L. T. Erwin. The funds from their sale were used to build the Erwin Ditch for irrigation on the Yakima Reservation. In 1911 some Wenatchees scheduled for removal took homesteads on their ancestral lands, but those lands were valuable for irrigation, which, with other problems that the Wenatchees faced in holding them, hastened their alienation from their original owners. In the spring of 1911 some of those Wenatchees relinquished their holdings to join others of their people already on the Colville Reservation in taking allotments on that confine. By 1915 twelve quarter sections originally allotted to Indians near Cashmere were subdivided into nearly 200 tiny tracts.

In 1959 about 153 Indians on the Colville Reservation were classified as Wenatchees, and 115 more were listed as living off the reservations. Those 1959 figures may have included some of the Sinkiuses. In 1970 only 33 Wenatchee-Sinkiuses were reported. They and their close neighbors have been estimated to have numbered over 1,000 in 1780.

Wenatchee

Pete Judge, a Wenatchee Indian, circa 1910. Judge's people lived along the Wenatchee River in central Washington. The Wenatchees were forced off their lands by white settlers. Some of them went to the nearby Colville Reservation. Courtesy of the North Central Washington Museum Association.

For Wenatchee claims see **Confederated Tribes of the Colville Reservation, Washington.**

Suggested Readings: Walter Cline et al., *The Sinkaietk, or Southern Okanagon, of Washington,* ed. Leslie Spier, American Anthropology Association, General Series in Anthropology, no. 6 (Menasha, Wis.: George Banta Publishing Co., 1938); John Hermilt and Louis Judge, "The Wenatchee Indians Ask Justice," *Washington*

Historical Quarterly 16, no. 1 (January, 1925); Robert H. Ruby and John A. Brown, *Half-Sun on the Columbia: A Biography of Chief Moses* (Norman: University of Oklahoma Press, 1965); Cashmere, Wash., Public Schools, *The Wenatchi Indians: Guardians of the Valley*, ed. Richard D. Scheuerman (Fairfield, Wash., Ye Galleon Press, 1982); James A. Teit, "The Middle Columbia Salish," *University of Washington Publications in Anthropology* 2, no. 4 (1928).

WHISKAH
(Coastal Division, Salishan)

The Whiskahs lived in present-day southwestern Washington. Although autonomous, they were perhaps similar linguistically to the Lower Chehalises, and they shared with them a similar history. They were also closely related to the Wynoochees. They were classified by the ethnologist John R. Swanton as a village of the Humptulipses only because of their location near that tribe. (See **Humptulips, Lower Chahalis,** and **Wynoochee.**)

WILLAMETTE VALLEY CONFEDERATED TRIBES

The Willamette Valley Confederated Tribes of Indians were composed of descendants of the tribes who signed a treaty with the United States on January 10, 1855. The confederation included all the Kalapuyan peoples except the Yoncallas, plus the Molalas, the Clackamases, the Clowwewallas, and the Watlalas. The confederation, which no longer exists, was primarily a political organization to seek compensation for their lost lands.

WILLAPA
(See **Shoalwater Bay.**)

WISHRAM
(Upper Chinookan Division of Chinookan)

The Wishrams were the "Echeloots" whom the American explorers Meriwether Lewis and William Clark visited on their westward trek in 1805. Their name is derived from a Yakima word. The lands of this Upper Chinookan tribe extended along the Columbia north bank from about ten miles above The Dalles to about ten miles below them. Their main village was at Spearfish (present-day Wishram, Washington), where in 1906 the Spokane Portland & Seattle Railway established a siding, called Spedis for a Wishram

Wishram

A Wishram girl, Eagle Feather, in costume. The photograph was one of many taken of Indian people by Lee Moorhouse around the turn of the century. Some Wishrams were integrated with other tribesmen on the Yakima Reservation of south-central Washington.

chief. By the estimates of Lewis and Clark and others, near the beginning of the nineteenth century the Wishrams proper represented between 6 and 10 percent (an estimated 1,000 to 1,600 souls) of the total Upper Chinookan population. It has been suggested that the 1782–83 smallpox epidemic killed about half the Wishrams. With other Chinookans, they also suffered population losses from other diseases, such as the intermittent fever that broke out in 1829.

The Wishrams depended heavily for their subsistence on the salmon that they caught where the Columbia River narrows at The Dalles. They preserved the fish in baskets containing up to a hundred pounds each, not only for their own consumption but also for trade to the other peoples who flocked there in salmon seasons, making it perhaps the foremost native mart and mecca of the Pacific Northwest. Like other Columbia River peoples, they observed strict "first-salmon" rituals. Located between the coastal and the interior regions of the Pacific Northwest, they exhibited cultural traits from both regions. Around the middle of the eighteenth century they showed evidence of integration with the Shahaptian peoples on their east by utilizing mat-covered lodges as well as their own lodges made of planks which were typical of the coastal peoples. In winter they lived in the semisubterranean houses that were common among the peoples of the interior, whose dress they also came to emulate. Like others of the lower Columbia River and the Northwest Coast, the Wishrams paid considerable attention to disposing of their dead, whom they placed in rectangular grave houses of planks and poles on islands in the Columbia River. The class distinctions among Wishrams resembled those so evident among the coastal peoples, who were grouped into upper, middle, and lower ranks. Included in the lower class were slaves, whom Wishrams held not only to enhance the position of their owners but also, as importantly, to exchange for goods which were carried to them over routes stretching from the Rocky Mountains to the Pacific Ocean and from Canada to the Spanish-Mexican borderlands. Even before they had seen the whites, the Wishrams had obtained their goods in trade.

The Wishrams' unfriendliness to whites developed, it appears, in proportion to the whites' presence on the Columbia River, where they threatened the Wishrams' mercantile dominance. In 1811, the tribe showed hostility to Astorian fur traders who sought their services as porters over a ten-mile stretch around Celilo Falls. In the following year they attacked an Astorian party, nearly killing one of its members. The Wishrams' resistance to whites weakened as the Hudson's Bay Company increased its control over the Columbia, as their population declined and the number of whites increased, and under the influence of the Methodist Wascopam Mission founded in 1838 in their lands. The Wishrams' hostility was not entirely directed toward whites; for ages they had opposed natives raiding them from up and down the Columbia and the Northern Paiutes from the southern interior.

Under leaders such as the Dreamer chief Colwash, the Wishrams opposed removal to a reservation. In contrast to the natives of the Columbia south bank, who removed to the Warm Springs Reservation in north-central Oregon, some Wishrams between 1860 and 1865 moved to the Yakima Reservation in Washington Territory, which they alternated with their former homes to subsist on the fisheries. Several families, avoiding the reservation, remained in their homelands along the Columbia. A 1910 census listed 274 Wishrams. In 1962, 10 were reported in Washington.

Suggested Readings: David French, "Wasco-Wishram," in Edward H. Spicer, ed., *Perspectives in American Indian Culture Change* (Chicago: University of Chicago Press, 1961); Leslie Spier and Edward Sapir, "Wishram Ethnography," *University of Washington Publications in Anthropology* 3, no. 3 (1930).

WYNOOCHEE
(Coastal Division, Salishan)

The Wynoochees lived on the river bearing their name, a tributary of the Chehalis River in southwestern Washington state. The Wynoochees and their Whiskah neighbors have been classified on occasion as belonging to the Lower Chehalis tribe, because of their linguistic and cultural closeness to it. Washington Superintendent of Indian Affairs Samuel Ross, in a September, 1870, report, stated that the Wynoochees and the Whiskahs, like others of the Chehalis watershed, were probably once one people, who over time had divided to form two separate tribal identities. Ross counted the Wynoochees and the neighboring Hoquiams, Satsops, and Whiskahs at 350, under a chief named Sam. The ethnologist John R. Swanton classifies the Whiskahs as a village of the Humptulips tribe. Frederick Webb Hodge classifies them as a Chehalis subdivision. The ethnologist George Gibbs noted that Wynoochees had few associations with whites in 1853. Then, after the period of United States–Indian treaty-making between 1854 and 1856, their isolation broke down as they received gifts from government officials. Some of these they exchanged for liquor, as they did the wages that they earned by working for oyster companies on Willapa Bay. Today the Wynoochees no longer exist as a tribe.

YAHUSKIN
(See **Northern Paiute** and **Klamath**.)

YAKIMA
(Shahaptian)

The Yakimas were one of the most numerous of the Shahaptian-speaking peoples. Their 1780 population has been estimated at 3,000. Even so, the numbers recorded by early nineteenth-century observers were excessive because they included other native groups.

According to John R. Swanton, the name Yakima means "runaway." Another ethnologist, Frederick Webb Hodge, stated that the native name of Yakimas was Waptailmin, or Pakiutlema, meaning "people of the gap." Union Gap south of present-day Yakima, Washington, was the site of their main village, Pa'kiut ("hills together"). An authority on the Yakimas, L. V. McWhorter, stated that Spokane and Nespelem natives conferred the name Yah-ah-kima on the portion of the tribe known as the Upper Yakimas, who were frequently also called the Kittitas ("rock people"). Some believe that Yakima is a modification of Yah-ah-ka-ma, meaning "a growing family" or "a tribe expansion." Other meanings ascribed to the tribal name are "black bear," "big belly," or "the pregnant ones." Some elderly Yakimas believe the last meaning derived from the spectacle of refugee women during the Yakima War of 1855–56.

The Yakimas lived in the watershed of the Yakima River, their primary stream in central and south-central Washington. The Yakima River begins in the Cascade Mountains and is joined by other streams, such as the Tieton, the Cowiche, the Toppenish, and the Satus, as it flows southeast to join the Columbia near Richland, Washington. Besides the Upper Yakimas on the north,

the Lower Yakimas, or Yakimas proper, occupied the lower Yakima watershed, from the ancient Selah Village (just north of present-day Yakima) south to present-day Prosser. The Upper Yakimas, also called the Kittitas, occupied the upper Yakima valley north of Selah and the Kittitas Valley. Besides the river and an Indian reservation, a county and a city on U.S. Highway 97 and Interstate 82 bear the Yakima name.

When elderly Yakimas were asked about their origins, they replied that red men were the first on earth, and that they were followed by water and finally, by wood. Among the Yakima traditions are stories of the Flood and of prophets dying for three days and returning to earth and predictions of the coming of the black-robed Roman Catholic priests. All of those indicate an early familiarity with Christianity such as could have come through direct or indirect ties with the American Southwest, where Spanish priests had established missions. Christianity may also have come to the Yakimas from Salish speakers who had contacts with Catholic Iroquois Indians or French-Canadian Catholics in the early nineteenth century. The Yakimas came into direct contact with whites in 1805–1806, when they met Lewis and Clark. Soon after that, other white travelers and traders passed through the Yakimas' lands, and in the late 1830s and 1840s they came under the ministrations of Catholic priests.

Among both Indians and whites, the Yakimas had a reputation for stressing individuality in their society. Fishing was perhaps their most important means of subsistence,

Yakima

Yakima Indian doctors, photographed by Lee Moorhouse, circa 1900. The populous Sha-haptian-speaking Yakimas have produced a long line of prophets, shamans, and other religious leaders. Native religions, such as the Pompom, the Feather, and the Shaker, continued into the twentieth century alongside those introduced by whites. Courtesy of the Yakima Indian Nation Cultural Center.

followed by gathering roots and berries and hunting. Some historians claim that the Yakimas obtained horses from the peoples of the Great Basin through Cayuse Indian intermediaries sometime around 1730. In any event, with horses they were able to hunt buffalo on the plains, though they did not pursue them to the same extent that the interior Salish peoples did, or as much as the Nez Percés, who were also Shahaptian

273

speakers. The Yakimas did not hunt buffalo at the expense of their traditional food gathering.

As white settlement of the interior progressed, the Yakimas were among Indians who treated with Washington Territorial Governor and Superintendent of Indian Affairs Isaac Stevens at the Walla Walla council. The Yakima headmen who signed the Yakima Treaty on June 9, 1855, represented various lower-middle Columbia River bands. Despite opposition to the treaty, fourteen tribes under the Yakima standard ceded to the United States about ten million acres of present-day central Washington for their main reservation, which was less than 1,250,000 acres. They were also to receive the usual goods and services from the government in exchange for their lands. Designated under the treaty as the head Yakima chief, Kamiakin led a coalition of interior tribes against the Americans in what became known as the Yakima War of 1855–56. Despite some initial victories, the Yakimas and their allies were defeated in a key fight early in November, 1855, at Union Gap. During the war Yakima unity was disrupted by friction between Kamiakin's Lower Yakima faction and that of the Upper Yakimas, who regarded this son of a Palouse father as an outsider. After the treaty was ratified on March 8, 1859, the fourteen confederated tribes formed what Yakimas called the Yakima Nation. From then on the story of the Yakimas is interwoven with that of those tribes who composed the Yakima Nation of the Yakima Reservation under the Yakima, or Simcoe, Agency. See **Confederated Tribes of the Yakima Indian Reservation of Washington.**

Suggested Readings: See the suggested readings under **Confederated Tribes of the Yakima Indian Reservation of Washington.**

YAKIMA TRIBES OF THE YAKIMA RESERVATION
(See **Confederated Tribes of the Yakima Indian Reservation of Washington.**)

YAMEL
(Kalapuyan)

The Yamels, or Yamhills, comprised six bands who spoke the Tualatin-Yamhill dialect, one of three Kalapuyan dialects. Their name originated from a native word meaning "a ford." The Yamhill River flows east through Yamhill county to the Willamette River in northwestern Oregon. A town and a county also bear the tribal name Yamhill.

The Yamels suffered the severe population losses experienced by other Kalapuyan speakers. In 1849, when whites had taken most of their lands, Oregon Territorial Governor Joseph Lane, visited the Yamels and counted only ninety souls. By 1910 they had been reduced to five. On April 24, 1851, they met in council with commissioners authorized by Congress to treat with them for their lands. At that time they numbered fifty-four persons. They refused the commissioners' proposal that they move east of the Cascade Mountains, as did other Kalapuyan peoples, stating their wish for a reserve in their homelands, where for generations they had gathered native grains and roots from the soil, lakes, and marshes. At that time about thirty Yamel families lived on the tribal lands. Government agents promised that houses would be built for them on a proposed reserve. Apparently the commissioners did not make a similar promise to other Kalapuyan peoples.

After a treaty was signed on May 2, 1851, Oregon Superintendent of Indian Affairs Anson Dart tried to make the Yamels and their fellow Kalapuyans resettle on the agreed-upon reservation, though the treaties directing them to do so remain unratified. With nonratification of the treaties, operations to resettle the Yamels out of the way of whites came to an end. In 1854, however, under pressure from the increasing number of whites, the tribe was asked to renegotiate. Along with the Molalas and a few Clackamasas they met at Dayton, Oregon Territory, on January 4, 1855, with Oregon Superintendent of Indian Affairs Joel Palmer to sign a treaty (10 Stat. 1143). By its terms the Yamels agreed to live in the Willamette valley until the government established a suitable reservation for them. Such a reserve, the 60,000-acre Grand Ronde, was established on June 30, 1857, in the tribe's ancestral homelands in the upper Yamhill River country. There were forty-seven Yamels on the reservation in 1870.

Suggested Readings: S. A. Clarke, *Pioneer Days of Oregon History* (Portland, Ore., 1905); Leo J. Frachtenberg, *Ethnological Researches Among the Kalapuya Indians, Smithsonian Miscellaneous Collections 65*, no. 6 (1916); J. A. Hussey, *Champoeg: Place of Transition* (Portland: Oregon Historical Society, 1964); Harold Mackey, *The Kalapuyans: A Sourcebook on the Indians of the Willamette Valley* (Salem, Ore.: Mission Hill Museum Association, Inc., 1974); W. W. Oglesby, "The Calapoyas Indians" (188?), Mss. P-A 82, Bancroft Library, University of California, Berkeley; James L. Ratcliff, "What Happened to the Kalapuya? A Study of the Depletion of Their Economic Base," *Indian Historian* 6, no. 3 (Summer, 1973).

Yamel

The Yamels, popularly called Yamhills, spoke a dialect of the Kalapuyan language. This male adult Kalapuyan speaker was sketched in the early 1840s by A. T. Agate, who was among the United States Navy explorers under Lt. Charles Wilkes. Reproduced from Charles Pickering, The Races of Men and Their Geographical Distribution *(1863), courtesy of Harold Mackey.*

YAQUINA
(Yakonan)

The Yaquinas occupied territory along the central Oregon coast on the river that today bears their name. A bay also bears the tribal name. Like so many coastal and riverine peoples of the Pacific Northwest, their tribal organization was informal. There were several villages in which one or two headmen held positions because of their wealth, which was measured primarily in dentalia shells and slaves. The headmen's authority was weak, but each village had longstanding rules, traditions, values, and attitudes that bound the leaders and followers together. Shamans sought powers not only to cure but also to divine the causes of troubles such as poor salmon runs, which they sought to remedy by entering streams with poles to stimulate the runs. Although the Yaquinas had seen white men and had traded with them, most of their Euro-American goods had been obtained indirectly. Trade increased with the presence of Hudson's Bay Company traders along the Yaquinas' coasts in the 1820s. In 1910 the Yaquinas numbered but nineteen souls. No one today speaks the Yaquina language.

With the Upper Coquilles, Tututnis, Chetcos, Siletzes, Nechesnes, and Alseas, the Yaquinas, as Siletz Reservation inhabitants, were in the first group of nontreaty Indians to be awarded claims by the United States, which did not ratify a treaty made with those tribes in 1855. In 1888 and 1893 a Senate subcommittee on Indian Affairs recognized the Siletz Indians' claim, but it was not until August 26, 1935, that legislation was passed (49 Stat. 810) enabling them to bring suit in the Court of Claims against the government (Case No. 45230). In instituting that suit, the tribes presented every possible shred of documentary evidence that they could assemble to prove that their claim was based on an involuntary and uncompensated appropriation of lands by the government. In their presentation they applied lessons learned from the Miluk and Hanis Coos, the Siuslaws, and the Kuitshes (Lower Umpquas), who in a

1938 ruling had lost an award for their alienated lands because of improper presentation of the evidence, which had rested largely on the oral testimony of individual Indians. By taking advantage of the lessons learned from that ruling, the Yaquinas and other tribes on April 2, 1945, received an award of $3,128,900. Because of a Supreme Court ruling on April 6, 1951, they were, however, disallowed interest monies. The Coquilles received $847,190.40 of that award; the Tututnis, $465,225; and the Chetcos, $489,085. As confederated "Tillamook" tribes, the Nechesnes, Siletzes, Yaquinas, and Alseas shared $1,327,399.20.

Their claim for $10 million was settled with that award.

Suggested Readings: Stephen Dow Beckham, *The Indians of Western Oregon: This Land Was Theirs* (Coos Bay, Ore.: Arago Books, 1977); J. O. Dorsey, "Indians of the Siletz Reservation," *American Anthropologist* 2 (1889); William Eugene Kent, *The Siletz Indian Reservation, 1855–1900*, Master's thesis, 1973, Portland State University, Oregon.

YONCALLA
(Kalapuyan)

The Yoncalla dialect was one of three Kalapuyan dialects. The modern tribal name, Yoncalla, is derived from their name for themselves. The tribe was divided into two bands. Their homelands lay south of the Willamette valley on Elk and Calapooya creeks, between present-day Oakland and Drain, Oregon. Elk and Calapooya creeks are tributaries of the Umpqua River, an affluent of the Pacific Ocean. A town near Drain today bears the name Yoncalla. Like other Kalapuyan speakers, the Yoncallas were pressured not only by whites entering their lands but also by Klickitat Indians from north of the Columbia River, who entered the Willamette valley and pushed as far south as the Umpqua valley after the 1830s. During the 1820s the Yoncallas were

visited by the Hudson's Bay Company fur men Alexander R. McLeod and Thomas McKay and by brigades of their firm.

On November 29, 1854, the Yoncallas and Umpquas signed a treaty with United States officials (10 Stat. 1125, ratified March 3, 1855). They agreed to remove to a reservation where and when the government deemed best and to receive allotments there at the president's discretion. Monies received from improvements in their homelands were to be spent on permanent improvements on their reservation. In the fall of 1855, during the later stages of the Rogue Wars, Oregon Superintendent of Indian Affairs Joel Palmer gathered together the noncombatant tribes in southern Oregon. The Yoncallas and the Upper Umpquas agreed to confederate with the Southern Molalas, who in turn agreed to the association in a December 21, 1855, treaty (12 Stat. 981, ratified March 8, 1859). Palmer then ordered those three tribes removed north to the headwaters of the Yamhill River, where the Grand Ronde Reservation was to be established for them. They began their trek to that place on January 10, 1856, arriving on February 2 after enduring hardships. Not all of them removed. Those under Chief Halotish and a few Upper Umpquas under their chief, Napesa, remained in their Umpqua valley homelands under the protection of white settlers, especially Meshak Tipton and Jesse Applegate, who set aside portions of their farms for them. Three decades later a small Yoncalla remnant still farmed there, living in the manner of whites and sending their children to local schools. Descendants of those Yoncallas, with descendants of the Upper Umpquas, on April 3, 1950, were awarded $377,177.16 for the loss of their homelands by a decision of the Court of Claims (Case No. 45231). This award represented the principal of $67,820 plus interest and deductions for offsets. In 1910 the original Yoncallas had numbered only ten.

Suggested Readings: S. A. Clarke, *Pioneer Days of Oregon History* (Portland, Ore., 1905); Leo J. Frachtenberg, *Ethnological Researches Among the Kalapuya Indians,* Smithsonian Institution, *Miscellaneous Collections* 65, no. 6 (1916); Anne Applegate Kruse, *The Halo Trail: The Story of the Yoncalla Indians* (Drain, Ore., 1954); Harold Mackey, *The Kalapuyans: A Sourcebook on the Indians of the Willamette Valley* (Salem, Ore.: Mission Mill Museum Association, Inc., 1974); W. W. Oglesby, "The Calapooyas Indians," [188?], mss. P-A 82, Bancroft Library, University of California, Berkeley; James L. Ratcliff, "What Happened to the Kalapuya? A Study of the Depletion of Their Economic Base," *Indian Historian* 6, no. 3 (Summer, 1973).

Yoncalla

This Yoncalla Indian, like so many others of his race in the late nineteenth and the early twentieth century, posed for a photographer (who may have provided white men's clothing for the sitting).

Index

Burials: 97, 131, 161, 186, 209, 261, 265
Burns, Ore.: 9, 156
Burns Paiute Indian Colony: 9
Butte Creek (Rogue River tributary): 237

Cache Valley Indians: 192, 194, 199, 200
Calamoxes: 240
Calapooya Creek: 10, 254, 276
Calapooya Indians: 10, 11, 90
California & Oregon Land Company: 93
Calvin, E. D.: 61
Camano Island: 90, 212, 214
Camas Prairie: see Kansas (Camas) Prairie
Canada and Canadian border: 18, 35, 42, 87, 97,
     111, 112, 133, 147, 150, 179, 188, 203–205, 266,
     270
Canoes and canoeing: 4, 18, 28, 79, 86, 113, 128,
     131, 134, 209, 226, 262
Captain, The (Umpqua chief): 135, 136
Capes: Alava, 128; Farello, 19; Flattery, 81, 125,
     161, 171; Lookout, 50
Carr Inlet: 166, 226
Carson, Kit: 134
Carter, Jimmy (president): 52
Cascades, The (of Columbia River): 21, 22, 264
Cascade Mountains: 3, 5, 17, 27, 60, 61, 67, 69, 71,
     75, 91, 95, 102, 110, 130, 137, 140, 150, 153,
     155, 165, 183, 185, 204
Cathlamet Indians: 11, 12, 31, 257, 258
Cathlapotles: 13
Cayuse Indians: 13–15, 17, 52, 95, 137, 240, 250,
     251, 259, 260
Celilo Falls of Columbia River: 54, 56, 62, 148, 239,
     240, 264, 270
Ceremonials: 19, 125, 231, 261; first salmon, 4, 30,
     174, 270; potlatch, 178, 209, 228, 231; secret
     society, 27, 171, 211; sun dance, 100; wolf dance,
     171; see also Prophet Dance
Chambers, Thomas: 224
Champoeg, Ore.: 3, 137
Charley, George A. (Shoalwater chief): 191
Charlo (Flathead chief): 77, 88
Chastacostas: 16, 49, 237, 247
Chatham, HMS (ship): 24
Chehalises: see Kwaiailks; Lower Chehalises
Chehalis River: 40, 101, 102, 105, 106, 185, 271
Chelamelas: 17
Chelans: 17, 18, 43
Chepenafas: 18, 19
Chetco Indians: 19–21, 49, 63, 143, 247, 276
Chetco Jennie (Chetco Indian): 246
Chetco River: 19, 246
Chewelahs: 86
Cheyennes: 81
Chieftaincy: see classes
Chilleuk (Lummi chief): 111
Chilliwacks: 153
Chilliwists: 129
Chilluckittequaw: 21, 22, 265
Chilwitses: 208
Chimakums: 22, 23, 27, 171, 209, 249
Chinook jargon: 238
Chinooks: 11, 23–25, 30, 31, 40, 48, 51, 103, 105,

107, 131, 171, 240, 257, 258
Chinoose (Humtulips chief): 83
Chirouse, Eugene Casimir, O.M.I. (missionary):
     111, 213, 225, 244, 245
Chocktoot (Paiute chief): 57, 58
Chopunnishes: 144
Chowitshoot (Lummi chief): 179
Christianity: see churches; missions
Chualpays: 35
Churches: American Board of Commissioners for
     Foreign Missions, 15, 146, 203, 218; Baptist, 196;
     Congregational, 84; Church of God, 245; Church
     of Jesus Christ of Latter-day Saints (Mormon),
     196, 200, 245; Episcopal, 196; Methodist, 3, 32,
     150, 264; Native American, 196; Pentecostal, 211,
     220, 245; Presbyterian, 54, 147, 220; Roman
     Catholic, 3, 48, 54, 57, 58, 141, 147, 152, 168,
     186, 196, 212, 213, 220, 245, 272; Shaker
     (Indian), 54, 57, 82, 84, 141, 152, 170, 171, 174,
     177, 209, 211, 221, 222, 245
Civilian Conservation Corps: 89
Clackamases: 25, 26, 32, 110, 137, 268, 275
Clackamas River and valley: 25, 26
Clackstar Nation: 29
Clahcllellahs: 265
Clahnaquahas: 142
Clallam Bay: 27, 30
Clallams: 23, 26–29, 81, 84, 106, 107, 125, 126,
     164, 165, 170, 209–12, 214, 216, 224, 248, 249
Clamons: 23, 235
Claplanhoo, Maquinna Jongie (Makah chief): 126
Clark, Harry A.: 59
Clark, William: 12, 21, 24, 29, 30, 32, 64, 76, 95,
     105, 129, 142, 144, 155, 171, 200, 208, 239–41,
     243, 257, 259, 265, 266, 268
Classes: 174, 198, 231, 248, 270; chieftaincy, 51,
     145, 146, 153; slavery, 5, 30, 56, 69, 107, 110,
     125, 131, 134, 153, 172, 184, 206, 235, 241, 259,
     264; shamans, 4, 65, 174, 221
Clatsops: 11, 25, 29–31, 40, 47, 48, 171, 243, 257,
     258
Clearwater River: 32, 145, 146
Cleveland, Grover (president): 40, 50
Clothing: 5, 7, 91, 107, 110, 131, 134, 183, 214,
     225, 235, 241
Clowwewallas: 31, 32, 137, 268
Coast-No (Molala chief): 137
Coast Range: 3, 4, 50, 79, 96, 235, 240, 241
Coast Rogues: see Rogues
Coeur d'Alênes: 32–34, 87
Coeur D'Alene Tribe, Coeur D'Alene Reservation: 35
Columbia (ship): 49, 238
Columbia Indians: 44
Columbia Plateau: 23, 145, 162, 204, 265
Columbia Indians: 44
Columbia River: 3, 9, 37, 69, 74, 99, 143, 148, 155,
     166, 170, 171, 182, 185, 188, 202, 239, 248
Colvile, Andrew: 36
Colville River and valley: 35, 87
Colvilles: 35–37, 42, 87, 188, 202
Colville, Wash.: 35, 220
Colwash (Dreamer chief): 270
Commencement Bay (Tacoma): 166, 222
Confederated Salish & Kootenai Tribes of the

283

285